1978
The Supreme Court Review

1978

The

"Judges as persons, or courts as institutions, are entitled to
no greater immunity from criticism than other persons
or institutions . . . [J]udges must be kept mindful of their limitations and
of their ultimate public responsibility by a vigorous
stream of criticism expressed with candor however blunt."
—*Felix Frankfurter*

". . . while it is proper that people should find fault when
their judges fail, it is only reasonable that they should recognize the
difficulties. . . . Let them be severely brought to book,
when they go wrong, but by those who will take the trouble
to understand them."
—*Learned Hand*

THE LAW SCHOOL

THE UNIVERSITY OF CHICAGO

Supreme Court Review

EDITED BY

PHILIP B. KURLAND

AND GERHARD CASPER

THE UNIVERSITY OF CHICAGO PRESS

CHICAGO AND LONDON

INTERNATIONAL STANDARD BOOK NUMBER: 0-226-46431-8

LIBRARY OF CONGRESS CATALOG CARD NUMBER: 60-14353

THE UNIVERSITY OF CHICAGO PRESS, CHICAGO 60637

THE UNIVERSITY OF CHICAGO PRESS, LTD., LONDON

© 1979 BY THE UNIVERSITY OF CHICAGO. ALL RIGHTS RESERVED. PUBLISHED 1979

PRINTED IN THE UNITED STATES OF AMERICA

CONTENTS

DANIEL D. POLSBY

F.C.C. v. NATIONAL CITIZENS COMMITTEE FOR BROADCASTING AND THE JUDICIOUS USES OF ADMINISTRATIVE DISCRETION

I. Partnership Shares

To judge from the Supreme Court opinion, *F.C.C. v. National Citizens Committee for Broadcasting* (NCCB),[1] was an ordinary case of judicial review of an administrative agency rule. The Federal Communications Commission (FCC) had decided after a long proceeding that diversity of ownership in the various media of mass communications was important enough to rule that owners of daily newspapers should not, in the future, be licensed to operate

Daniel D. Polsby is Associate Professor of Law, Northwestern University.

AUTHOR'S NOTE: Several of the cases discussed herein were before the Federal Communications Commission during my tenure as counsel to Glen O. Robinson, who served as Commissioner from 1974 through 1976. Robinson prepared opinions in these cases, usually dissenting. My participation in drafting those opinions was substantial, and the reader should discount for my bias. Grateful acknowledgment must be made to Professor Robinson and to J. Roger Wollenberg and Joel Rosenbloom of the District of Columbia bar for sharing with me their private correspondence concerning a thesis of Robinson's, published as *The Judicial Role*, in COMMUNICATIONS FOR TOMORROW: POLICY PERSPECTIVES FOR THE 1980s 415 (G. Robinson ed. 1978). William T. Lake of the District of Columbia bar helped me to clarify and formulate a number of the points made herein. The Aspen Institute for Humanistic Studies provided the quiet place and studious atmosphere in which this paper was written. None of the foregoing is chargeable with anything said herein. Indeed, Robinson would probably demur to almost all of it as "rest[ing] simply on verbal filigree." *The Judicial Role, supra*, at 420.

[1] 98 S. Ct. 2096 (1978).

broadcasting stations within the newspaper's community. Consistent with its longstanding practice in similar proceedings, the agency made its rule prospective only. Existing newspaper-broadcasting combinations would not be ordered dissolved (with a few minor exceptions). But no new combinations would be allowed to come into existence under the FCC's rule.

The Supreme Court was unanimous, and, on its face, its opinion is without special interest to administrative or constitutional law. Since the goals of promoting diversity are well within the agency's power and the means chosen to effectuate those goals are not unreasonable, the use of a grandfather clause to avoid the necessity of ordering wide-scale divestitures of broadcast stations by newspapers was not an arbitrary manifestation of administrative discretion. Therefore the order of the agency is affirmed in all respects.

But the case assumes a larger significance when evaluated in context. The judgment which it reviewed, that of the United States Court of Appeals for the District of Columbia Circuit, was of sweeping and ambitious import. The lower court had found the FCC's defense of the status quo to be arbitrary and capricious within the meaning of the Administrative Procedure Act and had remanded the docket to the agency to repair this defect. It left little doubt, moreover, that it did not consider the FCC to be at large either to reconsider the cross-ownership policy or merely to refit the same rule with a tidier or more persuasive memorandum of justification. Rather, the Court of Appeals found in the notion of diversity of communications media ownership—which in a related context Judge Learned Hand had called "closely akin to, if indeed it is not the same as, the interest protected by the First Amendment"[2]—a requirement that the FCC justify on reasonable grounds any departure from actions which maximize diversity of communications media ownership. In short, the grandfather clause must be deleted and newspapers must not continue to be licensed to operate television or radio stations hereafter unless the agency explains why the public interest will be served by such variance from the norm of diversity.

The judgment of the Court of Appeals represented what was probably the boldest extension of judicial power over the substantive rulemaking competence of an independent administrative agency. Had the Supreme Court left this judgment undisturbed, the *NCCB*

---

[2] United States v. Associated Press, 52 F. Supp. 362, 372 (S.D.N.Y. 1943), aff'd 326 U.S. 1 (1945).

case, far from being the footnote that it is, would unmistakably have been a license for the District of Columbia Circuit Court to continue to explore a wider and deeper involvement in the substantive policies of administrative agencies. The involvement of the D.C. Circuit in the burgeoning of administrative government has been pronounced over the past generation and, especially, the past decade. In part, no doubt, this increasing involvement has been brought about by judges who have, for the most part, sought out opportunities to affect the course of public policy by rejecting traditionally narrow constructions of standing, ripeness, mootness, and other similar prudential limitations of the judicial power. But an activist disposition is hardly the entire story. The presence of the federal judiciary—and particularly the D.C. Circuit—in the thick of federal administrative policymaking has often been commanded by Congress. Statutory schemes as diverse as the National Environmental Policy Act, the Occupational Safety and Health Act, the Safe Drinking Water Act, the Endangered Species Act, and numerous other laws have made the institution of judicial review a basic, if not the most important, element in guiding the exercise of administrative discretion.[3] In the narrow sense of the term, there is seldom any "law" to apply in characterizing various exercises of administrative discretion once certain basic considerations, such as the agencies' jurisdiction in a given matter, have been decided. But the courts, and most particularly the D.C. Circuit, have not taken the narrowest possible view of their role in the process. They have developed a conception of themselves that amplifies the congressional judgment that Courts of Appeals do, indeed, have an important part to play in the administrative process.

The District of Columbia Court of Appeals' *NCCB* opinion was an integral part of its developing self-definition. The Supreme Court's reversal must be considered in relation to that self-conception. Especially when read in light of a case decided only two months earlier, *Vermont Yankee Nuclear Power Corp. v. Natural Resources Defense Council, Inc.*,[4] the *NCCB* case is an important event in the evolution of the judicial role in administrative government. The Court of Appeals had gone too far, had done (or tried to do) too much, according to the Supreme Court.

---

[3] See McGowan, *Congress and the Courts*, 62 A.B.A.J. 1588 (1976).
[4] 435 U.S. 519.

In one sense, to reflect on the proper role for the courts in administrative government is a sterile scholastic exercise. However hard we try, we are not likely to find the theorem which justifies the exercise of judicial or administrative discretion. But, by looking closely at the principles by which discretion is parceled out, we may at least discover the limits of principle fixing the perimeters.

There are, conventionally, two broad questions here. One of them deals with the proper judicial role in the formation of substantive policies; the other concerns the function of a reviewing court in shaping and determining the administrative procedures through which these policies are made. Congress has contemplated and the courts have recognized that in each of these spheres, the reviewing court is entitled to a measure of authority. What the measure of that authority should be in each sphere is debated with vehemence. For the debate is one about political power. One of the assumptions commonly entertained in administrative law (and one that I share) is that the exercise of administrative discretion is a zero-sum game. If more discretion is allocated to the agency, the scope of the judicial function is necessarily less. The converse is necessarily equally true.

In the procedural sphere the most important text is *Vermont Yankee*, which very complexly combines reasons of policy and principle with supposed congressional purposes—either to deprive the Court of Appeals of its long asserted role in influencing agency procedures in the interest of fundamental fairness[5] or, a related congressional concern, to promote the interest of the fundamental political legitimacy of the agency's ultimate product.[6] But the procedural role of a reviewing court is one which I propose to discuss only briefly here. My purpose is to sketch the substantive role that the Court of Appeals has staked out for itself in the formation of administrative agency policy. In particular, I am concerned with the relationship of the FCC with the D.C. Circuit, where most of that agency's review petitions are filed. The give and take between these two branches of government often concerns what both recognize as freedom of speech issues of unfeigned constitutional

---

[5] See Walter Holm & Co. v. Hardin, 449 F.2d 1009 (D.C. Cir. 1971); International Harvester Co. v. Ruckleshaus, 478 F.2d 615 (D.C. Cir. 1973).

[6] See Home Box Office, Inc. v. F.C.C., 567 F.2d 9 (1977); Aeschliman v. United States Nuclear Regulatory Comm'n, 547 F.2d 622 (1976), reversed sub nom. Vermont Yankee Nuclear Power Corp. v. Natural Resources Defense Council, Inc., 435 U.S. 519 (1978).

stature. How the pie of discretion is divided between them will often decide how these issues will be determined. My conclusion is that the court can seldom, if ever, defensibly upset the agency's decisions on how the First Amendment relates to communications policy. And, because the shaping of constitutional policy seems to be a place where a legislative role for the judiciary could most logically be thought to exist, the implication is that the judicial role in all substantive policymaking by agencies should be small. The *NCCB* case carries the seeds of this conclusion. It also suggests that the judicial role should be almost indeterminately small. I assert that these consequences would be an unfortunate development.

II. THE AGENCY AND COURT OPINIONS

To understand the larger meaning of *NCCB*, it is helpful to attend first to its smaller meaning. Here one must not only look carefully at the proffered basis for the agency's action but also contextually locate that action within the complex of related FCC policies.

The FCC's concern with "diversification"—*i.e.*, placing limits on the amount of concentration of control in the commercial broadcast industries—goes back almost forty years. In 1941, the Commission enacted its so-called chain broadcasting rules which forbade any one person from operating more than one network at the same time.[7] In the same year, the Commission published rules which forbade anyone from owning more than one AM radio station in a single market.[8] In 1953, the Commission imposed an absolute limit on the number of broadcast properties that a single person might own, regardless of whether any of these were located in a single city. In 1964 and again in 1970, the multiple ownership rules were changed again to favor increasing diversity of ownership. The 1970 rule prohibited common ownership of a radio station and a VHF (Channels 2 through 13) TV station in the same community. All of these decisions proceeded, more or less explicitly, upon two

---

[7] See National Broadcasting Co. v. United States, 319 U.S. 190 (1943).

[8] The rule, generally stated, forbade the licensure of the same person to more than one frequency in a given "service." AM, FM, and TV are each different "services." This would have prohibited one licensee from operating two FM or TV stations as well. At that time, however, these services were still embryonic and of small practical consequence.

related but different premises, one rooted in antitrust policy and the other in First Amendment theory.

In 1970 the Commission issued the *First Report and Order* of the multiple ownership docket in which the *NCCB* matter became the second.[9] The 1970 order announced the so-called one-to-a-market principle which, as eventually modified on reconsideration,[10] prohibited a single applicant from being licensed to operate a VHF TV station in the same market where it was licensed to operate a radio station. Consistent with the Commission's invariable past practice in multiple-ownership rulemaking, the 1970 order was prospective only—*i.e.*, it allowed all existing television-radio combinations to remain in place indefinitely and required that they be broken up only if the ownership of the combined entity changed hands. The Commission explained its 1970 order on two grounds: to foster maximum competition in broadcasting and to promote diversification of programming sources and points of view. Moreover the Commission was concerned with these objectives both in local markets and on a national scale.[11]

If both antitrust principles and First Amendment considerations were on the Commission's mind, however, it is fair to say that the free-speech implications of what it was doing were paramount. The Commission said:[12]

> Basic to our form of government is the belief that "the widest possible dissemination of information from diverse and antagonistic sources is essential to the welfare of the public." Associated Press v. United States, 326 U.S. 1, 20 (1945). Thus, our Constitution rests upon the ground that "the ultimate good desired is better reached by free trade in ideas—that the best test of truth is the power to get itself accepted in the competition of the market." Justice Holmes dissenting in Abrams v. United States, 250 U.S. 616, 630 (1919).
>
> These principles, upon which Judge Learned Hand observed that we had staked our all, are the wellspring, together with the

---

[9] 18 Pike & Fischer, R.R.2d 1735 (1970).

[10] 21 P. & F. 1551 (1971).

[11] Thus the rules contained both "duopoly" prohibitions—forbidding the ownership of more than one station in one market—and "concentration of control" prohibitions, setting an overall limit on the number of stations which could be licensed to a single person or entity.

[12] 18 P. & F. at 1740.

concomitant desire to prevent undue economic concentration, of the Commission's policy of diversifying control of the powerful medium of broadcasting. For, centralization of control over the media of mass communications is, like monopolization of economic power, per se undesirable. The power to control what the public hears and sees over the airwaves matters, whatever the degree of self-restraint which may withhold its arbitrary use.

The nature of the Commission's concern, then, is evident; but the degree of its concern is difficult to overstress. It went on to declare:[13]

A proper [Commission] objective is the maximum diversity of ownership that technology permits in each area. We are of the view that 60 different licensees are more desirable than 50, and that even 51 are more desirable than 50. In a rapidly changing social climate, communication of ideas is vital. If a city has 60 frequencies available but they are licensed to only 50 different licensees, the number of sources for ideas is not maximized. . . . In our view, as we have made clear above, there is no optimum degree of diversification, and we do not feel competent to say or hold that any particular number of outlets of expression is "enough."

There is more in the same vein, but it is repetitive. The diversity issue, clearly enough in the Commission's analysis, is a "motherhood" issue. It is important in itself and is seen as important to a variety of other fundamental values as well. Nevertheless, the Commission's chairman, Dean Burch, criticized his colleagues for trivializing an important issue. Whatever the value and importance of the underlying public interests at stake in protecting diversity of ownership in the structure of the broadcasting industry, Burch argued, the part of that interest addressed by a concern for television-radio combinations was not very great and, indeed, was perhaps trifling.

While multiple ownership may be a problem in some small markets without many aural services, Burch said, in most large markets —where the majority of the population resides—diversification of ownership in radio is already ample. "In the Washington metropolitan area there are 37 aural services; in New York, 59, in Chicago, 61. . . . There is a plethora of aural services in all significant markets. Thus, while separating TV from AM or FM might make a

---

[13] *Id.* at 1741–43.

contribution in a few cases, it is clearly far from the heart of the problem."[14]

The heart of the problem, according to Burch, was the cross-owned VHF-television-newspaper combination:[15]

> There are only a few daily newspapers in each large city and their numbers are declining. There are only a few powerful VHF stations in these cities and their numbers cannot be increased. Equally important, the evidence shows that the very large majority of people get their news information from these two limited sources.

The Commission issued a further notice of proposed rulemaking on the same day that the *First Report and Order* was published, and it was Burch's lamp which guided the commission's path on the *Second Report and Order*. Prospectively, the owners of daily newspapers would be ineligible for licensure to operate broadcast stations in the community where their newspaper was circulated. This rule was to enhance competition both in economic markets and in the markets for ideas.[16] As with the *First Report and Order*, the free speech values were seen as the greater: "If our democratic society is to function, nothing can be more important than insuring that there is a free flow of information from as many divergent sources as possible."[17]

As before, however, the Commission's rhetorical commitments considerably overmatched its resolution to act.[18] In particular, its failure to order the generalized retroactive application of the rule

---

[14] *Id.* at 1759–60.

[15] *Id.* at 1760.

[16] 50 F.C.C.2d 1046, 1048 (197x).

[17] *Id.* at 1079. Similar sentiments were expressed *id.* at 1074.

[18] It may seem puzzling that not infrequently there is a considerable gap between what the agency purports to be doing and what it actually does. The reason for this gap is simple enough. The Commission's Reports and Orders are drafted in bureaus by lawyers who generally have little direct contact with the decisionmakers, *i.e.*, the commissioners. The draftsmen rely on the general principles which favor one result or policy over another and are almost always aware of, if not sensitive to, the logical implications of the rules they develop for the larger policies of the national government, and some effort is typically made to refer the agency's rules to that larger context. By contrast, the commissioners are generally political in approach. They care for results and not dicta minted "downstairs," which are, often as not, left unread or only skimmed by them. Results are sometimes changed at the last minute with only minimal changes in the underlying Report and Order being made. Hence, the agency's words and deeds do not always make a comfortable fit.

betrayed an awareness that something less was at stake in the cross-ownership arena than the survival of democracy in this hemisphere. And still open was the question, What precisely was moving the Commission to act at all? Was this problem serious? If it was as serious as the Commission's language suggested, how could the divestiture remedy be shunned? And if the divestiture remedy was to be avoided, what was the justification for the Commission's actions? There was in its order a certain unpersuasiveness, as partly reflected in two matters, one small, the other large. The small matter is reflected in a tragicomic exception the Commission made to the general prospectivity of its order. In a few so-called egregious cases, divestiture would be required within five years. While the communications oligopolies in highly concentrated markets like New York, Chicago, Atlanta, San Francisco, and Washington, D.C. were to remain unaffected by the Commission's prodiversity sentiments,[19] no such leniency would be shown to the monopolies in Owosso, Michigan; Norfolk, Nebraska; Effingham, Illinois; and a handful of other similar small communities. The conveyed impression of an administrative agency at its work is decidedly unattractive: It is a bulldog of stern principle toward the weak, a spaniel of complaisance toward the strong.

In a larger sense a feeling of administrative arbitrariness—or at least a failure to have thought the issue through—is conveyed by the explanations put forward by the agency for not ordering wide-scale divestitures. The reasons given by the agency for its diffidence were a fear of impairing the stability and continuity of local broadcasting service and the related concern that large-scale divestiture could do injury to the FCC's expressed policy favoring the local ownership of broadcast stations. But these reasons stand up to analysis very poorly. The local ownership policy, for example, has never been thought of by the Commission as much more than a decision rule for choosing

---

[19] At the time the Commission spoke, Washington, D.C. was one of the most concentrated large communications markets in the country. One network-affiliated station was owned and operated by the NBC network, the second affiliate was owned by the city's morning newspaper, and the third by the afternoon paper. An independent VHF station was owned by Metromedia, one of the largest group owners. All of the network-affiliated stations had powerful AM radio affiliates as well. Several other major markets were similarly concentrated. The shape of the industry at that time is described and analyzed in BAER, GELLER, GRUNDFEST, & POSSNER, CONCENTRATION OF MASS MEDIA OWNERSHIP: ASSESSING THE STATE OF CURRENT KNOWLEDGE (1974); and BAER, GELLER, & GRUNDFEST, NEWSPAPER-TELEVISION STATION CROSS-OWNERSHIP: OPTIONS FOR FEDERAL ACTION (1974).

between two otherwise identically qualified applicants for the same frequency.[20] Even in this limited application the Commission has all but abandoned local ownership as a criterion on which anything of importance should be allowed to turn.[21] After all, broadcast stations are managed and programmed by full-time staffs. The economic, sociological, and related concerns which are supposed to affect station performance should remain constant no matter where the capital to buy the station came from. This policy then, will bear little weight as a justification for doing anything let alone refraining from implementing a policy whose success is said to constitute a condition for the proper functioning of a democratic society.

The Commission's professed concern with dislocation and discontinuity of operation is likewise difficult to credit. It is hard to see how a divestiture order carrying a five-year grace period, itself subject to protraction by waiver for good cause, would be likely to create any serious disruption in the operation of a broadcast station. Stations are never static affairs: management, programming, sales, and technical personnel change; news and weather people come and go; every fall, winter, and spring, program schedules are shuffled. These normal incidents of change in the everyday life of a station need not be and generally are not disruptive in themselves. Neither does a change in ownership need to be disruptive. Of course it may be. New owners, with their new brooms, could, if they chose to do so, march through newly acquired properties sweeping away all continuity with the past and nurturing new promise for the future. Not surprisingly, few new owners have seen such radicalism to be in their financial interest. There is nothing which compels them to break sharply with the traditions of the past. Yet, if such changes are believed to be in the interest of the new ownership because it will attract a larger or more contented audience or for other similar reasons, this would hardly be "disruptive" but would rather merit being called an "innovation" or "improvement," nothing for the FCC necessarily to abjure in radio or television. The point is not, of course, that creating opportunities for new owners is a good in itself. There is no reason to believe this apart from certain assumptions about the intrinsic goodness of ownership diversity. But neither is it an evil. The Commission's fear of disruption apparently has its

---

[20] 1 F.C.C.2d 393 (1965).
[21] Cowles-Florida Broadcasting, Inc., 60 F.C.C.2d 372 (1976).

source in a fear that new owners will somehow damage the public interest in some undefined way, possibly because they simply will not know quite how to operate the station. But, of course, none of this follows plausibly from a divestiture order with a generous compliance schedule.[22]

The Commission's proffered justifications for grandfathering existing cross-owned combinations were intrinsically unpersuasive. When these justifications are juxtaposed with the First Amendment penumbrae which the Commission invoked to explain the underlying rule, they begin to seem worse than unpersuasive. They begin to seem "arbitrary and capricious," not only as those words are used in common speech but also as they are used in the judicial review provisions of the Administrative Procedure Act.[23] And this, in substance, was the argument of the Court of Appeals in the *NCCB* case.

It was, in particular, the Commission's First Amendment hyperbole which fixed the attention of the Court of Appeals. If, as the Commission had said, "nothing can be more important than insuring" diversity, then why should such speculative and ill-supported considerations such as "economic dislocation" or "diminution of local ownership" overbear this value? Even while recognizing that the Commission probably could not be held literally to its own puffing, the court concluded that, "at the least, consistency would call for ordering divestiture absent a showing of greater public interest harm."[24]

There was indeed ample justification in the Commission's poorly written document for the reviewing court to object. The conventional judicial response would have been to remand the docket to the

---

[22] The Commission also expressed the fear that any rule which required wide-scale divestitures would place unacceptable demands on the nation's equity capital markets, bidding up interest rates, and perhaps requiring financial sacrifices by existing owners. Given the historic profitability of commercial television, however, it seems improbable that raising capital to buy a station would be a difficult task. Given the size of American capital markets, it seems farfetched to imagine that these would be dislocated or injured by the sale of even a large number of broadcasting stations over a five-year period. And, as for financial losses by existing owners—even assuming it appropriate for the Commission to make much of this sort of entirely private burden—it is hard to see why any great sacrifices should occur. A station would bring approximately the capitalized value of its expected revenue stream. Existing owners should realize this sum and would not be "injured" in any economic sense if they did.

[23] 5 U.S.C. § 706(2)(A).

[24] 555 F.2d 938, 963 (D.C. Cir. 1977).

agency and to require it to take the "hard look" at the problem required by law,[25] either to change its result to conform to its views or to change its expressed views to something more nearly consistent with its result.[26] The court did not take this approach, however, but rather found, both in the Communications Act[27] and in the First Amendment, a prodiversity presumption of sufficient strength to establish the newspaper–broadcast station cross-ownership prohibition as a presumptive baseline of policy from which deviations must be considered abnormal as a matter of law and consequently in need of justification. The Commission, in short, must explain not its newly adopted policy but rather the grandfather clause which forms an exception to it.

Taking this prodiversity presumption of law on its own terms, several questions of policy come to mind. How strong is this presumption and how far does it radiate? If the FCC must require the dissolution of newspaper broadcast station combinations unless there exist specific reasons for not doing so, must it similarly require all so-called multiple owners—licensees of more than one broadcast station—to dissolve their holdings as well, unless there exist specific reasons for not so doing? Should the Commission attempt to discourage network programming in the name of diversity, unless there exist specific reasons for not so doing?[28] Must the entire structure of the broadcasting industry be reconstructed to conform to the presumption of diversity, unless there exist specific reasons for not so doing?

It would be impractical, to say the least, to take the court's logic to the extremes of its implications and an ordinary charitable reading of its opinion would not suggest that this be done. But neither is

---

[25] Greater Boston Television, Inc. v. F.C.C., 444 F.2d 841 (D.C. Cir. 1969).

[26] In any event, the agency is usually thought to be entitled to rethink its position in light of the guidance furnished by the reviewing court. In F.C.C. v. Pottsville Broadcasting Co., 309 U.S. 134, 145 (1940), the Supreme Court said: "An administrative determination in which is embedded a legal question open to judicial review does not impliedly foreclose the administrative agency, after its error has been corrected, from enforcing the legislative policy committed to its charge."

[27] The Commission is charged to "encourage the larger and more effective use of radio in the public interest." 47 U.S.C. § 303(g).

[28] Indeed, the Commission already has a limited policy to this very effect. See 47 C.F.R. § 73.658(k). For an explanation of this policy see Second Report and Order (Docket No. 19622), 50 F.C.C.2d 829 (1975). Does some constitutional theophany require the agency to go further still?

there a means available for deciding just what the court's presumption should mean, for there is not much precedent for reviewing tribunals doing what the court did here, *i.e.*, ordering that an agency rule—the product of an informal rulemaking under the Administrative Procedure Act—be drafted around a presumption of law erected by the court. In effect, the court orders that a particular rule be adopted. An administrative policy of some specificity but of an undetermined reach is simply teased out of the generalities of the statute and the First Amendment. Whatever the merits of the rule itself, it is a dramatic example of judicial legislation and not merely of the sort long recognized as appropriate in common law determinations,[29] but of a different sort, one which draws from a reservoir of discretion which, at least apparently, has been entrusted by the legislature to an independent administrative agency.

Whether or not this is an appropriate role for the court to play in the administrative process, it is certainly not one arrived at by accident. The Court of Appeals's opinion in *NCCB* is not a sport. One of the achievements of the Court of Appeals over the past decade has been gradually to fashion a vocabulary and self-conception consistent with a substantial participation in both the procedures of the agencies whose decisions it reviews and their substantive judgments. It would be misleading to suggest that this self-conception is refined enough to describe precisely. The often voluminous opinions produced by the Court attest to the uncertainties which the judges entertain about their proper role. Yet it is possible to see in the cases decided by the Court an unfolding self-definition, different both in nuance and atmosphere and quite possibly different in some concrete ways as well, from any normal conception of judicial review.

III. The Partnership Doctrine

What I call the "normal" conception of judicial review of administrative decisions does contain, for reasons mentioned earlier, a considerable element of legislative judgment. But it seems generally understood that the narrowness of the judicial role is or ought to be a far more prominent feature of the process than its breadth. This inference, at all events, can be gathered from the Supreme Court's

---

[29] See, *e.g.*, the discussion by Hand, J., in *Associated Press*, 52 F. Supp. at 370.

opinion in *Citizens to Preserve Overton Park v. Volpe*,[30] as well as from numerous other sources.[31] Notwithstanding this general understanding—which Glen Robinson would dismiss as more or less mandatory "expressions of judicial piety [similar to] statements that courts are the 'guardians of liberty,' 'defenders of justice,' and so on"[32]—the Court of Appeals has often gone beyond anything that could be realistically described as a narrow conception of its role. It has ranged far and involved itself in both substantive and procedural areas of administrative discretion and practice. It has not done so surreptitiously but to the full accompaniment of various proffered apologia for the part it has gradually come to play. For example, in *Calvert Cliffs Coordinating Committee, Inc. v. United States Atomic Energy Comm'n*,[33] the Court spoke of itself in terms the Constitution relates to the Executive—to take care that the laws are faithfully executed:[34]

> [I]t remains to be seen whether the promise of [the National En-
> vironmental Policy Act] will become a reality. Therein lies the
> judicial role. . . . Our duty . . . is to see that important legislative
> purposes, heralded in the halls of Congress, are not lost or mis-
> directed in the vast hallways of the federal bureaucracy.

And in *Environmental Defense Fund, Inc. v. Ruckelshaus*, the Court said that where administrative action "touches on fundamental personal interests in life, health and liberty"—and a great many agency decisions obviously do—"the court invokes a standard of 'strict judicial scrutiny of administrative action.' "[35] This "strict scrutiny"—the echo from the vocabulary of the Supreme Court equal protection doctrine cannot be accidental—is to operate both to "require administrative officers to articulate the standards and principles that govern their discretionary decisions in as much detail

---

[30] 401 U.S. 402, 416 (1971).

[31] Wright, *The Courts and the Rulemaking Process: The Limits of Judicial Review*, 59 CORNELL L. REV. 375, 396–97 (1974); Bazelon, *Coping with Technology through the Legal Process*, 62 CORNELL L. REV. 817, 828 (1977); Leventhal, *Environmental Decision-making and the Role of the Courts*, 122 U. PA. L. REV. 509, 511–12 (1974); Paper, *Judicial Scrutiny of the F.C.C.: The Illusion of Usurpation*, 52 B. U. L. REV. 659, 664 (1972).

[32] Robinson, *The Judicial Role*, in ROBINSON, ED., COMMUNICATIONS FOR TOMORROW: POLICY PERSPECTIVES FOR THE 1980s 415, 420 (1978).

[33] 449 F.2d 1109 (D.C. Cir. 1971).

[34] *Id.* at 1111.

[35] 439 F.2d 584, 598 (D.C. Cir. 1971).

as possible" and "to ensure that the administrative process itself will confine and control the exercise of discretion."[36] That the Court understood itself to be undertaking an essentially new departure in its relation with the agencies can hardly be doubted. It said:[37]

> We stand on the threshold of a new era in the history of the long and fruitful collaboration of administrative agencies and reviewing courts. For many years, courts have treated administrative policy decisions with great deference, confining judicial attention primarily to matters of procedure. On matters of substance, the courts regularly upheld agency action, with a nod in the direction of the "substantial evidence" test, and a bow to the mysteries of administrative expertise. Courts occasionally asserted, but less often exercised, the power to set aside agency action on the ground that an impermissible factor had entered into the decision, or a crucial factor had not been considered. Gradually, however, that power has come into more frequent use, and with it, the requirement that administrators articulate the factors on which they base their decisions.

The Court has never attempted to reduce its views on its proper relationship to a single rigorous statement. Terms have sometimes been used with minor inconsistencies from opinion to opinion, but the general idea that emerges can be legitimately traced to some influential dicta in *Greater Boston Television Corp. v. F.C.C.*, which asserted that "agencies and courts together constitute a 'partnership' in furtherance of the public interest, and are 'collaborative instrumentalities of justice.' "[38] The *Greater Boston* opinion goes on to sug-

---

[36] *Ibid.*

[37] *Ibid.* As was noted by Judge Harold Leventhal, the Supreme Court's opinion in *Overton Park* ratifies at least a portion of this apology for an expanded judicial function— *i.e.*, the part dealing with a court's competence to "probe the mind of the administrator" in order to satisfy itself that the decision was based on a consideration of the relevant factors—what Judge Leventhal would call a "hard look." See WAIT Radio v. F.C.C., 418 F.2d 1153, 1157 (1969); Pikes Peak Broadcasting Co. v. F.C.C., 422 F.2d 671, 682 (1969). See Leventhal, note 31 *supra*, at 512. *Overton Park*, however, hardly catches the expansive spirit of the Court of Appeals's opinion in *Environmental Defense Fund*.

[38] 444 F.2d 841, 851–52 (1969). The notion of courts and agencies in "partnership" was probably original with Professor Louis L. Jaffe, who states that this theme is central in his classic JUDICIAL CONTROL OF ADMINISTRATIVE ACTION vii (1965). The "collaborative instrumentalities of justice" language is drawn from the opinion of Justice Frankfurter in United States v. Morgan, 313 U.S. 409, 422 (1941), which, ironically, was meant to counsel a narrow rather than an expansive attitude toward judicial review: "[I]t was not the function of the court to probe the mental processes of the Secretary. . . . Just as a judge cannot be subjected to such a scrutiny . . . so the

gest the practical and intellectual grounds on which the partnership is to rest. The Court must undertake:[39]

> [a] study of the record . . . even as to the evidence on technical and specialized matters, for this enables the court to penetrate to the underlying decisions of the agency, to satisfy itself that the agency has exercised a reasoned discretion, with reasons that do not deviate from or ignore the ascertainable legislative intent. . . .
>
> Its supervisory function calls on the court to intervene not merely in the case of procedural inadequacies, or bypassing of the mandate in the legislative charter, but more broadly if the court becomes aware, from a combination of danger signals, that the agency has not really taken a 'hard look' at the salient problems, and has not genuinely engaged in reasoned decision-making. . . .
>
> The court is in a real sense part of the total administrative process, and not a hostile stranger to the office of first instance. . . .

Occasionally the Court of Appeals has spoken of its role in the partnership as a two-edged instrument. In the *Texas Gulf Coast Area Natural Gas Rate Cases*, the Court suggested that "[i]n judicial review of administrative regulation courts have a dual role, of supervision of administrative agencies and of responsible partnership in the public interest."[40] A few months later in *Holloway v. Bristol-Myers Corp.* a similar statement appears suggesting that the judicial function is "one related to the administrative process—in part supervisory and in part collaborative."[41] Such dicta are ambiguous, of course, and settle nothing in themselves. But they do seem to correspond with something palpable in the behavior of the Court. Not only has the Court's reviewing behavior been of the conventional kind, the judicial function inherited from the common law and the Administrative Procedure Act, that of ascertaining "consistency with law and legislative mandate."[42] The Court has also, in a number of cases, assumed and exercised powers beyond the traditional, manifested a

---

integrity of the administrative process must be equally respected. . . . It will bear repeating that although the administrative process has had a different development and pursues somewhat different ways from those of courts, they are to be deemed collaborative instrumentalities of justice, and the appropriate independence of each should be respected by the other."

[39] 444 F.2d at 850–52.

[40] 487 F.2d 1043, 1067 (D.C. Cir. 1973)

[41] 485 F.2d 986, 1002 (D.C. Cir. 1973).

[42] 444 F.2d at 851.

willingness to prescribe procedures for the agency that are not mandated by statute but rather deduced from the premise of "fairness" and required the enforcement of substantive policies that are referable neither to the Constitution nor anything ascertainably embedded in a statute. The source of this extra power is understood to be inherent in the relationship between court and agency or in the idea of judicial power. The *NCCB* case is only the latest instance. At least one other is worth extended discussion.

Similar to *NCCB* in its substantive focus and nearly as dramatic are the format change cases[43] in which the Court of Appeals, over a number of years, has consistently refused to allow the FCC's interpretation that the Communications Act does not require the agency to assume a protective attitude toward so-called unique radio entertainment formats in the interest of "program diversity." This matter remains a bone of contention between the Court and the agency. The cases are extraordinary illustrations of a court willing to expand its own function at the expense of the agency's discretion, to make remote inferences of policy from amorphous and general statutory language, and to go beyond mere oversight of the agency's work product to an extended collaborative dialogue with the Commission over what its substantive policies ought to be.

So far, the cases which have progressed as far as judicial review have all arisen in the context of the proposed sale of a radio station (an assignment application), where the acquiring applicant informs the agency that it intends to abandon the station's existing entertainment format, usually either of classical or "progressive rock" music, to try something else, usually commercial popular music. The Communications Act requires the agency to hold a hearing before granting an assignment if any substantial matter of fact is in controversy concerning whether the public interest will be served if the application is granted. The FCC has invariably taken the view that allegations that some particular program format subserves the interest of diversity, and thus the public interest, amount to open invitations for it to regulate programming, and has declined on those grounds to

---

[43] Citizens Committee to save WEFM v. F.C.C., 506 F.2d 246, 252 (D.C. Cir. 1974) (en banc); Lakewood Broadcasting Service, Inc. v. F.C.C., 478 F.2d 919 (D.C. Cir. 1975); Citizens Committee to Keep Progressive Rock v. F.C.C., 478 F.2d 926 (D.C. Cir. 1973); Hartford Communications Committee v. F.C.C., 467 F.2d 408 (D.C. Cir. 1972); Citizens Committee to Preserve the Voice of Arts in Atlanta v. F.C.C., 436 F.2d 263 (D.C. Cir. 1970).

hold hearings at the instance of various community groups—"public interest groups" or "private pressure groups"—which do not want their favorite music to disappear from the air.

In support of its views, the Commission has made reference to several distinct reasons of policy, some of which have strong constitutional overtones. There is the question of how a format is to be defined together with the related question, What makes a format "unique"? *i.e.*, a special contributor to the diversity of program choices in a given market. If this definition cannot be made reasonably intelligible, then there is simply no feasible way to pursue the further and more complex questions concerning the relation between this term and program diversity. But pinning down an acceptable or workable definition of a format, or a unique format, turns out to be a serious difficulty indeed. As then-Commissioner Robinson observed in 1976:[44]

> What makes one format unique makes all formats unique. If subjectivity is to be an important determinant of what makes a format "unique" (or, in other terms, what makes it a net contributor to diversity), how are we to avoid the fact that even with respect to formats which objectively seem identical, people— radio listeners—can and do make distinctions. For example, in most large markets, there are a number of middle-of-the-road formats which seem identical on any objective or quantifiable basis; yet they are far from interchangeable to their respective audiences. Indeed, if people did not distinguish among these stations, there would be no reason for them to co-exist—and little economic likelihood that they would. Questions of pacing and style, the personalities of on-the-air talent (both individually and in combination with one another) all contribute to those fugitive values that radio people call a station's "sound" and that citizens' groups (and, alas, appellate judges) call format. [A]ny format is unique; from which it follows, all must be preserved.

The very essence of the inquiry is so subjective that it would be impossible for an agency to pursue it fairly, *i.e.*, with regularity or perceived consistency in the application of its criteria. The inability to manage an essentially subjective issue in a fair way furnishes, in itself, an adequate justification for the agency's policy.

Several other reasons, similarly persuasive, favor the agency's position. There is, for example, the guess that a restrictive format-

---

[44] 57 F.C.C.2d at 594–95 (1976).

change policy could prove to be counterproductive. It would take a courageous (and solvent) licensee to begin experimenting with a format that it might not be able to abandon later without first going through a hearing—a form of litigation which can easily cost several hundred thousand dollars which is nearly as much as an average radio station is worth. Thus a restrictive format-change policy could work to the long-term detriment of the very diversity it would seek to promote.

Furthermore, if the agency is required to observe the equation between the public interest and a diversity of program formats, it would be unreasonable, if not actually oppressive, for it to do so only when an assignment application raised the problem. The principle of the format-change cases cannot be confined to assignment applications alone for there is nothing about the context of an assignment that gives the Commission special powers or responsibilities that do not equally belong to a consideration of any other "application" as that term is employed by the Communications Act. Hence it follows that the Commission must be equally concerned, must equally convene a hearing in an otherwise routine license renewal, if some question were raised as to whether the licensee's programming had adequately contributed to diversity during the preceding license term. Furthermore, there is the question whether the Commission could justify proceeding on an *ad hoc* basis at all, that is, by ordering this station to continue or to discontinue some type of programming without giving some thought to spreading the burdens of diversity among all the competitors in the market. As Robinson suggested:[45]

> [E]lementary considerations of fair play as well as constitutional principles of equal protection would seem to forbid the Commission from placing on any one licensee the full weight of the obligation to promote diversity without imposing an equivalent burden of obligation to the public interest in diversity on its competitors. . . . I can see no escape from market-by-market allocation proceedings which would determine what array of formats a particular community required, together with which station would be allowed to use which format.

Such allocation proceedings, obviously, would have the most serious free-speech consequences, for they would place the agency in the position not only of dictating program content to licensees but

---

[45] *Id.* at 599.

also of punishing deviation from the programming prescribed. In *Columbia Broadcasting System, Inc. v. Democratic National Committee*,[46] the Supreme Court agreed with the FCC that an agency directive to licensees to accept controversial editorial advertising—which the Court of Appeals had declared to be a First Amendment obligation of both the Commission and the broadcasters—would seriously threaten to draw the Commission into day-to-day supervision of broadcaster programming decisions and Fairness Doctrine compliance, with deleterious First Amendment consequences that the Commission was entitled to attempt to avoid as a matter of congressionally conferred discretion. It is hard to imagine that the consequences of format regulation could be less serious or that the agency's discretion to steer around constitutional pitfalls in this area would be any less than that recognized by the Supreme Court in *Columbia Broadcasting*.

Whatever the constitutionality of the administrative consequences of the Court of Appeals's *WEFM* decision, it certainly cannot be defended as an inexorable, or even a reasonably probable, extrapolation from the Communications Act. Between the statute and the Court's opinion are many noncompulsory steps whose measure constitute the size of the administrative discretion to which the Court has laid claim. The Communications Act has two provisions on which the Court's argument turns: § 309(a), which obliges the agency to find, before granting an application, that the public interest will be served by that action; and § 309(e), which requires the agency to hold a hearing if there exists any substantial and material question of fact pending whose resolution the public interest finding cannot be made. Does a format change raise a substantial and material question of fact concerning whether the public interest will be served by the agency's grant of an assignment application? That question is simply a roundabout way of probing the FCC's discretion to interpret the Communications Act and to make qualitative and quantitative estimates of the costs likely to be encountered by the agency's enforcement of a restrictive format-change policy. The "fact" supposed to be in controversy includes the assertion that format diversity is a part of the statutory public interest. The agency had determined that several consequences would flow from recognizing that fact in the way that the Court of Appeals had repeatedly insisted: that it would be expensive for the agency, that it

---

[46] 412 U.S. 94, 126–27 (1973).

would probably be self-defeating in its own terms, and that it would be contrary to the policies of the anticensorship provision of the Communications Act[47] as well as menacing to the First Amendment. How the format diversity question relates to the public interest, then, is or is not a fact depending upon whether the Court may properly override the agency's judgment respecting these determinations of policy.

In conventional principle, the Court should affirm the Commission's decision if, speaking plainly, the agency has been "not unreasonable."[48] The Court of Appeals's *WEFM* holding, then, if it is to be taken as proceeding from that conventional principle, must involve the assertion that the agency's reading of the Communications Act and its selection of policies and educated guesses about the probable risks and consequences of adopting this or that particular policy have fallen below the "not unreasonable" standard. The agency is entitled to be affirmed if it is not unreasonable in supposing that a restrictive format-change policy may undermine program diversity in the long run by deterring licensees from experimenting with novel entertainment formats, licensees fearing that once they had begun carrying such a format, the public interest might be interpreted to forbid its *ad libitum* abandonment. Likewise, the agency is entitled to be affirmed if it was not unreasonable in reading the anticensorship section of the Communications Act to restrain it from inquiry, at least in the prohibitively expensive context of a hearing, into the entertainment formats proposed to be offered by a licensee or a prospective licensee. Finally, the agency ought to be affirmed if it not unreasonably believed that the consequences of a restrictive format-change policy might "chill" the free speech of broadcasters and disturb the correlative interests of the public. The agency's decision, that format diversity cannot be accounted as a fact pertaining to the public interest, simply integrates all of the foregoing conclusions.

To suggest that the Court did indeed find the agency unreasonable

---

[47] Section 326 provides: "Nothing in this chapter shall be understood or construed to give the Commission the power of censorship over the radio communications or signals transmitted by any radio station, and no regulation or condition shall be promulgated or fixed by the Commission which shall interfere with the right of free speech by radio communication." 47 U.S.C. § 326.

[48] Ethyl Corp. v. Environmental Protection Agency, 541 F.2d 1, 68, 69 (D.C. Cir. 1976) (Leventhal, J.).

on each or any of the foregoing synapses of policy strains credulity. The Court of Appeals's decision not to accept the agency's definition of what constitute facts can only be understood (unless one wishes to strain credulity) by parsing the Court's judgment into holding that it is not the Commission but the Court of Appeals that is the better arbiter of these matters. Whether or not this decision appropriately allocates functions between the two institutions, it evidently displays an aspect of the court-agency relationship that cannot be justified in the conventional language of judicial review of administrative action.

IV. WHO SHOULD DECIDE?

Both *WEFM* and *NCCB* reflect a consistent premise concerning the allocation of substantive policy-making discretion between the agency and the reviewing court. The premise bespeaks a broad role for the judicial part of the partnership and no principle has been discussed that would seem to impeach this distribution of power. After all, the courts as much as administrative agencies speak for the public. They should be at least as "expert" as a regulatory commission in expounding constitutional values. If they recognize some important ("fundamental") value on which an agency seems not to place sufficient importance, what objection should there be to the Court of Appeals intervening with its presumably refined notions of policy?

The primary reason for preferring the agencies' decisions derives from democratic theory. Compared to courts, agencies are "closer to the people," and "more politically responsive." These fictitious constructs have some relationship to reality. But the "democratic legitimacy" point is, for the skeptical observer, much too complex to be accepted offhandedly. Agencies are both formally and informally "responsive" to congressional committee chairmen,[49] who are in turn responsive to the members of their committees. Every member of Congress is concerned with and influenced by public opinion—at least as manifested in his own district. Few members of appropriations or oversight committees, however, run for reelection on their administrative policy stands. Agencies are responsive to important officers of the executive branch—especially

---

[49] Dean Ernest Gellhorn describes the congressional influence over FCC policymaking as "limited and reactive." See Gellhorn, *The Role of Congress*, in ROBINSON, note 32 *supra*, at 445, 447.

the president—if strong views about agency policies are entertained or expressed there. Agencies also respond to the views of their professional staffs, to the expressions and needs of the industries which they regulate, to what they believe the newspapers will say about them and what they are doing, to how they believe the Court of Appeals will react, and to their own notions of what society's welfare requires. Agencies do have a niche in a complex political machinery. Their practices and procedures can unblushingly, if somewhat poetically, be referred to as "democratic" inasmuch as they do constitute a rational part of a larger democratic context. Agencies are not, however, representative in themselves. Furthermore, if the agency is democratic, the Court of Appeals would be democratic for many of the same reasons. Courts too are responsive, it might be argued, even if not to precisely the same things. They do respond to argument based on important principles: to constitutional values and to fundamental rights. Certainly they respond to what they believe the newspapers will say. Proverbially, they follow the election returns, and at all events, their membership, just as with commissioners, is replenished from time to time by presidential appointment. Some people, indeed—the true believers in the theory that regulated industries "capture" and "manipulate" the administrative agencies—might even regard judicially shaped administrative policies as superior in legitimacy to those fashioned by the agencies themselves.

To satisfy those who express doubt about the superior democratic legitimacy of administrative agencies, we have to find another reason for preferring the agencies' judgment. Perhaps a reviewing court should defer to an agency's substantive policy decisions because there is generally nothing to be gained by not deferring. This answer can be tested in the context of the *NCCB* case. Here, if anywhere, is an administrative policy with constitutional overtones. And it is with constitutional policies, if anywhere, that the judiciary would seem to have some "expertise" superior to that of administrative agencies.

It will help to clarify the discussion to look first at an old and influential case which bears many substantive similarities to the newspaper–broadcast station cross-ownership issue. In *United States v. Associated Press*[50] the district court found a First Amendment presumption similar to that asserted by the Court of Appeals in *NCCB*

---

[50] Note 2 *supra*.

to determine the outcome of an antitrust action. In *Associated Press*, the Justice Department had brought an antitrust action alleging that the members of the Associated Press (AP) had conspired unreasonably to restrain commerce and create monopoly in violation of the Sherman Act. The members of AP were newspapers. Every member was required to subscribe to the association's bylaws which, among other things, forbade members from sharing any news with nonmember newspapers and placed serious obstacles in the way of nonmembers joining the association—at least if a direct competitor of an applicant were already enrolled in the association.

Judge Learned Hand writing for the majority of the district court had little difficulty in finding that the bylaws were in effect an agreement whose purpose was to restrict interstate commerce. But to find a Sherman Act violation, the restraint "must be 'unreasonable' in the sense that the common law understood that word."[51] Were the association's restraints, then, unreasonable? The court found the matter not free from doubt:[52]

> [I]f this were a case of the ordinary kind: the production of fungible goods, like steel, machinery, clothes or the like, it would be a nice question whether the handicap on those excluded from the combination should prevail over the claims of the members to enjoy the fruits of their foresight, industry and sagacity. But in that event the only interest we should have to weigh against that of the members would be the interest of the excluded newspapers. . . . However, neither exclusively, nor even primarily, are the interests of the newspaper industry conclusive; for that industry serves one of the most general interests: the dissemination of news from as many different sources, and with as many different facets and colors as is possible. That interest is closely akin to, if indeed it is not the same as, the interest protected by the First Amendment.

In short, a combination which might be reasonable in another industry was unreasonable in the newspaper business because of its incidental effect on a First Amendment interest—the unrestrained operation of "a multitude of tongues" for (changing the metaphor) "it is only by crosslights from varying directions that full illumination can be secured."[53]

---

[51] 52 F. Supp. at 368, citing Standard Oil Co. v. United States, 221 U.S. 1 (1911).

[52] 52 F. Supp. at 372.

[53] *Ibid.*

The district court was exceptionally careful to indicate that this determination was a matter of discretion which it proposed to resolve according to its own perception of the applicable standards. "Courts must proceed step by step, applying retroactively the standard proper for each situation as it comes up, just as they do in the case of negligence, reasonable notice, and the like."[54] Hand did not shy away from the issue:[55]

> Certainly such a function is ordinarily "legislative"; for in a legislature the conflicting interests find their respective representation, or in any event can make their political power felt, as they cannot upon a court. The resulting compromises so arrived at are likely to achieve stability, and to be acquiesced in: which is justice. But it is a mistake to suppose that courts are never called upon to make similar choices: i.e., to appraise and balance the value of opposed interests and to enforce their preference. The law of torts is for the most part the result of exactly that process, and the law of torts has been judge-made, especially in this very branch. Besides, even though we had more scruples than we do, we have here a legislative warrant, because Congress has incorporated into the Anti-Trust Acts the changing standards of the common law, and by so doing has delegated to the courts the duty of fixing the standard for each case. Congress might have proceeded otherwise; it might have turned the whole matter over to an administrative tribunal, as indeed to a limited extent it has done to the Federal Trade Commission. But, though it has acted, it has left these particular controversies to the courts, where they have been from very ancient times.

The conclusion of the court of appeals in *NCCB* was not formally dissimilar from that of the district court in the *Associated Press* case. Some act which might otherwise be discretionary with the actor is limited by the overriding requirements of free speech. If the *Associated Press* court reached the right result and the *NCCB* court reached the wrong result, the explanation must lie in some differences between the judicial role in shaping common law versus that role in administrative law. But one must not be too swift to conclude that in the cross-ownership case and other FCC concerns Congress had "turned the whole matter over to an administrative tribunal" for determination. It had not. The FCC's legislative mandate—to enlarge the uses of radio communications in the public interest—is

---

[54] *Id.* at 368.

[55] *Id.* at 370.

broad enough to endow the agency with a wide-sweeping discretion. By the same token the reviewing court is endowed with a comparably broad discretion by the comparably general terms of the judicial review provisions of the Administrative Procedure Act:[56]

> The delegation of legislative power ultimately transfers power not only to agencies but also to courts that supervise the exercise of agency power. This may seem contradictory. In theory, as statutory terms of agency power and discretion broaden, the justification for judicial interference, at least on substantive or jurisdictional grounds, becomes more limited. However, when such terms (or their judicial construction) become so broad as to lose all practical significance, an agency and its supervisory courts enjoy ample room to share the power that the legislature has relinquished.

It begs the question, then, to assert that the matter has been wholly turned over to an administrative tribunal.[57] Indeed, the presumption is the other way—that reviewing courts may have their say, whatever it properly is, unless there is "no law to apply."[58] In the case of the cross-ownership issue, at least as the Court of Appeals saw it, not only was there law to apply, but constitutional law at that, a field in which the preeminent expertise of a court must be presumed. Additional explanation must be necessary, then, to understand wherein the Court of Appeals erred.

Perhaps the explanation, or a part of it, lies in where each court is located in the decisional process. Judge Hand's court was the one of first instance and rested its decision on an estimate of the consequences of its decision on the values to which it gave priority. The constitutional issues bound up in much of substantive FCC policy

---

[56] Robinson, *The Federal Communications Commission: An Essay on Regulatory Watchdogs*, 64 VA. L. REV. 169, 176 (1978). Judge Carl McGowan has expressed a similar point: "If federal judges hold a great potential of power to impose their views on many aspects of the modern economy, it is surely the Congress that has made them so by its penchant for combining broad delegation of lawmaking authority with sweeping, albeit sometimes inexpertly conceived, provisions for judicial review." McGowan, note 3 *supra*, at 1590.

[57] On this point I disagree with Lewis J. Paper, recently appointed assistant general counsel of the FCC whose 1972 article, note 31 *supra*, at 664–65, does assume this assertion, especially in its provocative suggestion that separation of powers problems arise when legislative authority is given to the judiciary.

[58] See Citizens to Preserve Overton Park v. Volpe, note 30 *supra*; Wheelabrator Corp. v. Chafee, 455 F.2d 1306 (D.C. Cir. 1971).

are often more complicated and in greater logical tension because of the explicit statutory basis for the "collective" free-speech interest formulated by the Supreme Court in *Red Lion Broadcasting Co. v. F.C.C.*[59] than in *Associated Press*. Thus, as the decision maker of first instance, the *Associated Press* court was in a position analogous to that of the FCC in the *NCCB* case. Could the district court's opinion in *Associated Press* have stood up to an authoritative assertion that First Amendment interests are better served by allowing newspapers to combine in order to maximize their profitability than by requiring them to share the product of their collaboration with their competitors? Obviously not. But the court seemingly conceived that it had the authority to decide how the antitrust laws and the First Amendment would intermesh.

The cross-ownership issue entails numerous, important, and sometimes conflicting free-speech related values. To begin with, there is the multitude of tongues version of free speech which assumes that different speakers will produce different accounts of the world from which people may pick and choose, or triangulate, whatever reality they prefer.[60] This is an honored conception of the First Amendment, but it is also somewhat abstract. From the viewpoint of the person in the street, a more useful version of "diversity" might imply a wide range of program choices. As Professor Peter Steiner demonstrated more than twenty-five years ago, diversity, in the sense of wide-

---

[59] 395 U.S. 367 (1969).

[60] "News is history; recent history, it is true, but veritable history, nevertheless; and history is not total recall, but a deliberate pruning of, and calling [sic] from, the flux of events. Were it possible by some magic telepathy to reproduce an occasion in all its particularity, all reproductions would be interchangeable; the public could have no choice, provided that the process should be mechanically perfect. But there is no such magic; and if there were, its result would be immeasurably wearisome, and utterly fatuous. In the production of news every step involves the conscious intervention of some news gatherer, and two accounts of the same event will never be the same. Those who make up the first record—the reporters on the spot—are themselves seldom first hand witnesses; they must take the stories of others as their raw material, checking their veracity, eliminating their irrelevancies, finally producing an ordered version which will evoke and retain the reader's attention and convince him of its truth. And the report so prepared, when sent to his superiors, they in turn 'edit,' before they send it out to the members; a process similar to the first. A personal impress is inevitable at every stage; it gives its value to the dispatch, which without it would be unreadable. So much for those items which actually appear in all the larger news services, and which include all events of major interest. But these are not all: the same personal choice which must figure in preparing a dispatch, operates in deciding what events are important enough to appear at all; and about that men will differ widely; as we often find, when one service 'carries' what others have thought too trivial; or may indeed have missed altogether." 52 F. Supp. at 372.

ranging program choices, can be pursued much more effectively by a monopolist than by competitors.[61] Steiner's argument, which I must truncate without pretending to do it justice, rests on a number of highly plausible assumptions, some of the most important of which are: that a broadcaster, whether a monopolist or a competitor, will attempt to maximize the number of its listening audience at any given time; that programming is a "free good" to listeners except for the opportunity costs associated with listening; that listeners distinguish program "types" and have preferences among them; and that stations simultaneously producing the same type of programming will divide among them the audience that prefers that type of programming. Given these assumptions, a competitor may often calculate that there is more to be gained by securing a fractional share of the very large audience that clusters around the median of taste than by monopolizing the allegiance of some subaudience which forms a much smaller portion of the whole. A monopolist—one who controlled all the available frequencies—with the same incentive to maximize its total audience, would pursue an entirely different strategy. Assuming its intuition were adequate to discriminate among the various types of programming that would be perceived by the audience as distinct, it would have no interest in competing with itself by placing the same type of program material on more than one frequency. On the contrary, it would attempt to employ each frequency to reach a different segment of the audience, thus yielding a more "diverse" result.

It is an interesting question of constitutional and/or statutory interpretation whether Steiner's insights about the diversity generating properties of the industry structure dictated by the Communications Act should be imputed to the Congress which enacted that statute eighteen years before Steiner's article. Surely the argument is original with Steiner. Just as surely, however, the congressional decisions (1) to place radio licenses in the hands of many competitors rather than a single public or private monopolist; (2) to make advertising rather than direct audience payment the industry's economic base; and (3) to structure the industry largely around local markets, has "caused" the present reality in which (among other things) middle-of-the-road and "bubble-gum music"[62] formats

---

[61] Steiner, *Program Patterns and Preferences, and the Workability of Competition in Radio Broadcasting*, 66 Q. J. ECON. 194 (1952).

[62] *I.e.*, music of special interest to younger teenaged listeners.

abound in most cities, while minority tastes in radio programming—
e.g., classical music—are represented sporadically or unstably, if at
all. If it is proper to hold that Congress necessarily "foresees" and
thus "intends" effects which will ensue (given the durable premise
that commercial licensees will try to maximize profits) naturally and
probably from the economic characteristics of the statutes which it
enacts, what follows is more than merely a different ground on which
to disagree with the Court of Appeals's opinion in *WEFM*. This
interpretation, if it is accepted, implies a congressional "intention"
to subordinate the program-diversity speech interest to the inconsistent speech interest of dispersing the control of the broadcasting
industry into many hands in many markets. This argument was not
made to the Court of Appeals in *NCCB*. Had it been, it might have
given the court a somewhat stronger plank on which to stand in
reaching its decision. The court, although it relied on the policies of
the Communications Act for a part of its justification for the diversity presumption which it declared, did not have a persuasive
rationale for preferring that diversity interest to any of the other free-
speech related interests.

Some critics would probably reject the imputation to the Congress
of an intention that it could not possibly have intended. Those
critics would point out that it takes a fiction—the notion that large
legislative assemblies can ordinarily be said, in any meaningful sense,
to be capable of intending anything[63]—and compounds it. But even
if one accepts imputations of intention such as the one suggested
above, the cross-ownership issue (in common with communications
policy more generally) contains a number of other speech-related
interests which elude any logical ordering.

Another diversity interest, related to the First Amendment in
several credible but conflicting ways, is the conception of broadcast
stations as advertising outlets—unquestionably their most accurate
characterization in economic terms. To the extent that a broadcaster, who also owns a newspaper, has "power" in the local advertising market, he will be in a position to pursue the conventional
monopolist's strategy of constricting the supply of his product
(advertising space, either in the newspaper, or on the broadcast
station, or both) and raising its price to advertisers. To the extent
that this is done, advertisers' communication with the public—a

---

[63] See Arrow, Social Choice and Individual Values (1951); Dahl, A Preface
to Democratic Theory 34–62 (1956).

free-speech interest not less important for its recent recognition—
will be inhibited by being made more expensive. Thus monopoly
works against free-speech interests. On the other hand, the reduction
of advertising in the newspaper and especially on television might be
thought to increase audience satisfaction with the product—arguably
a First Amendment interest and at all events an interest closely pertaining to free speech.[64]

Yet another free-speech interest, heavily relied on by the National
Association of Broadcasters (NAB) in its brief to the Supreme
Court, for which there exists plenty of authority, is tapped by the
assertion that the government:[65]

> may not deny a benefit to a person on a basis that infringes his
> constitutionally protected interests—especially his interest in
> freedom of speech. For if the Government could deny a benefit to
> a person because of his constitutionally protected speech or as-
> sociations, his exercise of those freedoms would in effect be
> penalized and inhibited.

Here, of course, it could be said that the FCC was conditioning the
availability of a broadcast license on an applicant's willingness to
forego a First Amendment interest—that of publishing a daily newspaper in the market where the broadcast license is sought. The NAB
argued:[66]

> Ironically, if the [cross-ownership] regulations had taken a
> more limited approach toward promoting diversity, their un-
> constitutionality would perhaps have been more readily apparent.
> For example, if the FCC promulgated a regulation denying broad-
> cast licenses to all local publishers who refused to adopt a right-
> of-reply policy [like the one held invalid in *Miami Herald Pub-
> lishing Company v. Tornillo*] in their newspapers, surely the court
> would not have hesitated to strike it down. Yet, since the regula-
> tions here have gone considerably further—since they have

---

[64] Robinson's dissent to the Commission's order was the only place where this economic effect was discussed. And he conceded: "These benefits from the exercise of market power must be candidly acknowledged as possible partial offsets against the potential
economic efficiency in the allocation of resources which increased competition can be
expected to stimulate." 50 F.C.C.2d at 1113, 1116.

[65] Perry v. Sinderman. 408 U.S. 593, 597 (1972). To the same effect are, *e.g.*, Elrod v.
Burns, 427 U.S. 347 (1976); Garrity v. New Jersey, 385 U.S. 493 (1967); Spevack v.
Klein, 385 U.S. 511 (1967); Sherbert v. Verner, 374 U.S. 398 (1963).

[66] N.A.B. Brief, p. 32.

categorically refused licenses to those same publishers on the
ground that they chose to publish at all—the [Court of Appeals]
has lent them unqualified approval.

The argument has logical force. And the easy refutation—that while
one may have a constitutional right to publish a newspaper, one has
no such right to a broadcast license—is regarded by cogent authority
as unacceptable.[67] How shall this value, then, be accounted for and
rank ordered as against other values in the First Amendment sphere?

Finally, the possibility that highly profitable television stations
might subsidize financially shaky newspapers is a sort of pro free-
speech value, and practically speaking, it may well be the most important First Amendment interest of all.[68] The First Amendment
and its corollaries are evidently everywhere and enlisted on both
sides of the cross-ownership question. How then, in the welter of
crosscurrents shall anyone go about pronouncing which version of
the shibboleth represents the authentic strain?

Obviously this is not the sort of question that can possibly be dealt
with by reference to expertise of any kind, neither the agency's
expertise in regulating its industry nor the court's expertise in
constitutional policy and statutory interpretation. The important
legal question is not so much what is decided but who is entitled to
decide.

In the absence of any authoritative rendition of which value
should take precedence—some clear Supreme Court precedent or a
conventional understanding about a particular hierarchy of constitutional values—it requires only a moderate positivist bias to conclude
that, practically speaking, one value is as good as another. The
Commission and the Court of Appeals may differ concerning which

---

[67] In McAuliffe v. Mayor of New Bedford, 155 Mass. 216 (1892), where a policeman
challenged the city's right to fire him for violating a regulation which prohibited soliciting
political contributions while on duty, Justice Holmes wrote: "The petitioner may
have a constitutional right to talk politics, but he has no constitutional right to be a
policeman." *Id.* at 220. Professor William Van Alstyne persuasively shows that the
statement, if accepted as a rule, leads to untenable results. *The Demise of the Right-
Privilege Distinction in Constitutional Law*, 81 HARV. L. REV. 1439 (1968). See also
NOWAK, ROTUNDA, & YOUNG, CONSTITUTIONAL LAW 478–80 (1978); ROBINSON &
GELLHORN, THE ADMINISTRATIVE PROCESS 653 (1974).

[68] This assertion requires one to accept as true the notion that newspapers are a
superior vehicle of free speech—a common prejudice which I share. It also assumes that
people in the broadcasting business will be somewhat more likely than, say, people in
the hardware or dry-cleaning business to cross-subsidize a failing newspaper with
profits from the other business. I believe this also, but do not pretend that I can prove it.

values should be prior to others. But given the impossibility of showing which viewpoint is the better, allowing the reviewing court's judgment to supersede that of the agency would not increase the odds of improving the justice or virtue of a given result, *i.e.*, if there is such a thing as justice and virtue apart from the decisions social institutions make about them—something that even a moderate positivist would probably find difficult to imagine. It would simply amount to deciding that this judgment belonged to the court and not to the agency.

I do not suggest that there is anything intrinsically nonsensical about such a decision. Just as there is no *a priori* reason for preferring the judgment of the court to that of the agency in making the choice of which free-speech interests to subordinate to which others, there is similarly no special reason for preferring the judgment of the agency to that of the court. Answering the question who gets to decide these policies is accomplished, not by disputation, but by authority.

The Supreme Court has taken the view that Congress has left the fundamental ordering of values to the agency's discretion. Moreover, the consideration that appears to determine this result is the very characteristic I have noted above concerning free speech in this context—the logical inconsistencies of the various policies and interests which can be found in or extracted from the First Amendment, and the irrefragably subjective, if not arbitrary, character of most orderings of those policies and interests in importance.

In *Business Executives Move for Vietnam Peace v. F.C.C.*,[69] the Court of Appeals reversed an agency determination that a licensee was within its rights (notwithstanding its quasi-fiduciary relation to the public) to pursue a policy of rejecting out of hand proffers of paid advertisements of an editorial or otherwise noncommercial character. One of the Commission's chief reasons for characterizing this policy as within the licensees' discretion was an apprehension that, in view of the Fairness Doctrine,[70] the agency would be irresistibly

---

[69] 450 F.2d 642 (D.C. Cir. 1971).

[70] The Fairness Doctrine obliges licensees both to identify diverse topics of public interest and importance and to select and present various perspectives on these and on any other controversial matters of public importance that may arise in the course of a station's programming. Editorial advertisements, to the extent that they contain controversial matters of public importance, trigger a station's Fairness Doctrine obligations. See generally, *Report and Order* (Docket No. 19260), 48 F.C.C.2d 1 (1974).

drawn into an ever-increasing scrutiny and regulation of licensee programming practices which would affect the speech of licensees and the First Amendment interests of both licensees and the general public. The Court of Appeals, however, rejected this argument by pointing out that the would-be advertisers, whose messages pertained to the Vietnam War also had First Amendment rights, just as the public had a right to hear their views.

The Supreme Court reversed the Court of Appeals and reinstated the decision of the agency in *Columbia Broadcasting System, Inc. v. Democratic National Committee.*[71] It rejected the lower court's argument at the most fundamental level, by denying that the Court of Appeals, rather than the FCC, should define what free speech in broadcasting should mean. The Court likened this definitional process to a "tightrope" between "the various interest in free expression of the public, the broadcaster, and the individual."[72] And implicit in its opinion is the assumption that, notwithstanding the palimpsest of constitutional concerns and values, this business belongs to the legislative authority and is a matter to which the judicial competence has little to add.

The *NCCB* case is similar to that presented in *Columbia Broadcasting*. No decision, by any institution of government (and for that matter no decision not to decide) could fail to ramify to the First Amendment, exalting some of its values and associations and depreciating others. If the proper course is befogged in principle with a high degree of uncertainty, the agency must be given a wide latitude for its discretion otherwise the grounds on which it is reversed will never be explicable as occasions when the agency's choice was "unreasonable," leaving one the unseemly—if not unrealistic—alternative, that the court's decision was more pretextual than principled.

Where the uncertainties have been of a factual character, the Court of Appeals has been quick to defer to the administrative discretion, as, for example, in *Ethyl Corp. v. Environmental Protection Agency*,[73] where the Court of Appeals makes the apparently paradoxical but ultimately persuasive argument that the acknowledged uncertainty concerning whether airborne lead "will endanger" the

---

[71] 412 U.S. 94 (1973).

[72] *Id.* at 117, 122.

[73] 541 F.2d 1 (D.C. Cir. 1976).

public health within the meaning of § 211(c) (1) (A) of the Clean
Air Act gives the EPA an extra measure of discretion in promulgating motor fuel additive standards whose premise is that such lead will
indeed endanger the public.[74] The discretion-amplifying aspect of
uncertainty, perhaps, is equally applicable where the uncertainties
concern the rank-ordering of values rather than the ascertainment of
fundamentally unknowable facts.

V. Conclusion

The Supreme Court has not taken an express position on the
propriety of the partnership metaphor. But there are clear intimations in its *NCCB* opinion that this, as well as kindred evocations of
a broad judicial role in the administrative process, may no longer be
tolerable. The Court affirmed in its entirety an agency order that was
only lamely and inconsistently justified. Whatever one thinks of the
judgment reached by the Court of Appeals, there was ample justification for the agency to be required to rethink its decision and if not to
change its cross-ownership rule, at least to redraft its opinion to give
a clearer account of its reasons.

It would probably be better to rely on some entirely different
mechanism for the control of administrative discretion if the judicial
role does not extend at least to ascertaining whether the agency has
some intelligible reason for doing whatever it is doing. "Better no
judicial review at all than a charade that gives the imprimatur without the substance of judicial confirmation that the agency is not
acting unreasonably."[75]

The Supreme Court's judgment in *NCCB* may be read to shrink
the judicial role considerably. There is, admittedly, little express
discussion in the Court's opinion of the proper relationship between

---

[74] "Questions involving the environment are particularly prone to uncertainty·
Technological man has altered his world in ways never before experienced or anticipated·
The health effects of such alterations are often unknown, sometimes unknowable. While
a concerned Congress has passed legislation providing for protection of the public
health against gross environmental modifications, the regulators entrusted with the
enforcement of such laws have not thereby been endowed with a prescience that removes
all doubt from their decision making. Rather, speculation, conflicts in evidence, and
theoretical extrapolation typify their every action. How else can they act, given a
mandate to protect the public health but only a slight or nonexistent data base upon
which to draw?" 541 F.2d at 24.

[75] Ethyl Corp. v. Environmental Protection Agency, 541 F.2d 1, 69 (1976) (Leventhal, J.).

the judicial and administrative authorities. Perhaps the sulphur and brimstone of the Court's opinion in *Vermont Yankee*,[76] where the Court of Appeals's assertion of authority concerned the agency's procedures rather than its policies, was meant to be applicable to the *NCCB* situation *a fortiori*. In *Vermont Yankee*, the Court said that the lower court "fundamentally misconceives the nature of the standard of review of an agency rule,"[77] and was guilty of "Monday morning quarterbacking,"[78] of "run[ning] riot,"[79] and being "Kafkaesque."[80] No similar sonorities emerge from the *NCCB* opinion. Its dun-colored holding is simply that "the weighing of policies under the 'public interest' standard is a task that Congress has delegated to the Commission in the first instance, and we are unable to find anything . . . that would require the Commission to 'presume' that its diversification policy should be given controlling weight in all circumstances."[81] The Commission's arguments are rehearsed solemnly and equally solemnly pronounced to be in the discretionary perimeter of reasonableness. Those who cannot accept either the sufficiency of the Commission's explanation of its rule, or that the Supreme Court's own reasoning powers have become impaired, will naturally seek for an explanation of *NCCB* which relies on neither proposition. One such possible explanation would look at the FCC's *Report and Order* as a pawn in a bigger contest between the Court of Appeals and the Supreme Court on the proper scope of judicial review.

There would be ample reason for the Court to refrain from embarking on any protracted metaphysical discussion of the limits of administrative discretion which it would expect the Court of Appeals hereafter to observe. There is no rigorous way to discuss in the abstract how discretion shall be parcelled out between a court and an agency. But the vagueness of the boundaries which divide the respective roles of agency and court may be taken by the latter in one of two opposite ways. A court may consider that, inasmuch as the

---

[76] Vermont Yankee Nuclear Power Corp. v. Natural Resources Defense Council, Inc., see note 4 *supra*.

[77] 435 U.S. at 547.

[78] *Ibid.*

[79] *Id.* at 557.

[80] *Ibid.*

[81] *Id.* at 2120.

limits of its discretion are fugitive and imprecise, it must be careful in what it says and does so that it may not overstep its bounds. Or it may conclude that, inasmuch as no one can say for certain where the judicial function ends, it may not end at all, at least until the Court of Appeals has established as a matter of "law" which substantive legislative policies it wants to have followed. The message of the Supreme Court may now be that it is better to have no judicial review at all—nothing, at least, beyond the purely perfunctory—if the reviewing court insists that the gossamer character of the restraints on its discretion can be taken to mean that actually there were no restraints. The Court of Appeals, in its haste to reassert its hegemony as a policymaker, neglected its regular duties and squandered the opportunity to get the agency to face the cross-ownership question with reasonable clarity of mind. The Supreme Court—possibly to emphasize its disapproval of the lower court's ambitious policy-making claims—squandered the same opportunity by affirming the agency's order *in toto*.

If one takes the Supreme Court's *NCCB* opinion as an authoritative pronouncement that the FCC's cross-ownership opinion constituted "reasoned decision-making" as a matter of administrative law, it is difficult to imagine how scatterbrained an administrative agency would have to be to entitle a reviewing court to remand a problematic docket for a "hard look." And if one reads the *NCCB* opinion simply as a message to the Court of Appeals to back away from the policy role which it has asserted, it remains difficult to guess what the future vitality will be of the "partnership" notion and the collaborative relationship of court and agency which it postulates and symbolizes. One way or the other, the Court of Appeals must evidently refine and rationalize its part of the partnership. Some justifications for a judicial role conceived of in this way seem to me, although subtle in probable effect, entirely salutary. If used parsimoniously and with an awareness of the territorial problems which arise when two wills inhabit an effectually unbounded field, the partnership notion can be—as it has been—an influential and constructive presence within administrative agencies. This principle tends to enlist on the side of candor in the explanation of discretionary decisions and thus serves to produce more openness in government. Agencies are apt to take more care in what they say—which can occasionally affect not only what is said but what is done—if there is a chance that the reviewing court may vacate the decision, not only when it discerns procedural inadequacy or departure from the mandate of the Congress, but also when it "becomes aware, from a combination of danger signals, that the agency has not really taken a 'hard look' at the salient problems, and has not genuinely engaged in reasoned decision-making."[82] And even if this cautionary effect is only marginal, it is a tendency which points administrative government in the direction of care and lucidity, and therefore an influence that should not be dismissed lightly.

---

[82] Greater Boston Television Inc. v. F.C.C., 444 F.2d 841, 850 (1970).

MICHAEL LES BENEDICT

PRESERVING FEDERALISM: RECONSTRUCTION AND THE WAITE COURT

I. National Sovereignty, State Rights, and State Sovereignty

It has become a commonplace of American history that the Chase and Waite Courts subverted Congress's post–Civil War Reconstruction legislation. A typical reading is that the Court engaged in a "judicial counterrevolution," a "judicially-directed perversion of what the abolitionists tried to write into the Constitution," the most "striking instance in American constitutional history of outright judicial disregard for congressional intent."[1] Historians and legal scholars, in recognition that the postwar constitutional amendments were designed to write an antislavery theory of American rights into the Constitution, have damned the Court, essentially for two reasons. First, because the Court was so restrictive in its construction of the Fourteenth Amendment's Privileges and Immunities Clause. Second, because the Court gutted Republican efforts to make the national government the guarantor of citizens' rights. The vehicle for this subversion, it is charged, was the doctrine of "State

Michael Les Benedict is Associate Professor of History, Ohio State University.

[1] Gressman, *The Unhappy History of Civil Rights Legislation*, 50 Mich. L. Rev. 1323, 1339 (1952); Pritchett, The American Constitution 712 (2d ed. 1968).

action."[2] While this criticism has flourished since the 1930s, John Mabry Matthews and Charles Warren had earlier described the same judicial misbehavior, except that, on the whole, Matthews and Warren approved of it.[3]

No feat of revisionism can turn the Waite Court of the 1870s and 1880s into a firm and unflinching defender of black peoples' rights. But the fact is that the modern criticism distorts our constitutional history. It fails to distinguish the position of the Waite Court from its successors, accepting, for instance, the reactionary decisions of the Fuller Court in civil rights cases as logical extensions of Waite Court doctrines, which they were not. Moreover, the modern criticism proceeds from the assumptions of a constitutional theory of nationalism that is indigenous to our age, presumes that Reconstruction legislation proceeded upon the same theory, and judges the Supreme Court's nationalism against that standard. Historians of Reconstruction, however, are beginning to realize that Civil War–era Republicans adhered to a concept of nationalism far less expansive than what has since emerged. They fought for the Union they had known and loved, a Union in which the authority of the national government was balanced against the rights of the States. And they fought for freedom. After victory they wanted to make the rights inherent in that freedom secure, but they wanted to secure them within the old federal framework. As southern whites contested every inch of freedom's advance, it became ever more apparent that the Republicans' commitments both to federalism and

[2] BETH, THE DEVELOPMENT OF THE AMERICAN CONSTITUTION, 1877–1917 191–99 (1971); BLAUSTEIN & ZANGRADO, CIVIL RIGHTS AND THE NEGRO: A DOCUMENTARY HISTORY 246–69 (1968); 2 BOUDIN, GOVERNMENT BY JUDICIARY 94–150 (1932); FRANKLIN, FROM SLAVERY TO FREEDOM 331–32 (3d ed. 1967); HARRIS, THE QUEST FOR EQUALITY 58, 82–91 (1960); KELLY & HARBISON, THE AMERICAN CONSTITUTION 462–65 (5th ed. 1976); KLUGER, SIMPLE JUSTICE 62–65 (1976); LOGAN, THE BETRAYAL OF THE NEGRO 105–24 (1965); MAGRATH, MORRISON R. WAITE 130–49 (1963); MILLER, THE PETITIONERS 85–164 (1966); MITCHELL & MITCHELL, THE BIOGRAPHY OF THE CONSTITUTION 304–10 (2d ed. 1975); RODELL, NINE MEN 165–67 (1955); Boudin, Truth and Fiction about the Fourteenth Amendment, 16 N.Y.U. L. REV. 19 (1938); Note, Section 1983 and Federalism, 90 HARV. L. REV. 1133 (1977); Gaffnev, History and Legal Interpretation—Early Distortion of the Fourteenth Amendment by the Gilded Age Court, 25 CATH. U. L. REV. 207, 236–47 (1972); Graham, Our "Declaratory" Fourteenth Amendment, in GRAHAM, EVERYMAN'S CONSTITUTION 295 (1968); Kinoy, The Constitutional Right of Negro Freedom, 21 RUTGERS L. REV. 387 (1967); Woodson, Fifty Years of Negro Citizenship as Qualified by the United States Supreme Court, 6 J. NEGRO HIST. 1 (1921).

[3] MATTHEWS, LEGISLATIVE AND JUDICIAL HISTORY OF THE FIFTEENTH AMENDMENT 97–126 (1909); 2 WARREN, THE SUPREME COURT IN UNITED STATES HISTORY 533–48, 600–18 (rev. ed. 1926).

to security of rights were in conflict, and they were forced to make an agonizing choice between them. The Supreme Court under Chase and Waite was faced with the same dilemma. Responding to it, the Justices did not bow to racism, betray nationalism, and revive discredited theories of federalism. They made the same effort as did the Republicans to preserve the balance of the old federal system, to protect the States' rights which had been an implicit element of nationalism as it had been understood for fifty years, and at the same time to recognize in Congress enough power to protect civil rights. In the process they reached surprisingly liberal conclusions about congressional power under the postwar Amendments, given the dominant ideas of federalism which provided the context in which they operated.

The essential difference between modern constitutional nationalism and that prevalent at the time of the Civil War was the latter's acceptance of the notion that there was a reserved area of State jurisdiction beyond the competence of national authority. Modern constitutional doctrine reflects the Supreme Court's conclusions in *United States v. Darby*—the deathblow to "dual federalism"—that the jurisdiction of the State governments is defined by that of the national, that the Tenth Amendment "states but a truism that all is retained which has not been surrendered."[4]

The focus of our attention has shifted dramatically from where it was when Americans went to war in 1861. The earlier era was State centered. In practical terms this was reflected in the small effect of national government on Americans' daily lives. From birth to death the only federal officials most Americans were likely to see in peacetime were their postmaster and a pension agent. Both were local men appointed for political services rendered in their own communities.[5] In political terms it was reflected in the continued domination from the 1830s to the eve of war of a political party founded upon a narrow conception of national power. And in legal-constitutional terms it was reflected in the acceptance, even among those who favored energetic national government, of the principles of what Edward S. Corwin identified as "dual federalism."

The basic doctrine of dual federalism—what we identify today as

---

[4] 312 U.S. 100, 124 (1941). See Corwin, *The Passing of Dual Federalism*, 36 Va. L. Rev. 1 (1950); Note, *supra* note 2, 90 Harv. L. Rev. at 1156–90.

[5] Hyman, A More Perfect Union 7–14 (1973); Paludan, A Covenant with Death 11–20 (1975).

"States' rights"—was, in Corwin's words, that "the coexistence of the states and their power is of itself a limitation upon the national power."[6] As originally fashioned by Andrew Jackson, other Democratic statesmen and politicians, and the Taney Court from principles articulated by Jefferson and Madison, it proceeded upon the assumption that the States had been sovereign before the ratification of the Constitution; that the Union was an indissoluble compact in which some sovereign jurisdiction was taken from the States and delegated to the national government; that the States retained sovereign jurisdiction in other areas and were therefore the equals of the national government in the federal system; that each of these governments had a complete, independent structure with which to exercise its powers and could not require the other to administer its laws; that the powers of each government were completely distinct and independent with each supreme in its own sphere; that the Tenth Amendment confirmed this structure and guaranteed that national powers would not be interpreted in such a way as to subvert the reserved sovereign jurisdiction of the States; and that the Supreme Court was the umpire of the federal system with the duty to protect the sovereignty of each government from encroachment by the other.[7] (Corwin did not coin the phrase "dual federalism" until the 1930s. Earlier he referred to a "moderate states rights" doctrine, to distinguish it from Calhounite "state sovereignty.")[8] Those who advocated broad expansion of the national role from the Progressive to the New Deal eras—especially Corwin himself—argued that this doctrine of dual federalism had subverted the nationalistic principles expounded by the Marshall Court. But in reality, most Americans had accepted dual federalism as implicit in those principles.

For most pre–Civil War nationalists, the crucial determinant of the constitutionality of national legislation was its purpose. Early nationalists like Marshall and Hamilton were determined to prevent

---

[6] Corwin, *The Power of Congress to Prohibit Commerce*, 18 CORN. L. Q. 477, 482 (1933).

[7] See CORWIN, THE COMMERCE POWER VERSUS STATES RIGHTS (1936); CORWIN, NATIONAL SUPREMACY: THE TREATY POWER V. STATE POWER (1913); Corwin, note 4 *supra*; Corwin, note 6 *supra*.

[8] For a good statement of dual federalist principles, see Schroth, Dual Federalism in Constitutional Law 376–80 (1941) (unpublished Ph.D. dissertation, Princeton University). Schroth, like his mentor Corwin, frequently confuses "dual federalism" with "state sovereignty."

an exaggerated commitment to State jurisdiction from inhibiting the national government from exercising its authority effectively. They stressed the sovereign authority of the national government to fulfill the purposes for which it was created. While they did not articulate the limits upon national jurisdiction very clearly, those limits were plainly there. "Let the end be legitimate, let it be within the scope of the constituton, and all means which are appropriate, which are plainly adapted to that end . . . are constitutional,"[9] wrote Marshall in his most celebrated enunciation of nationalist constitutional theory. This is something quite different from the modern gloss which has sustained a national police power and which might be stated, "Let the means be legitimate, let them be within the scope of the constitution, and all ends which are achieved by those means are constitutional." Although Marshall condoned the framing of legislation to carry out mandated objectives in such a way as to promote more general goals, it is plain that the constitutionality of such legislation depended "on their being the natural, direct, and appropriate means, or the known and usual means, for the execution of the given power."[10] Over and over again in his opinions and his extrajudicial defenses of them, Marshall defined the powers of the national government in terms of their purpose, deducing their constitutionality from the postulate that "in America, the powers of sovereignty are divided between the government of the Union, and those of the states. They are each sovereign with respect to the objects committed to it, and neither sovereign with respect to the objects committed to the other."[11] Although Marshall and his colleagues stressed the national sovereignty aspect of these principles to sustain national legislation against attacks based on State sovereignty, he left no doubt that the sword could cut both ways. In *McCulloch v. Maryland*, Marshall stated plainly: "Should congress under the pretext of executing its powers, pass laws for the accomplishment of objects, not entrusted to the government, it would become the painful duty of this tribunal . . . to say that such an act was not the law of the land."[12] Legal scholars have recognized re-

---

[9] McCulloch v. Maryland, 4 Wheat. 316, 421 (1819).

[10] GUNTHER, ED., JOHN MARSHALL'S DEFENSE OF McCULLOCH V. MARYLAND 186 (1969).

[11] 4 Wheat. at 410.

[12] *Id.* at 423.

cently that the divergence between the Marshall and Taney Courts on matters of federalism has been exaggerated, but they have emphasized primarily the Court's continued commitment to national supremacy.[13] The foregoing suggests that the Taney Court's concern for the integrity of State jurisdiction was also implicit in the decisions of its predecessor. Although it is unclear whether Marshall would have accepted all the doctrines of dual federalism, and it is certain that Story rejected most of them, most Americans did not recognize in them any fundamental inconsistency with nationalist principles.[14] Even while disagreeing vigorously with strict constructionists over where the line between national and State jurisdiction lay, a nationalist like Edward Everett agreed that there was "a wise and happy partition of powers between the national and state governments, in virtue of which the national government is relieved from all odium of administration."[15] Webster too admitted the necessity for keeping "the general government and the State government each in its proper sphere."[16] It was that consideration which

---

[13] BAXTER, THE STEAMSHIP MONOPOLY: GIBBONS V. OGDEN, 1824 117–18 (1972); FRANKFURTER, THE COMMERCE CLAUSE UNDER MARSHALL, TANEY AND WAITE 46–73 (1937); Garvey, The Constitutional Revolution of 1837 and the Myth of Marshall's Monolith, 18 W. POL. Q. 27 (1965); KELLY & HARBISON, note 2 supra, at 282, 331; SCHMIDHAUSER, SUPREME COURT AS FINAL ARBITER IN FEDERAL-STATE RELATIONS, 1789–1937 50–79 (1958); SCHWARTZ, FROM CONFEDERATION TO NATION 7, 26–28, 33–37 (1973).

[14] Marshall surely would have disagreed with the Taney Court dicta in various Commerce Clause cases that inspection laws, immigration regulations, and the like were, by definition, exercises of police power and, therefore, not subject to congressional commerce regulation. See Gibbons v. Ogden, 9 Wheat. 1 (1824), and Willson v. Blackbird Marsh Creek Co. 2 Pet. 245 (1829), and compare New York v. Miln, 11 Pet. 102 (1837); BALDWIN, A GENERAL VIEW OF THE ORIGIN AND NATURE OF THE CONSTITUTION AND GOVERNMENT OF THE UNITED STATES 181–97 (1837); The License Cases, 5 How. 504 (1847); The Passenger Cases, 7 How. 283 (1845); and Groves v. Slaughter, 15 Pet. 449 (1841).

Marshall did take a distinctly dual federalist view of Congress's taxing power, when he announced that "Congress is not empowered to tax for those purposes which are in the exclusive province of the states." Gibbons, 19 Wheat. at 199; GUNTHER, note 8 supra, at 100.

Story was consistent in his rejection of dual federalism. STORY, COMMENTARIES ON THE CONSTITUTION OF THE UNITED STATES §§ 1063–66, §§ 1254–1322, §§ 955–89, §§ 1072–89 (1833). But see Prigg v. Pennsylvania, 16 Pet. 539 (1842). Story believed that "new men and new opinions have succeeded" the nationalistic ones that he and Marshall shared, and he contemplated resigning his place on the Taney Court. 2 STORY, ED., LIFE AND LETTERS OF JOSEPH STORY 527–29 (1851).

Gerald Gunther has indicated that there were limits to Marshall's nationalism, GUNTHER, note 10 supra, at 19–21. William H. Hatcher noted, but could not explain, a weakening in the Marshall Court's nationalism in its later years. Hatcher, John Marshall and States' Rights, 3 S.Q. 207 (1965).

[15] Quoted in PALUDAN, note 5 supra, at 14–15.

[16] WEBSTER, THE GREAT SPEECHES AND ORATIONS OF DANIEL WEBSTER 272 (Whipple ed. 1889).

led him to urge adherence to a strict conceptual differentiation between national regulations of interstate commerce and state police
powers affecting commerce, such as inspection and quarantine laws;
toll-road, ferry, and bridge regulations; and restrictions on black
immigration. "If all these be regulations of commerce," he warned,
"does it not admit the power of Congress . . . upon all these minor
objects of legislation, . . . acknowledg[ing] the right of Congress
over a vast scope of internal legislation, which no one has heretofore
supposed to be within its powers" and subjecting "all State legislation over such subjects . . . to the superior power of Congress, a
consequence which no one would admit for a moment."[17] Thus, on
the eve of Civil War, even the Republican party, the political heir
to the nationalist sentiments of the Federalists and Whigs, acknowledged the obligation to preserve "the rights of the States . . . invio-
late . . . , and especially the right of each State to order and control
its own domestic institutions . . . exclusively, 'rights' essential to that
balance of power on which the perfection and endurance of our
political fabric depends."[18]

It was not the doctrine of dual federalism, or "State rights," that
threatened to disrupt the Union in 1861, but rather that of "State
sovereignty." While this theory of federalism involved many principles similar to those expressed by dual federalists with the strictest
notions of national power, permitting legal and especially political
cooperation of adherents of the two theories within the Democratic
party, it differed on the crucial question of where authority lay to
define constitutional powers. Even the most extreme dual federalist
acknowledged the Supreme Court as the ultimate arbiter of the
federal system. State sovereignty exponents, convinced that sovereignty was indivisible and therefore that the Union was merely a
league of sovereign states, insisted that the people of the individual

---

[17] Like most Americans in an age of inactive government, Webster did not recognize
the inconsistency between such statements and his Storyesque argument in defense of the
protective tariff that there could be no inquiry into the motive with which Congress
levied duties and imposts once the power was conceded. He may have been blinded to
the implications of such an argument because he, like Story, believed protection of
domestic industry to be within the acknowledged scope of foreign commerce power and
not an indirect benefit of that power. See *id.* at 321.

[18] The phrasing comes from resolutions two and four of the Republican national plat-
form of 1860. PORTER & JOHNSON, NATIONAL PARTY PLATFORMS, 1840–1956 32 (1956).
For similar descriptions of pre–Civil War legal theory in regard to federalism, see
BENNETT, AMERICAN THEORIES OF FEDERALISM 168–69 (1964); Note, *supra* note 2,
90 HARV. L. REV. at 1138–41.

States had the ultimate right to define the boundaries of the federalism.[19] Moreover, by the 1850s southern adherents of State sovereignty were challenging other fundamental tenets of dual federalism, insisting that as an agent of sovereign states the national government was obligated to use its power to promote the interests of all of them and never to oppose the interests of any of them. Thus, they challenged the cherished notion of their closest allies that the national and State spheres were distinct and independent.[20] When applied to the national government's power to govern United States territories, the conflict disrupted the Democratic party. When State sovereignty doctrines were expressed in the form of nullification and secession, the fundamental differences with even the most anti-national-power dual federalists became apparent, as northern Democrats rallied to the flag. In terms of constitutional theory, the Civil War was fought between the concepts of State sovereignty and what we would now identify as State rights.

Historians have accurately perceived in the legislation of the Civil War years an application of constitutional nationalism much more similar to our own than what had gone before—a "Blueprint for Modern America," as one termed it.[21] Even as they fought to maintain national supremacy, northerners divided on whether the very existence of sovereign States imposed some limitation upon the jurisdiction of the national government. Under the pressure of war, Republicans seemed to repudiate the idea, justifying confiscation, emancipation, construction and operation of railroads and telegraphs, and supervision and care of large populations as "necessary and proper" uses of the war power. At the same time they took a modern view of the taxing and spending power, repudiating dual federalist limitations upon it, and reconfirmed interpretations of national authority over interstate and foreign commerce that justified protective tariffs and national support for internal improvements. Traditionalists, mostly Democrats but also conservative ex-

---

[19] BAUER, COMMENTARIES ON THE CONSTRUCTION, 1790–1860 (1952); BENNETT, note 18 *supra*, at 108–59; 4 BEVERIDGE, THE LIFE OF JOHN MARSHALL 309–96 (1919); CARPENTER, THE SOUTH AS A CONSCIOUS MINORITY, 1789–1861 (1930); HAINES, THE AMERICAN DOCTRINE OF JUDICIAL SUPREMACY 285–344 (1959); MUDGE, THE SOCIAL PHILOSOPHY OF JOHN TAYLOR OF CAROLINE 60–76, 133–44 (1939); SPAIN, *The Political Thought of John C. Calhoun* (1968); Note, *Judge Spencer Roane of Virginia: Champion of States' Rights—Foe of John Marshall*, 66 HARV. L. REV. 1242 (1953).

[20] Bestor, *State Sovereignty and Slavery: A Reinterpretation of Proslavery Constitutional Doctrine, 1846–1860*, 54 J. ILL. H. SOC'Y 1 (1961).

[21] CURRY, BLUEPRINT FOR MODERN AMERICA (1968).

Whigs and Republicans, responded with a barrage of denunciation in the press, Congress, political oratory, legal arguments and court opinions, and treatises on constitutional law.[22]

Even as they set precedents for modern nationalism, however, Republicans could not shake off their commitment to older notions of federalism. Republican reliance upon a broad interpretation of national war powers to sustain their legislation enabled them to isolate the peacetime restrictions from wartime experience. When the war ended Republican leaders urged: "During the prevalence of the war we drew to ourselves here as the Federal Government authority which had been considered doubtful by all and denied by many of the statesmen of this country. That time . . . has ceased and ought to cease. Let us go back to the original condition of things, and allow the States to take care of themselves."[23]

This commitment to State rights within the federal system seriously compromised Republican efforts to establish full freedom and equality for the newly freed slaves. Historians now recognize that every Reconstruction-era effort to protect the rights of citizens was tempered by the fundamental conviction that federalism required that the day-to-day protection of the citizen had to remain the duty of the States.[24] Direct national control of the South and early super-

---

[22] See HYMAN, note 5 *supra* at 156–70, 207–62; RANDALL, CONSTITUTIONAL PROBLEMS UNDER LINCOLN (1951); PALUDAN, note 5 *supra* at 109–69; BURGESS, THE CIVIL WAR AND THE CONSTITUTION, 1859–1865 (1901); SILBEY, A RESPECTABLE MINORITY 62–88 (1977). Democrats invited the cooperation of all opponents of Republican policies during the war and after, often denominating themselves Conservatives, announcing "that the aim and object of the Democratic party is to preserve the Federal Union and the rights of the States unimpaired." PORTER & JOHNSON, note 18 *supra*, at 34; SILBEY, *supra*, at 138 and *passim*.

[23] CONG. GLOBE, 39th Cong., 1st Sess., 2446 (1866). These remarks were made by James W. Grimes, one of the most important Republican Senators and a member of the Joint Committee on Reconstruction, which framed the Fourteenth Amendment, in the course of opposing a bill that would have established a national quarantine during the cholera epidemic of 1866—a clear exercise of a national "police" power under the authority of the Commerce Clause. The bill failed, with Republicans dividing and Democrats almost unanimously opposed. See Benedict, *Contagion and the Constitution: Quarantine Agitation from 1859 to 1866*, 25 J. H. MED. & ALLIED SCI. 177 (1970). See also the similar remarks of Fessenden, the chairman of the Joint Committee on Reconstruction, CONG. GLOBE, 39th Cong., 1st Sess., 27–28 (1866); PALUDAN, note 5 *supra*, at 28–48; Benedict, *Preserving the Constitution: The Conservative Basis of Radical Reconstruction*, 61 J. AM. H. 65 (1974) [hereinafter *Preserving the Constitution*.]

[24] BELZ, A NEW BIRTH OF FREEDOM 113–37, 157–82 (1976); *Preserving the Constitution;* HYMAN, note 5 *supra*, at 282–306, 414–542; KELLER, AFFAIRS OF STATE 37–73 (1977); Kelly, *Comment on H. M. Hyman's Paper*, in HYMAN, NEW FRONTIERS OF THE AMERICAN RECONSTRUCTION 40 (1966); PALUDAN, note 5 *supra;* Note, note 2 *supra*, 90 HARV. L. REV. at 1141–47.

vision of the transition from slave to free labor were considered temporary and justified on grounds expressly contrived to avoid setting precedents dangerous to the future balance of federalism.[25] As to the permanent protections for Americans' rights, despite arguments to the contrary by those modern legal scholars who write in the tradition of a new nationalism, all the evidence of the congressional discussions, the ratification debates, and the public controversy indicates that Republicans intended the States to retain primary jurisdiction over citizen's rights. They attempted to write into the Constitution an obligation that antislavery theorists already believed incumbent on the States: the requirement that they protect all citizens equally in fundamental human rights. They did not intend the national government to replace the States in fulfilling that obligation. Throughout the early years of Reconstruction, the focus of Republican concern was active State discrimination against blacks in basic rights. Republicans stressed over and over again that if the States simply performed their constitutional obligations to protect citizens equally in basic rights, the Reconstruction legislation and Amendments would work no substantial change in the federal system.[26]

---

[25] *Preserving the Constitution.*

[26] See, *e.g.*, CONG. GLOBE, 39th Cong., 1st Sess., 1785 (1866) (Sen. Stewart); *id.* at 476, 600 (Sen. Trumbull); Letter from Ohio Governor Jacob D. Cox to Andrew Johnson (March 22, 1866); Schurz, *The Logical Results of the War*, in 1 SPEECHES, CORRESPONDENCE, AND POLITICAL PAPERS OF CARL SCHURZ 377 (F. Bancroft, ed. 1913). For a clear indication of how State-centered Republicans understood the Fourteenth Amendment to be, see Fairman, *Does the Fourteenth Amendment Incorporate the Bill of Rights? The Original Understanding*, 2 STAN. L. REV. 5, especially 41–134 (1949). The evidence is all the more persuasive because Fairman was dealing with a different question—the scode of rights protected, not which government was to do the protecting. See also *Preserving the Constitution, passim.*

An excellent insight into the framers' early interpretation of the national government's power to enforce the provisions of the Fourteenth Amendment is revealed by Representative John A. Bingham, explaining the meaning of the original version, worded to give Congress direct, positive power to make laws necessary and proper to protect the civil rights. Insisting that State officials were obligated to protect the rights enumerated in the Bill of Rights, he argued: "The question is, simply, whether you will give by this amendment to the people of the United States the power, by legislative enactment, to punish officials of States for violations of the oaths enjoined upon them by their Constitution? That is the question, and the whole question. The adoption of the proposed amendment will take from the States no rights that belong to the States. They elect their Legislatures; they enact their laws for the punishment of crimes against life, liberty, and property; but in the event of the adoption of this amendment, if they conspire together to enact laws refusing equal protection to life, liberty, or property, the Congress is thereby vested with powers to hold them to answer before the bar of the national courts for the violation of their oaths and of the rights of their fellow-men." CONG. GLOBE, 39th

Since Americans believed that the main purpose of government was to protect citizens against wrongs perpetrated by others, Republicans believed that by banning State discrimination they were guaranteeing positive protection to freed slaves. "The presumption was that these States would be obedient to the Constitution and the laws," James G. Blaine remembered.[27] "But for this presumption, legislation would be but idle play, and a government of laws would degenerate at once into a government of force. In enacting the Reconstruction laws, Congress proceeded upon the basis of faith in Republican government."[28] Had southerners only fulfilled this naive expectation, the sanguine prophecy made by Ohio's conservative Republican Governor Jacob Dolson Cox might have come true: "If the Southern people will . . . do right themselves, by legislation of their own which shall break down distinctions between classes . . . , the law itself would become of little practical moment . . . and a very short time would make it a practically dead letter."[29]

Cong., 1st Sess. 1090 (1866). The wording of the proposed amendment at this time was: "That Congress shall have power to make all laws which shall be necessary and proper to secure to the citizens of each State all the privileges and immunities of citizens in the several States, and to all persons in the several States equal protection in the rights of life, liberty, and property." *Id.* at 1033–34. Thus, with an amendment apparently worded to give Congress the broadest possible range of powers, its author intended it to operate upon State laws and State officials, not to authorize Congress to establish a general criminal code.

[27] 2 BLAINE, TWENTY YEARS OF CONGRESS 466 (1886).

[28] *Ibid.* The Lockean conviction that "the great and chief end of . . . men uniting into commonwealths and putting themselves under government, is the preservation of their property," by which is meant the individual's "life, liberty and estate," was an axiom of American constitutional thought, enshrined in the Declaration of Independence's avowal that all men were endowed "with certain unalienable Rights" and "[t]hat to secure these rights Governments are instituted among men." See LOCKE, TWO TREATISES ON GOVERNMENT 163–84 (Cook ed. 1947). See also THE FEDERALIST 35 (Rossiter ed. 1961); WILSON, THE WORKS OF JAMES WILSON 171–72 (McCloskey ed. 1967); CHIPMAN, PRINCIPLES OF GOVERNMENT 55–56 (1833); 1 LIEBER, MANUAL OF POLITICAL ETHICS 156–57 (Woolsey ed. 1890) (Joseph Story called this work "the fullest and most correct development of the theory of what constitutes the States that I have ever seen." *Id.* at 3.), 1 LEGGETT, A COLLECTION OF THE POLITICAL WRITINGS OF WILLIAM LEGGETT 162 (Sedgwick ed. 1840); MULFORD, THE NATION: THE FOUNDATIONS OF CIVIL ORDER AND POLITICAL LIFE IN THE UNITED STATES 285–88 (1870); RAWLE, A VIEW OF THE CONSTITUTION OF THE UNITED STATES OF AMERICA 89, 92 (2d ed. 1829); WEDGEWOOD, THE GOVERNMENT AND LAWS OF THE UNITED STATES 66–68 (1867); YOUNG, THE CITIZEN'S MANUAL OF GOVERNMENT AND LAW 17–21 (rev. ed. 1858). Justice Bushrod Washington had placed "protection by the government" at the very head of the list of citizens' privileges and immunities in his celebrated opinion in Corfield v. Coryell, 6 Fed. Cas. 546, 551 (# 3,230) (C.C.E.D. Pa. 1823).

[29] Letter from Jacob D. Cox to Andrew Johnson (March 22, 1866).

It was not until the Ku Klux Klan violence of 1868 through 1872 that Republicans began to recognize that superficially equal laws did not guarantee full protection of rights. As early as 1870 they began to pass laws making it a crime punishable in national courts for individuals to infringe upon citizens' right to vote whether or not they acted under State authority,[30] despite the fact that the Fifteenth Amendment was worded as a prohibition upon States just as the Fourteenth Amendment was.

By 1871, when they passed the so-called Ku Klux Klan Act, Republicans had developed a carefully reasoned constitutional argument that State failure to protect rights guaranteed by the Fourteenth and Fifteenth Amendments amounted to such State action as justified congressional intervention. And that intervention could take the form of positive congressional enactments to punish individual wrongdoers.[31] Even this interpretation, however, stressing as it did the States' primary jurisdiction over crimes, put a tremendous strain upon Republicans. It seemed to encroach upon the heart of State jurisdiction. Key leaders, like Lyman Trumbull, the author of most of the Reconstruction legislation of the 1860s, abandoned the party over the issue. Even as he pressed for direct national punishment of ordinary crimes where States failed to act, John A. Bingham, the chief author of the Fourteenth Amendment, exclaimed, "God forbid . . . that by so legislating we would strike down the rights of the State . . . . I believe our dual system of government essential to our national existence."[32] No one who reads the debates over the Ku Klux Klan Act can fail to be impressed with the effort Republicans made to reconcile their desire to afford protection to citizens in the South with the contours of the federal system they wanted to preserve, one with "a clear and well defined line between the powers of the General Government and the powers of the States."[33]

---

[30] Enforcement Act of 1870, 16 Stat. 140 (1870).

[31] Avins, *The Ku Klux Klan Act of 1871: Some Reflected Light on State Action and the Fourteenth Amendment*, 11 St. Louis U.L.J. 331 (1967); Harris, note 2 *supra*, at 41–53. An excellent summary of the development of the arguments may be found in the reader's guide section of Avins, The Reconstruction Amendments' Debates: The Legislative and Contemporary Debates in Congress on the 13th, 14th, and 15th Amendments xx–xxiv (1967).

[32] Cong. Globe, 42d Cong., 1st Sess., app. 84 (1871).

[33] Representative Charles Williard, *id.* at app. 187; Lionel A. Sheldon, *id.* at 368–69; Jesse H. Moore, *id.* at app. 112; John B. Hawley, *id.* at 382; Garfield, *id.* at app. 150–53;

The suspension of the privilege of the writ of *habeas corpus* in
South Carolina in 1872, the direct interference of the national government to settle disputed elections results in the South in 1872–73
and 1874–75, and especially the 1875 purge of Democrats from
contested seats in the Louisiana State legislature at the point of
federal bayonets made it ever more difficult to reconcile protection
of rights in the South with the federal system Americans wanted
to preserve. An old abolitionist expressed the simple but tragic truth
when he wrote as Republicans gave up the struggle: "We never
contemplated when we took the freed blacks under the protection
of the North that the work was to be for an unlimited time. We
hoped that if for a few years we lent them a helping hand, self
interest, if not a sense of right, would prompt the Southern whites
to do their duty by them."[34]

Americans' desire to preserve the old balance of federalism was
reflected in the post–Civil War writings of legal scholars and political philosophers. Before the war, exaggerated notions of State
rights enervated the national government and finally almost destroyed it, the respected jurist Isaac F. Redfield wrote in 1867:
"The great danger now will be that things will rush in the opposite direction, and the central authority from being limited and
straitened in all its powers and functions, . . . will be in danger of
absorbing all the important functions of governmental administration."[35] The most important legal thinker of the post–Civil War
era, Michigan Judge Thomas M. Cooley, echoed him: "The proper
boundary between national and state powers . . . has been found
so satisfactory that we have willingly endured a war in its defence.
The cost of that war has been in vain if at its conclusion we propose to treat that boundary as a shadow line which none need regard."[36] The Civil War killed State sovereignty, and the postwar
era saw the growing influence of the "organic theory" of American nationalism posited most influentially before the war by Francis

Burton H. Cook, *id*. at 485–86; Horatio C. Burchard *id*. at app. 313–15; Note, note 2
supra, 90 Harv. L. Rev. at 1156.

[34] Letter from Francis Cope to Laura Towne (November 19, 1877), reprinted in
Rose, Rehearsal for Reconstruction 403–04 (1964).

[35] Redfield, *The Proper Limits between State and National Legislation and Jurisdiction*,
15 Am. L. Reg. 193, 197 (1867).

[36] Cooley, *The Legal Aspects of the Louisiana Case*, 1 S.L. Rev. (n.s.) 18, 42 (1875).

Lieber. These nationalists asserted that American nationality pre-
dated the Constitution. They argued that the Constitution ema-
nated from an entire people rather than from States or even the
people of the States. But their conclusion also sustained the doctrines of dual federalism. The people of the United States created
both State and national governments. "The two together constitute
the government of the United States," explained Orestes A. Brownson: "The powers of each are equally sovereign . . . . In their respective spheres neither yields to the other. In relation to the matters
within its jurisdiction, each government is independent and supreme
in regard of the other."[37] Another influential nationalist legal scholar
put it more succinctly: "Within their respective spheres, these two
classes of governments are as independent as though they represented different nations."[38] As a recent investigator has observed,
"The nationalist commentators of the post–Civil War era were able
to reconcile their uncompromising hostility to the Confederacy . . .
with an ardent advocacy of their own particular version of state
rights. Indeed, it seemed at times that their nationalism consisted
almost solely in their attacks upon the doctrines of nullification and
secession."[39] No wonder, then, that as he left Faneuil Hall after

---

[37] BROWNSON, THE AMERICAN REPUBLIC, ITS CONSTITUTION, TENDENCIES AND
DESTINY 234, 256 (1865).

[38] Pomeroy, *The Force Bill*, 12 THE NATION 268, 269 (1871).

[39] Larsen, *Nationalism and States' Rights in Commentaries on the Constitution after the
Civil War*, 3 AM. J.L. HIST. 360, 366 (1959). For a similar conclusion, see PALUDAN,
note 5 *supra*, at 219–73; and McCurdy, *Legal Institutions, Constitutional Theory, and the
Tragedy of Reconstruction*, 4 REV. AM. HIST. 203 (1976). Walter H. Bennett concluded
that postwar constitutional theory elevated the United States to the plane of sovereign
equality with the States. BENNETT, note 18 *supra*, at 179–81. For what might be called
"state rights nationalism," see BROWNSON, note 37 *supra*; POMEROY, AN INTRODUCTION
TO THE CONSTITUTIONAL LAW OF THE UNITED STATES (1870), and Pomeroy, *The Supreme Court and Its Theory of Nationality*, 12 THE NATION 445 (1871); HARE, AMERICAN
CONSTITUTIONAL LAW (1889); HURD, THE THEORY OF OUR NATIONAL EXISTENCE, AS
SHOWN BY THE GOVERNMENT OF THE UNITED STATES SINCE 1861 (1881). Cooley was
one of the few nationalist constitutional commentators to adhere to the notion that the
people of the individual states had created the Union, but his acceptance of national
supremacy was as thorough as that of other analysts. COOLEY, A TREATISE ON CONSTITU-
TIONAL LIMITATIONS (2d ed. 1871); Cooley, *The Guarantee of Order and Republican
Government in the United States*, 2 INT'L REV. 57 (1875).

With the works of these legal scholars, compare the analysis of Timothy Farrar, a
Civil War nationalist with ideas more similar to our own. According to Farrar, the
States derived their power not from preexisting sovereignty but from the Constitution.
Since the national government determines whether a subject is under national or state
jurisdiction, it is the United States which is sovereign and not the State government. Like
modern constitutional nationalists, Farrar scouted the notion of implied limitations upon

Charles Sumner delivered his intensely nationalistic lecture, *Are We a Nation?* Sumner's senatorial colleague, Henry Wilson, grumbled, "The States are something still."[40]

II. THE COURT, THE AMENDMENTS, AND FEDERALISM

It was this State-centered nationalism, held in common with different degrees of commitment (especially when compared to the necessity to protect freedmen's rights) by Democrats and Republicans, politicians and jurists, that the Supreme Court articulated in the years following the Civil War. Both the States and the United States held equal places in our scheme of government, each with independent authority within its sphere of jurisdiction—"an indestructible Union, composed of indestructible States," as the Court expressed it in one of its most memorable phrases.[41] And the Constitution imposed just as great a duty to protect and maintain the integrity of the State governments as the national government. "The Supreme Court has thus . . . placed the nation and the States upon the same footing," nationalist constitutional commentator John Norton Pomeroy wrote happily. "As we have in this theory the greatest security for the nation, we have also the greatest security for the several States."[42]

The consequence of such concern for the integrity of State as well as national jurisdiction was the continued adherence to the doctrines of dual federalism. As early as 1864 Republican State courts in Indiana, Wisconsin, and Michigan were applying dual federalist glosses to the doctrines enunciated by Marshall in *McCulloch v. Maryland*, holding unconstitutional provisions of the federal internal revenue code levying stamp taxes upon State court

---

national power arising from preexisting State sovereignty. "All state rights and powers must be carved out of what the people of the United States have left after having delegated the powers of the Constitution [to the national government]. . . . They have given no right to anybody, to come in competition with their own supreme law, or any power lawfully exercised under it." Farrar, *State Rights*, 21 NEW ENGLANDER 695, 723 (1862).

[40] 4 PIERCE, MEMOIR AND LETTERS OF CHARLES SUMNER 335 (1893).

[41] Texas v. White, 7 Wall. 700, 725 (1868). For a full appreciation of the state-centeredness of the Supreme Court doctrine expressed in this case, read Lane Cty. v. Oregon, 7 Wall. 71 (1868), decided at the same Term and in conjunction with it.

[42] Pomeroy, note 39 *supra*, at 445. Chase wrote Pomeroy that the opinion reflected many of Pomeroy's ideas. POMEROY, note 39 *supra*, at 521n.

writs, State tax deeds, or surety bonds required of State officers,[43] despite the fact that the Constitution limits the national taxing power only by requiring that taxes be levied directly and for common defense, payment of debts, or the national welfare. With Cooley and future Republican Senator Isaac Christiancy concurring, Michigan Supreme Court Justice James V. Campbell justified such rulings in sweeping dual federalist language: "Our whole system is based upon the principle that local affairs must be administered by state authority. . . . The same supreme power which established the departments of the general government, determined that the local governments should also exist for their own purposes. . . . Each of these several agencies is confined to its own sphere, and all are . . . independent of other agencies, except as thereby made dependent. There is nothing in the constitution which can be made to admit of any interference by Congress with the secure existence of any State authority within its lawful bounds. And any such interference by the indirect means of taxation, is quite as much beyond the bounds of the national legislature, as if the interference were direct and extreme."[44]

Cooley endorsed this principle of State immunity from taxation in his *Constitutional Limitations*.[45] Four different United States Attorneys General expressed similar opinions between 1867 and 1871.[46] And the Supreme Court concurred in *Collector v. Day* in 1871[47] and *United States v. R.R. Co.* in 1873.[48] Even while affirming Congress's power to tax State-chartered banks out of existence in one of the most nationalistic decisions of the nineteenth century, the Court agreed that "there are . . . certain virtual limitations [upon the taxing power] arising from the principles of the Constitution itself. . . . It would undoubtedly be an abuse of the power . . . if exercised for

---

[43] Warren v. Paul, 22 Ind. 279 (1864); Jones v. Estate of Keep, 19 Wis. 369 (1865); Sayles v. Davis, 22 Wis. 217 (1867); Fifield v. Close, 15 Mich. 505 (1867); State ex rel. Lakey v. Garton, 32 Ind. 1 (1869).

[44] Fifield v. Close, 15 Mich. at 509.

[45] COOLEY, note 39 *supra*, at 482–83.

[46] The Attorneys General did not hold provisions of the internal revenue laws unconstitutional, but opined that Congress could not have intended to include States and municipalities among taxable corporate bodies because of the principle involved. 12 OP. ATT'Y GEN. 277 (1867); 12 OP. ATT'Y GEN. 376 (1868); 13 OP. ATT'y GEN. 67 (1869); 13 OP. ATT'Y GEN. 439 (1871).

[47] 11 Wall. 113 (1871).

[48] 17 Wall. 322 (1873).

ends inconsistent with the limited grants of power in the Constitution."[49] Thus the Court rejected Story's views and took the same position that would overturn the Agricultural Adjustment Act some sixty-five years later.[50]

The Justices also displayed a disposition to sustain State police regulations in the 1870s and 1880s. Quick to overturn State interferences with foreign or interstate commerce for the mere purpose of raising revenue and interferences with the free travel of United States citizens,[51] the majority put safety, moral, and health regulations under much milder scrutiny. The Court denied that the "original package rule" of *Brown v. Maryland*[52] meant that the national commerce power superseded State prohibition laws or that national licensing of lottery-ticket or liquor sales to raise money displaced State bans on such sales.[53] It held that States could ban corporations chartered in other States from doing business within their boundaries and that businesses engaged in interstate commerce could be charged more for licenses than those whose business was limited to States or municipalities.[54] The Court sustained broad State taxing authority against charges that State and municipal levies inhibited interstate or foreign commerce.[55] It protected States' power to tax dividends on national bank shares.[56] It followed the precedent of *Willson v. Blackbird Creek Marsh Co.*[57] rather than the *Wheeling*

---

[49] Veazie Bank v. Fenno, 8 Wall. 533 (1870). Although the Court held that it could not question the reasonableness of the exercise of legislative power where it is expressly granted, it also relied heavily upon Congress's power to regulate the currency as justification for the tax. The Court was plainly uncomfortable with the implications of the broader argument.

[50] United States v. Butler, 297 U.S. 1 (1936). See also the dual federalist dicta pervading Justice Field's rejection of State court power to enforce writs of habeas corpus on behalf of those claimed to be held by national authority. *Tarble's Case*, 13 Wall. 397, especially at 406–08 (1872).

[51] E.g., Crandall v. Nevada, 6 Wall. 35 (1867); Ward v. Maryland, 12 Wall. 163 (1871); *Case of the State Freight Tax*, 15 Wall. 232 (1873); Henderson v. Mayor of New York, 92 U.S. 259 (1875).

[52] 12 Wheat. 419 (1827).

[53] McGuire v. Commonwealth, 3 Wall. 387 (1866); Pervear v. The Commonwealth, 5 Wall. 475 (1867). See also *The License Tax Cases*, 5 Wall. 462 (1867).

[54] Paul v. Virginia, 8 Wall. 168 (1869); Osborne v. Mobile, 16 Wall. 479 (1873).

[55] Waring v. The Mayor, 8 Wall. 110 (1869); Woodruff v. Parham, 8 Wall. 123 (1869); *Cases of the State Tax on Ry. Gross Receipts*, 15 Wall. 284 (1873).

[56] Van Allen v. Assessors, 3 Wall. 573 (1866); National Bank v. Commonwealth, 9 Wall. 353 (1870).

[57] 2 Pet. 245 (1829).

Bridge case[58] to sustain the State's authority to charter the building of railroad bridges across tidal waters.[59] And, in a forerunner to the *Granger Cases*,[60] the Justices ruled that State requirements that railroads set and post rates once a year, punishing those who levied charges in excess of the stated tariff, were legitimate exercises of the police power rather than commerce regulations.[61]

Constitutional historians recognize that the majority of the Justices adopted a similarly restrained view of the Due Process Clause of the Fourteenth Amendment in the early years of its construction. Despite persistent efforts to set it up as the protector of "vested rights" against legislative infringement, they refused to enforce the Clause as a restraint upon the substance of laws.[62] As late as 1889, Charles A. Kent instructed a college audience, "Many as are the suits in which its jurisdiction rests on the allegation of such a conflict, in perhaps no case has the judgment of the State court been reversed on this ground."[63]

The Supreme Court's construction of the legislation and constitutional amendments of the Reconstruction era must be understood within the context of this State-centered nationalism. For if Republican legislators ultimately came to see that their desire to protect

---

[58] Pennsylvania v. Wheeling & Belmont Bridge Co., 13 How. 518 (1851).

[59] Gilman v. Philadelphia, 3 Wall. 713 (1866).

[60] 94 U.S. 113 (1877).

[61] R.R. Co. v. Fuller, 17 Wall. 560 (1873).

[62] The most famous in this line of decisions were the *Granger Cases*, Munn v. Illinois and its sister cases, 94 U.S. 113 (1877). In 1878 a frustrated Justice Miller noted the number of due process cases being filed despite the Court's consistent rebuffs, complaining, "There is here abundant evidence that there exists some strange misconception of the scope of this provision, as found in the Fourteenth Amendment."Davidson v. New Orleans, 96 U.S. 97, 104 (1878). The complaint was repeated by—of all people—Justice Field in Missouri Pac. Ry. v. Humes, 115 U.S. 512, 519–20 (1885). See KELLY & HARBISON, note 2 *supra*, at 468–88, although with hindsight the authors stress how doctrines of "substantive due process" slowly developed rather than how long that development took. See also FAIRMAN, MR. JUSTICE MILLER AND THE SUPREME COURT, 1862–1890 179–206 (1939); MAGRATH, note 2 *supra*, at 173–203.

For the relationship of the doctrine of "vested rights"—the idea that there were strict limitations upon legislative power over property rights—and "substantive due process," see Corwin, *The Doctrine of Due Process of Law Before the Civil War*, 24 HARV. L. REV. 366, 460 (1911); Corwin, *The Basic Doctrine of American Constitutional Law*, 12 *Mich. L. REV.* 247 (1914).

[63] Kent, *Constitutional Development in the United States, as Influenced by Decisions of the Supreme Court since 1864*, in COOLEY, HITCHCOCK, BIDDLE, KENT, & CHAMBERLAIN, CONSTITUTIONAL HISTORY OF THE UNITED STATES AS SEEN IN THE DEVELOPMENT OF AMERICAN LAW 232 (1889).

rights was at war with their desire to preserve federalism, the Court had to face that dilemma even earlier, and in its starkest aspect, in the *Slaughter-House Cases* of 1873.[64]

The *Slaughter-House Cases* brought into focus the Fourteenth Amendment's potential for revolutionary change in American federalism in a way the black-rights-oriented legislation of Congress simply had not. The doctrines the lawyers for the New Orleans butchers advocated were aimed at more than the Crescent City Live-Stock and Slaughter-House Company's "monopoly" (which was in reality no monopoly at all). Their arguments attacked State legislation regulating the State lottery, municipal gas supply, levee repair, funding of the State debt, "prodigal expenditures and jobs innumerable."[65] The Fourteenth Amendment was designed to protect individuals from State invasion of all citizens' fundamental rights and immunities, broadly construed, they insisted. Assume a narrower purpose and "the State may deny individual rights and liberties, and claim to perform all the offices and duties of society, and under the names of socialism, communism, and other specious pretences, control all the revenues and labor of the State."[66] The argument for broad protection for citizens' privileges and immunities under the Fourteenth Amendment was no effort to secure the rights of black Americans. It was an invitation to the Court to write the "vested rights" doctrine into the Constitution through the Privileges and Immunities Clause in 1873 as they would write it into the Due Process Clause twenty years later. Defendant's counsel saw this clearly: "The result of the argument against the validity of this charter must . . . be this: that the 14th amendment does not prohibit State legislatures from passing acts of municipal legislation which abridge the privileges and immunities of citizens, provided such acts appear to be reasonable, but does prohibit the passing of acts which appear to be unreasonable; that it is for this court to determine whether such acts are reasonable or unreasonable."[67]

---

[64] 16 Wall. 36 (1873).

[65] Argument for Plaintiff, *Slaughter-House Cases*, 21 L. ED. at 395–99.

[66] Brief for Plaintiff upon Reargument, *Slaughter-House Cases*, 83 U.S. (16 Wall.) 36 (1873), in 6 KURLAND & CASPER (EDS.), LANDMARK BRIEFS AND ARGUMENTS OF THE SUPREME COURT OF THE UNITED STATES: CONSTITUTIONAL LAW 639, 669 (1975) [hereinafter LANDMARK BRIEFS].

[67] Brief for the Defendants, 6 LANDMARK BRIEFS at 587, 601.

Moreover, this proposition was being posited in an era of active congressional civil rights legislation, long before the Supreme Court became the most active protector of rights among the branches of the national government. Although the butchers' lawyers avoided the issue, there was no convincing reason why Congress should not accept the same invitation so temptingly offered the Justices. Even proponents of the broad view worried about such a revolution in the federal system. John Norton Pomeroy tried to demonstrate that the rights secured by the Privileges and Immunities Clause could be enforced only by the judiciary, but he was not very convincing. What was convincing was the terrible consequence he predicted from such an assumption of jurisdiction by Congress: "If the Democratic party should come to power, it is certainly within the range of possibilities that it should endeavor to uphold and sustain the liquor interest by Congressional legislation directed against State prohibitory and license laws. . . . [T]he State laws could be declared void; the States enacting and sustaining them could be described as 'abridging the privileges and immunities of citizens of the United States' . . . " Likewise, Congress could protect privileges and immunities by nullifying Sabbath laws or restrictions against church endowments.[68]

It is in light of the commitment of Americans generally to the idea that the States had a reserved area of jurisdiction that the query in Justice Miller's majority opinion must be read: "Was it the purpose of the fourteenth amendment . . . to transfer the security and protection of all the civil rights [broadly defined] . . . from the States to the Federal Government? . . . [W]as it intended to bring within the power of Congress the entire domain of civil rights heretofore belonging exclusively to the States?"[69] If so, "Congress . . . may pass laws . . . limiting and restricting the exercise of legislative power by the States, in their most ordinary and usual functions," and the Supreme Court would be "constitute[d] a perpetual censor upon all legislation of the States, on the civil rights of their own

[68] Pomeroy, *Political Precedents*, 12 THE NATION 300, 301 (1871); Pomeroy, *Police Duty*, 12 *id.* at 284–85; Pomeroy, *The Rights of Citizens*, 12 *id.* at 335–36. In his dissenting opinion in *Slaughter-House*, Bradley insisted that the Amendment would virtually be self-executing, but did not echo Pomeroy's strictures against congressional authority. 16 Wall. at 123–24.

[69] 16 Wall. at 77.

citizens, with authority to nullify such as it did not approve as consistent with those rights."[70]

Given such possibilities, it is not surprising that the majority of the Justices sought to avoid what seemed to many the obvious meaning of the Fourteenth Amendment's Privileges and Immunities Clause. And given the doctrines of dual federalism that the Court had already endorsed in *Collector v. Day*, it is not surprising that they found the way out in the notion that Americans held privileges and immunities as citizens of the United States different from those they held as citizens of the individual States.

Constitutional historians have severely criticized the *Slaughter-House* decision for nullifying the plain meaning of the Fourteenth Amendment's Privileges and Immunities Clause as defined by its framers.[71] As early as 1879, a critic wondered what fiery old Thaddeus Stevens's reaction would have been if told that all he had intended to secure through that clause were the rights of ex-slaves to protection on the high seas, to travel freely between States, or to petition the government.[72] There can be no doubt that the point was well made. Whatever Republicans intended "privileges and immunities of citizens of the United States" to mean, it was more than that. But Stevens would have been just as incredulous to learn that he had given Congress or the Supreme Court the power to nullify Louisiana's regulations of slaughterhouses, and that is the nub of the conundrum the Court faced. As the *American Law Review* understood, the problem in construing the Amendment's provisions was to "apply their letter . . . to new states of fact not contemplated by Congress nor the legislatures that made them."[73]

Critics of the *Slaughter-House Cases* argue that the Court majority ignored the well-known intent of the Fourteenth Amendment and that Miller's eloquent articulation of its "one pervading purpose," to secure full liberty to blacks, was merely "a strategic ob-

---

[70] *Id.* at 78.

[71] KELLY & HARBISON, note 2 *supra*, at 476; Beth, *The Slaughter-House Cases Revisited*, 23 LA. L. REV. 487 (1963); Graham, *Our "Declaratory" Fourteenth Amendment*, in GRAHAM, EVERYMAN'S CONSTITUTION, note 2 *supra*, at 319–35; MILLER, note 2 *supra*, at 102–69; 4 BOUDIN, note 2 *supra*, at 94–150.

[72] Royall, *The Fourteenth Amendment: The Slaughter-House Cases*, 4 S.L. REV. (n.s.) 558, 576n (1878).

[73] Note, 8 AM. L. REV. 732 (1873).

fuscation of the issues."[74] But it was those who contended for the broad interpretation of privileges and immunities who had to concede they were innovating. "It is possible that those who framed the article were not themselves aware of the far reaching character of its terms," Justice Bradley admitted in his circuit court decision sustaining the butchers.[75] "Yet, if the amendment, as framed and expressed, does in fact bear a broader meaning, and does extend its protecting shield over those who were never thought of when it was conceived and put in form . . . , it must be presumed that the American people, in giving it their imprimatur, understood what they were doing."[76] The butchers' Democratic counsel insisted they were compelled on principle to "assume" a broader meaning for the Amendment than the merely "partisan" one that might be attributed to it.[77] It was the Court majority and the defendant's lawyers, on the other hand, who argued, "So far as can be judged by the public debate upon the subject, it was certainly never intended or contemplated that this Amendment should receive such a construction." "Have Congress and the whole nation been deceived?" they asked. "Have they done what they did not intend to do?"[78]

In virtually eliminating the Privileges and Immunities Clause as a source of national power to protect citizens' rights, Miller and the lawyers for the Slaughter-House "monopoly" insisted that they intended no subversion of black men's liberty. As noted, Miller was eloquent upon the "one pervading purpose" of the Amendment to protect black rights, and several of the "monopoly's" lawyers were active radical Republicans.[79] Their conviction that the well-known

---

[74] Beth, note 71 supra, at 501.

[75] Live-Stock Dealers and Butcher's Ass'n v. Crescent City Live-Stock Landing and Slaughter-House Co., 15 Fed. Cas. 649, 652 (# 8,408) (C.C.D. La. 1870).

[76] Ibid.

[77] Note 66 supra, at 657, 668.

[78] Argument for the Defendant, 21 L. Ed. 399, at 401 (1873); Brief for Defendant, Slaughter-House Cases, in 6 LANDMARK BRIEFS at 603–04; Brief for Defendant on Reargument, id. at 726–27; 16 Wall. at 67–72.

[79] 16 Wall. at 71. Among defendant's counsel were Thomas J. Durant, a Louisiana radical who had pressed for black suffrage as early as 1864, and Matthew Hale Carpenter, Republican Senator and floor manager of the Civil Rights Act of 1875. Miller himself, a conservative Republican, was impelled to support congressional Reconstruction legislation by southern subversion of freedmen's liberty after the war. FAIRMAN, note 62 supra, at 189–93.

purpose of the Amendment "was to secure all citizens and persons the same rights as white citizens and persons"[80] suggests that they placed primary reliance upon its Equal Protection Clause.[81] That ultimately proved to be a weak reed, but there is no reason to believe that a broader definition of the Privileges and Immunities Clause would have provided any stronger support for black rights. The real obstacle to protection for those rights was the Court's insistence that they were protected only against State infringement and not against individual violence. The Privileges and Immunities Clause was subject to the same limitation, and those who sustained a broad view of it made clear that they interpreted it the same way.[82]

Moreover, those who advocated a broad interpretation of privileges and immunities intended to leave their definition to the vagaries of the judiciary, just as "due process of law" would be subject to judicial construction decades later. The implications are obvious in the result of *Bradwell v. Illinois*,[83] decided only the next day. In that case three of the four Justices who advocated the broader view of privileges and immunities in Slaughter-House concluded that a regulation barring women from practicing law was a "reasonable" exercise of the State police power. It was consistent with "the divine law of the Creator," which made woman's "paramount destiny and mission . . . to fulfill the noble and benign offices of wife and mother."[84] The same "divine law" could be—and would be—cited to ordain "reasonable" regulations of the privileges and immunities of freedmen.[85]

Just as the almost universal desire of Americans to preserve the basics of the federal system impelled the Justices to avoid the revolutionary potential of the Privileges and Immunities Clause of the

---

[80] Argument for the Defendant, 21 L. Ed. at 402.

[81] See also Miller's discussion of that Clause. 16 Wall. at 81.

[82] *Id.* at 83*ff.*

[83] 16 Wall. 130 (1873).

[84] *Id.* at 141.

[85] In 1880 and 1881 Justices Field and Clifford would deny that the right to sit upon a jury was included even within the broad category of privileges and immunities of citizens of the States. Ex parte Virginia, 100 U.S. 339, 365–66 (1880); Neal v. Delaware, 103 U.S. 370, 406 (1881).

Fourteenth Amendment, it led them to adopt the doctrine of "State action." As early as 1872 they had demonstrated their concern that a broad interpretation of Reconstruction-era legislation might subvert the reserved area of State jurisdiction. In *Blyew v. United States*[86] they had considered the Civil Rights Act's removal provisions, which permitted transfer of cases from State to national courts when they "affected" a person whose rights as defined by the Act were denied. The victim of a crime was not a party legally "affected" in the culprit's prosecution, the Court ruled, nor were witnesses who could not testify in the case because of their color. Once again the Court's opinion reflected the concern for State authority that pervaded its pre-Reconstruction cases: "It will not be thought that Congress intended to give to the District and Circuit Courts jurisdiction over all causes both civil and criminal . . . . And yet if all those who may be called as witnesses in a case, were intended to be described in the class of persons affected by it . . . , there is no cause either civil or criminal of which those courts may not take jurisdiction . . . [because] such an allegation might always be made."[87]

In case after case in the 1870s and 1880s the Justices construed the Reconstruction Amendments and legislation in light of these considerations. The practical results in individual cases still shock the researcher—the release of Blyew and his confederate, who butchered an innocent black woman in paranoid expectation of a race war; the freeing of the Colfax rioters, who had massacred defenseless, fleeing blacks.[88] One cannot help but suspect that had the Court been more sensitive to blacks' rights, they would have found the grounds upon which to do justice. But that does not mean that the Justices were motivated by the desire to cement the Union with the blood of the Negro, as some scholars have alleged.[89] It was the duty of the States, not Congress, to punish such outrages, they insisted. To hold otherwise "would be to clothe congress with power to

---

[86] 13 Wall. 581 (1872).

[87] *Id.* at 592.

[88] United States v. Cruikshank, 92 U.S. 542 (1876). United States v. Harris, 106 U.S. 629 (1883), also involved southern white rioters.

[89] MAGRATH, note 2 *supra*, at 136–49; Scott, *Justice Bradley's Evolving Concept of the Fourteenth Amendment from the Slaughter-House Cases to the Civil Rights Cases*, 25 RUTGERS L. REV. 552, 564–69 (1971); Kinoy, note 2 *supra*, at 396–97.

pass laws for the general preservation of social order in every state."[90]

When one assesses the Supreme Court's decisions within the context of the doctrines of dual federalism accepted by most Americans in the nineteenth century, however, what is remarkable is the degree to which the Court sustained national authority to protect rights rather than the degree to which they restricted it. In fact, although the Justices found fault with indictments and ruled Reconstruction legislation unconstitutional for excessive breadth, they made clear that with the exception of a few of the *Civil Rights Cases*,[91] every single prosecution brought before them could have been sustained by an appropriate national law. In the very decisions that released southern defendants as well as in those that affirmed their convictions, the Court rejected nearly all the arguments against national enforcement of rights put forward by its opponents. The Justices adhered to the doctrine of "state action" under the Fourteenth Amendment—the crucial element in the maintenance of the federal system they believed in. They repudiated every other restriction.

In Congress, in political platforms, campaign literature and oratory, and finally in legal briefs, arguments, and opinions, opponents of Reconstruction legislation developed a catalogue of limitations upon national authority to protect civil and political rights that truly would have nullified the constitutional amendments had it been accepted, and caused incalculable embarrassment to modern federal civil rights protection, much of which is still based upon the Reconstruction-era laws.

They insisted that the Thirteenth Amendment itself did no more than abolish the institution of slavery. Legislation authorized by its enforcement provision could reach nothing more than peonage and coolyism. Thus if the Fourteenth Amendment had not been passed, the Civil Rights Act of 1866 would have been unconstitutional.[92] If the Thirteenth Amendment did not give Congress power to pro-

---

[90] Bradley in United States v. Cruikshank, 25 Fed. Cas. 707, 710 (# 14,897) (C.C.D. La. 1874).

[91] 109 U.S. 3 (1883).

[92] E.g., Cong. Globe, 39th Cong., 1st Sess., 623 (1866) (Rep. Kerr); *id*. at 628 (Rep. Marshall); *id*. at 499 (Sen. Cowan); *id*. at 1156 (Rep. Thornton); *id*. at 476 (Sen. Saulsbury); Bowlin v. Kentucky, 65 Ky. 5 (1867); People v. Brady, 40 Cal. 198 (1870).

tect rights, the Fourteenth and Fifteenth Amendments did little more, according to the conservative argument. Not only were the prohibitions of the Fourteenth and Fifteenth Amendments aimed only at States, they were aimed at States only in their corporate capacities. Thus, they operated directly upon offending State laws, rendering them immediately null and void, but could not authorize criminal or civil action against State officers who carried out those laws. In a federal system in which State and nation were equally sovereign, neither government could impose duties on the officers of the other.[93] And that was even more certainly true if the officer's act was not sanctioned by State law or was in actual contravention of it.[94] Moreover, it was a plain violation of the Constitution to make the same act both a State and a national crime, so no offense against a State law could be prosecuted by the national government merely by giving it another name.[95]

All these positions were grounded in the notion of State independence from national impositions that the Supreme Court itself had recognized in *Collector v. Day* and *United States v. R.R. Co.* But the commitment to maintaining the State's primary jurisdiction over protection of rights against individual infringement, embodied in the State action doctrine, led inexorably to an even more extreme conclusion—that despite provisions directly affirming congressional power to enforce the Amendments by appropriate legislation, Congress had no more power to enforce Fourteenth and Fifteenth Amendment prohibitions than it had to enforce the Constitution's Obligation of Contracts or Ex Post Facto Clauses. In quintessential dual federalist argument against the constitutionality of the 1871 Enforcements Acts, Justice Field's brother, David Dudley Field,

---

[93] CONG. GLOBE, 41st Cong., 2d Sess., 3667, appendix, 422 (1870) (Sen. Fowler); *id.* 42d Cong., 1st Sess., app. 231 (1871) (Sen. Blair); *id.* at appendix, 217 (Sen. Thurman formerly chief justice of the Ohio Supreme Court); Brief for Petitioner, Ex parte Virginia, 8 LANDMARK BRIEFS 113–24; Brief for Defendants, United States v. Cruikshank, 7 *id.* at 340; Biddle, *Indictment of Judge Coles*, 6 S.L. REV. (n.s.) 206, 216–20 (1880); Justices Field and Clifford, dissenting in Ex parte Virginia, 100 U.S. at 349–70, and in Ex parte Clarke, 100 U.S. 399, 404–22 (1880). The argument was also made, apparently, by defense counsel in United States v. Given, 25 Fed. Cas. 1329 (# 15,211 C.C.D. Del. 1873). It is implicit in Bowlin v. Kentucky, 65 Ky. 5, 7–14 (1867) (Williams, J. concurring), and State v. Rash, 1 Houston's Crim. Rep. 271 (Del. 1867).

[94] CONG. GLOBE, 41st Cong., 2d Sess., 472–73 (1870) (Sen. Casserly); United States v. Jackson, 26 Fed. Cas. 563 (# 15,459) (C.C.D. Cal. 1874).

[95] CONG. GLOBE, 41st Cong., 2d Sess., 3674 (1870) (Sen. Thurman); *id.*, 42d Cong., 1st Sess., 572 (1871) (Sen. Stockton).

established the underpinnings of such a position: "Congress . . . is judge of the means to be chosen for attaining a desired end, only in this sense, that it must choose *appropriate* means . . . such as are not *expressly or by implication prohibited.* . . . There are many limitations upon the choice of means beyond those which are expressed. They are implied from the nature of the government. . . . The right to declare an act invalid, because incompatible with the Constitution, applies with the same effect where the incompatibility relates to the implied, as where it relates to the express limitations of the Constitution."[96] With every justification Field was able to cite *Collector v. Day* as authority for this argument—"The case itself is the strongest possible example of an implied limitation upon the powers of Congress. Its power to tax is apparently unlimited, and it had passed an act, by the terms of which the salary of a State judge was liable to taxation, but this court pronounced the act unconstitutional, because, in the exercise of an express power, Congress had transgressed the implied limitations."[97] Given the nature of the American federal system, what could Congress do, then, if a State violated the Fourteenth or Fifteenth Amendments? The conclusion Field offered echoed the position Democrats had taken since the introduction of enforcement legislation: "The answer must be, Congress may do nothing whatever, beyond providing judicial remedies in federal courts for parties aggrieved by deprivation of their rights. Beyond this there is no alternative between doing nothing or doing everything, between leaving the States alone or destroying them altogether. Congress cannot do everything, because that would be the annihilation of the States; therefore it can do nothing, beyond providing the judicial remedies here indicated. . . . [A]n act of a State in violation of the prohibitions of the amendments would be a nullity. . . . Congress, being authorized to enforce the prohibitions by appropriate legislation, the natural, the true, and the only constitutional mode of enforcement, is by the judicial remedies to establish and enforce the nullity."[98]

---

[96] 7 Landmark Briefs 430–31. Cooley referred to similar "implied restrictions" upon congressional power, in Cooley, The General Principles of Constitutional Law in the United States of America 97 (1880).

[97] 7 Landmark Briefs 432–33.

[98] *Id.* at 441–43. See also Thurman's closely reasoned argument against the constitutionality of the 1871 Enforcement Act. Cong. Globe, 42d Cong., 1st Sess., 216, 221–22 (1871), an elaboration of a notion he expressed earlier in opposition to the 1870 En-

Justices Field and Clifford accepted David Dudley Field's argument, going further and finding unconstitutional even the judicial remedy embodied in the 1866 Civil Rights Act's removal provisions. Unconstitutional State laws must be reversed upon appeal to the Supreme Court from State tribunals, they insisted. This "gives to the Federal courts the ultimate decision of Federal questions without infringing upon the dignity and independence of the State courts. By it harmony between them is secured [and] the rights of both Federal and State governments maintained."[99]

The majority of the Justices, however, rejected every one of these arguments. In the process they construed the Amendments in a fashion surprisingly similar to the Court's interpretations of the past twenty years.

First, the Justices never rejected absolutely and without cavil Republican legislators' contentions that Congress might protect rights directly when they were violated by individuals in consequence of State inaction rather than action. Justices Strong and Woods, on the contrary, sustained the Republican position in circuit court decisions shortly after the passage of the 1870 and 1871 Enforcement Acts.[100] In his two seminal Reconstruction-law opinions, the circuit court decision in *United States v. Cruikshank*[101] and the Supreme Court decision in the *Civil Rights Cases*,[102] Justice Bradley spoke, not only in terms of States' primary jurisdiction over private infringement of individual rights, but of the duty of States to protect persons against such infringements and the presumption that they were fulfilling that duty in the absence of allegations to the contrary. Woods expressed a similar presumption when he spoke for the Court in *United States v. Harris*, holding unconstitutional a portion of the 1871 Enforcement Act.[103] In a

---

forcement Act. *Id.*, 41st Cong., 2d Sess., 3664 (1870). See Senator Davis's similar argument, *id.* at 3667; *id.* 42d Cong., 1st Sess., appendix, 49 (1871) (Rep. Kerr).

[99] Virginia v. Rives, 100 U.S. 313, 324–28, 338 (1880); Ex parte Virginia, 100 U.S. 339, 349–70 (1880).

[100] United States v. Given, 25 Fed. Cas. 1324 (# 15,210) (C.C.D. Del. 1873); United States v. Hall, 26 Fed. Cas. 79 (# 15,282 C.C.D. Ala. 1871). Woods had not yet been appointed to the Supreme Court when he delivered his opinion. See also the opinion of Judge Bradford in United States v. Given, 25 Fed. Cas. 1328 (# 15,211) (C.C.D. Del. 1873), which put the "state inaction" argument even more forcefully than did Strong.

[101] 25 Fed. Cas. 707, 710, 714 (# 14,897) (C.C.D. La. 1874).

[102] 109 U.S. 3, 14 (1883).

[103] 106 U.S. 629, 639 (1883).

thorough study of the Court's Reconstruction Amendment opinions, Laurent B. Frantz has made about as strong an argument as possible that such language meant that the Court would have sustained direct congressional protection of civil rights upon demonstration of State dereliction,[104] and he may be right, although there is much to suggest he is not.

A jurist's conviction that the Fourteenth Amendment restated the State's positive duty to provide full protection of the laws did not necessarily mean that he believed Congress could remedy its failure to fulfill it. The nationalist constitutional commentator Pomeroy, who did share this conviction, denied that State dereliction activated national authority. "If the good and valid laws which legislatures have enacted are not fully administered, there is no legal remedy to be obtained . . . from Congress . . . ; redress must be found alone in a change of officers through the ordinary processes of election and appointment," he insisted.[105] While the Court never repudiated the notion in words as direct as David Dudley Field's— "State inaction . . . is no cause for federal action"[106]—neither did it repeat Woods's dictum from his days as district judge that "denying includes inaction as well as action, . . . the omission to protect, as well as the omission to pass laws for protection."[107] It would have been easy to do either.

The Court did, however, reject totally the contention that the Fourteenth Amendment referred to the action of States only in their corporate capacities. As early as 1870 federal judges were sustaining prosecutions of State officers for failures to administer State laws equally, whether or not the laws were discriminatory on their face.[108] In circuit court in 1873 Justice Strong upheld the conviction of a tax collector who refused to accept a black man's tender of taxes required to vote under State law.[109] Seven years later he delivered the Court's opinion that even State judges were liable to con-

---

[104] Frantz, *Congressional Power to Enforce the Fourteenth Amendment against Private Acts,* 73 YALE L. J. 1353 (1964).

[105] Pomeroy, *Rights of Citizens,* note 68 *supra,* at 335.

[106] Note 98 *supra,* at 437.

[107] United States v. Hall, 26 Fed. Cas. 79, 81 (# 15282) (C.C.D. Ala. 1871).

[108] McKay v. Campbell, 16 Fed. Cas. 157 (# 8,839) (D.C.D. Ore. 1870); United States v. Petersburg Judges of Election, 27 Fed. Cas. 506 (# 16,036) (C.C.E.D. Va. 1874).

[109] United States v. Given, 25 Fed. Cas. 1324 (# 15,210) (C.C.D. Del. 1873).

viction for carrying out unfairly nonjudicial functions imposed by superficially equal State laws.[110] Moreover, in a cognate case, Strong made clear that even if a State officer deprived a person of a right in direct contravention of State law, such a violation would both make him "liable to punishment at the instance of the State and under the laws of the United States."[111] At the same time the Court upheld congressional laws aimed directly at State officers' interference with voting rights at federal elections.[112]

While we might take such decisions for granted today, within the context of nineteenth-century federalism these were bold rulings indeed. (In fact, from around 1900 until *United States v. Classic* in 1941[113] the federal courts refused to sustain prosecutions or suits against State officers for civil rights violations that apparently violated State as well as national laws.[114]) The laws the Court thus sustained asserted "a power inconsistent with, and destructive of, the independence of the States," Field and Clifford insisted in dissent.[115] "The right to control their own officers, to prescribe the duties they shall perform, without the supervision or interference of any other state authority . . . is essential to that independence."[116]

In response Strong and Bradley, speaking for the majority in different cases, went to the verge of repudiating the entire notion of dual sovereignty. In language that the Roosevelt Court would echo sixty years later, Strong rejected the idea of "implied limitations" on congressional authority. "The prohibitions of the Fourteenth Amendment are directed to the States," he answered, "and they are to a degree restrictions of State power. It is these which Congress is empowered to enforce, and to enforce against State action, however put forth. . . . Such enforcement is no invasion of State sovereignty. No law can be, which the people of the United States have, by the Constitution of the United States, empowered Congress to enact."[117]

---

[110] Ex parte Virginia, 100 U.S. 339 (1880).

[111] Virginia v. Rives, 100 U.S. 313, at 321 (1880).

[112] Ex parte Siebold, 100 U.S. 371 (1880); Ex parte Clarke, 100 U.S. 399 (1880).

[113] 313 U.S. 299 (1941).

[114] Note, note 2 *supra*, 90 HARV. L. REV. at 1160–61n, 1167–69.

[115] 100 U.S. at 409.

[116] *Ibid.*

[117] Ex parte Virginia, 100 U.S. 339, 346 (1880).

Such language rebuffed the argument that Congress was limited to providing judicial remedies for State violations of the constitutional amendments. "It seems often overlooked that a National Constitution has been adopted in this country, establishing a real government therein, operating upon persons and territory and things," Bradley observed in rebutting the narrow view of national power.[118] At the same time he attacked the sentiment that lay at the foundation of dual federalism, confronting the "mistaken notions with regard to the relations which subsist between the State and national Governments."[119] The national government "is, or should be, as dear to every American citizen as his State Government is," he insisted.[120] "[I]f we allow ourselves to regard it as a hostile organization, opposed to the proper sovereignty and dignity of the State Governments, we shall continue to be vexed with difficulties as to its jurisdiction and authority. . . . Both are essential to the preservation of our liberties and the perpetuity of our institutions. But, in endeavoring to vindicate the one, we should not allow our zeal to nullify or impair the other."[121] With justification, Field perceived in such reasoning "a new departure."[122] In the less restrained world of journalism, the editor of a newspaper established in 1880 to boost Field's presidential ambitions, exploded, "They are revolution. They are a complete overthrow of our institutions."[123]

Even more enlightening is the reasoning by which the Supreme Court tried to sustain national authority to protect individual rights directly without permitting precedents that might later destroy the established lines between State and national power. The Justices did this through doctrines first propounded by Bradley in his circuit court opinion in *Cruikshank*.[124] In that prosecution the United States district attorney for Louisiana, James Beckwith, sought the convictions of the Grant Parish rioters under section six of the Enforcement Act of 1870, which made it illegal for two or more people to

---

[118] Ex parte Siebold, 100 U.S. 371, 393–94 (1880).

[119] *Ibid.*

[120] *Ibid.*

[121] *Ibid.*

[122] Ex parte Clarke, 100 U.S. 399, 414 (1880).

[123] *Richmond Daily Commonwealth*, March 5, 1880.

[124] 25 Fed. Cas. 707 (# 14,897) (C.C.D. La. 1874).

injure or threaten any citizen "with intent to prevent or hinder his free exercise and enjoyment of any right or privilege granted or secured to him" by the United States Constitution or laws. The indictment alleged several counts of murder with the intent to deprive the victims of various rights secured by the Constitution—to bear arms, to assemble peaceably, to equal protection of the laws, to enjoyment of life and liberty unless deprived of them by due process of law, to rights secured by the State and national constitutions because of their color, the right to vote, and all the privileges and immunities of citizens of the United States.

The defendants' lawyers attacked the constitutionality of the law itself, insisting it usurped the States' jurisdiction over individual crimes. Bradley agreed that the Fourteenth Amendment prohibited State action only and that protection of rights was primarily the duty of the States. Any other holding "would be to clothe congress with power to pass laws for the general preservation of social order in every state."[125] Yet despite these strictures, he upheld the law as an exercise of congressional power, not under the Fourteenth Amendment, but under the Thirteenth and Fifteenth.

The Thirteenth Amendment, Bradley asserted, involved more than the mere nullification of the formal institution of slavery. It implied the vesting of the positive rights of freedom. Therefore it authorized Congress "to make it a penal offense to conspire to deprive a person of, or hinder him in, the exercise and enjoyment of the rights and privileges conferred by the 13th amendment and the laws thus passed in pursuance thereof."[126] So not only was Congress freed of the "State action" limitation by Bradley's construction, but the "rights and privileges" protected by the Enforcement Act were those of citizenship in general, not the limited ones the Supreme Court perceived incident to United States citizenship in *Slaughter-House*. Still committed to preserving the basic demarcations of the federal system, Bradley carefully defined the power he was conceding: Congress could punish directly only those offenses perpetrated to deprive persons of rights because of race, color, or previous condition of servitude, not offenses motivated by ordinary malice or greed. As an example, he cited the case where a freedman sought to lease and cultivate a farm but was prevented from doing

---

[125] *Id.* at 710–11.

[126] *Id.* at 711.

so on account of his color by whites. "It cannot be doubted that this would be a case within the power of Congress to remedy and redress. It would be a case of interference with that person's exercise of his rights as a citizen because of his race."[127] If, however, the same offense were motivated by other considerations, "without any design to interfere with his rights of citizenship or equality before the laws, as being a person of a different race or color . . . , it would be an ordinary crime, punishable by the state law only."[128] Thus, in 1875, Bradley construed the Thirteenth Amendment in a manner not revived by the Twentieth-Century Supreme Court until it decided *Jones v. Mayer* in 1968.[129]

Bradley went even further, concluding that the "rights and privileges" directly protected by the Enforcement Act included voting rights. Since the Amendment simply states that the citizen's right to vote "shall not be denied or abridged by the United States or any State" on account of race or previous condition, Bradley was interpreting away what seems to be another State action limitation. Despite its unusual formulation, Bradley asserted, the Fifteenth Amendment "confers a right not to be excluded from voting by reason of race, color, or previous condition of servitude."[130] In essence it was "a constitutional extension of the civil rights bill, conferring upon the emancipated slave . . . another specific right" of citizenship.[131] Just as in the case of Thirteenth Amendment rights, "Congress has the power directly to enforce the right and punish individuals for its violation,"[132] no matter what the State does in the premises. "There is no essential incongruity in the coexistence of concurrent laws, state and federal, for the punishment of the same unlawful acts."[133]

But once again, Bradley carefully defined Congress's jurisdiction. The "right and privilege" protected by the Enforcement Act was the right not to be deprived of the power to vote because of color.

---

[127] *Id.* at 712.

[128] *Ibid.*

[129] 392 U.S. 409 (1968). See Casper, *Jones v. Mayer: Clio, Bemused and Confused Muse,* 1968 SUPREME COURT REVIEW 89.

[130] United States v. Cruikshank, 25 Fed. Cas. 707, 712 (# 14.897) (C.C.D. La. 1874).

[131] *Ibid.*

[132] *Id.* at 713.

[133] *Ibid.*

Congress did not acquire general power to regulate voting from the Fifteenth Amendment.[134]

Having defined Congress's powers in such a way as to sustain broad authority to protect rights, Bradley found the individual counts of the indictment wanting. Some claimed an intent to violate rights not guaranteed or secured by the Constitution; others were too vague. But the biggest obstacle was the very ground upon which Bradley had protected national power. Under his construction, the Colfax rioters must have intended to violate their victims' rights on account of their color or previous condition of servitude in order to be convicted. Because Beckwith had failed to allege that motivation, convictions were reversed on counts that otherwise would have been sustained. "Perhaps such a design may be inferred from the allegation that the persons injured were of the African race . . . . But it ought not to have been left to inference; it should have been alleged."[135] Throughout his discussion of the individual counts, Bradley—having conceded so much to Congress—seemed intent on assuring that the counts of the Colfax rioters' indictment transgress by not one inch over what he had reserved to the States.[136]

The Court endorsed Bradley's expansive view of congressional authority to enforce the Fifteenth Amendment against individual infringements of the rights to vote in both *United States v. Reese*[137] and *United States v. Cruikshank*,[138] agreeing that Congress could punish private offenses against citizens' voting rights so long as they were motivated by race or previous condition of servitude. In *Reese*, the Court ruled unconstitutional two provisions of the 1870 Enforcement Act. One punished State officials who at any election refused to accept ballots from voters who had been denied the opportunity to meet voting qualifications by others on account of their race. The other punished anyone who tried to interfere with any citizen's effort to meet voting qualifications. Although the second provision posited no State action, the Court did not rule it unconstitutional on those grounds. Nor did the Justices accept the argument that Congress could impose no duties on officers of the

---

[134] *Id.* at 714.

[135] *Id.* at 715.

[136] *Ibid.*

[137] 92 U.S. 214 (1876).

[138] 92 U.S. 542 (1876).

"independent" State sovereignties. Still less did they accept David Dudley Field's argument, made on behalf of Cruikshank, that Congress could do no more than provide judicial remedies. Instead, Waite took the position which Bradley had developed in his *Cruikshank* circuit court opinion. Although the citizen's right to vote does not emanate from the national government and the government therefore has no general power over it, the Amendment "has invested citizens with a new constitutional right which is in the protecting power of Congress. The right is exemption in the exercise of the elective franchise on account of race, color, or previous condition of servitude."[139] The two Enforcement Act provisions were unconstitutional, not because of any State action requirements, but because they did not require the allegation that offenses be motivated by the race or previous condition of the victims. It was true that the indictments themselves alleged the requisite motivation. But that could not cure the defect. The statute covered offenses both within and without congressional jurisdiction. Like Bradley, having conceded Congress direct power in an area at the heart of State jurisdiction, the Court was unwilling to concede one inch more. Reese and his codefendants were released, not because Congress lacked authority to punish them, but because it "ha[d] not as yet provided by 'appropriate legislation' for the punishment of the offense."[140]

In *Cruikshank*,[141] Waite once more followed Bradley's construction of the Fifteenth Amendment, holding invalid the counts of the indictment alleging intent to deprive voting rights for failure to allege racial motivation, rather than for lack of State action. Waite again sustained Congress's power to protect voting rights against racially motivated private assaults two years later, while trying the Ellenton, South Carolina, rioters on circuit.[142] And Justice Woods reaffirmed the Bradley construction in 1883 in *United States v. Harris*,[143] while holding a provision of the 1871 Enforcement Act unconstitutional because it did not require racial motivation for the offense against voting rights that it punished. As in

---

[139] United States v. Reese, 92 U.S. 214, 218 (1876).

[140] *Id.* at 221.

[141] United States v. Cruikshank, 92 U.S. 542 (1876).

[142] United States v. Butler, 25 Fed. Cas. 213 (No. 14,700) (C.C.D.S.C. 1877).

[143] 106 U.S. 629 (1883).

Reese, the fact that such motivation was alleged in the indictment and proved could not rescue the Act itself. Once again, the offenders would have been liable to conviction for the same acts under a properly drawn statute.

The Court went further in sustaining congressional power to protect voting rights. In his *Reese* opinion, Waite expressly limited to local and State elections his argument that States retained general authority over voting, implying broader congressional power over federal elections.[144] As in the Ellenton riot case he tried on circuit in 1878, he ruled that in federal elections Congress had plenary power to protect the rights of all voters against individual interference whether motivated by racial hostility or not.[145] And the entire Court took the same view in the 1880s,[146] sustaining convictions of white voting officials and rioters for precisely the same acts alleged in *Reese* and *Cruikshank.*[147] Thus the Waite Court established Congress's power to protect voting rights against private infringement in State and local elections in any case where the offense was racially motivated, and on any grounds whatever in federal elections.

It is not clear whether the whole Court immediately accepted Bradley's recognition of broad congressional power to enforce the Thirteenth Amendment. Bradley's colleagues certainly did not reject it when his *Cruikshank* opinion came before them a year later.[148] Waite's majority opinion sustaining Bradley's circuit court judgment is unclear on the grounds on which the Justices upheld the constitutionality of the Enforcement Act provisions before them. Waite, however, followed Bradley's analysis of the specific counts closely, and Bradley did not write a separate opinion, suggesting that he saw nothing inconsistent between Waite's views and his own. In *United States v. Harris,*[149] where a lynch mob was accused of killing their victims with intent to deny their right to equal protection of the laws, Justice Woods tested the provisions of the Enforcement Act against Congress's power to protect rights di-

---

[144] 92 U.S. at 216, 218.

[145] United States v. Butler, 25 Fed. Cas. 213 (No. 14,700) (C.C.D.S.C. 1877).

[146] Ex parte Siebold, 100 U.S. 371 (1880); Ex parte Clarke, 100 U.S. 399 (1880); Ex parte Yarbrough, 110 U.S. 651 (1884).

[147] United States v. Reese, 92 U.S. 214 (1875); United States v. Cruikshank, 92 U.S. 542 (1876).

[148] United States v. Cruikshank, 92 U.S. 542 (1876).

[149] 106 U.S. 629 (1883).

rectly under the Thirteenth Amendment, but without committing the whole Court to Bradley's views. "Even if the Amendment is held to be directed against the action of private individuals," he wrote, "the law under consideration covers cases both within and without the provisions of the Amendment" because it does not require racial motivation for the offense. Therefore, under the rule of construction enunciated in *Reese*, the law fell.[150]

But if the Court did not endorse Bradley's views unequivocally in *Cruikshank* or *Reese*, it certainly acquiesced in them when he wrote the opinion striking down the Civil Rights Act of 1875. In the famous (or perhaps infamous) *Civil Rights Cases*,[151] Bradley tested the law against both the Fourteenth and the Thirteenth Amendments. Rejecting arguments that the businesses and institutions covered by the act were quasi-state agencies, he held the law unwarranted by the Fourteenth Amendment on State action grounds.[152] But when it came to treating the Thirteenth Amendment, Bradley took advantage of the opportunity to write his expansive views of that Amendment—the heritage of the antislavery legal argument—squarely into the Court's opinion. "It is true, that . . . the Thirteenth Amendment may be regarded as nullifying all State laws which establish or uphold slavery. But it has a reflex character also, establishing and decreeing universal civil and political freedom throughout the United States; and it is assumed, [by those upholding the law,] that the power vested in Congress to enforce the article by appropriate legislation, clothes Congress with power to pass all laws necessary and proper for abolishing all badges and incidents of slavery in the United States."[153] Bradley conceded

---

[150] 106 U.S. at 640–41. Woods added that this particular offense—acting with intent to deprive persons of equal protection of the laws—could not be punished under Thirteenth Amendment authority in any case, even if the law required racial motivation. Since only governments can pass laws, he wrote, denial of their protection by individuals could be accomplished only by violating a law. "[I]f, therefore, we hold that [the law] . . . is warranted by the Thirteenth Amendment, we should . . . accord to Congress the power to punish every crime by which the right of any person to life, property, or reputation is invaded." *Id.* at 643. This is a troubling *dictum*, directly counter to Bradley's *dictum* in the circuit court *Cruikshank* opinion, 25 Fed. Cas. at 715, implying that a count alleging such an offense, if racially motivated, could be sustained if its specifications were made clear. For example, Bradley's *dictum* would sustain, and Woods's would condemn, a national antilynching law.

[151] 109 U.S. 3 (1883).

[152] *Id.* at 8–19.

[153] *Id.* at 20.

the truth of the assumption,[154] but then rejected the proposition that denial of equal accommodations and privileges was an incident of slavery.[155]

Bradley's problem was that his own interpretation of the Thirteenth Amendment threatened to justify national punishment of any private invasion of a citizen's rights where race was the motive, to sustain a national criminal code protecting blacks against ordinary crimes against life and property. He apparently felt impelled to draw the line somewhere. In his cruel sentence—"When a man has emerged from slavery, . . . there must be some stage in the progress of his elevation when he takes the rank of a mere citizen, and ceases to be the special favorite of the laws, and when his rights as a . . . man, are to be protected in the ordinary modes by which other men's rights are protected"[156]—Bradley, it would seem, was referring to stages of law, not time. Direct national legislation protecting basic rights inherent in freedom was legitimate; legislation protecting more elevated rights was not. Moreover, Bradley believed that State courts had held the common law to require equal access for all citizens to inns and public conveyances. Any change in that requirement would have to be made by statute. He implied that if such statute caused an unjust discrimination, it would violate the Fourteenth Amendment.[157] And he carefully avoided any suggestion that Congress lacked authority to pass a similar law restricted in its application to interstate conveyances and United States territory and the District of Columbia.[158]

A recent analyst has stated aptly that "both the majority position in the *Civil Rights Cases* and the Harlan dissent . . . were fashioned by Joseph Bradley."[159] Like Bradley, Harlan rejected the *Slaughter-House Cases'* narrow conception of congressional authority under the Fourteenth Amendment to protect rights of citizenship.[160] But

[154] *Id.* at 20–21, 23.

[155] *Id.* at 23–25.

[156] *Id.* at 25.

[157] *Ibid.*

[158] *Id.* at 19.

[159] Scott, note 89 *supra*, at 564.

[160] Harlan went about it a different way. Instead of rejecting the Court's differentiation between rights of United States citizens and rights of State citizens, Harlan argued that Congress had power to protect rights under the first clause of the Amendment defining citizenship. 109 U.S. at 46–48.

that was a lost cause. Harlan's dissent challenged Bradley most powerfully by accepting Bradley's own views of the Thirteenth Amendment. "The Thirteenth Amendment, it is conceded, did something more than to prohibit slavery as an *institution*, resting upon distinctions of race, and shielded by positive law," Harlan wrote.[161] "My brethren admit that it established and decreed universal *civil freedom*. . . . They admit . . . that there are burdens and disabilities, the necessary incidents of slavery, which constitute its substance and visible form; that Congress, by the [Civil Rights] Act of 1866, passed in view of the Thirteenth Amendment, . . . undertook to remove certain burdens and disabilities . . . and secure to all citizens of every race and color . . . those fundamental rights which are the essence of civil freedom . . . ; that under the 13th Amendment . . . legislation, so far as necessary and proper to eradicate all forms and incidents of slavery and involuntary servitude may be direct and primary, operating upon the acts of individuals, whether sanctioned by state legislation or not."[162] Harlan recognized what most scholars have not; to reverse Bradley's judgment it was not necessary to challenge his construction of the constitutional amendments. It was merely necessary to challenge his definition of the "incidents" of slavery.[163]

In sum, then, the Supreme Court's construction of congressional power under the constitutional amendments hardly subverted Republican intent. Committed, as were nearly all Americans of the time, to maintaining the State's primary jurisdiction over criminal offenses, endorsing the basic concepts of dual federalism, the Court still managed to sustain Congress's power to protect directly citizens' fundamental civil and political rights. That Congress did not take advantage of that opportunity reflected the fact that other issues had become more important to a majority of Americans than protection of civil rights. One should not forget, however, that the first time Republicans regained control over all three branches of

---

[161] *Id*. at 34.

[162] *Id*. at 35–36.

[163] Citing *Reese* and *Cruikshank*, Harlan pointed to the Court's own recognition, based upon the theories Bradley articulated in his circuit court *Cruikshank* opinion, that emancipation had created a national privilege not to be deprived of rights on account of color— that racial discrimination was the most fundamental "incident" of slavery. "If, then, exemption from discrimination in respect of civil rights, is a new constitutional right, . . . why may not the nation . . . protect and enforce that right?" he asked. *Id*. at 50.

the national government after 1874, they attempted to pass a law to protect voting rights according to the guidelines set by the Waite Court. It was draconian enough to be called the Force Act of 1890—the direct heir of the Force Act of 1871.[164]

Nearly all of the Waite Court's assertions of broad congressional power under the Thirteenth and Fifteenth Amendments were *dicta*. It was this that permitted the Fuller Court to ignore them in later years. One need only compare the Court's opinion in *Williams v. Mississippi*[165] with Strong's language in *Strauder* and *Ex parte Virginia* to recognize the magnitude of the change.[166] In *James v. Bowman*,[167] the Fuller Court ignored the Waite Court's *dicta* and held the Fifteenth Amendment subject to the same State action limitations as the Fourteenth. In doing so, the Justices overturned a district court decision to the contrary[168] which had been based squarely upon the *dicta* in *Cruikshank*, *Reese*, and *Harris*. The Court merely announced that the Fifteenth Amendment incorporated the same limitations as the Fourteenth and then cited the Waite Court's Fourteenth Amendment opinions as authority. In *Barney v. City of New York*,[169] it held that offenses of State officers in violation of State law could not constitute State action. And in a series of cases it refused to provide relief to blacks disenfranchised under the new southern constitutions of the 1890s and early 1900s.[170] Once again, one need only compare the Fuller Court's language with that of the Waite Court in *Ex parte Yarbrough* to appreciate the difference in the attitudes of the Justices.

Of course neither black Americans nor radical Republicans felt

---

[164] Hirshon, Farewell to the Bloody Shirt 200–33 (1962).

[165] 170 U.S. 213 (1898).

[166] In this case the Fuller Court ignored the obvious discrimination in the administration of Mississippi's new voting laws of the 1890s, accepting the State's argument that they purged from the voting rolls persons with certain "characteristics," not persons of a certain race. Thus all-white juries chosen from the purged voting lists did not violate the Constitution.

[167] 190 U.S. 127 (1903).

[168] United States v. Lackey, 99 Fed. 952 (D.C.D. Ky. 1900).

[169] 193 U.S. 430 (1904). It is not clear that the Court intended to preclude national authority in all such circumstances in this property-rights case, but it was so interpreted. See Note, note 2 *supra*, 90 Harv. L. Rev. at 1160–61n.

[170] Mills v. Green, 159 U.S. 651 (1895); Giles v. Harris, 189 U.S. 475 (1903); Jones v. Montague, 194 U.S. 147 (1904); Selden v. Montague, 194 U.S. 153 (1904); Giles v. Teasley, 193 U.S. 146 (1904).

much like thanking the Waite Court for sustaining congressional power while they released southern killers and election riggers. Democrats and "liberal" or "Mugwump" Republicans demanding sectional reconciliation at the price of black rights praised Court decisions that protected "State rights" by releasing undoubted criminals upon technicalities of statutory construction. It was in their interests politically to ignore the fact that these decisions were based on technicalities, that beneath the surface most of Congress's power to protect rights remained unimpaired. But when one steps back from the immediate political circumstances of the decisions, when one assesses them in light of contemporary doctrines of federalism rather than our own, one reaches a more balanced conclusion. No one can accuse the Justices of the Waite Court of wearing their hearts upon the sleeves of their robes, but they left a heritage of sanctioned congressional power over civil rights that was ignored by their immediate successors and only recently resurrected, without credit to them, by the new abolitionists of the mid-twentieth century.

PETER WESTEN

RICHARD DRUBEL

TOWARD A GENERAL THEORY
OF DOUBLE JEOPARDY

Of all procedural guarantees in the Bill of Rights, the principle of double jeopardy is the most ancient. It is "one of the oldest ideas found in western civilization,"[1] with roots in Greek, Roman, and canon law.[2] What Blackstone said of double jeopardy in the eighteenth century can be traced to what Demosthenes said 2,000 years earlier: "[T]he laws forbid the same man to be tried twice on the same issue."[3]

Peter Westen is Professor of Law, University of Michigan. Richard Drubel is law clerk to Judge Louis F. Oberdorfer, United States District Court for the District of Columbia.

AUTHORS' NOTE: The authors would like to thank Gerald Rosberg for commenting upon an earlier draft; Edward Cooper and Jerold Israel for donating their time and insights during the preparation of this article; and Frank Easterbrook for his generosity both in sharing his wisdom and in helping to rationalize the developing jurisprudence of double jeopardy.

[1] Bartkus v. Illinois, 359 U.S. 121, 151 (1959) (Black, J., dissenting).

[2] For a history of double jeopardy see FRIEDLAND, DOUBLE JEOPARDY 5-15 (1969); SIGLER, DOUBLE JEOPARDY: THE DEVELOPMENT OF A LEGAL AND SOCIAL PHILOSOPHY 1-37 (1969).

[3] DEMOSTHENES 589 (Vance transl. 1962), quoted in United States v. Jenkins, 490 F.2d 868, 870-71 (2d Cir. 1973), aff'd, 420 U.S. 358 (1975). Cf. 4 BLACKSTONE, COMMENTARIES *335: "[It is] a universal maxim of the common law of England, that no man is to be brought into jeopardy of his life, more than once for the same offense."

One might suppose that an idea of such antiquity by now would have been thoroughly refined and simplified, but that is not so. Although the language of double jeopardy is "plain,"[4] it presents problems that are "both subtle and complex"[5] and encompasses a body of doctrine that is in an acknowledged state of "confusion."[6] The Supreme Court now concedes that its decisions "can hardly be characterized as models of consistency and clarity"[7] and yet proceeds to compound the confusion by overruling two separate lines of cases including one that was launched with considerable fanfare just three years ago.[8]

Significantly, this shift cannot be attributed to recent changes in the Court's membership.[9] The problem, rather, is that the individual Justices have yet to develop coherent positions of their own. One Justice acknowledges that he has "reexamined" his "assumptions"[10]

---

[4] Crist v. Bretz, 98 S. Ct. 2156, 2159 (1978).

[5] Ibid.

[6] Burks v. United States, 98 S. Ct. 2141, 2149 (1978) (hereinafter Burks). See also Sanabria v. United States, 98 S. Ct. 2170, 2187 (1978) (hereinafter Sanabria) (Blackmun, J., dissenting). Cf. Note, 24 MINN. L. REV. 522 (1940): "The riddle of double jeopardy stands out today as one of the most commonly recognized yet most commonly misunderstood maxims in the law, the passage of time having served in the main to burden it with confusion upon confusion."

[7] Burks, 98 S. Ct. at 2146.

[8] Burks, 98 S. Ct. 2141, overruling cases following Bryan v. United States, 338 U.S. 552 (1950); United States v. Scott, 98 S. Ct. 2187, 2191 (1978) (hereinafter Scott), overruling cases based on United States v. Jenkins 420 U.S. 358 (1975) (hereinafter Jenkins). Mr. Justice Rehnquist, who wrote the opinion for the Court in Jenkins, later said of Jenkins that it was intended to provide "explicit guidance" to the lower courts by providing a " 'bright line' analysis" for deciding double jeopardy cases. Lee v. United States, 432 U.S. 23, 36 (1977) (hereinafter Lee). Last Term, in writing the Opinion for the Court in Scott, Mr. Justice Rehnquist admitted that "We believe we pressed too far in Jenkins." 98 S. Ct. at 2198–99.

[9] "The inconsistency and ambiguity of the Court's mistrial decisions thus are due only in part to changing personnel on the Court and changing attitudes toward law enforcement requirements; to some extent they reflect a genuine uncertainty among the Justices concerning the nature of the competing interests and the appropriate way to reconcile them." Schulhofer, Jeopardy and Mistrials, 125 U. PA. L. REV. 449, 472 (1977). Double jeopardy is not one of the areas of criminal procedure in which recent appointees have replaced more liberal predecessors. If anything, the Burger Court has expanded the scope of constitutional protection under the Double Jeopardy Clause. See, e.g., Burks, 98 S. Ct. 2141; Brown v. Ohio, 432 U.S. 161 (1977) (hereinafter Brown); United States v. Martin Linen Supply Co., 430 U.S. 564 (1977) (hereinafter Martin Linen); Breed v. Jones, 421 U.S. 519 (1975) (hereinafter Breed); Ashe v. Swenson, 397 U.S. 436 (1970) (hereinafter Ashe); Waller v. Florida, 397 U.S. 387 (1970). See also Israel, Criminal Procedure, the Burger Court and the Legacy of the Warren Court, 75 MICH. L. REV. 1319, 1352–55 (1977).

[10] Lee, 432 U.S. at 37 (Rehnquist, J., concurring).

about double jeopardy within the past year. A majority are persuaded to "reexamine"[11] and "overrule"[12] a position they had embraced with enthusiasm a few years before. Another bloc decides to set a case for reargument in order to reexamine the validity of "a long line of precedent"[13] and ends up adhering to original precedent. In short, there has been "some shift in emphasis"[14] in the Court's view of double jeopardy not because of shifting alliances among Justices with clearly defined positions but because of uncertainty among the individual Justices about the proper meaning of the concept of double jeopardy.

Nor are these problems likely to disappear. During the decade 1965–75, the Court rarely decided more than three double jeopardy cases per year and in some years decided none at all. Within the last two Terms the Court has decided a total of twenty cases with opinion[15] and remanded numerous others for reconsideration. In the course of one decision the Court reserved three separate questions for future consideration.[16] Thus, far from being able to say that "the end of our problems . . . is finally in sight,"[17] the Court finds that its "exposure to the various facets of the double jeopardy clause" has

---

[11] *Scott*, 98 S. Ct. 2187.

[12] *Id.* at 2191, overruling *Jenkins*, 420 U.S. 358.

[13] Crist v. Kline, 434 U.S. 981 (1977) (Marshall, J., dissenting from order restoring case to the calendar for reargument), decided following argument *sub nom.* Crist v. Bretz, 98 S. Ct. 2156 (1978) (hereinafter *Crist*).

[14] Finch v. United States, 433 U.S. 676, 680 (1977) (hereinafter *Finch*) (Rehnquist, J., dissenting).

[15] Arizona v. Washington, 98 S. Ct. 824 (1978) (hereinafter *Washington*); *Burks*, 98 S. Ct. 2141; *Crist*, 98 S. Ct. 2156; Greene v. Massey, 98 S. Ct. 2151 (1978) (hereinafter *Greene*); *Sanabria*, 98 S. Ct. 2170; Simpson v. United States, 98 S. Ct. 909 (1978) (hereinafter *Simpson*); Swisher v. Brady, 98 S. Ct. 2699 (1978) (hereinafter *Swisher*); *Scott*, 98 S. Ct. 2187; United States v. Wheeler, 98 S. Ct. 1079 (1978) (hereinafter *Wheeler*); Abney v. United States, 431 U.S. 651 (1977) (hereinafter *Abney*); Brown v. Ohio, 432 U.S. 161 (1977); *Finch*, 433 U.S. 676; Harris v. Oklahoma, 433 U.S. 682 (1977) (hereinafter *Harris*); Jeffers v. United States, 432 U.S. 137 (1977) (hereinafter *Jeffers*); Lee, 432 U.S. 23; United States v. Kopp, 429 U.S. 121 (1976) (hereinafter *Kopp*); *Martin Linen*, 430 U.S. 564; United States v. Morrison, 429 U.S. 1 (1976) (hereinafter *Morrison*); United States v. Rose, 429 U.S. 5 (1976) (hereinafter *Rose*); United States v. Sanford, 429 U.S. 14 (1976) (hereinafter *Sanford*). See also Rinaldi v. United States, 434 U.S. 22 (1977) (federal courts should cooperate with the Justice Department in enforcing the *Petite* policy against the federal prosecution of defendants who have already been prosecuted in State court for the same offense).

[16] *Greene*, 98 S. Ct. at 2154–55 nn.7, 9–10.

[17] United States v. Weller, 401 U.S. 254, 255 n.1 (1971), quoted in *Scott*, 98 S. Ct. at 2190–91.

"vastly increased."[18] It is deeply engaged in a "continuing struggle to create order and understanding out of the confusion of [a] lengthening list of . . . decisions on the double jeopardy clause."[19]

The failure is at the level of fundamental theory, and it touches everything the Court does. Sometimes the Court is said to be using a " 'bright line' analysis";[20] sometimes it is said to be using a "balancing test."[21] A defendant's interest in finality is sometimes "subordinate"[22] to the public's interest in accurate prosecution; again it is said to be "absolute."[23] The "heart" of double jeopardy is sometimes identified as the ban on reprosecution following conviction;[24] in other cases it is said to be the ban on reprosecution following acquittal.[25] These paradoxes are the product of what the Court has aptly recognized as its own "conceptual confusion."[26]

The keystone of the theory proposed in this article is that the principle of double jeopardy serves not one, but three distinct interests. In ascending degrees of importance, they are: (1) an interest in finality which may be overcome relatively easily; (2) an interest in avoiding double punishment which comes armed with a presumption in the defendant's favor; and (3) an interest in nullification—*viz.*, an interest in allowing the system to acquit against the evidence—which is absolute. These three interests are all loosely connected to the notion of ending litigation, and it is this connection that provides textual justification for bringing them under the common "rubric"[27] of double jeopardy. But they are conceptually distinct and should be separately addressed.

---

[18] *Scott*, 98 S. Ct. at 2191.

[19] *Sanabria*, 98 S. Ct. at 2187 (Blackmun, J., dissenting). *Cf.* Schulhofer, note 9 *supra*, at 457: "Double jeopardy doctrine thus remains riddled with loopholes of varying conceptual coherence and uneven pragmatic justification."

[20] *Lee*, 432 U.S. at 36 (Rehnquist, J., concurring).

[21] *Finch*, 433 U.S. at 680 (Rehnquist, J., dissenting).

[22] *Washington*, 98 S. Ct. at 830.

[23] *Burks*, 98 S. Ct. at 2147 n.6.

[24] *Jeffers*, 432 U.S. at 150.

[25] *Martin Linen*, 430 U.S. at 569. This same principle has also been referred to as "perhaps the most fundamental rule in the history of double jeopardy jurisprudence." *Scott*, 98 S. Ct. at 2193, quoting from United States v. Ball, 163 U.S. 662, 671 (1896) (hereinafter *Ball*).

[26] *Burks*, 98 S. Ct. at 2149.

[27] *Crist*, 98 S. Ct. at 2166 (Powell, J., dissenting).

One must proceed by identifying the respective interests served by the prohibition of double jeopardy and then assign them pertinent weights. In this respect, cases involving multiple interests are no different or more difficult than cases involving a single interest. For purposes of exposition, however, it may be useful first to analyze the three interests in contexts in which they arise singly and then to consider them in combination.

I. Reprosecution Following Mistrial: The Interest in Finality

There are several reasons for starting with the problems of mistrials. For one, mistrials present in pure form what is often taken to be the central value of double jeopardy, *viz.*, the defendant's interest in getting the proceedings over with once and for all. Furthermore, the problems of reprosecution following mistrial arise more frequently than other double jeopardy problems and, consequently, the Court has had more experience and its analysis of this aspect of double jeopardy is more mature. Finally, the prohibition on reprosecution following a mistrial was the last to be incorporated under the rubric of double jeopardy. Thus, it is now understood that the scope of double jeopardy was originally confined to certain common-law pleas that a defendant could raise to bar further litigation following a final judgment—principally the pleas of *autrefois acquit* and *autrefois convict*—and that it did not protect defendants from being reprosecuted following proceedings that terminated before a verdict.[28] It is also understood, however, that the Court has since constitutionalized a separate rule at common law against dismissing the jury before verdict and subsumed the new rule under

---

[28] "The Fifth Amendment guarantee against double jeopardy derived from English common law, which followed then, as it does now, the relatively simple rule that a defendant has been put in jeopardy only when there has been a conviction or an acquittal—after a complete trial. . . . And it is clear that in the early years of our national history the constitutional guarantee against double jeopardy was considered to be equally limited in scope. . . . But this constitutional understanding was not destined to endure. Beginning with this Court's decision in *United States* v. *Perez*, it became firmly established by the end of the 19th Century that a defendant could be put in jeopardy even in a prosecution that did not culminate in a conviction or acquittal, and this concept has been long established as an integral part of double jeopardy jurisprudence." *Crist*, 98 S. Ct. at 2159–60. See also *id.* at 2163–66 (Powell, J., dissenting). It is usually said, following Blackstone, that the principle of double jeopardy was limited to the common-law pleas of *autrefois acquisit* and *autrefo convict*. See United States v. Wilson, 420 U.S. 332, 340 (1975) (hereinafter *Wilson*). Sometimes, however, following Lord Coke, it is

the rubric of double jeopardy.[29] Consequently, the mistrial cases are a useful reminder that double jeopardy serves more than one purpose and that although the purposes may be loosely "related,"[30] they are also conceptually "separate."[31]

A. THE NATURE OF THE DEFENDANT'S INTEREST

In trying to discover the controlling values, the problem is not to catalog the various possibilities but to identify the one that best explains the Court's decisions. The most famous and oft quoted list of double jeopardy values comes from Justice Black's opinion for the Court in *Green v. United States*.[32] Although *Green* arose in the context of an acquittal, Justice Black's opinion is regularly taken as a starting point for analyzing mistrial cases.[33] He suggested that double jeopardy is designed to protect defendants from three kinds of abuse.[34]

> The underlying idea, one that is deeply ingrained in at least the Anglo-American system of jurisprudence, is that the State with all its resources and power should not be allowed to make repeated attempts to convict an individual for an alleged offense, thereby [1] subjecting him to embarrassment, expense and ordeal and [2] compelling him to live in a continuing state of anxiety and insecurity, as well as [3] enhancing the possibility that even though innocent he may be found guilty.

In addition to these three protections, a fourth makes a frequent appearance in mistrial cases—[4] a defendant's "valued right to have his trial completed by a particular tribunal."[35] An analysis will show

---

said that double jeopardy also includes the plea of pardon. See *ibid.*; *Scott*, 98 S. Ct. at 2191; see also Comment, *Twice in Jeopardy*, 75 YALE L.J. 262, n.1 (1965) (double jeopardy also includes the common-law plea of *autrefois attaint*).

[29] The history of the process by which this "separate rule of English practice" became "absorbed in this country" into the Double Jeopardy Clause is set forth at length by Mr. Justice Powell in his dissenting opinion in *Crist*, 98 S. Ct. at 2163–66. Mr. Justice Powell does not object to the fact that this "separate rule" is now subsumed under the "rubric" of the Double Jeopardy Clause, because if it had not been deemed part of the Double Jeopardy Clause, "we might well have come to regard [it] as an aspect of due process." *Id.* at 2165.

[30] *Scott*, 98 S. Ct. at 2194.

[31] *Ibid.*

[32] 355 U.S. 184 (1957) (hereinafter *Green*).

[33] See *Crist*, 98 S. Ct. at 2160; *Scott*, 98 S. Ct. at 2192; *Washington*, 98 S. Ct. at 829 n.13; United States v. Dinitz, 424 U.S. 600, 606 (1976) (hereinafter *Dinitz*).

[34] 355 U.S. at 187–88.

[35] Wade v. Hunter, 336 U.S. 684, 689 (1949) (hereinafter *Hunter*).

that number [1] is ordinarily insufficient either alone or in combination with the other values to explain the mistrial cases; that [2] and [4] are essentially equivalent to one another; but that [2] and [3], though insufficient in themselves, together provide a coherent rationale for mistrial cases.

Mr. Justice Powell has taken the position that the first value—*viz.*, the value in protecting a defendant from the "embarrassment" and "expense" of repeated litigation—is largely immaterial. With respect to the embarrassment and expense of being subjected to repeated proceedings, he says, there is no significant difference between the burden of pretrial proceedings and the burden of the trial itself, because it is just as embarrassing and financially burdensome to endure repeated preliminary examinations and bail hearings and other pretrial hearings as to endure repeated trials. Yet the law of double jeopardy draws a marked distinction between pretrial proceedings which the State may interrupt and repeat without justification, and trial proceedings which may not be stopped and started again except for reasons of "manifest necessity."[36] Consequently, so the argument goes, whatever it is that supports this distinction, it cannot simply be the alleged desire to protect defendants from embarrassment and expense.[37]

There is force to the Powell argument, but it does not follow that

---

[36] The term "manifest necessity" is used here to emphasize that the burden on the State of justifying a mistrial over the defendant's objection is a heavy one, but beyond that the term is almost useless. As it now stands, manifest necessity is used in too many different settings to be of any descriptive value. One thing is certain: " 'Necessity' cannot be interpreted literally." *Washington*, 98 S. Ct. at 831. Indeed, the term is not even useful to describe those cases in which, because of some calamity, it is physically impossible to proceed with a trial, because the constitutional effect depends on the cause of the calamity. If the State is not to blame for the calamity, the defendant can be reprosecuted. See *Hunter*, 336 U.S. 684. If the calamity was caused by deliberate harassment or overreaching, however, the defendant is immune from reprosecution. See notes 115, 117–18, *infra*. The difficult case, of course, is the case in which it cannot be determined whether the calamity was caused by deliberate overreaching. It remains to be seen whether doubts are to be resolved there in favor of reprosecution or in favor of immunity. Whatever the answer, however, it will not be facilitated by incantation of the term "manifest necessity." For a similar point, see Schulhofer, note 9 *supra*, at 490.

[37] "Defendants may . . . move for various rulings on the indictment and on the admissibility of evidence before trial. These motions, in practical terms, may decide the defendant's case. They sometimes may require a devotion of time, energies, and resources exceeding that necessary for the trial itself. Yet it has never been held that jeopardy attaches as of the making or deciding of pretrial motions. . . . It is clear, then, that the central concern of the double jeopardy clause cannot be regarded solely as protecting against repeated expenditures of the defendant's efforts and resources." *Crist*, 98 S. Ct. at 2168 (Powell, J., dissenting).

embarrassment and expense fall totally outside the scope of double jeopardy. It is true that the burden of embarrassment and expense is insufficient to explain why the State must "shoulder"[38] the "heavy"[39] burden of justifying repeated trials (in contrast to repeated pretrial proceedings). But it is a mistake to assume that embarrassment and expense have no double jeopardy implications whatsoever. Even Mr. Justice Powell is willing to say that intentional prosecutorial harassment by repeated and unnecessary pretrial proceedings, simply to expose a defendant to public humiliation and crushing financial expense is unconstitutional.[40] If so, embarrassment and expense are sufficient by themselves—at least in extreme cases—to trigger the protection of double jeopardy.

Nonetheless, the defendant's interest in avoiding embarrassment and expense, though constitutionally protected, is insufficient to explain the "heavy"[41] burden of justification the State bears once the trial itself has commenced. To explain that burden, we must turn to value number (2), *viz.*, the defendant's interest in not having to live "in a continuing state of anxiety and insecurity,"[42] because that is an interest that does become more acute once the trial commences. To be sure, a defendant possesses a genuine and legitimate interest in finality from the very outset of the proceedings including the period

---

[38] *Washington*, 98 S. Ct. at 830.

[39] *Ibid.*

[40] *Crist*, 98 S. Ct. at 2168 (Powell, J., dissenting): "The due process clause would protect such a defendant . . . against prosecutorial abuse." To be sure, Mr. Justice Powell would prefer to subsume this protection under the Due Process Clause, rather than the Double Jeopardy Clause, presumably because it contains a lesser degree of protection than the rules generally associated with the Double Jeopardy Clause. But this decision on where to place a certain protection is largely a matter of convenience. After all, one can view the Double Jeopardy Clause in its entirety as a part of the Due Process Clause without having to alter one's views of its scope. See Benton v. Maryland, 395 U.S. 784, 793–96 (1969) (hereinafter *Benton*). Thus, the important determination is whether a particular rule of procedure should be constitutionalized in the first place. Nor is it untidy to subsume the Powell "due-process" rule under the umbrella of double jeopardy simply because it possesses a less rigorous standard than other rules of double jeopardy. Indeed, the Justice recognizes that much the same thing has occurred with the common-law rule—now constitutionalized—that a jury may not be dismissed before verdict. 98 S. Ct. at 2163–66. This latter rule is less "absolute" than the separate rule against retrying a defendant after an acquittal, yet both are easily accommodated under the umbrella of double jeopardy. Thus, if it makes conceptual sense to bring the constitutional rule on mistrials under the rubric of double jeopardy, it makes equal conceptual sense to bring the constitutional rule on intentional harassment under it.

[41] *Washington*, 98 S. Ct. at 830.

[42] *Green*, 355 U.S. at 187–88.

before trial.[43] But his interest in finality becomes particularly acute with the commencement of trial because it is then that he first becomes "subjected to the hazards of . . . conviction."[44] It is then, when the potential "risk"[45] and the "personal strain"[46] are the greatest that a defendant suffers most from a continuing state of anxiety and insecurity.[47]

Before an analysis of this interest in finality, however, it may be useful to turn to value (4), *i.e.*, the defendant's "valued right to have his trial completed by a particular tribunal."[48] Although the Court has never explored the nature of this valued right,[49] there are several possible interpretations. One is that a defendant has a constitutional interest in having his case resolved by a tribunal that he perceives to be "favorably disposed to his fate."[50] This suggestion finds no support in the Court's decisions. Assume, for example, that a case, having been assigned to a judge whom the defendant considers favorable, is reassigned to another judge before the trial commences. Or assume that a juror whom the defendant perceives to be favorable is excused and replaced by an alternate juror for no compelling reason. Whatever else may be objectionable about such changes, they can hardly be said to violate double jeopardy. Accordingly, "the [defendant's]

---

[43] One of the reasons a defendant has a Sixth Amendment right to a speedy trial is "to minimize anxiety and concern accompanying public accusation." United States v. Ewell, 383 U.S. 116, 120 (1966).

[44] *Green*, 355 U.S. at 187.

[45] Serfass v. United States, 420 U.S. 377, 391 (1975) (hereinafter *Serfass*); see also Price v. Georgia, 398 U.S. 323, 329 (1970) (hereinafter *Price*).

[46] *Abney*, 431 U.S. at 661; see also United States v. Jorn, 400 U.S. 470, 479 (1970) (hereinafter *Jorn*) (Harlan, J.).

[47] This explains why the State can almost always put a defendant to trial following a preliminary proceeding that presents no risk of final conviction. See, *e.g.*, Ludwig. v. Massachusetts, 427 U.S. 618, 630–32 (1976) (defendant can be tried in a court of general jurisdiction following conviction in a prior summary proceeding provided he has an absolute right to set aside the initial conviction by demanding a trial *de novo*); Collins v. Loisel, 262 U.S. 426, 429 (1923) (defendant can be tried following a preliminary examination); Kepner v. United States, 195 U.S. 100, 130–31 (1904) (hereinafter *Kepner*) (defendant can be tried following a pretrial challenge to the indictment); *cf.* *Breed*, 421 U.S. at 533 (defendant cannot be put through two separate trials for no good reason, if each trial confronts him with the risk of final conviction).

[48] *Hunter*, 336 U.S. at 689.

[49] "[T]he Court today does not explore the reasons supporting valuation of this particular right, merely announcing that it is 'valued.' " *Crist*, 98 S. Ct. at 2166 n.13 (Powell, J., dissenting).

[50] *Jorn*, 400 U.S. at 486 (Harlan, J.).

interest in having his 'trial completed by a particular tribunal' must refer to some interest other than retaining a fact-finder thought to be favorably disposed toward the defendant."[51]

Another meaning is more likely. A defendant has a valued right to have his trial completed by a particular tribunal, not because he has a constitutional interest in the identity of any particular tribunal, but because he has an interest in being able "to conclude his confrontation with society"[52] once it has begun. Once a trial begins, a defendant has a legitimate interest in getting the trial over with "once and for all."[53] It follows, therefore, that he also has an interest in continuing with "the first jury"[54] impaneled in the case because changing the jury means interrupting the trial. To that extent, the defendant's interest in retaining the particular tribunal with which he began is merely an incident of his primary interest in being able to complete the trial itself.

Interestingly, if this valued right is part of a defendant's larger interest in finality, it falls squarely within the traditional purposes of double jeopardy.[55] But in that event it cannot be distinguished from value (2), namely, the value in relieving a defendant's anxiety and insecurity by swiftly bringing to an end "the period of unresolved accusation of wrongdoing."[56] In short, if it is valid to say that a defendant has a right to have his trial completed by a particular tribunal, it is because he has a more general interest in "being able, once and for all, to conclude his confrontation with society."[57]

At one time there was reason to believe that this interest in finality was sufficient of itself to give a defendant the right to resist a

---

[51] *Crist*, 98 S. Ct. at 2169 (Powell, J., dissenting); see also Schulhofer, note 9 *supra*, at 504.

[52] *Jorn*, 400 U.S. at 486 (Harlan, J.).

[53] *Ibid.*

[54] *Ibid.*

[55] "The Fifth Amendment's prohibition against placing a defendant 'twice in jeopardy' represents a constitutional policy of finality for the defendant's benefit in federal criminal proceedings." *Jorn*, 400 U.S. at 479 (Harlan, J.).

[56] *Scott*, 98 S. Ct. at 2201 (Brennan, J., dissenting).

[57] *Jorn*, 400 U.S. at 486 (Harlan, J.). This "valued right" is only a part of the defendant's larger interest in finality, because it does not guarantee a defendant that his proceedings will end with the first tribunal; it merely gives him an opportunity to have the proceedings ended by means of a verdict of not guilty. If the defendant is convicted and his conviction reversed on appeal, the State may be able to insist on putting him to trial a second time. See text *infra*, at notes 120–21.

mistrial provided he could show that the mistrial was attributable to some error on the State's part.[58] In *Downum v. United States*,[59] for example, the Court appeared to hold that once a proceeding has begun and, hence, once the defendant has an interest in "having his trial completed by the particular tribunal summoned to sit in judgment on him,"[60] the State cannot abort the proceedings simply by showing that it has a legitimate prosecutorial interest in starting all over. After the jury had been sworn in *Downum* the prosecution moved for a mistrial over the defendant's objection, arguing that, inadvertently, the State's key witness had not been served with a subpoena and had failed to appear. The Court recognized that there was a "public interest"[61] in abating the proceedings, *viz.*, the interest in allowing the prosecution to postpone the trial until its key witness was ready to testify. Nonetheless, considering that the prosecution itself was responsible for the defect in the proceedings, the Court held that the defendant's interest in being able to proceed with the trial was paramount to the public interest in plenary presentation of the State's case. As a result, some authorities took *Downum* to mean that once a trial has commenced, " 'manifest necessity' [for overriding the defendant's interest in finality] cannot be created by errors on the part of the prosecutor or judge" but, rather, "must arise from some source outside their control."[62]

---

[58] Theoretically, of course, it could be argued that a defendant's interest in finality is so strong that it ought to override the State's interest in prosecution, even where the State itself is not responsible for the fact that first proceeding ended in a mistrial. Indeed, Justice Murphy, in dissent, seems to have taken this extreme position. See *Hunter*, 336 U.S. at 694. But the Court has never adopted this view. On the contrary, it has emphatically taken the position that "the double jeopardy provision of the Fifth Amendment . . . does not mean that every time a defendant is put to trial before a competent tribunal he is entitled to go free if the trial fails to end in a final judgment." *Id.* at 688. This explains why a defendant can constitutionally be subjected to a second trial if the first proceeding fails to result in a final judgment through no fault of the government's. See, *e.g.*, *Hunter, supra;* Thompson v. United States, 155 U.S. 271 (1894); Logan v. United States, 144 U.S. 263 (1892); Simmons v. United States, 142 U.S. 148 (1890); United States v. Perez, 9 Wheat. 579 (1824).

[59] 372 U.S. 734 (1963).

[60] *Id.* at 736.

[61] *Ibid.*

[62] Illinois v. Somerville, 410 U.S. 458, 483 n.2 (1973) (hereinafter *Somerville*) (Marshall, J., dissenting). See also *id.* at 471–77 (White, J., dissenting). This position, that a defendant cannot be retried following a mistrial declared over his objection because of errors on the government's part, was embraced by certain members of the Court both before and after *Downum*. See United States v. Tateo, 377 U.S. 463, 473 (1964) (hereinafter *Tateo*) (Goldberg, J., dissenting); Gori v. United States, 367 U.S. 364, 370–73 (1961) (hereinafter *Gori*) (Douglas, J., dissenting).

The Court has since repudiated this expansive view of *Downum*, holding in *Illinois v. Somerville*[63] that a defendant's finality interest in proceeding to judgment is sometimes not sufficient to override " 'the public's interest' "[64] in full and accurate prosecution, even where the State itself is responsible for the defect in the first proceeding. *Somerville* is worth examining in detail because it represents the Court's current view of the defendant's interest in finality.

After the jury had been impaneled and sworn, the prosecution became aware of a jurisdictional defect in the indictment that could not be cured by amendment or waiver. The defect was such that if the trial were to proceed and the defendant convicted, he would almost certainly be able to upset the conviction at will. Accordingly, the prosecution moved for mistrial, arguing that it should not have to proceed with a case that it could no longer win and might forever lose if the defendant were acquitted. The defendant acknowledged, in turn, that the prosecution had a legitimate interest in avoiding a trial that it could never win and might even lose. But he relied on *Downum* for the proposition that because the prosecution itself was responsible for the defect in the first proceeding, his interest in being able to proceed with the trial was paramount.

The Court rejected the defendant's argument by rejecting his construction of *Downum*. It was true, the Court said, that the defendants in *Downum* and *Somerville* each had a constitutional interest "in having [his] fate determined by the jury first impaneled."[65] It was also true that the prosecution in each case was responsible for the defect in the initial proceeding. Moreover, it was true that Downum's interest in finality was held to override the public's interest in full and plenary prosecution. But the same did not follow for Somerville because the error in his case was different. What distinguished the two cases was that the defect that caused the mistrial in *Downum*, i.e., the failure of a prosecution witness to appear at trial, is the kind of error that "lend[s] itself to prosecutorial manipulation"[66] because it can be used in bad faith "to allow the prosecution an opportunity to strengthen its case."[67] The defect in

---

[63] 410 U.S. 458 (1973).

[64] *Id.* at 463, quoting from *Hunter*, 336 U.S. at 689.

[65] 410 U.S. at 471.

[66] *Id.* at 464.

[67] *Id.* at 469.

Somerville, however, was a jurisdictional error of the kind that taints the prosecution's case from the outset and, hence, cannot be manipulated to abort a trial because it is not proceeding favorably for the prosecution.[68]

Somerville shows that a defendant's interest in finality is not sufficient to override the State's legitimate interest in avoiding an improvident acquittal by being able to abort a proceeding in which its prosecutorial position is fundamentally impaired. This issue divided the dissenters in *Somerville* from the majority. The dissenters took the position that "the defendant's interest in submitting his case to the initial jury" was itself "sufficient"[69] to entitle the defendant to resist a mistrial. The Court rejected that position holding that, even though the prosecution was responsible for the defect in its case, the defendant's interest in finality was not sufficient to override " 'the public interest' "[70] in interrupting the case and starting afresh.

Thus, none of the three possible rationales for the mistrial cases

---

[68] By "manipulation" the Court apparently means the deliberate introduction of an error for the purpose of gaining a tactical advantage over the defendant. There are two kinds of manipulation: (1) After a trial has begun, a prosecutor may discover that the trial is not proceeding favorably to his cause, and, therefore, may introduce an error in order to cause a mistrial and allow himself to start over. (2) Before a trial has begun, a prosecutor may "build in" an error knowing full well that it will cause a mistrial, but hoping to discover as much as he can about the defendant's case in the meantime. A built-in error of the *Somerville* variety cannot be used for the first purpose because it makes a mistrial inevitable, long before the prosecutor knows whether the trial is proceeding favorably to his cause and without regard to whether he would prefer to continue with the trial. On the other hand, the built-in error in *Somerville* might have been manipulated for the second purpose if the prosecutor had not brought it to the trial court's attention as early as he did. Since he brought the error to light before hearing any of the defendant's evidence, in neither respect could it be said that the *Somerville* error was capable of manipulation of the facts of the case.

The defendant in *Lee*, 432 U.S. 23, detected a built-in error at the very outset of the trial, but the judge, instead of ruling upon it immediately, continued with the trial, allowing the defendant to outline the nature of his defense, and then declared a mistrial before allowing the case to go to the jury. The defendant argued that the combination of the prosecutor's built-in error and the judge's delay in ruling on his motion raised the possibility of manipulation by allowing the prosecutor to obtain a preview of his defense. The Court rejected the argument on the ground that the defendant was "himself to blame" for the timing of the judge's ruling. He not only failed to request a continuance to enable the judge to rule immediately, but he allowed the judge to rule on the motion before submitting the case to the jury. 432 U.S. at 28, 33–34. Thus, the defendant himself may be responsible for failing to detect the built-in error at the outset or for allowing the case to continue until a mistrial is declared. See *Serfass*, 420 U.S. at 394.

[69] 410 U.S. at 473 (White, J., dissenting).

[70] *Id.* at 462, quoting from *Hunter*, 336 U.S. at 691.

is sufficient by itself to give a defendant the right to resist a mistrial. There still remains value (3), from Justice Black's opinion in *Green*, that a State "should not be allowed to make repeated attempts to convict an individual for an alleged offense, thereby . . . enhancing the possibility that even though innocent he may be found guilty."[71] Of course, it must be remembered that *Green* involved an acquittal, rather than a mistrial, and that its reference to the danger of convicting innocent defendants may be confined to that context. Nonetheless, it can be argued that the State should not be able to interrupt and recommence criminal proceedings in order to obtain "a tactical advantage"[72] over a defendant who would otherwise be found innocent. The State should not be allowed either to abort proceedings in order to shop for a more favorable trier of fact, or to correct deficiencies in its case, or to obtain an unwarranted preview of the defendant's evidence. Indeed, that appears to be what the Court in *Somerville* had in mind when it referred to the dangers of manipulation.

Unfortunately, this rationale, too, fails to explain the mistrial cases. This can be illustrated by contrasting pretrial proceedings with the trial itself. As far as manipulation is concerned, the dangers exist to the same degree before a trial has commenced as afterward. Yet the strict protections of double jeopardy do not "attach" until after the trial has commenced.[73] Consequently, while manipulation may be a factor in the law of double jeopardy, it does not explain why the scope of protection is so much greater once the trial has commenced.

The obvious solution is that the combination of the defendant's interest in finality and his separate interest in being protected from manipulation explains the mistrial cases. Thus the State does not have to show manifest necessity for interrupting pretrial proceedings, because the defendant's interest in finality does not become sufficiently acute until the trial itself commences. Moreover, even after the trial has commenced, and even after the defendant has substantial interest in getting the trial over with, the defendant does not have a right to resist a mistrial unless the defect causing the mistrial is one that could be "manipulated . . . to allow the prosecution an opportunity to

---

[71] *Green*, 355 U.S. at 187–88.

[72] *Washington*, 98 S. Ct. at 832.

[73] *Crist*, 98 S. Ct. at 2168 (Powell, J., dissenting). See note 36 *supra*.

strengthen its case."[74] On the other hand, if the trial has commenced, and if the cause of the mistrial is one that could be manipulated to abort a proceeding that is not going favorably to the prosecution, the State may not secure a mistrial over the defendant's objection.

This analysis explains *Arizona v. Washington*,[75] the most recent
of the cases involving a mistrial over the defendant's objection.
After the trial commenced, the prosecutor moved for a mistrial on
the basis of certain improper and prejudicial remarks by defense
counsel in his opening statement to the jury. The defendant opposed
the motion for a mistrial, arguing that the prejudicial effects of his
remarks could be cured by cautionary instructions. The trial judge
evidently disagreed because he declared a mistrial and ordered the
case to be retried. After being convicted, the defendant appealed,
arguing that the first proceeding should not have been aborted over
his objection. The Court affirmed the conviction. It recognized that
the defendant had "a constitutionally protected interest"[76] in " 'being
able, once and for all, to conclude his confrontation with society

---

[74] *Somerville*, 410 U.S. at 469. It must be said that the thesis advanced here is difficult
to square with *Jorn*, 400 U.S. 470. It might be argued that the defendant in *Jorn* had a
right to resist a mistrial because the judge acted "irresponsibly" and thus raised an
inference that his ruling was designed to give the prosecution a tactical advantage. See
note 83 *infra*. This inference is untenable on the facts of *Jorn*, however, because it is
obvious from the record that the judge was not acting in the interests of the prosecution.
Since *Jorn* was a case like *Somerville* in which the error could not be attributed to manipulation, the mistrial should have been without prejudice to the State's ability to retry the
defendant. The Court has described *Jorn* as a case in which the judge's decision was
"erratic," suggesting that the defendant had a right to proceed with the trial because
there was simply no good reason to declare a mistrial. *Somerville*, 410 U.S. at 469. But
this misconceives the nature of the interests that must be balanced in the mistrial cases.
It is not enough to say that the trial judge's decision in *Jorn* served no legitimate purpose,
because that is always true of the prosecutorial or judicial error on which a mistrial is
based. There was no good reason for the prosecutor's error in *Somerville* or for the
judge's error in *Gori*, 367 U.S. 364. The question is not whether the State had a good
reason for committing the error, but whether, once the error has occurred, the State's
interest in being able to start again overrides the defendant's interest in finality. If the
State's interest in having a fresh start was sufficient to overcome the prosecutor's
inexcusable error in *Somerville*, it should have been sufficient to overcome the judge's
inexcusable error in *Jorn*. Of course, the judge in *Somerville* made a deliberate judgment
on whether to proceed with the trial, while the judge in *Jorn*, by acting precipitously,
did not deliberate at all. But that is simply another way of saying that one was a prosecutorial error and the other was a judicial error. The double jeopardy question does not
arise in either case until the defendant is brought to trial a second time, and at that point
the question is whether the State's interests in retrial outweigh the defendant's interests
in finality, given the nature of the State's error.

[75] 98 S. Ct. 824 (1978).

[76] *Id.* at 835.

through the verdict of [the first] tribunal,' "[77] but held that the defendant's interest was "subordinate"[78] to the "public interest in affording the prosecutor one full and fair opportunity to present his evidence to an impartial jury."[79]

Washington supports the view that it is the combination of the defendant's interest in ending a proceeding once and for all and his interest in being protected from manipulation that gives a defendant the right to resist a mistrial. True, the defendant could show that he had a constitutional interest in proceeding with the first jury, but he could not show that the declaration of mistrial was based on manipulated error. Obviously, insofar as the mistrial was based on defense counsel's own prejudicial comments, there was no error on the government's part at all, no reason why it should have to bear the risk of loss.[80] The better argument, of course, was that the judge overreacted in declaring a mistrial and that the mistrial was based on the judge's failure to utilize less drastic alternative devices for curing the effects of the opening statement. This was a forceful argument, because if, indeed, the judge erred in declaring a mistrial, it was the kind of error that could be manipulated in bad faith to abort a proceeding that was progressing favorably for the defendant.

The Court rejected the argument, holding that the trial judge acted well within his "discretion"[81] in declaring a mistrial. There are two ways to explain the Court's opinion. One, the trial judge had no feasible alternative under the circumstances and a mistrial was the only adequate response. In that event, there was no error at all on the judge's part. Two, although the trial judge overreacted, his decision was admittedly a close one,[82] and because there is less danger of manipulation by a judge than by a prosecutor, it can be assumed that he acted in good faith.[83] In that event, although the

---

[77] *Id.* at 835, quoting from *Jorn*, 400 U.S. at 486 (Harlan, J.).

[78] 98 S. Ct. at 830.

[79] *Id.* at 830.

[80] See note 58 *supra.*

[81] 98 S. Ct. at 835.

[82] The Court emphasized that the trial judge did not act "irrationally or irresponsibly" but rather proceeded "responsibly and deliberately." *Ibid.*

[83] If this is the rationale, it means the Court is drawing a distinction between judicial error and prosecutorial error. In the case of prosecutorial error, where the risk of manipulation is high, one may be justified in adopting a "prophylactic rule" of presuming manipulation from any error that is capable of manipulation. See *Somerville*, 410 U.S. at 482 n.1 (Marshall, J., dissenting). In the case of judicial error, where the risk of

mistrial was based on an error by the State, the error was not the product of manipulation.

B. THE TIME AT WHICH JEOPARDY ATTACHES

The time at which jeopardy attaches is said to be " 'the linchpin for all double jeopardy jurisprudence.' "[84] Yet it too is the source of considerable disagreement. Last Term, for example, the Court granted certiorari to decide whether the rule in federal cases, that jeopardy attaches at the time when the jury is sworn, should also apply in State court cases. After hearing argument, the Court set the case for reargument on the question whether the federal rule itself should be changed, over the dissent of Mr. Justice Marshall who argued that the Court was " 'reaching out' for a vehicle to change" the "well-established"[85] rule for federal cases. In the end the Court voted five to four to adhere to the existing federal rule and to hold it applicable to State proceedings as well as federal.[86]

The answer to the question—When does jeopardy attach?— depends on one's purpose in asking the question. If the purpose is to identify the first point in time at which a defendant is capable of suffering constitutional injury, the answer is, at the very beginning. Suppose, for example, that a prosecutor subjects the defendant to repeated and burdensome pretrial proceedings—such as repeated bail or probable-cause hearings—solely for the purpose of causing him embarrassment, anxiety, and expense. In all likelihood the defendant could demonstrate that he had suffered constitutional injury at that point in time, and even that the injury was of the kind

---

manipulation is less, it may not be appropriate to presume that manipulation did occur merely from the fact that it could have occurred. Instead, it may be appropriate to look to the circumstances of the error and presume manipulation only if it appears that the judge acted "irrationally or irresponsibly." *Washington*, 98 S. Ct. at 835. The Court has lent support to this distinction by observing in *Washington* that "strict scrutiny" is appropriate in the event of certain prosecutorial errors. *Id*. at 832. This distinction may also explain why in *Gori*, where the error was committed by the trial judge rather than the prosecutor, the Court refused to presume that the error was a product of manipulation and, instead, determined from the circumstances of the error that it was made "in the sole interest of the defendant." But see *Jorn*, 400 U.S. 470.

[84] *Crist*, 98 S. Ct. at 2162, quoting from the opinion below, 546 F.2d 1336, 1343 (9th Cir. 1977).

[85] Crist v. Cline, 434 U.S. 981 (1977) (Marshall, J., dissenting from order restoring case to the calendar for reargument).

[86] *Crist*, 98 S. Ct. at 2156.

prohibited by the Double Jeopardy Clause.[87] In that respect, jeopardy could be said to attach whenever the prosecutor or trial judge is capable of subjecting a defendant to intentional harassment.[88]

Usually, however, the purpose of the question is not to decide at what point a defendant is capable of suffering constitutional injury but to decide at what point the risks of injury are so great that the government should have to "shoulder"[89] the "heavy"[90] burden of showing manifest necessity for repetitious proceedings. To be sure, if a defendant can prove that he is the victim of intentional harassment he should be entitled to relief at any stage of the proceedings, but the burden of proof is on him and it is a difficult burden to sustain. At some point during the proceedings, however, the burden shifts and it is the government that must shoulder the burden of justifying repetitious proceedings. That is the point in time—the point at which the burden shifts from the defendant to the prosecution—that jeopardy is usually said to attach. But this is circular unless it is known why this burden should suddenly shift from the defendant to the prosecution. The answer is that the burden shifts when the defendant's two protected interests, *i.e.*, his interest in finality and his interest in being protected from manipulation, become particularly acute. This point is sometime after a case is called for trial and before the final judgment is entered, because it is then that the "risk of conviction"[91] and, hence, the "personal strain"[92] to the defendant is the greatest. It is also during that time that the greatest "opportunity" exists for "prosecutorial overreaching."[93]

On a clean slate, one could record a variety of different tests for defining the attachment of jeopardy. Thus to establish a fixed rule, one could arbitrarily designate a variety of points between the calling of a case for trial and the entry of final judgment when jeopardy could

---

[87] See note 40 *supra*.

[88] See Coleman v. State, 35 So. 937, 939 (Miss. 1904); see also Note, *Statutory Implementation of Double Jeopardy Clauses: New Life for a Moribund Constitutional Guarantee*, 65 Yale L.J. 339, 357–59 (1956); Note, *Trial by Persistence*, 4 Stan. L. Rev. 537 (1952).

[89] *Washington*, 98 S. Ct. at 830.

[90] *Ibid*.

[91] *Price*, 309 U.S. at 329.

[92] *Jorn*, 400 U.S. at 479 (Harlan, J.).

[93] *Crist*, 98 S. Ct. at 2162 (Blackmun, J., dissenting).

reasonably be deemed to attach.[94] Alternatively, one could apply a "sliding" test according to which the further a trial proceeds—and, therefore, the greater the defendant's personal strain and the greater the prosecution's opportunity for manipulation—the more justification would be required for terminating the trial.[95]

The Court has opted for a fixed rule, holding that jeopardy attaches when the jury is sworn in a case tried to a jury, and when the first witness is sworn in a case tried to a judge. In that respect, there is something "arbitrary"[96] about the Court's decision, if by arbitrary one means that the decision is essentially "an exercise in line drawing"[97] and that the Court could have drawn the line equally well somewhere else. But saying that is very different from saying that the Court's rule lacks constitutional justification. On the assumption that there is institutional value in having a fixed rule (as opposed to a sliding rule), the Court's bifurcated rule not only serves the policies of double jeopardy as well as any other,[98] but also has the further historical advantage of being "a settled part of federal constitutional law."[99]

C. THE RESULTING BALANCE

Thus far we have identified the two interests that work in combination to give a defendant a right to resist a mistrial, and we have further identified the point in time at which the right is said to at-

---

[94] The Court enumerated several of the possibilities in a footnote including the point at which selection of the jury begins and the point at which the State first makes out a prima facie case against the defendant. *Crist*, 98 S. Ct. at 2162 n.16.

[95] "The United States alternatively proposes a due process sliding 'interest balancing test' under which the further the trial has proceeded the more the justification is required for a mid-trial termination." *Ibid*.

[96] *Id*. at 2161.

[97] *Ibid*.

[98] It is perfectly rational to apply different rules according to whether a case is tried to a judge or to a jury. After all, since the purposes of double jeopardy are to safeguard the defendant's interest in finality and to protect him from manipulation, the rules for the "attachment" of jeopardy should be tailored to serve those purposes. In a case tried to a judge, the defendant does not invest any effort in the proceedings, nor does the prosecutor have any opportunity for manipulation, until the first witness is sworn. In cases tried to a jury, on the other hand, the defendant not only makes a physical and psychological investment in the selection of a jury, but the selection of the jury also gives the prosecutor opportunities for manipulation in the event that he does not like the configuration of the final panel. Accordingly, the purposes of double jeopardy are served by having different rules in the two types of cases. That is not to say one could not rationally draw the line somewhere else. See Schulhofer, note 9 *supra*, at 512–24.

[99] *Crist*, 98 S. Ct. at 2162.

tach. As a consequence, a defendant is entitled to immunity from reprosecution following a mistrial if he can show that the mistrial was intentionally triggered by the State for the tactical purpose of strengthening the prosecution's case. Moreover, if the defendant can make such a showing, it makes no difference whether the mistrial was granted on his motion or someone else's. In either event, he is entitled to immunity from reprosecution.[100]

Realistically, however, it is very difficult for a defendant to prove that a mistrial was triggered by intentional overreaching. In most cases, therefore, the question is whether a defendant is entitled to relief if the most he can show is that the mistrial was based on an error that was capable of being manipulated in order "to achieve a tactical advantage over the accused."[101] The answer depends on how much weight one wants to accord the defendant's interest in finality. At one extreme, a defendant should be immune from reprosecution following a mistrial whenever he can show that the mistrial was based on an error that was capable of manipulation, even where he responded to the error by requesting the mistrial himself.[102] At the other extreme, a defendant is never entitled to immunity unless he can show that the mistrial was not only capable of being manipulated but also was actually manipulated to give the State a tactical advantage.[103]

The Court has rejected both of these "bright line"[104] extremes and has adopted what has been called a "balancing test."[105] If a mistrial is based on an error by the State that could be manipulated to strengthen the prosecution's case, a defendant is entitled to immunity from reprosecution if he opposes the mistrial, but not if he

---

[100] "The Double Jeopardy Clause does protect a defendant against governmental actions intended to provoke mistrial requests and thereby to subject defendants to the substantial burdens imposed by multiple prosecutions. It bars retrials where 'bad-faith conduct by judge or prosecutor' threatens the '[h]arassment of an accused by successive prosecutions or declaration of a mistrial so as to afford the prosecution a more favorable opportunity to convict' the defendant." *Dinitz*, 424 U.S. at 611; see also *Jorn*, 400 U.S. at 485 n.12 (1971) (Harlan, J.); *Tateo*, 377 U.S. at 468 n.3; United States v. Martin, 561 F.2d 135, 138–41 (8th Cir. 1977).

[101] *Washington*, 98 S. Ct. at 832.

[102] This appears to be the position that Mr. Justice Brennan would take. See *Dinitz*, 424 U.S. at 613.

[103] This appears to be the position that Mr. Justice Clark would have taken. See Downum v. United States, 372 U.S. 734, 742 (1963).

[104] *Jorn*, 400 U.S. at 486 (Harlan, J.).

[105] *Finch*, 433 U.S. at 680 (Rehnquist, J., dissenting); *Somerville*, 401 U.S. at 477 (Marshall, J., dissenting).

requests it.[106] What this means, of course, is that in the event of manipulable error, a defendant has an intermediate remedy. He has no right to demand a mistrial with prejudice, because by requesting a mistrial he exposes himself to reprosecution. But he does have a right to resist a mistrial and to insist that the trial proceed to a verdict. He has what Justice Harlan called an "option to go to the first jury and, perhaps, end the dispute then and there with an acquittal."[107]

This option is significant in two ways. First, it is an explicit compromise, or balance, between the "vital competing interests of the government and the defendant."[108] The balance gives the defendant less than he desires because it forces him to make what has been termed a " 'Hobson's choice.' "[109] That is, if the prosecutor or court makes an error that provides grounds for a mistrial, the defendant is forced to decide between requesting a mistrial without prejudice, thereby "giving up his first jury"[110] and consenting to be reprosecuted, or opposing a mistrial and thereby continuing with a trial that is "tainted by prejudicial, judicial or prosecutorial error."[111]

This solution also gives the prosecutor less than he desires, because it means that in the event of manipulable error he must continue with a case that he can no longer win. That is, once a prosecutor or judge commits the kind of error that is grounds for a mistrial, the trial becomes "tainted"[112] and the defendant becomes entitled to a reversal if he is eventually convicted.[113] Accordingly, if a defendant has an option to proceed with the trial while preserving his claim of error, it means that he has something to win and little to lose. If he is acquitted despite the taint, he succeeds in ending the case once and for all; if he is convicted, his conviction will be reversed and he will be given a second opportunity—this time error-

---

[106] See *Scott*, 98 S. Ct. at 2195; *Dinitz*, 424 U.S. at 600; *Tateo*, 377 U.S. at 467 (1964).

[107] *Jorn*, 400 U.S. at 484 (Harlan, J.).

[108] *Id.* at 486.

[109] "[T]raditional waiver concepts have little relevance where the defendant must determine whether or not to request or consent to a mistrial in response to judicial or prosecutorial error. In such circumstances, the defendant generally does face a 'Hobson's choice' between giving up his first jury and continuing the trial tainted by prejudicial judicial or prosecutorial error." *Dinitz*, 424 U.S. at 609.

[110] *Ibid.*　　　　　　[111] *Ibid.*　　　　　　[112] *Ibid.*

[113] To say that an error is grounds for a mistrial means that it is the kind of error that cannot be cured by cautionary instructions; by the same token, to say that an error cannot be cured by cautionary instructions means that it is ordinarily grounds for reversal.

free—to obtain an acquittal. In sum, although the defendant's interest in finality is not sufficient to give him immunity from reprosecution whenever the State commits a manipulable error, it is sufficient to give him the right to proceed to a final verdict "and, perhaps, end the dispute then and there with an acquittal," while at the same time preserving his claim of error in the event he is convicted.[114]

Second, this solution is a mirror image of the balance that now exists in the law of double jeopardy in the context of reprosecution following conviction. A defendant who has been tried and convicted is entitled to a reversal of his conviction and to immunity from reprosecution upon a showing that his original trial was tainted by acts of deliberate harassment or overreaching.[115] But he is not entitled to immunity from reprosecution simply on showing that his original trial was tainted by the kind of error that lends itself to manipulation. Rather, he stands in the same position then as a defendant who decides at midtrial to proceed to a final judgment in the face of a manipulable error: Although he can be retried, he has meanwhile had an opportunity to go to the first jury and possibly end the case with an acquittal while having preserved his claim of error for appeal following his conviction.[116]

---

[114] It could be argued, even in the case of manipulable error, that a defendant should be obliged to choose between standing on his claim of error (and thus requesting a mistrial), or standing on his right to proceed with the trial (and thus "waiving" his claim of error). But that would give a prosecutor an incentive to commit error if a trial were not proceeding favorably to his cause. This situation should be distinguished from *Somerville*, where the error was not the kind that would "lend itself to prosecutorial manipulation," 410 U.S. at 464, and did not pose the danger of giving the prosecutor an incentive to commit error at trial. See note 68 *supra*. If the error had not also been "jurisdictional," the defendant in *Somerville* could have been forced to choose between standing on the error or standing on his right to proceed with the trial. As it was, the jurisdictional error was not one that the defendant could waive, so the trial court was justified in declaring a mistrial over the defendant's objection. If the error had been waivable, however, and if the defendant had been willing to waive the error in order to proceed with the trial, then he would be entitled to immunity from reprosecution if trial court acted "irrationally" in proceeding to declare a mistrial over his objection. See note 82 *supra*.

[115] United States v. McCord, 509 F.2d 334, 348–51 (D.C. Cir. 1974) (*en banc*); Commonwealth v. Manning, 367 N.E.2d 635 (Mass. Sup. Jud. Ct. 1977); Commonwealth v. Wilkinson, 21 Crim. L. Rep. 2301 (July 6, 1977) (Pa. Ct. Comm. Pleas).

[116] "[T]he crucial difference between reprosecution after appeal by the defendant and reprosecution after a *sua sponte* judicial mistrial declaration is that in the first situation the defendant has not been deprived of his option to go to the first jury and, perhaps, end the dispute then and there with an acquittal." *Jorn*, 400 U.S. at 484 (Harlan, J.). There is one situation in which a defendant at trial is in a different position from a

The considerations are the same both for reprosecution following
a mistrial and reprosecution following conviction. In each case one
must balance the defendant's interest in finality against "the public
interest in assuring that each defendant shall be subject to a just
judgment on the merits of his case."[117] Thus, when a trial is tainted
by deliberate overreaching, the defendant's interest in finality overrides "the societal interest in law enforcement"[118] and the defendant
is entitled to immunity from reprosecution regardless of whether a
mistrial is granted at his request at trial or whether the resulting
conviction is reversed at his request on appeal.[119] On the other hand,
if the trial is tainted by an error which, though capable of manipulation, cannot be proved to have been manipulated, the balance is
different. There the defendant is not entitled to immunity from
reprosecution, whether he proceeds by requesting a mistrial or by
requesting reversal of his conviction on appeal, because immunity
comes at "too high a price"[120] to society. Justice Harlan said it
best:[121]

---

defendant following conviction, *i.e.*, where the prosecution commits a nonmanipulable
error. If the error is not detected until the case is on appeal, or if it is detected but not
acted on by the trial judge, the defendant will have enjoyed both the opportunity to go
to first jury and, perhaps, be acquitted, and at the same time preserve his claim of error
on appeal. If, on the other hand, the error is noticed during the course of the trial, then
the defendant can be forced to choose between standing on the error or standing on his
right to continue with the trial. The reason for this distinction, of course, is that in the
case of nonmanipulable error, the defendant's interest in finality is not sufficient, by
itself, to override the State's interest in terminating a case that it can no longer win and
yet might lose.

[117] *Scott*, 98 S. Ct. at 2199. This interest has also been referred to as "society's interest
in giving the prosecution one complete opportunity to convict those who have violated
its laws," *Washington*, 98 S. Ct. at 832; "society's . . . valid concern for insuring that
the guilty are punished," *Burks*, 98 S. Ct. at 2149; "[the government's] very vital
interest in enforcement of criminal laws," *Jorn*, 400 U.S. at 479 (Harlan, J.); "the
societal interest in punishment of one whose guilt is clear," *Tateo*, 377 U.S. at 466; and
"the public's interest in fair trials designed to end in just judgments," *Hunter*, 336 U.S.
at 689.

[118] *Jorn*, 400 U.S. at 484 (Harlan, J.); see also United States v. Kessler, 530 F.2d
1246, 1255–56 (5th Cir. 1976).

[119] See notes 115, 117–18, *supra*.

[120] *Jorn*, 400 U.S. at 480 (Harlan, J.); see also *Tateo*, 377 U.S. at 466: "Corresponding
to the right of an accused to be given a fair trial is the societal interest in punishing
one whose guilt is clear after he has obtained such a trial. It would be a high price indeed
for society to pay were every accused granted immunity from punishment because of
any defect sufficient to constitute reversible error in the proceedings leading to conviction."

[121] *Jorn*, 400 U.S. at 483–84 (Harlan, J.).

> Certainly it is clear beyond question that the double jeopardy clause does not guarantee a defendant that the government will be prepared, in all circumstances, to vindicate the social interest in law enforcement through the vehicle of a single proceeding for a given offense. Thus, for example, reprosecution for the same offense is permitted where the defendant wins a reversal on appeal of a conviction. *United States* v. *Ball,* 163 U.S. 662 (1896). . . . The determination to allow reprosecution in these circumstances reflects the judgment that the defendant's double jeopardy interests, however defined, do not go so far as to compel society to so mobilize its decision-making resources that it will be prepared to assure the defendant a single proceeding free from harmful governmental or judicial error.

Nonetheless, although a defendant is not entitled to claim a mistrial with prejudice whenever the State makes such an error, he is entitled to resist a mistrial declared over his objection because he has a right (if he so chooses) to proceed with the trial despite the error. Again, this means that he is in the same position as a defendant who is retried following the reversal of his conviction on appeal: He is entitled "to go to the first jury and, perhaps, end the dispute then and there with an acquittal"[122] and yet demand a new trial if he is convicted.

The resulting solution is that in the event of manipulable error a defendant has a right to proceed with the trial if he so desires. This is a pragmatic compromise between the defendant's interest in finality and society's interest in prosecution. It imposes some burden on society, because it forces the prosecution to proceed with a case that it can no longer win and might possibly lose, yet the burden is still less than giving the defendant automatic immunity from reprosecution. By the same token, the solution imposes some burden on the defendant's interest in finality because it puts the defendant to the "Hobson's choice" of giving up his chance for an acquittal by the first jury or proceeding with a tainted trial, yet the burden on the defendant is still less than declaring a mistrial over his objection

---

[122] 400 U.S. at 484; see also *Tateo,* 377 U.S. at 473 (Goldberg, J., dissenting): "In this country . . . a defendant may be retried after reversal because of errors at the trial—including errors in instructions, in rulings on the evidence, in admitting confessions, or in permitting prejudicial comments or conduct by the prosecutor. But, in such instances, the realities are that, notwithstanding the errors, the defendant has had a jury trial, albeit not the error-free jury trial to which by law he is entitled."

or forcing him to waive the error as a condition for proceeding with the trial.[123]

Ultimately, this also explains why a defendant can be reprosecuted if a mistrial is granted at his own request. To do otherwise—to treat the ruling as a mistrial with prejudice—would be to grant the defendant the kind of immunity that is considered "too high a price to pay" for the defendant's interest in finality.[124] By requesting a mistrial, the defendant foregoes the only right to which he is entitled, the right to choose to go forward and perhaps be acquitted by the first jury impaneled in the case.[125]

To conclude, a defendant has a constitutional interest in finality, a cognizable interest in seeing that criminal proceedings against him are resolved once and for all. But this interest is not absolute and must be balanced against society's interest in conducting further proceedings. In some contexts, where society's interest is weak, the defendant's interest in finality may prevail.[126] In the context of mis-

---

[123] See note 114 *supra*. Even if a defendant knows that his chances for acquittal are reduced by the taint of reversible error, he may still consider it in his interest to proceed in the hope that he will nonetheless prevail. See *Tateo*, 377 U.S. at 474 (Goldberg, J., dissenting): "Many juries acquit defendants after trials in which reversible error has been committed, and many experienced trial lawyers will forego a motion for a mistrial in favor of having his case tried by the jury." Accord *Dinitz*, 424 U.S. at 608. Moreover, it should not be feared that defendants will abuse this "option" of proceeding with the trial while also preserving a claim of error, because the defendant proceeds at some risk. Commission of the error almost always reduces the defendant's chances of an acquittal. Yet by proceeding with the trial, the defendant is forced to disclose his defense to the prosecution and thus make it easier for the prosecution to prevail against him the second time around should the first trial end in a conviction. *Id.* at 608, 610.

[124] *Jorn*, 400 U.S. at 480 (Harlan, J.).

[125] "If that right to go to a particular tribunal is valued, it is because . . . the defendant has a significant interest in the decision whether or not to take the case from the jury when circumstances occur which might be thought to warrant a declaration of mistrial. Thus, where circumstances develop not attributable to prosecutorial or judicial overreaching, a motion by the defendant for a mistrial is ordinarily assumed to remove any barrier to reprosecution, even if the motion is necessitated by prosecutorial or judicial error." *Id.* at 485. See also cases cited in note 123 *supra*.

[126] See, *e.g.*, *Breed*, 421 U.S. 534. The defendant in *Breed*, a juvenile, challenged the constitutionality of a two-step procedure in California for adjudicating juvenile delinquency. The first step was an omnibus hearing that combined the functions of a transfer hearing and an adjudicatory hearing—giving the judge an option either to enter a final finding of guilt or innocence or to transfer the proceeding to an adult court for trial *de novo*. The defendant, whose case was transferred for trial *de novo* following a complete adjudication in the first instance, challenged the procedure, arguing that it forced him to go through two complete trials in order to get a final adjudication of his guilt or innocence. He also argued that the state had no significant interest in combining the transfer hearing with the adjudicatory hearing and, thus, in forcing him to go through

trials and retrials following conviction, where finality is balanced against "the public's interest in fair trials designed to end in just judgments,"[127] the defendant's interest can be relatively easily outweighed.[128] Thus the defendant is not entitled to demand a mistrial with prejudice unless he can make a showing of deliberate harassment or overreaching. In all other cases, he is entitled to no more than to proceed with the first trial (subject always to being retried if he is convicted and his conviction reversed on appeal), and even there his right to proceed with the first trial is limited to cases in which the defect in the first proceeding is capable of manipulation.

II. REPROSECUTION FOLLOWING CONVICTION: THE PROHIBITION OF DOUBLE PUNISHMENT

The essential teaching of *United States v. Ball*[129] is that the Double Jeopardy Clause does not prohibit the State from retrying a defendant following an erroneous conviction.[130] The defendant's interest in finality must yield to the public interest in law enforcement.[131] The Double Jeopardy Clause "does not preclude the govern-

---

two separate adjudicatory hearings, because it could have served its purposes equally well by conducting the transfer hearing before the final adjudicatory hearing. The Court agreed, holding that the State procedure violated the " 'constitutional policy of finality' " by subjecting the defendant to two trials where one would have served the State's interest equally well. For further illustrations of cases in which the State had no significant interest that would outweigh the defendant's interest in finality, see text *infra*, at notes 334–49.

[127] *Hunter*, 336 U.S. at 689.

[128] See, *e.g.*, United States v. Castellanos, 478 F.2d 749 (2d Cir. 1973) (third trial allowed after two hung juries); United States v. Persico, 425 F.2d 1375, 1385 (2d Cir. 1970) (fifth trial upheld after two mistrials and two reversals). But see Preston v. Blackledge, 332 F. Supp. 681 (E.D.N.C. 1971) (double jeopardy bars retrial after four hung juries).

[129] 163 U.S. 662 (1896).

[130] With respect to a defendant who succeeds in reversing his conviction on appeal, the Double Jeopardy Clause provides no protection whatever against reprosecution unless he can show deliberate harassment or overreaching. See notes 115, 117–18, *supra*. That is not to say that a defendant's finality interest has no constitutional protection at all following a conviction, because there are cases in which the State has no significant interest in subjecting a defendant to further proceedings following a conviction. See note 126 *supra*. The problems of finality, however, are conceptually distinct from the problems of double punishment and should be studied separately. For discussion of a case that combines the problems of double punishment and finality, see text *infra*, at notes 334–49.

[131] See text *supra*, at note 121.

ment's retrying a defendant whose conviction is set aside because of an error in the proceeding leading to conviction."[132]

Yet it is also a basic maxim that double jeopardy "protects [a defendant] against a second prosecution for the same offense after conviction."[133] In the context of retrial following conviction, the Double Jeopardy Clause may protect some interest besides the defendant's interest in finality. The principal interest, we submit, is that underlying the historical plea of *autrefois convict*, namely, to protect the defendant from being subjected to double punishment for the same offense.

A. THE MEANING OF DOUBLE PUNISHMENT

The principle that a person may not be punished twice for the same offense was first noted by the Court in *Ex parte Lange*.[134] Lange was convicted of an offense which carried a maximum penalty of either one-year imprisonment or a $200 fine, but he was mistakenly sentenced both to pay a fine of $200 and to serve one year in prison. When the error was brought to the trial judge's attention, he set aside the original sentence and imposed a fresh sentence of one year in prison, without, however, taking into account that the defendant had already fully paid the $200 fine. The Court reversed the prison sentence holding that even though the fine had been paid pursuant to an illegal sentence, to punish the defendant further was to punish him twice in violation of the Double Jeopardy Clause: "If there is anything settled in the jurisprudence of England and America, it is that no man can be twice lawfully punished for the same offense."[135]

At the very least, therefore, *Lange* stands for the proposition that it violates double jeopardy to subject a defendant to two separate and complete penalties for an offense that carries a maximum of only

---

[132] *Tateo*, 377 U.S. at 465.

[133] North Carolina v. Pearce, 395 U.S. 711, 717 (1969) (hereinafter *Pearce*). See also *Wilson*, 420 U.S. at 343: "when a defendant has been once convicted and punished for a particular crime, principles of fairness and finality require that he not be subjected to the possibility of further punishment by being again tried or sentenced for the same offense."

[134] 18 Wall. 163 (1873).

[135] *Id*. at 168. For an explanation as to why the defendant was entitled to full credit for the $200 fine even though the original sentence was void, see *id*. at 174–75.

one penalty. But the Court's rationale in *Lange* was not limited to cases in which the resulting punishment is twice what the legislature intends. Rather, the Court held the sentence invalid because it exceeded the maximum that the legislature contemplated.[136] In other words, insofar as a defendant was subjected to punishment in excess of what the legislature intended, he was "doubly" punished in violation of the Double Jeopardy Clause.

This reading of *Lange* was later confirmed in *North Carolina v. Pearce*.[137] One of the defendants in *Pearce* was convicted and sentenced to ten years in prison under a statute providing for a maximum of thirty-years imprisonment. After he had served two and a half years of the sentence, his conviction was reversed, and he was retried and convicted. This time he was sentenced to 25 years in prison with no credit for the two and a half years he had already spent in prison. He sought review in the Supreme Court, arguing among other things[138] that it violated double jeopardy to deny him credit on the new sentence for the time he had already served for the same offense. The Court agreed: "We hold that the constitutional guarantee against multiple punishments for the same offense absolutely requires that punishments already exacted must be fully 'credited' in imposing sentence upon a new conviction for the same offense."[139]

Pearce confirmed the suggestion in *Lange* that a person suffers double punishment whenever his sentence is excessive under the domestic law.[140] Thus, if the lawful domestic sentence was twenty-five

---

[136] "We are of opinion that when the prisoner, as in this case, by reason of a valid judgment, had fully served one of the alternative punishments to which alone the law subjected him, the power of the court to punish further was gone." *Id.* at 176; see also *id.* at 168, 175.

[137] 395 U.S. 711 (1969).

[138] The defendant was the respondent in the companion case, *Simpson v. Rice*, which the Court decided together with *Pearce*. The defendant also argued that it violated double jeopardy to impose a higher sentence following his original trial. The Court rejected the argument holding that the Double Jeopardy Clause does not preclude a court from giving a defendant a higher sentence the second time than he was given originally. 395 U.S. at 719 n.14, 719–21. Accord: Chaffin v. Stychcombe, 412 U.S. 17, 23–24 (1973). The Court agreed, however, that the higher sentence violated due process, because the sentence was imposed under circumstances which suggested that it was a vindictive effort to punish the defendant for appealing his original conviction.

[139] 395 U.S. at 718–19.

[140] "The constitutional violation is flagrantly apparent in a case involving the imposition of a maximum sentence after reconviction. Suppose, for example, in a jurisdiction

years in prison, the defendant did not have to show that he was subjected to twice that. It was enough to show that by denying him
credit for the two and a half years he had already served in prison,
the trial judge imposed a total sentence of 27½ years, or two and a
half years in excess of the lawful sentence. The resulting sentence
violated double jeopardy because, by denying the defendant credit
for time already served for the same offense, the trial judge required
him to serve two and a half years of his lawful twenty-five-year
sentence twice.

Pearce makes clear, too, that the protection against double punishment is not limited to penalties in excess of legislative authority but
also extends to "excessive" penalties as defined by the body possessing final sentencing authority under the domestic law. *Pearce's*
sentence of 27½ years in prison was still less than the legislative
maximum of thirty years. If double jeopardy served only to prohibit the courts from imposing penalties greater than the maximum
defined by the legislature, the sentence in *Pearce* should have been
affirmed. By reversing the sentence, the Court implicitly held that
double jeopardy also prohibits the courts from imposing penalties
that are excessive as defined by the sentencing authority. Thus,
because the sentencing judge had made a lawful determination that
the appropriate sentence for the defendant was twenty-five years in
prison, it was excessive and, therefore, a violation of double jeopardy, to subject the defendant to what was effectively a 27½ year
term.[141]

Finally, *Pearce* is significant because it shows that in the area of
double punishment, doubts are to be resolved in favor of the defendant. The State had argued that the sentence of twenty-five years
without credit ought to be affirmed because it was functionally
equivalent to a sentence of 27½ years with credit—a sentence the

---

where the maximum allowable sentence for larceny is 10 years imprisonment, a man
succeeds in getting his larceny conviction set aside after serving three years in prison.
If, upon reconviction, he is given a ten-year sentence, then, quite clearly, he will have
received multiple punishments for the same offense. For he will have been compelled
to serve separate prison terms of three years and 10 years, although the maximum
single punishment for the offense is 10 years imprisonment." *Id.* at 718.

[141] "The constitutional violation is flagrantly apparent in a case involving the imposition of a maximum sentence after reconviction. . . . Though not so dramatically evident,
the same principle obviously holds true whenever punishment already endured is not
fully subtracted from any new sentence imposed." *Ibid.*

judge could have imposed, and, indeed, may have wished to impose.[142] The Court rejected the argument by refusing to assume that the sentencing judge's silence indicated that he wanted to impose a total sentence of 27½ years. The Court said that if the judge had wanted to impose a total sentence of 27½ years, he could have done so by imposing the sentence and then crediting it for the time already served.[143] Yet it is equally possible that is what he intended when he imposed a twenty-five-year sentence without credit. Equally possible is that the judge thought the appropriate sentence was no more than twenty-five years, and that he imposed a twenty-five-year sentence without credit because of a mistaken assumption that because the prior sentence was entered and served pursuant to an invalid conviction, it had to be disregarded.[144] In ordering that the defendant be given credit, the Court thus made a constitutional judgment that the ambiguity in the judge's sentence must be construed in favor of lenity in order to avoid the potential risk of double punishment.[145]

---

[142] The state argued that the sentencing judge may have intended that the defendant spend a full twenty-five years in prison starting from the date of his second conviction. If that was the judge's intent, he could have proceeded in two ways: He could have imposed a 27½-year sentence with credit for the time already served, or he could have done what he did—impose a twenty-five year sentence without credit for the time served. In each case the purpose and effect would be the same. Accordingly, so the argument went, since the former approach would have been constitutionally valid, the latter should be, too.

[143] "In most situations, even when time served under the original sentence is fully taken into account, a judge can still sentence a defendant to a longer term in prison than was originally imposed. That is true with effect to [the case] before us. . . . In [this] case credit for the 2½ years served was not given, but even if it had been, the sentencing judge could have reached the same result that he did reach simply by sentencing Rice to 27½ years in prison." *Id.* at 719 n.14.

[144] The sentencing judge in *Lange*, note 134 *supra*, made precisely that mistake. The judge did so because of the mistaken assumption that the original sentence was completely void and, therefore, had to be disregarded in imposing a new and valid sentence. 18 Wall. at 174–75. It is possible that the judge in *Pearce* made the same mistake and denied the defendant credit not because he wanted to, but because he believed he had to.

[145] The sentencing judge in *Pearce* specifically denied the defendant credit for the time he had already served. In many cases, however, the trial judge is silent, and the appellate court must then decide what kind of inference to draw from the judge's silence. Although some pre-*Pearce* cases held to the contrary, *e.g.*, Bryans v. Blackwell, 387 F.2d 764 (5th Cir. 1967), *Pearce* appears to require that the ambiguity be resolved in the defendant's favor in order to avoid the risk of double punishment. What that means, of course, is that the appellate court must assume that the trial judge did not give credit. A related issue arises in the context of credit a defendant receives for time served in jail before conviction. *Compare* Staph v. United States, 367 F.2d 326 (D.C. Cir. 1966) (assumed that credit was given), *with* Law v. Wainwright, 264 So.2d 3 (Fla. Sup. Ct. 1972) (assumed that credit was not given). This analogy should not be pressed too far, however, because the source of the two claims to credit are significantly different: In the

Thus, once offenses are determined to be the "same" for double jeopardy purposes, it is double punishment to subject a defendant to a penalty in excess of what the domestic authorities determine to be the appropriate penalty for that offense. Moreover, in deciding what the domestic authorities have determined the appropriate sentence to be, doubts are to be resolved in favor of the defendant.

B. THE MEANING OF "SAME OFFENSE"

The problem of identifying the standard that determines whether offenses are the same for double jeopardy purposes can arise in two basic contexts. There are "double-description"[146] cases, i.e., cases in which the domestic law contains more than one statute for describing what is determined to be a single offense for double jeopardy purposes. For example, a certain course of conduct may be simultaneously described as a statutory offense in its own right and also as a lesser-included offense within some other statutory offense. In addition, there are so-called unit-of-prosecution[147] cases. These are the converse of the double-description cases. Here it is not that the same course of conduct is proscribed by more than one statute but that the same statute may fragment a defendant's conduct into more than one offense. For example, if a pickpocket steals $500 in a jurisdiction that makes it a felony to steal $100 dollars or more, the unit of prosecution may be defined as the theft of $100 or as the theft of everything in the wallet. If the unit of prosecution is the theft of $100, the pickpocket could be punished for five separate violations of the statute. On the other hand, if the unit of prosecution

---

cases based on *Pearce*, the defendant has a constitutional claim to credit under the Double Jeopardy Clause. In the presentence cases, he has no right to credit under the Double Jeopardy Clause, because presentence time is not "punishment," and it is questionable whether he has a constitutional claim under any other clause. But see Schornhorst, *Presentence Confinement and the Constitution: The Burial of Dead Time*, 23 HAST. L.J. 1041 (1972). The fact that a presumption does not operate in a defendant's favor in the presentence cases does not mean that it should not operate in the cases based on *Pearce*.

[146] *Cf.* Gore v. United States, 357 U.S. 386, 392 (1958) (hereinafter *Gore*) (whether two statutes describe two separate offenses or are "merely different descriptions of the same offense"). See also In re Nielsen, 131 U.S. 176 (1889).

[147] The term "unit of prosecution" appears to have been used by the Court first in United States v. Universal C.I.T. Credit Corp., 344 U.S. 218, 221 (1952) (hereinafter *C.I.T.*). The question in such cases is "whether conduct constitutes one or several violations of a single statutory provision." Callanan v. United States, 364 U.S. 587, 597 (1961) (hereinafter *Callanan*). See also Bell v. United States, 349 U.S. 81, 83 (1955) (hereinafter *Bell*); In re Snow, 120 U.S. 274 (1887).

is the theft of the wallet, he could be prosecuted only for a single violation of the statute.

The potential for double punishment exists in both situations. If a defendant is convicted and given cumulative sentences for committing an offense that simultaneously violates two separate statutes, he may be able to show that the two statutes describe what is essentially the same offense for double jeopardy purposes and, therefore, that his simultaneous conviction and punishment for both exceed what the domestic law prescribes as the penalty for committing one of them. Conversely, if a defendant is convicted and given cumulative sentences for multiple violations of a single statute, he may be able to show that the court has fragmented into multiple units what is a single unit of prosecution for double jeopardy purposes and that his cumulative sentences, therefore, exceed what the domestic law prescribes as the appropriate sentence for a single unit.

This brings us back to the question: What is the standard for determining whether offenses are the same for double jeopardy purposes?[148] There are several possibilities. First, it can be argued that the Double Jeopardy Clause imposes no limitation on the legislature's definition of an offense, but rather incorporates by reference whatever the legislature defines as an "offense" for punishment purposes.[149] Thus, if the domestic law defines robbery and bank robbery as separate offenses to be punished cumulatively, a defendant who commits a single act of bank robbery can be punished under both statutes, because, by definition, the two offenses are not the same. Similarly, if a single statute defines the unauthorized opening of mailbags as separate offenses to be punished cumulatively, a defendant who opens several mailbags in the course of a single robbery can be punished for each unauthorized opening because, again by definition, each unit is a separate offense.[150] In both cases,

---

[148] Our purpose here is to determine whether offenses are the "same" for the purpose of imposing multiple punishment, not for the purpose of deciding whether a defendant can be subjected to multiple prosecutions following a conviction or to multiple prosecutions following an acquittal. The purposes of the Double Jeopardy Clause differ from one context to the other and, therefore, so, too, does the definition of an "offense." See Note, *Twice in Jeopardy*, note 28 *supra*, at 267, 302. But see *Sanabria*, 98 S. Ct. at 2184; *Brown*, 432 U.S. at 161, 166 (1977).

[149] "The ban on multiple punishment imposes a limitation on judicial interpretation of substantive criminal law. It forbids penalizing an accused more severely than the law provides, through the device of finding that he has committed several violations of substantive law where only one exists." Note, note 88 *supra*, at 340.

[150] See Ebeling v. Morgan, 237 U.S. 625 (1915).

the defendant's rights under the Double Jeopardy Clause proceed from legislative intent.[151]

The foregoing thesis has force. Nonetheless, as stated in its strongest form—that the Double Jeopardy Clause imposes no restrictions whatsoever on the legislature's definition of offenses—it contradicts a handful of decisions that the Double Jeopardy Clause does inhibit legislative authority in this area.[152]

Second, it can be argued that the Double Jeopardy Clause contains an independent standard of its own for defining whether offenses are the same. Insofar as this thesis assumes that "same offense" has substantive content that is independent of domestic law as defined by the legislature, it demands more of the Double Jeopardy Clause than it is capable of supplying.

With respect to unit-of-prosecution cases, the argument assumes that the Double Jeopardy Clause is capable of reducing the concept of a criminal offense to its smallest rational unit, or atom, beyond which further fragmentation cannot occur without creating a "doubling effect." The difficulty with this assumption is that the size of any unit of prosecution depends on the legislature's purpose in making it an offense, and purposes of punishment are notoriously diverse.[153] Consequently, until it can be said that only one of the various purposes of punishment is constitutionally acceptable, units of prosecution cannot be judged by any single constitutional standard.[154]

---

[151] The Court, at times, comes close to embracing this view. See *Sanabria*, 98 S. Ct. at 2181; *Brown*, 432 U.S. at 165.

[152] See, *e.g.*, *Brown*, 432 U.S. at 161; *Jeffers*, 432 U.S. at 154–58 (plurality opinion); Iannelli v. United States, 420 U.S. 770, 785–86 nn.17–18 (1975) (hereinafter *Iannelli*.)

[153] The Supreme Court recognizes the constitutional validity of several different purposes of punishment, including retribution, Gregg v. Georgia, 428 U.S. 153, 183 (1976) (plurality opinion); deterrence, *id.* at 186–87; Furman v. Georgia, 408 U.S. 238, 307–08 (1972) (Stewart, J., concurring); incapacitation, Roberts v. Louisiana, 428 U.S. 325, 334 (1976) (White, J., dissenting); and rehabilitation, Williams v. New York, 337 U.S. 241, 247–48 (1949).

[154] Suppose, for example, that a defendant enters a bank, discovers that four tellers are unexpectedly on duty, and robs them all. Whether the defendant's conduct should be defined as a single act of robbery or as four separate robberies depends upon one's purpose in making robbery a crime. If the purpose is to make the punishment fit the evil nature of the defendant's mind as he entered the bank, the defendant's conduct will be defined as one robbery; if the purpose is to deter defendants from entering banks for the purpose of committing robbery, it will probably be defined as a single robbery; if the purpose is to give defendants who had already robbed one teller an incentive to desist from robbing others, it will be treated as four robberies; and if the purpose is to make the punishment fit the consequences of the defendant's actions, it will also be

To be sure, it may be possible to hypothesize units of prosecution that are so fragmented that to punish each separately would constitute excessive punishment. But in that event, the fragmentation would be invalid because the Eighth Amendment already prohibits the State from subjecting a defendant to excessive punishment.[155] In other words, once it is determined that a defendant can constitutionally be punished for his conduct as a whole, the manner in which his conduct is divided into separate units for purposes of calculating his total sentence is of no constitutional significance except for deciding whether the total sentence is excessive; and that is a subject for decision under Eighth Amendment and not the Double Jeopardy Clause.[156]

The same point can be made with respect to the double-description cases, where a single act by a defendant violates more than one statute. The argument assumes that the legislature has multiplied into many statutory offenses what is really only one offense. The flaw, however, is to assume that there is an objective basis for determining the maximum number of statutory offenses implicit in a single course of conduct. There is simply no way to make sense out of the notion that a course of conduct is "really" only one act, rather than two or three, or, indeed, as many as one likes.[157] Of course, it may again be possible to hypothesize a situation in which the multiplication of statutes results in excessive punishment. But, here too, the statutes would be unconstitutional under the Eighth Amendment rather than the Double Jeopardy Clause.

---

defined as four. In short, unless the Double Jeopardy Clause is capable of deciding that one, and only one, of the foregoing purposes of punishment is legitimate, it cannot decide which is the appropriate unit of prosecution.

[155] See Weems v. United States, 217 U.S. 349 (1910). See generally Note, *Constitutional Law—Cruel and Unusual Punishments—Eighth Amendment Prohibits Excessively Long Sentences*, 44 FORD. L. REV. 637 (1975).

[156] With respect to a defendant who steals $10, for example, there is no functional difference between punishing the entire theft by sixty days, or the theft of each separate dollar by six days, or the theft of each penny by six minutes. In each case the constitutional question is whether the total penalty the defendant receives is excessive in light of his conduct. And that is an Eighth Amendment question, not a question under the Double Jeopardy Clause: "The punishment appropriate for the diverse federal offenses is a matter for the discretion of Congress, subject only to constitutional limitations, more particularly the Eighth Amendment. Congress could no doubt make the simultaneous transportation of more than one woman in violation of the Mann Act liable to cumulative punishment for each woman so transported. The question is: did it do so?" *Bell*, 349 U.S. at 82–83.

[157] This point was made very ably in Comment, note 28 *supra*, at 276.

To illustrate, assume that a defendant who robs a bank is simultaneously prosecuted for the separate offenses of armed robbery and bank robbery. If each robbery statute contains an element the other robbery statute lacks, one must determine whether it serves any legitimate purpose to prosecute and punish the defendant under one statute if he is already being prosecuted and punished under the other. If it does serve a purpose, then multiple prosecutions cannot be said to violate either the Eighth Amendment or the Double Jeopardy Clause. On the other hand, if no such purpose is served, or if one statute is identical to the other, then one must further decide whether the combined sentence the defendant receives for his act of robbery is excessive under the circumstances. If it is excessive, it is invalid under the Eighth Amendment itself. If it is not excessive, however, and if it does not violate the Eighth Amendment, it should not violate the Double Jeopardy Clause either.[158]

Previous attempts to define offenses other than by reference to the legislature's intent have all failed. The experience in California provides the best example. The California legislature tried to codify the prohibition against punishing a person twice for the same offense by providing that "an act . . . which is made punishable in different ways by different provisions of [the penal] code may be punished under either of such provisions, but in no case . . . under [both]."[159]

---

[158] See Note, note 28 *supra*, at 302; Comment, note 88 *supra*, at 364. It might be argued that double jeopardy prohibits the State from using two identical statutes to punish a defendant for the same offense, because the existence of two identical statutes gives the prosecutor too much discretion with respect to the selection of a charge. There are two problems with this argument. First, it fails to explain why the Double Jeopardy Clause should be deemed to regulate this one narrow area of prosecutorial discretion while the great body of discretion to prosecute falls outside the scope of constitutional review. See, *e.g.*, Shade v. Commonwealth, 394 F. Supp. 1237 (M.D. Pa. 1975); People v. McCollough, 57 Ill.2d 440, 313 N.E.2d 462 (1974); KAMISAR, LAFAVE & ISRAEL, MODERN CRIMINAL PROCEDURE 834–64 (4th ed. 1974). Second, and more importantly, it fails to explain why such discretion should be prohibited even on statutory grounds, much less constitutional grounds. After all, there is a legitimate reason for giving a prosecutor a choice to proceed under one of two statutes that are identical in every way except punishment—*viz.*, to permit him to tailor the seriousness of the charge to the seriousness of the offense. See, *e.g.*, Berra v. United States, 351 U.S. 131 (1956). If the State can authorize a prosecutor to choose between identical statutes carrying different sentences, as in *Berra*, it can also authorize a prosecutor to choose between proceeding under either one or two statutes that are identical in every way including punishment. In each case the purpose of the delegation is to enable the prosecutor to tailor the seriousness of the charge to the seriousness of the offender. See, *e.g.*, Cichos v. Indiana, 385 U.S. 76 (1966).

[159] CALIF. PEN. CODE § 654 (West 1970). For a clear and persuasive analysis of the problems presented by the statute, see Johnson, *Multiple Punishment and Consecutive Sentences: Reflections on the Neal Doctrine*, 58 CALIF. L. REV. 357 (1970).

The State courts have had endless difficulty defining an "act" for the purpose of the statute. Sometimes an act is defined by the physical nature of the defendant's conduct;[160] sometimes by the nature of his intended objective;[161] and sometimes by the nature of the resulting harm.[162] In the end, the effort has raised "excruciatingly difficult technical questions"[163] and produced a doctrine that is "difficult to apply"[164] and has "no apparent relationship to any sentencing policy or philosophy."[165] The same is true in other states.[166]

A third position recognizes that the Double Jeopardy Clause imposes no limitation on what the legislature may define as an offense but provides a limitation on how the legislature defines offenses. The result would be a constitutional presumption against imposing multiple punishment where the legislature may have intended a defendant to be punished only once, the presumption to be rebuttable by a clear and persuasive showing of legislative intent to the contrary.[167]

This presumption is a constitutional equivalent of what the Court calls the "rule of lenity"[168]—the rule of statutory construction the Court regularly employs to resolve doubts about multiple punish-

---

[160] As Professor Johnson points out, however, the trouble with this approach is that "any incident of physical conduct can be divided indefinitely into its component parts." *Id.* at 363.

[161] Again, as Johnson notes, "One may describe a concept like the defendant's objective as broadly or narrowly as one wishes." *Id.* at 365.

[162] There is one test that can be formulated in a coherent way—namely, to treat offenses as separate for double jeopardy purposes if each furthers a distinct legislative policy. See Note, *Consecutive Sentences in Single Prosecutions: Judicial Multiplication of Statutory Penalties,* 67 YALE L.J. 916, 929–31 (1958). But if the rule is stated in this form, it is no different from a rule that simply incorporates by reference whatever the legislature has defined an offense to be, and, in that event, the rule is no longer a limitation on what the legislature may do. See Johnson, note 159 *supra,* at 366–67.

[163] Johnson, note 159 *supra,* at 360.

[164] *Id.* at 377.

[165] *Ibid.*

[166] See Comment, *The Texas Carving Doctrine,* 6 AMER. J. CRIM. L. 57 (1978); Note, *One Transaction—One Conviction: The Texas Carving Doctrine,* 25 BAYLOR L. REV. 623 (1973); Comment, *Double Jeopardy—Defining the Same Offense,* 32 LA. L. REV. 87, 100 (1971); Note, *Multiple Prosecution and Punishment of Unitary Criminal Conduct,* 56 MINN. L. REV. 646 (1972).

[167] We are not the first to suggest that as to double punishment the Double Jeopardy Clause does no more (and no less) than create a presumption that the legislature intended conduct to be punished only once. For an original development of this idea, see Comment, note 28 *supra,* at 316.

[168] *Gore,* 357 U.S. at 391.

ment. The rule of lenity was first invoked in *Bell v. United States*,[169] a unit-of-prosecution case. The question in *Bell* was whether a defendant, who had transported two women on a single trip in the same automobile for purposes of prostitution, was guilty of one violation of the Mann Act or two. The Court recognized that Congress had the constitutional power to make the transportation of each woman a separate offense. But if Congress did not so intend, to construe the statute to allow multiple units of prosecution would cause the defendant to be punished twice for conduct that Congress intended to punish only once. Because of the ambiguity in the statute, and because the ambiguity created a risk of double punishment, the Court resolved the uncertainty by presuming that Congress intended the defendant to be punished only once. Justice Frankfurter explained this statutory presumption:[170]

> When Congress leaves to the Judiciary the task of imputing to Congress an undeclared will, the ambiguity should be resolved in favor of lenity. And this is not out of any sentimental consideration, or for want of sympathy with the purpose of Congress in proscribing evil or anti-social conduct. It may fairly be said to be a presupposition of our law to resolve doubts in the enforcement of a penal code against the imposition of a harsher punishment. This in no wise implies that language used in criminal statutes should not be read with the saving grace of common sense. . . . It merely means that if Congress does not fix the punishment for a federal offense clearly and without ambiguity, doubt will be resolved against turning a single transaction into multiple offenses.

The rule of lenity also applies in double-description cases where the same conduct violates more than one federal statute.[171]

The rule of lenity is more than a rule of statutory construction, it is a "presupposition of our law."[172] With regard to the constitutional requirement that a defendant have notice of what is defined as

---

[169] 349 U.S. 81 (1955).

[170] *Id.* at 83–84. The Court later characterized its decision in *Bell* as follows: "We held that the transportation of more than one woman as a single transaction is to be dealt with as a single offense, for the reason that when Congress has not explicitly stated what the unit of offense is, the doubt will be judicially resolved in favor of lenity." *Gore*, 357 U.S. at 391.

[171] See, *e.g.*, *Simpson*, 98 S. Ct. at 914; *Callanan*, 364 U.S. at 596.

[172] *Bell*, 349 U.S. at 83.

criminal conduct, the rule is grounded in the Due Process Clause and requires that penal statutes be strictly construed.[173] With regard to the constitutional prohibition on punishing a defendant in excess of legislative command, it is a principle of double jeopardy and requires that vague or ambiguous statutes be resolved leniently to prevent zealous prosecutors and timorous judges from perceiving two offenses where the legislature intended only one.[174] Thus, while designed as a protection against prosecutorial and judicial abuse, the Double Jeopardy Clause acts as an indirect restraint on the legislature, because it demands a certain standard of clarity from the legislature before multiple punishment will be allowed. Although the Clause incorporates by reference whatever the domestic law defines as an offense, in the event of uncertainty as to what the domestic law intends, the Clause requires that doubts be resolved in favor of punishing a defendant only once and puts the burden on the domestic law to speak to the contrary in language that is "clear and definite."[175]

This presumption helps explain the Court's recent decisions in double punishment cases, including its contrasting decisions in *Iannelli v. United States*[176] and *Jeffers v. United States.*[177] The defendants in *Iannelli* were simultaneously tried on two separate counts. One count charged a substantive violation of 18 U.S.C. § 1955, a statute making it an offense to conduct an illegal gambling business involving five or more persons. The other count charged a conspiracy in violation of 18 U.S.C. § 361, alleging that the defendants had conspired to violate § 1955. The defendants were convicted on both counts and given separate sentences that together exceeded what they could have received on each count alone.[178] They appealed,

---

[173] See United States v. Bass, 404 U.S. 336, 347–48 (1971).

[174] With respect to the interpretation of statutes, this constitutional rule of lenity is an analogue to the constitutional presumption in *Pearce*, that ambiguities in judicial sentences be resolved in favor of defendants in order to avoid the risks of double punishment. See text *supra*, at notes 142–45.

[175] "[W]hen choice has to be made between two readings of what conduct Congress has made a crime, it is appropriate, before we choose the harsher alternative, to require that Congress should have spoken in language that is clear and definite." *C.I.T.*, 344 U.S. at 221–22 (a nonconstitutional decision).

[176] 420 U.S. 770 (1975).

[177] 432 U.S. 138 (1977).

[178] This was not true of Iannelli himself, but it was true of the other defendants. 420 U.S. at 772–73 n.4.

arguing that the conspiracy count and the substantive count were the same offense for double jeopardy purposes and, therefore, that sentencing them on both subjected them to double punishment in violation of the Double Jeopardy Clause.

The defendants looked to Wharton's Rule to provide the standard for determining whether a conspiracy count and substantive count are the same for double jeopardy purposes. Wharton's Rule states that "[a]n agreement between two persons to commit a particular crime cannot be prosecuted as a conspiracy when the crime is of such a nature as to necessarily require the participation of two persons for its commission."[179] The defendants argued that since § 1955 itself requires the participation of at least five persons for its commission, Wharton's Rule precluded them from being cumulatively punished both for violating § 1955 and for conspiring to violate § 1955. Moreover, so they argued, since the Double Jeopardy Clause incorporates Wharton's Rule as a standard for determining whether offenses are the same, double jeopardy prohibited the State from punishing them for both offenses even if that is what the legislature intended.

The Court rejected the defendant's argument that Wharton's Rule operates as a substantive limitation on what a legislature may define as an offense. Wharton's Rule is not a rule of double jeopardy that operates in the face of legislative intent to the contrary. It is a constitutional "presumption"[180] to be used as "an aid to the determination of legislative intent."[181] The Rule recognizes that the

---

[179] *Id.* at 773 n.5, quoting from 1 ANDERSON, WHARTON'S CRIMINAL LAW AND PRO-CEDURE § 89, at 191 (1957).

[180] 420 U.S. at 782.

[181] *Id.* at 786. There is admittedly some ambiguity in the Court's statement of the relationship between Wharton's Rule and the Double Jeopardy Clause. What the Court said—"the broadly formulated Wharton's Rule does not rest on principles of double jeopardy," 420 U.S. at 782—can be interpreted in two different ways. It may mean that Wharton's Rule has nothing to do with the Double Jeopardy Clause, however the Rule may be formulated. Or it may mean that Wharton's Rule is not a rule of double jeopardy if the Rule is "broadly formulated" to be a substantive limitation on the way that the legislature may define offenses, but that it is a rule of double jeopardy if formulated as a "presumption" for ascertaining what the legislature in fact intended. The latter construction is more likely. Wharton's Rule, as originally formulated, was explicitly and exclusively based on the Double Jeopardy Clause, as was the original case from which the Rule was derived. See WHARTON, CRIMINAL LAW 198 (2d ed. 1852), commenting on Shannon v. Commonwealth, 14 Pa. 226, 227 (1850). Even the government in *Iannelli* assumed that Wharton's Rule is a principle of double jeopardy. Brief for Respondent at 9–10. Moreover, the Court compared Wharton's Rule with the Blockburger Rule, see note 186 *infra*, stating that both served the "function" of

closer the relationship between a substantive offense and a conspiracy, the less likelihood there is that the legislature intends to
punish them separately, and, therefore, the greater the potential
danger of double punishment. Accordingly, the closer the relationship between the nature of the two offenses, the stronger the presumption in favor of single punishment. In every case, however, the
presumption can be rebutted by a showing of "legislative intent to
the contrary."[182]

For double jeopardy purposes, therefore, Wharton's Rule is a
specific application of the rule of lenity.[183] While Wharton's Rule
creates the presumption in favor of a single offense, it can be rebutted, as it was in *Iannelli*, by a showing of a "clear and unmistakable"[184] legislative intent that the substantive violation and the
conspiracy be punished as multiple offenses.

In *Jeffers*, in contrast, the legislative evidence was insufficient to
rebut the constitutional presumption in favor of a single offense.
The defendant in *Jeffers* was tried on two counts. In one count he
was charged with conspiring to distribute drugs in violation of 21
U.S.C. § 846, in the other with distributing drugs in concert with
five or more persons in violation of 21 U.S.C. § 848. He was convicted on both offenses and given multiple sentences which together
exceeded the maximum that he could have received on either count
alone. The question, therefore, was whether §§ 846 and 848 were
the same offense for purposes of the constitutional rule against a
double punishment.[185]

"identifying congressional intent to impose separate sanctions for multiple offenses arising in the course of a single act or transaction." 420 U.S. at 785 n.17. It could never be
said that the Blockburger Rule has nothing to do with the Double Jeopardy Clause.
The Blockburger Rule is a constitutional presumption for ascertaining legislative intent
regarding double punishment where circumstances suggest that the legislature may
have intended a defendent to be punished only once. See *Gore*, 357 U.S. 386. By drawing
an analogy between the two Rules, the Court in *Iannelli* suggests that Wharton's Rule,
like the Blockburger Rule, is a constitutional rule of construction for ascertaining
legislative intent.

[182] 420 U.S. at 785–86.

[183] For an effort to formulate other presumptive rules, like Wharton's Rule and the
Blockburger Rule, to give specific content to the rule of lenity, see Kirchheimer, *The
Act, the Offense, and Double Jeopardy*, 58 YALE L.J. 513, 515–24 (1949).

[184] 420 U.S. at 791.

[185] In addition to this question of multiple punishment, *Jeffers* also presented a question
of multiple prosecution, because the defendant was first tried and convicted on § 846
and only later on § 848. The Court divided on this latter question, the plurality holding
that the defendant had waived any objection to seriatim prosecution by asking that the

The argument for the defendant was based on the so-called Blockburger Rule,[186] that two offenses are the same for purposes of punishment unless each requires proof of a fact which the other does not. The defendant argued that § 846 was a lesser-included offense within § 848, and, therefore, the same as § 848 for purposes of the Blockburger Rule. Moreover, so the argument went, since the Double Jeopardy Clause incorporates the Blockburger Rule as a standard for determining whether offenses are the same, it prohibits the State from imposing multiple punishments for the two violations even if that is what the legislature intended.

A plurality of the Court ruled for the defendant but not on the basis of the stated argument. The plurality was willing to assume that § 846 was a lesser-included offense within § 848, and that the two offenses were the same for purposes of the Blockburger Rule.[187] Yet it refused to conclude on that basis alone that the Double Jeopardy Clause prohibited the imposition of multiple punishments for the two offenses. Instead, it said, even assuming that one is a lesser-included offense within the other, the question for double jeopardy purposes is "[w]hether Congress intended to punish each statutory violation separately."[188] To answer that question, the

---

two counts be served for purposes of trial. 432 U.S. at 152. Consequently, the plurality treated the case for double jeopardy purposes as if the defendant had been simultaneously tried and convicted on both counts, thus presenting only the question of multiple punishment. For the double jeopardy implications of multiple prosecutions following conviction, see text *infra*, at notes 334–49.

[186] The Rule takes its name from Blockburger v. United States, 284 U.S. 299, 304 (1932): "The applicable rule is that where the same act or transaction constitutes a violation of two distinct statutory provisions, the test to be applied to determine whether there are two offenses or only one, is whether each provision requires proof of a fact which the other does not." Although *Blockburger* itself was not a double jeopardy case, see *Simpson*, 98 S. Ct. at 916 (Rehnquist, J., dissenting), the rule to which it gave its name was taken verbatim from Gavieres v. United States, 220 U.S. 338, 342 (1911), which was a double jeopardy case.

[187] 432 U.S. at 149–51 (plurality opinion).

[188] *Id.* at 155 (plurality opinion). Even though it was willing to assume that the one offense was a lesser-included offense within the other, the plurality still insisted that the question remained "whether Congress intended to allow cumulative punishment for violations of §§ 846 and 848." 432 U.S. at 155. The plurality recognized the fact that one offense is entirely included in another is not conclusive proof that the legislature intended them to merge for purposes of punishment, but, at most, is merely strong evidence of such an intent. The plurality lends support to this view by referring with approval to the footnote in *Iannelli* where the Court described the Blockburger Rule as a rule of construction "for identifying congressional intent." 420 U.S. at 785, 786 n.17, cited favorably in *Jeffers*, 432 U.S. at 155. It is important to distinguish here between the constitutional standards for multiple punishment and the distinct standards for a multiple

plurality turned to legislative history and, finding it "inconclusive,"[189] presumed that Congress intended that the two violations be punished as a single offense. Accordingly, the plurality ordered that the sentence on the lesser offense be credited against his sentence on the greater.

Iannelli and *Jeffers* reinforce the conclusion that the Double Jeopardy Clause operates as a rebuttable presumption against multiple punishment. The Court rejected an invitation in each case to constitutionalize a rigid "rule" for determining what the domestic law may define as an offense. Yet the Court also refused to defer to the prosecutor's interpretation of the domestic law. Instead, while recognizing that legislative intent must ultimately control, the Court held that in order to create multiple offenses where it might have created only one, the legislature must speak in language that is "clear and unmistakable."[190] In *Jeffers*, where the presumption raised by the Blockburger Rule was strong and the legislative history inconclusive, doubt was resolved in favor of the defendant.[191] In *Iannelli*, where the presumption raised by Wharton's Rule was weaker and legislative history more explicit, the Court was forced to conclude that separate offenses were intended.[192]

III. Reprosecution Following Acquittal: The Interest in Nullification

The rule that a defendant may not be retried following an acquittal is said to be "the most fundamental rule in the history of double jeopardy jurisprudence."[193] It is also the most perplexing. It has caused the Court more difficulty in recent years and created sharper divisions among the Justices than any other facet of double

---

prosecution. Although the Blockburger Rule operates as nothing more than a rebuttable presumption for purposes of multiple punishment, it may have a stricter and more rigid application in the context of multiple prosecution. See text *infra*, at notes 334–49.

[189] 432 U.S. at 156 (plurality opinion).

[190] 420 U.S. at 791.

[191] The presumption created by the Blockburger Rule in *Jeffers* was strong because while it is conceivable that a legislature would want to punish a lesser-included offense separately, see note 329 *infra*, it is highly unlikely.

[192] The Court in *Iannelli* concluded that the presumption created by Wharton's Rule was weak in *Iannelli* because, unlike the paradigm offense of adultery, § 1955 does not require concerted criminal activity. 420 U.S. at 785.

[193] *Martin Linen*, 430 U.S. at 571.

jeopardy. More than half of the Court's cases in the past two Terms have involved acquittals, including the two major cases which overruled earlier decisions.[194] This is also the area in which the Court most frequently has reserved questions for future consideration.

The rule on acquittals is perplexing because it is seemingly implausible on its face. In contrast to mistrials and convictions, where a defendant's interest in finality is carefully "balance[d]"[195] against society's interest in law enforcement, the rule for acquittals is "absolute."[196] The rule accords "absolute finality"[197] to judgments of acquittal, "no matter how erroneous"[198] they may be. Thus, while society has an "interest" in the government's being able "to appeal from an erroneous conclusion of law,"[199] this interest is completely subordinated to the defendant's once he is acquitted, because in the area of acquittals "[t]here are no 'equities' to be balanced."[200] Defendants are explicitly allowed to "benefit"[201] from errors, no matter how serious, provided the errors lead to an acquittal. Acquittals are final, even if "egregiously erroneous."[202]

Thus, the fundamental question: Why does the law attach "particular significance"[203] to an acquittal? What is it that distinguishes an "acquittal" from, say, a mistrial or a dismissal? Is there any "talismanic significance"[204] to the label a trial judge puts on his ruling? Does the nature of a ruling depend upon the name it is given? Or does the name depend on its underlying nature?

The answer, of course, is that "[t]he word itself has no talismanic quality."[205] A ruling is not treated as final because it is called an acquittal, it is called an acquittal because it is treated as final. In order to identify the nature of an acquittal and the features that dis-

---

[194] See note 8 *supra*.

[195] See note 21 *supra*.

[196] *Burks*, 98 S. Ct. at 2147 n.6.

[197] *Id*. at 2150.

[198] *Ibid*.

[199] *Scott*, 98 S. Ct. at 2198 n.13

[200] *Burks*, 98 S. Ct. at 2147 n.6.

[201] *Wilson*, 420 U.S. at 352.

[202] Fong Foo v. United States, 369 U.S. 141, 143 (1962) (hereinafter *Fong Foo*).

[203] *Scott*, 98 S. Ct. at 2194.

[204] *Id*. at 2203 n.7.

[205] *Serfass*, 420 U.S. at 392.

tinguish it from a mistrial or a dismissal, one must first identify the reasons for according a ruling "absolute finality."

A. VERDICTS OF NOT GUILTY BY A JURY

The paradigm in the law of acquittals is the rule that a defendant may not be retried following a jury verdict of acquittal—a general verdict of "not guilty." Whatever uncertainties may otherwise exist in the area of acquittals, this much is certain: The Double Jeopardy Clause accords "absolute finality to a jury's verdict of acquittal."[206] Indeed, the rule is so universally accepted that no one seriously thinks to challenge it, and the Court has only once decided a case directly presenting the issue.[207] The Court has never fully explicated the reasons for treating jury verdicts of acquittal as final. Yet, without these reasons, it is impossible to determine whether other verdicts or other judicial rulings ought to enjoy comparable finality. The starting point, therefore, is to identify the reasons for a constitutional rule that insulates jury verdicts from review.

There are several possibilities. The rule may be designed to protect a defendant's expectation that a verdict of acquittal will be final. Defendants may have come to expect that jury acquittals will be final and, because of that expectation, may breathe the proverbial sigh of relief when acquitted by a jury. These expectations are important and worthy of respect.[208] Once the State creates such an expectation, so the argument goes, it cannot destroy the expectation by altering the ground rules and causing a defendant to be retried.

The trouble with this—as with all protections based on what people in fact expect—is that the State can alter the scope of protection simply by changing what people are allowed to expect.[209] If an

---

[206] *Burks*, 98 S. Ct. at 2150.

[207] See *Ball*, 163 U.S. at 666–71. The others are all cases in which a defendant was tried on more than one count and convicted on one and either explicitly or implicitly acquitted on another. See *Price*, 398 U.S. 323; *Benton*, 395 U.S. 784; *Green*, 355 U.S. 184; Palko v. Connecticut, 302 U.S. 319 (1938). *Cf. Ashe*, 397 U.S. 436.

[208] It has been said that "the substantive criminal law defines the behavior authorizing imposition of the most drastic sanction at the command of government on individual human beings." Allen, *Criminal Law and the Modern Conscientiousness: Some Observations on Blameworthiness*, 44 TENN. L. REV. 735, 737 (1977). For this reason the expectations, which the State creates in defendants regarding the disposition of criminal charges, are entitled to protection. See Western & Westin, *A Constitutional Law of Remedies for Broken Plea Bargains*, 66 CALIF L. REV. 471 (1978).

[209] In *Swisher*, for example, the defendant argued that the master's proposed findings of fact should be treated as final because defendants had come to expect them to be final.

expectation is created by rules of positive law, it can be changed, reduced, or even eliminated by the positive law. Thus, if a defendant's protected interest in finality depends entirely on his reliance on the domestic law of acquittals, his interest can be changed, or even eliminated, by altering the domestic law.[210] The State would then be free to adopt a rule, applicable prospectively, permitting (or even requiring) that defendants be retried following jury verdicts of not guilty that are determined to be erroneous.

The better argument is based, not on what people in fact expect, but on what they are entitled to expect.[211] This may be what the Court means when it says that a defendant has a "legitimate interest in the finality of a verdict of acquittal."[212]

Yet that simply poses the next question: Why should a defendant be entitled to rely on a verdict of acquittal, particularly if it can be shown to be egregiously erroneous? Why, if a defendant is not entitled to complain about retrial following an erroneous conviction, is he entitled to complain about being retried following an erroneous acquittal?

One move is to argue that a defendant has a legitimate interest in seeing that the "risk[s]"[213] of litigation are brought to an end once and for all. But that is also true of a defendant who has been wrongfully convicted. He, too, has an interest in seeing the litigation end; he, too, would prefer not to be retried. Yet his interest in finality is subordinated to "the public interest in assuring that each defendant shall be subject to a just judgment on the merits of his case."[214] If

---

The Court rejected the argument, noting that "[w]ithin the limits of jury trial rights, and other constitutional constraints, it is for the state, not the parties, to designate and empower the fact-finder and adjudicator." 98 S. Ct. at 2707.

[210] See TRIBE, AMERICAN CONSTITUTIONAL LAW 469 (1978): "to the extent that [legal protection of expectations] is cast exclusively in terms of the expectations that persons in fact entertain in reliance upon legal commitments expressly made by the sovereign, it is within the sovereign's power to hedge those commitments in order to cut the expectations down to any desired size"; Note, *A Reconsideration of the Katz Expectation of Privacy Tests,* 76 MICH. L. REV. 154, 157–64 (1977): "if the right of privacy is only as great as the expectation of privacy, then the government can vitiate the right simply by taking away all such expectations."

[211] "At stake [regarding the impairment of contracts] must be not only what people in fact expect upon examining the body of positive law, but also what they are entitled to expect, positive law to the contrary notwithstanding." TRIBE, note 210 *supra.*

[212] *Wilson,* 420 U.S. at 352.

[213] See note 45 *supra.*

[214] *Scott,* 98 S. Ct. at 2199.

so, the same follows, too, for an erroneous acquittal, because if it is treated as final, it deprives the public of "a just judgment on the merits of [the] case."

Now it is sometimes said that the two cases are distinguishable because by appealing his conviction, the defendant who was wrongfully convicted demonstrates that he has no genuine interest in finality or, if he has such an interest, that he is willing to waive it.[215] This argument is fundamentally misconceived. For one thing, it confuses the defendant's interest in taking an appeal with his interest in avoiding reprosecution. Of course, a defendant who is wrongfully convicted may want to appeal his conviction; but that does not mean he also desires to be retried if his appeal is successful. On the contrary, he wants precisely the same thing as the defendant who is acquitted—a guarantee that he will never again be retried. And there is nothing in logic or experience that requires him to forego one desire in order to fulfill the other.[216]

Furthermore, the argument misconceives the nature of the defendant's so-called waiver. It is true that once a defendant's conviction is set aside on appeal he has no right to object to being retried. But that is so, not because he has no objection, but because he is not allowed to object. His objection is disallowed because "the societal interest in punishing one whose guilt is clear"[217] overrides his interest in finality.[218] The same should follow, too, for the de-

---

[215] See *Ball*, 163 U.S. at 672. This notion, that a defendant's interest in the finality of an erroneous judgment of conviction is inextricably linked with his interest in the finality of the first trial, is reflected in a famous statement by Justice McLean. The Double Jeopardy Clause permits a defendant to be retried following reversal of his conviction, he said, otherwise it would "guarantee him the right of being hung, to protect him from the danger of a second trial." United States v. Keen, 26 Fed. Cas. 686, 690 (No. 15, 510) (C.C.D. Ind. 1839), quoted in *Scott*, 98 S. Ct. at 2194.

[216] See *Kepner* 195 U.S. at 135 (Holmes, J., dissenting). The best evidence of this is that in England a defendant can appeal an erroneous conviction without running the risk of being retried should the conviction be reversed. See *Tateo*, 377 U.S. at 473 (Goldberg, J., dissenting).

[217] *Tateo*, 377 U.S. at 466.

[218] The Court now recognizes that a defendant can be retried following the reversal of his conviction on appeal, not because he wants to "waive" his objection to retrial, but because he is required to waive it as a consequence of his conviction being set aside. See *Burks*, 98 S. Ct. at 2149; *Pearce*, 395 U.S. at 721 n.18. Significantly, the Court is very skeptical about the very notion and terminology of "waiver" in double jeopardy cases. See *Scott*, 98 S. Ct. at 2198; *Burks*, 98 S. Ct. at 2150; *Benton*, 395 U.S. at 811–12 (Harlan, J., dissenting); *Green*, 355 U.S. at 191–92. For an excellent analysis of waiver in the context of retrial following a reversed conviction, see Mayers & Yarbrough, *Bis Vexari: New Trials and Successive Prosecutions*, 74 Harv. L. Rev. 1, 6–7, 18–20 (1960).

fendant who is erroneously acquitted, because once the first defendant's conviction is set aside on appeal, the two defendants stand
in precisely the same position with regard to society's interest in
enforcing its laws.

Another argument is that a defendant has a greater interest in the
finality of acquittals than convictions because acquittals are favorable
to his cause and convictions are not. But that is a descriptive statement, not a normative explanation. It describes the operative difference between an acquittal and a conviction, but it does not explain
why a defendant should have a greater claim of right to immunity
from reprosecution following an erroneous acquittal than following
an erroneous conviction. To support a claim of right, a defendant
would have to show that his interest in resisting reprosecution following an erroneous acquittal is stronger—or that society's countervailing interest is weaker—than a defendant's interest in resisting
reprosecution following an erroneous conviction. Yet the interests
appear to be the same. The defendant in each case has an interest in
not being "subjected to the hazards of trial and possible conviction
more than once for an alleged offense."[219] Society in each case has an
interest in having "one complete [and error-free] opportunity to
convict those who have violated its laws."[220] If society's interest in
law enforcement overrides the defendant's interest in finality for
purposes of retrial following an erroneous conviction, it should, too,
following an erroneous acquittal. "A system permitting review of
all claimed legal errors would have symmetry to recommend it and
would avoid the release of some defendants who have benefited from
instructions or evidentiary rulings that are unduly favorable to
them."[221]

Indeed, if anything, a defendant has a greater claim of right to
immunity from reprosecution following a conviction than following
an acquittal. A defendant whose conviction is reversed on appeal

---

[219] *Green*, 355 U.S. at 187.

[220] *Washington*, 98 S. Ct. at 832.

[221] *Wilson*, 420 U.S. at 352. See also Palko v. Connecticut, 302 U.S. 319, 328 (1937):
"The state is not attempting to wear the accused out by a multitude of cases with
accumulated trials. It asks no more than this, that the case against him shall go on until
there shall be a trial free from the corrosion of substantial legal error. . . . If the trial
had been infected with error adverse to the accused, there might have been review at
his instance, and as often as necessary to purge the vicious taint. A reciprocal privilege . . .
has now been granted to the state. There is here no seismic innovation. The edifice of
justice stands, its symmetry, to many, greater than before."

knows that if the State had not caused his trial to be tainted by error, he might have been acquitted. Indeed, it is because he might have been acquitted that he is entitled to reversal; otherwise, the error would be treated as harmless. In contrast, a defendant whose acquittal is "based on an egregiously erroneous foundation"[222] knows that if error had not been introduced in his favor, he might have been convicted. Accordingly, if a defendant must bear the risk of being retried when the State introduces error against him, he should also have to bear the risk of retrial when error is introduced in his favor. Justice Holmes made this point seventy-five years ago: "[A defendant] no more would be put in jeopardy a second time when retried because of a mistake of law in his favor, than he would be when retried for a mistake that did him harm."[223] In short, if an acquittal is absolutely final in a way that erroneous convictions or mistrials are not, it cannot be because the defendant has a stronger interest in finality—or the government has a weaker interest in reprosecution. Wholly apart from a defendant's expectations, the rule on acquittals is sometimes defended on the ground that if the State has unlimited opportunities to retry a defendant following an acquittal, it may eventually find a jury willing to convict, no matter how innocent the defendant may be.[224] Unfortunately, this rationale does not explain the enormous scope of the rule on acquittals. It explains why the State may not retry a defendant who has been fairly and justly "acquitted following an errorless trial."[225] But it does not explain why that State may not retry a defendant whose acquittal is "egregiously erroneous" and whose claim of innocence remains seriously in doubt. If a defendant has a right to immunity following an egregiously erroneous acquittal, it cannot be because the acquittal is taken as evidence that he is actually innocent. It must be because retrial is thought to impose too great a burden on his ability to demonstrate his innocence. If so, however, the same is also true of the defendant who is retried following a reversed conviction because he, too, is presumed to be innocent.[226]

---

[222] *Fong Foo*, 369 U.S. at 143.

[223] *Kepner*, 195 U.S. at 135.

[224] Hoag v. New Jersey, 356 U.S. 464, 474–75 (1958) (Warren, C.J., dissenting).

[225] *Benton*, 395 U.S. at 810 (Harlan, J., dissenting).

[226] An erroneous acquittal is no greater proof of actual innocence than an erroneous conviction is proof of actual guilt. Nor, as between the two erroneous verdicts, is an

Still another argument is that retrial following an acquittal enhances the probability of conviction by allowing the prosecutor "to reexamine the weaknesses in his first presentation in order to strengthen the second."[227] But, again, the same thing occurs when the State is allowed to retry a defendant following a conviction. The justification for retrial in each case is to give society "one complete [and error-free] opportunity to convict those who have violated its laws."[228] Obviously, one of the incidental effects of retrial—regardless of whether it follows an acquittal, dismissal, mistrial, or conviction—is to place the prosecutor in a position to correct his mistakes. But if that is not too high a price to pay to allow the government to retry a defendant following an erroneous conviction, it should not be too high a price for retrial following an erroneous acquittal.

Again, it is argued that a government appeal from a jury verdict would intrude upon the jury's authority to find the facts. The obvious answer is that when an appellate court reverses a jury verdict for errors in the taking of evidence, the giving of instructions, or the conduct of the trial, it is not acting as a trier of fact. It is regulating the setting in which the jury can accurately find the facts. The same is true in civil cases. The Seventh Amendment forbids the appellate courts from "re-examin[ing]" any "fact" that has been "tried by a jury." Yet appellate courts may reverse jury verdicts for legal errors in civil cases without intruding upon the jury's constitutional prerogative to find the facts because, in reversing, they are not "re-examin[ing]" the "facts."[229]

There remains a persuasive rationale for the finality of verdicts of acquittal, namely, that a defendant may not be retried following an erroneous acquittal because the acquittal may be a product of the jury's legitimate authority to acquit against the evidence. To say that an acquittal is erroneous may mean one of several things. It may mean that the verdict contradicts the overwhelming weight of the evidence. That, however, provides no basis for reversing such a verdict in a system like ours in which the jury may acquit against the

---

erroneous acquittal greater proof of actual innocence than an erroneous conviction. They both rest on error that is so serious as to preclude one from knowing what the verdict would have been at an error-free trial.

[227] *Wilson*, 420 U.S. at 352.

[228] *Washington*, 98 S. Ct. at 832.

[229] Capitol Traction Co. v. Hof, 174 U.S. 1, 13 (1899).

evidence. An acquittal may also be erroneous if it is the product of defective fact-finding either because items of prosecution evidence were wrongly excluded or because the jury was wrongly instructed. But, again, so long as the jury's role is not limited to simple fact-finding—so long as it has the authority to acquit a defendant in spite of the facts—these errors may be immaterial. There is no way of knowing whether a jury, which has acquitted a defendant following "defective" fact-finding, would not have come to precisely the same conclusion regardless of the facts and instructions.[230]

The reason protection is extended to judgments of lenity by the jury is the same reason that the term "erroneous acquittal" is a misnomer. There are no identifiably erroneous acquittals because every such purported candidate, evaluated by a legal standard resting on the evidence, may be explained alternatively as an extralegal judgment by the jury to act against the evidence. The balance of interests that justifies appellate review and retrial in cases of convictions and mistrials is, therefore, inappropriate in cases of acquittal, not because the government has no legitimate interest in correcting errors in such cases, but because there are no identifiable errors to correct. The Double Jeopardy Clause thus allows the jury to exercise its constitutional function as the conscience of the community in applying the law: to soften, and in the extreme case, to nullify the application of the law in order to avoid unjust judgments.[231]

This is not the place for a systematic argument in favor of the proposition that the criminal jury has legitimate authority to nullify the law by acquitting against the evidence. To make that argument

---

[230] If this rationale of nullification explains the rule of finality for jury verdicts of not guilty, it also suggests an exception to the rule. Specifically, one could argue that the prosecution ought to be able to obtain a new trial if it can show that the evidence in its case which was wrongfully excluded would have also had a substantial bearing on a jury's willingness to be lenient. Of course, this raises the counterargument that a jury's decision to nullify is essentially lawless and, therefore, by hypothesis, not amenable to standards. But surely that is not so. It is no more lawless than a chief executive authority to pardon or grant clemency, which is not subject to judicial review. In each case, the authority is granted with some idea in mind of the kinds of factors and considerations that might bear on the exercise of leniency. It should be possible, therefore, to identify the kinds of evidence that in all reasonable likelihood might, or might not, have a bearing on the jury. Once those factors are identified, the only remaining issue is to define the standard that determines how much "fit" there must be between the evidence the jury actually heard and the evidence it might have heard at an error-free trial for a defendant to avoid a reversal.

[231] See text *infra*, at notes 234–36.

properly, one would have to explain why the doctrine is maintained so surreptitiously,[232] and what the relationship is between nullification and prevailing rules regarding evidence, closing argument, and jury instructions.[233] It suffices to say that at some level, at least, nullification is implicit in the constitutional notion of trial by jury, because nothing else explains why a criminal defendant has a right to resist a directed verdict of conviction,[234] why he has a right to insist on a general verdict (as opposed to special verdicts),[235] and why neither he nor the prosecutor has the right to challenge a

---

[232] See, *e.g.*, United States v. Dougherty, 473 F.2d 1113, 1130–37 (D.C. Cir. 1972) (Leventhal, J.) (a criminal jury has the "prerogative" to acquit against the evidence but not to be told that it has such a prerogative).

[233] See United States v. Moylan, 417 F.2d 1002, 1006 (4th Cir. 1969) (defendant has no right to have the jury instructed on its authority to nullify). See also *Sparf*, 156 U.S. 51 (defendant has no right to insist that the jury be instructed on its right to return a verdict on a lesser offense than the one charged in the indictment, if a finding on the lesser offense would not be supported by the evidence). *Sparf* is sometimes taken as authority for the proposition that a criminal jury has no right (as opposed to power) to acquit against the evidence. But *Sparf* can be read more narrowly. For further discussion of this issue, see Scheflin, *Jury Nullification: The Right to Say No*, 45 S. CALIF. L. REV. 168 (1972).

[234] It is well understood that it would violate a defendant's right to trial by jury for a judge to direct the jury to return a verdict of guilty, even if the evidence of guilt is "overwhelming." *Martin Linen*, 430 at 572–73. See also Carpenters v. United States, 330 U.S. 395, 408 (1947); Sparf v. United States, 156 U.S. 105–06 (1895) (hereinafter *Sparf*). This rule cannot be based on the authority of the jury to find the facts, because when a jury makes a finding in the face of overwhelming evidence that no reasonable person could disbelieve, it is not finding the facts. It is either acting irrationally, or it is nullifying the legal standard. See Curie, *Thoughts on Directed Verdicts and Summary Judgments*, 45 U. CHI. L. REV. 72 (1977). The persistence of this ruel, that a verdict of guilty cannot be directed against a defendant in a criminal case, is evidence that the criminal jury has legitimate authority to acquit against the evidence. It might be argued that the ban on directing a verdict against a criminal defendant is based on the stringent standard of proof in criminal cases and on the difficulty for a court in concluding that there is no doubt that the defendant is guilty. But judges do precisely that in bench trials, and appellate courts do, too, in evaluating errors for "harmlessness." See Harrington v. California, 395 U.S. 250, 254 (1969).

[235] It is also generally assumed that it would be unconstitutional for a judge, over a defendant's objection, to order the jury to return special verdicts as opposed to a general verdict. See *Sparf* 156 U.S. at 51, 80–81, 83, 87, 95 (1895); Heald v. Mullaney, 505 F.2d 1241, 1245 (1st Cir. 1974). Yet the very purpose of special verdicts is to confine the jury to a fact-finding function and to prevent it from nullifying the legal standard it is supposed to apply. See Skidmore v. Baltimore & Ohio R.R. Co., F.2d 54, 57–60, 66 (2d Cir. 1948) (Frank, J.). Accordingly, if a defendant has a constitutional right to object to special verdicts in a criminal case, it must be because the Sixth Amendment prohibits the judge from confining a jury to an exclusively fact-finding function. So, too, the rule that in certain cases the doctrine of collateral estoppel cannot be applied against a defendant, see Simpson v. Florida, 403 U.S. 384 (1971), must be based on the notion that the elimination of certain issues from jury consideration by collateral estoppel would prevent the jury from exercising its veto power based on the "whole story."

verdict for factual inconsistency.[236] It is also the only thing that explains why, though a defendant can be retried following an erroneous conviction, he cannot be retried following an erroneous acquittal.

B. FINDINGS OF NOT GUILTY BY A JUDGE IN A TRIAL TO THE BENCH

Moving from jury trials to bench trials, we discover that the rule for acquittals is said to be the same. Without explaining why the two cases should be treated as equivalent, the Court has assumed that a general finding of not guilty by a judge in a bench trial is entitled to the same degree of finality as a jury verdict of not guilty.[237]

Are there good reasons for treating a judge's finding of not guilty as final? The rule cannot be designed to indulge a defendant's selfish desire to benefit from a finding that terminates a case in his favor, because other kinds of favorable rulings by a judge are now appealable.[238] Nor can it be designed to spare a defendant the expense and anxiety of further proceedings on appeal, because he can be subjected to such burdens at least where further fact-finding would not be required.[239] Nor can it be designed to protect defendants who are actually innocent from being falsely convicted the second time, because the rule on acquittals operates even where the original finding of not guilty is based on " 'error, irrational behavior, or

---

[236] The principal justification for the rule, that a defendant may not challenge a verdict for inconsistency, is that the inconsistency may reflect the jury's decision to be lenient. See Dunn v. United States, 284 U.S. 390, 393 (1932). Obviously, if the only justification for such inconsistency is the jury's exercise of leniency, and if the jury has no "right" to exercise leniency, the appropriate disposition would be to reverse the verdict. The persistence of the *Dunn* rule is further evidence, therefore, that the jury's exercise of leniency is not a "power," but a "right," because if it did not have the right to be lenient, the appellate courts could deny it the power by reversing for inconsistency.

[237] *Jenkins*, 420 U.S. at 365: "Since the double jeopardy clause of the Fifth Amendment nowhere distinguishes between bench and jury trials, the principles given expression through that clause apply to cases tried to a judge." Accord, *Martin Linen*, 430 U.S. at 573. This is an inadequate explanation even on the Court's own terms. For the Double Jeopardy Clause likewise fails to set apart for special treatment a directed verdict of acquittal by a trial judge after a verdict of guilty by the jury, yet appeal and reversal of such an acquittal has been held constitutional by the Court. See *Wilson*, 420 U.S. 332. Until further expression by the Court of the reasons for according jury acquittals nonappealable finality and some explanation as to why these should apply to judicial acquittals, this issue cannot be deemed to have been seriously addressed by the Court.

[238] See, *e.g.*, *Sanford*, 429 U.S. 14 (government may appeal a favorable ruling by a judge on the merits of the case if the ruling occurs before trial commences).

[239] See, *e.g.*, *Wilson*, 420 U.S. 332.

prejudice on the part of the trial judge.' "[240] As for the remaining arguments based on expectations of finality or claims of innocence, they cannot be any more successful here than they are in the context of jury verdicts of not guilty.

This leaves for consideration the rationale advanced in support of the finality of jury acquittals: the authority of the fact-finder to acquit against the evidence. Yet there are fundamental differences between bench trials and jury trials with respect to nullification. For one thing, the source of the authority to nullify is different. With respect to jury trials, nullification has its source in the Constitution. It is the Sixth Amendment right to trial by jury that prohibits the court from directing a verdict against the defendant, or from entering judgment against him notwithstanding a verdict, or from taking an appeal from a jury verdict of not guilty.[241] With respect to bench trials, on the other hand, there is nothing in the Constitution that gives a trial judge the authority to nullify. The Due Process Clause gives a defendant a right to a "fair" trial by the bench.[242] That means that the judge must provide a fair process of fact-finding, not that he must be allowed to nullify the law by acquitting against the evidence. Accordingly, if trial judges have the authority to nullify, it is not because the Constitution requires it, but because the domestic law chooses to vest them with that authority.

Furthermore, the theoretical justifications for allowing juries to nullify do not all apply in bench trials. One explanation for the finality of jury verdicts is that it gives a defendant an opportunity for "community participation in the determination of guilt or innocence"[243] and allows the defendant to be judged by "the conscience of the community."[244] That is certainly not true of a verdict by a professional judge.[245] Another explanation is that a jury verdict is a

---

[240] *Scott*, 98 S. Ct. at 2201 (1978) (Brennan, J., dissenting), quoting from *Martin Linen*, 430 U.S. at 574.

[241] *Martin Linen*, 430 U.S. at 572–73. See also *Swisher*, 98 S. Ct. at 2712 n.8 (Marshall, J., dissenting).

[242] See Mayberry v. Pennsylvania, 400 U.S. 455 (1971); Tumey v. Ohio, 273 U.S. 510 (1927). There is some reason to believe that federal judges do not have the authority to acquit against the evidence, at least not where the decision is combined with special findings of fact. See United States v. Maybury, 274 F.2d 899, 902–03 (2d Cir. 1960).

[243] Duncan v. Louisiana, 391 U.S. 145, 156 (1968).

[244] United States v. Spock, 416 F.2d 165, 182 (1st Cir. 1969).

[245] See United States v. Maybury, 274 F.2d 899, 903 (1960): "[T]he judge is hardly the 'voice of the country.' even when he sits in the jury's place."

group decision arrived at after collective discussion. The decision of a single judge does not have the same legitimacy, which is why rulings of law by a trial judge are reviewable by other judges on an appellate basis.[246] Finally, jury nullification is acceptable, in part, because the decision to nullify can be concealed in the ambiguity of a general verdict.[247] That, again, is not true in bench trials, at least in jurisdictions where the trial judge is expected to make findings of fact and law.[248]

Nonetheless, there are still good reasons to vest trial judges with the authority to acquit against the evidence.[249] It enables the judicial system to temper the legislature's generalized standards of criminal responsibility with lenity in particular cases. It also places bench trials on an equal footing with jury trials and, thereby, not only enhances the stature of bench trials, but also encourages defendants to select them more often. In short, a jurisdiction may choose to make legitimate in law what already occurs in practice, *viz.*, that trial judges sometimes acquit for reasons of personal conscience, irrespective of the defendant's actual guilt.[250]

This notion, that a jurisdiction is not required but is nonetheless free to vest trial judges with the authority to nullify, suggests a role

---

[246] The reason why we forbid even a second jury from passing on the defendant's guilt or innocence is a slightly different facet of the same value underlying the finality of acquittals in general. That value, as we have seen, places great store in the community, as represented by the jury, acting as the ultimate point of contact between the law and the accused. This places a certain emphasis upon the jury as a body representative of the community from which it is drawn. Such a conception of the jury excludes the possibility that a second jury, or a succession of juries, will be in any better position to deal fairly with the defendant than was the first. For if any jury is the embodiment of the community at large, then each one is, and no more than a single jury ought to be necessary.

[247] See Calabresi, *Bakke: Lost Candor,* N.Y. Times, July 6, 1978, p. A-19.

[248] See, *e.g.,* F. CRIM. PROC. R. 23(c). The Supreme Court has implied *in dictum* that if a federal judge, in addition to making a general finding, also makes specific findings of fact and conclusions of law, his general finding is reviewable if the specific findings are determined to be in error. See *Jenkins,* 420 U.S. at 366–67. But *cf. Finch,* 433 U.S. 676. This suggests that federal judges have authority to acquit against the evidence only if they, too, conceal what they are doing in a general verdict.

[249] See NEWMAN, CONVICTION: THE DETERMINATION OF GUILT OR INNOCENCE WITHOUT TRIAL 148–51 (1966), discussing A.L.I., MODEL PENAL CODE § 2.12 (Proposed Official Draft, 1962).

[250] See, *e.g.,* People v. Werner, Criminal No. 58-3636, Cook Cty. Ct., Ill., Dec. 30 1958, noted in 34 NOTRE DAME L. REV. 460 (1959). Regardless of whether they are explicitly so characterized, judicial acquittals against the evidence are apparently a common, though largely unrecognized, phenomenon. See NEWMAN, note 249 *supra,* at 149.

for double jeopardy in both bench and jury trials. If a trial judge has domestic authority to acquit against the evidence, double jeopardy protects a defendant from being retried following a finding of not guilty that can be explained as a product of the judge's legitimate desire to nullify. On the other hand, if a trial judge has no domestic authority to nullify, double jeopardy ought not to insulate a defendant from being retried following a bench acquittal based on "error, irrational behavior, or prejudice on the part of the trial judge,"[251] because there is no coherent reason for doing so.

This rationale helps explain the otherwise contradictory results in *Kepner v. United States*[252] and *Swisher v. Brady*.[253] The defendant in *Kepner* was tried by a judge within a system in the Philippines that appeared to allow for factual review on the record by the appellate court. The trial judge heard evidence and found the defendant not guilty; the government appealed on the record; and the appellate court, making an independent review of the record, set aside the trial judge's findings and entered a judgment of conviction. The defendant in *Swisher*, a juvenile, was tried by a magistrate who was required to hear evidence and make proposed findings to be reviewed on the record by a juvenile judge. The magistrate heard evidence and made proposed findings, recommending that the defendant be adjudged not guilty; the magistrate transmitted the record to the juvenile judge along with his proposed findings and recommended order; the government filed exceptions to the magistrate's proposals; the juvenile judge, making an independent review of the record, rejected the magistrate's proposed findings and recommendation and entered a judgment of conviction.

The systems in *Kepner* and *Swisher*, as described, are strikingly similar. To be sure, the Court tried to distinguish them. *Kepner*, it said, was a case in which the trial magistrate was "authorized" to enter a "judgment" of not guilty which, absent an "appeal" and "appellate" reversal, was "otherwise binding."[254] *Swisher*, in contrast, was a case in which the trial magistrate served as a "master,"[255] making "proposed findings"[256] of not guilty which became binding only if accepted by the juvenile judge. As the dissenters in *Swisher* pointed out, however, this purported distinction is an

---

[251] See note 240 *supra*.

[252] 195 U.S. 100 (1903).

[253] 98 S. Ct. 2699 (1978).

[254] *Id.* at 2707–08 n.15.

[255] *Ibid.*

[256] *Ibid.*

empty "formalism."[257] The finding of not guilty in *Kepner* was no more "final" than in *Swisher*. It was final only if the government did not take exceptions, and, if the government did take exceptions, only if the higher court agreed with the finding on the record. Conversely, the magistrate's findings of not guilty in *Swisher* were as final as the findings in *Kepner*. For all practical purposes, the juvenile judge would enter judgment on the proposed findings, unless the government filed exceptions and, if it did, unless the juvenile court disagreed with the magistrate on the record.[258] In short, *Kepner* and *Swisher* were both systems in which the trial magistrate's findings were final only to the extent that they were not challenged by the government and not reversed on the record by a superior tribunal.

Kepner and *Swisher* are not easily reconciled. Indeed, if the system in *Kepner* operated as previously described, the decisions are inconsistent. In that event, *Swisher* must be understood to overrule *Kepner* and to hold, with Justice Holmes, that double jeopardy permits the State to appeal an erroneous verdict of not guilty, at least in bench trials.[259] Nonetheless, the cases can be reconciled by reinterpreting the scope of the domestic law in *Kepner*. The State law in *Swisher* clearly intended to deny trial magistrates the authority to acquit defendants against the evidence; the magistrates were not competent even to make final findings of fact. In *Kepner*, on the other

---

[257] *Id.* at 2710 (Marshall, J., dissenting).

[258] The record suggested that there were many masters for every single juvenile judge and that a single juvenile judge might receive records and proposed findings in several thousand cases a year. The record also supported the conclusion that given these problems of caseload, juvenile judges reviewed proposed findings of not guilty only in cases in which the State filed exceptions. See *id.* at 2711 n.5.

[259] In *Kepner*, a bench trial, Holmes, joined by Justices White, McKenna, and Brown, would have allowed the appellate court to review the trial judge's finding of not guilty. 195 U.S. at 134–37 (Holmes, J., dissenting). To be sure, the Court continues to deny that it is willing to embrace Holmes's notion of continuing jeopardy. See *Scott*, 98 S. Ct. at 2193 n.6. But if it is true that the domestic law in *Kepner* intended the trial judge's findings of not guilty to be reviewable, there is no rational way to distinguish *Kepner* from *Swisher* or to avoid the conclusion that Holmes has now triumphed. One might try to distinguish *Kepner* on the ground that it was not a constitutional decision at all, but merely a construction of an Act of Congress. See *Green*, 355 U.S. at 196–98, construing *Trono v. United States*, 199 U.S. 521 (1905). But the Court continues to insist that *Kepner* was decided under the Double Jeopardy Clause. *Wilson*, 420 U.S. at 346 n.15. One might also try to distinguish *Swisher* from *Kepner* on the ground that *Swisher* involved the trial of a juvenile, as opposed to an adult, offender. But the Court continues to insist, too, that as far as double jeopardy is concerned, there is no distinction between the rights of juvenile delinquents and adult criminal offenders. See *Breed*, 421 U.S. at 519.

hand, the original system of appellate review had been successively amended, first by Military Order No. 58, then by Act No. 194 of the Philippine Commission and, finally, by an Act of Congress of July 1, 1902, imposing on the Philippines certain accepted practices of American criminal procedure. One can interpret these statutes as a decision by Congress that, as a matter of domestic law, findings of not guilty in the Philippines should have the same degree of finality as such findings by federal judges within the continental United States. Indeed, that may have been what the Court in *Swisher* meant in saying that trial judges in the Philippines possessed, by statute, " 'the great and dangerous power of finally acquitting the most dangerous criminals.' "[260] If so, then the Court in *Kepner* was correct in concluding that double jeopardy barred the appeal, not because the Fifth Amendment required that bench verdicts be final, but because the domestic law chose to make them final.

C. RULINGS BY A JUDGE IN A TRIAL BY JURY

The next question is more complex: To what extent may a defendant, who is being tried by a jury, be retried following a ruling in his favor by the bench?[261] To answer this question, three things must be kept in mind. First, it is important to distinguish an acquittal within the law of judgments from an acquittal for purposes of double jeopardy. Within the law of judgments, an acquittal is a verdict of not guilty returned by the body acting as the trier of fact. For purposes of double jeopardy, an acquittal is a conclusory term used

---

[260] 98 S. Ct. at 2707–08 n.15, quoting from *Kepner*, 195 U.S. at 137 (Brown, J., dissenting). This interpretation of the statutes in *Kepner* is not implausible. It is true that Military Order No. 58 provided for appellate review, and that the Act of Congress of July 1, 1902 intended that some appellate review continue in effect. But it does not follow that Congress intended that there be review of findings of not guilty. Rather, Congress may simply have intended that the existing regime of appellate review continue with respect to appeals by defendants from findings of guilty. If so, then, as a matter of domestic law, Congress intended that the trial judge's findings of not guilty be final. See Note, note 88 *supra*, 65 YALE L.J., at 362. If this interpretation of the Act of Congress of 1902 is correct, it means that the appeal in *Kepner* not only violated the statute, but *a fortiori* violated the Double Jeopardy Clause, because the Double Jeopardy Clause incorporates by reference domestic definitions of finality.

[261] By a "ruling in a defendant's favor" we mean a ruling which, if correct, would terminate all prosecution of the defendant on the ground that the law precludes him from ever being legally convicted of the offense charged. See *Lee*, 432 U.S. at 30: "[T]he critical question is whether the order contemplates an end to all prosecution of the defendant for the offense charged"—that is, whether it is based on the ground "that the defendant simply cannot be convicted of the offense charged."

to describe rulings possessing the quality of finality. The Court has experimented with various definitions of acquittal for double jeopardy purposes, attempting to define the circumstances that justify treating a ruling as final. Our purpose here, too, is to explore those definitions in order to decide what ought to be called an acquittal for double jeopardy purposes. Until we discover how the term ought to be used for constitutional purposes, we shall use it here in its conventional sense to refer to a verdict of not guilty returned by the body acting as the trier of fact.

Second, the constitutional standards in this area are conceded to be in a state of flux. For many years the federal government had no statutory authority to appeal rulings favorable to the defense. It was not until 1970, when full statutory authority was granted, that the Court first began to explore the constitutional restraints that reside in the Double Jeopardy Clause.[262] The Court's initial attempts to define an acquittal were tentative, and the Court has since felt quite free to repudiate them. Thus, the Court recognizes that it has little experience in this area and candidly admits that as its experience grows, it considers itself free to correct its mistakes.[263] If experience shows that the present definition is unsound, it is fair to assume that the Court will correct it.

Third, the effect of a judge's ruling is sometimes compounded by its timing. A judge may rule for a defendant at three different points in time: (a) before the trial has commenced; (b) after trial has commenced but before the case has been submitted to the jury; and (c) after the case has been submitted to the jury. The problem of acquittals is present in all three cases, but the second case presents an additional problem of timing because the effect of the ruling, if reversed, is to deny the defendant an opportunity to have his case completed by the first impaneled jury. In order to isolate the problem of acquittals in its pure form, the timing problems presented by the second case will be reserved for later discussion.

1. *Justice Douglas's Definition.* Justice Douglas, in dissent, ad-

---

[262] The Omnibus Crime Control Act of 1970, 18 U.S.C. § 3731, was designed to allow the government to appeal in any case in which the disposition on appeal would not violate the Double Jeopardy Clause. See *Wilson*, 420 U.S. at 337. But see *Sanabria*, 98 S. Ct. at 2186 (Stevens, J., concurring); *Martin Linen*, 430 U.S. at 576 (Stevens, J., concurring). For the history of the prior statute governing government appeals, see United States v. Sisson, 399 U.S. 267, 307–08 (1970).

[263] See, *e.g.*, *Scott*, 98 S. Ct. at 2191.

vanced the rule in *Serfass v. United States*,[264] that the State may not take an appeal from a ruling that terminates a case in a defendant's favor if the ruling is based on facts from outside the indictment going to the merits of the case. The defendant in *Serfass*, having been indicted for failure to submit to induction into the armed forces, moved to dismiss the indictment on the ground that his local board had failed to give proper consideration to a late-ripened claim of conscientious objection. In support of his motion, he filed an affidavit and a stipulation concerning his claim of conscientious objection. The district court granted the motion based on these factual submissions, and the government appealed, arguing that the district court had applied an erroneous standard of law to the issue of late-ripened claims of conscientious objection. The defendant moved to dismiss the appeal, arguing that the Double Jeopardy Clause prohibited the government from reconsidering the trial judge's ruling of law, even if the ruling were conceded to be erroneous.

Justice Douglas, dissenting, would have ruled for the defendant on the basis of the stated rule, but he refrained from even attempting to relate the rule to the purposes of double jeopardy. His rule is not easy to justify. It is not designed to protect defendants who are legally innocent. If the district judge in *Serfass* truly erred in his construction of the law, he exonerated a defendant who may well have been legally guilty. Nor is the rule designed to prevent a prosecutor from getting a preview of the defendant's case or from correcting errors in his own presentation. If the prosecutor was correct that the defendant had no valid defense as a matter of law, the parties would have no occasion to relitigate the issue at trial. Nor is the rule designed to protect defendants from harassment. The rule would apply even where a prosecutor is merely trying to prevent an erroneous dismissal. More likely, Justice Douglas may have believed that once a defendant is fortunate enough to obtain a ruling which terminates a case in his favor, it would be cruel, somehow, to disappoint him, even if the ruling is determined to be erroneous as a matter of law.

The majority in *Serfass* rejected Douglas's proposed rule, holding

---

[264] 420 U.S. at 394. Some courts would go even farther than Douglas and bar appeals from any pretrial ruling based on facts from outside the record, regardless of whether the ruling goes to the merits of the general issue in the case. See, *e.g.*, United States v. McCreery, 473 F.2d 1381 (7th Cir. 1973) (ruling on the government's destruction of evidence).

that the Double Jeopardy Clause does not prevent the government from taking an appeal from a pretrial ruling in a defendant's favor even if the ruling is based on facts from outside the indictment.[265] The Court evidently concluded that there was no constitutional distinction between the ruling in *Serfass* and a ruling in a defendant's favor based on the indictment alone—a kind of ruling that has long been appealable.[266] More important still is what the Court left unsaid. It implicitly rejected the notion that a defendant is constitutionally entitled by claim of right to rely on an erroneous ruling of law simply because the ruling happens to terminate the case in his favor.

2. *The* Sisson *Definition.* The State may not take an appeal from a ruling of law that terminates a case in a defendant's favor, if the ruling is based on facts adduced at trial. This rule comes from *United States v. Sisson.*[267] It has sometimes been taken to be a constitutional definition of an acquittal for double jeopardy purposes.[268] *Sisson* was functionally equivalent to *Serfass* except that the trial judge first allowed the case to go to the jury and did not rule favorably on the merits of the defense until after the jury had returned a verdict of conviction. The rule in *Sisson* is closely akin to Justice Douglas's, except that it bars an appeal only if the facts supporting the ruling are developed at trial. Yet it is unclear why that should make a difference for double jeopardy purposes.[269] It cannot be based on the desire to protect defendants from the burdens of retrial, because, as in *Sisson* itself, the rule operates even where the jury's original verdict can be reinstated and no further trial is necessary. Nor, for the same reason, can it be based on the desire to prevent prosecutors from having a second opportunity to prove a defendant

---

[265] 420 U.S. at 392–93.

[266] See United States v. Brewster, 408 U.S. 501, 504–05 (1972); Taylor v. United States, 207 U.S. 120, 127 (1907).

[267] 399 U.S. at 288 (1970) (Harlan, J.). Although Harlan wrote only for himself and three others, he was joined by Black with respect to his definition of an acquittal. It is fair to say that a majority of the Court agreed on this "definition." Also, although the foregoing definition does not draw a distinction based on the nature of the ruling, the particular ruling in *Sisson* was based on the merits of the general issue in the case.

[268] See, *e.g.*, United States v. Jaramillo, 510 F.2d 808, 812 (8th Cir. 1975); United States v. Jenkins, 490 F.2d 868, 878 (2d Cir. 1973); aff'd on other grounds, 420 U.S. 358 (1975); Note, *Government Appeals of "Dismissals" in Criminal Cases*, 87 HARV. L. REV. 1822, 1827 (1974).

[269] Note, note 268 *supra*, at 1836.

guilty. At best it is based on the desire to protect defendants, who have already been tried, from the disappointment of having erroneous rulings in their favor set aside.

The Court rejected the *Sisson* rule in *United States v. Wilson*,[270] holding that *Sisson* was never intended to serve as a constitutional definition of an acquittal. The Double Jeopardy Clause, the Court said, does not bar the State from taking an appeal from a ruling in a defendant's favor if, as in *Sisson* and *Wilson*, the consequence of appealing is to reinstate the jury's verdict of guilty. Thus, the Court rejected the suggestion that a defendant's unadorned desire to benefit from an erroneous trial ruling in his favor is sufficient by itself to bar an appeal: "To be sure, the defendant would prefer that the government not be permitted to appeal, or that the judgment of conviction not be entered, but this interest of the defendant is not one that the double jeopardy clause was designed to protect."[271]

3. *The* Jenkins *Definition.* United States v. Jenkins[272] offered a third definition: The state may not take an appeal from an erroneous ruling that terminates a case in a defendant's favor if, as a consequence of the appeal, the defendant is retried. *Jenkins*, a conscientious objection case, was factually identical to *Serfass*, except that the trial judge in *Jenkins* based his ruling on the facts as they appeared at trial. The government appealed, arguing that the district judge had misinterpreted the law governing the local board's obligation to consider late-ripened claims of conscientious objection. The Court assumed that the ruling was based on "an erroneous legal theory," yet held that it could not be appealed. The appeal was barred because, if successful, it would result in "further proceedings . . . devoted to the resolution of factual issues going to the elements of the offense charged."[273]

The puzzling thing about *Jenkins* is the weight it placed on the defendant's desire to avoid retrial. It is true, of course, that if the appeal in *Jenkins* had been successful, the defendant would probably

---

[270] 420 U.S. at 348–51. The particular ruling held appealable in *Wilson* was not based on the merits of the general issue, but, rather, was based on an issue of preindictment delay. In *Jenkins*, 420 U.S. 358, however, a companion to *Wilson*, the Court said in dictum that if it were possible to reinstate a prior and valid finding of guilt, the *Wilson* rule would also apply in a case like *Jenkins* where the ruling was based on an issue relating to the defendant's guilt or innocence. 420 U.S. at 365. See *Scott*, 98 S. Ct. at 2193 n.7.

[271] *Jenkins*, 420 U.S. at 365.

[272] 420 U.S. 358 (1975).	[273] *Id*. at 370.

have been retried. In some cases that may enable a prosecutor to correct deficiencies in his case and obtain a preview of the defendant's evidence. Yet the same thing occurs every time a prosecutor is allowed to retry a defendant who is convicted and whose conviction is reversed on appeal. There society's interest in law enforcement is found to outweigh the defendant's interest in avoiding retrial, even though the prosecutor may himself be responsible for the error that tainted the original proceeding.

Interestingly, the Court has overruled *Jenkins* in *United States v. Scott*.[274] The defendant in *Scott* made a pretrial motion to dismiss the indictment with prejudice because of pretrial delay. The trial judge reserved his ruling in order to determine from the evidence at trial whether the delay had actually prejudiced the defendant. At the close of all the evidence, the judge granted the motion and dismissed the indictment with prejudice. The government appealed, arguing that the trial judge had applied an erroneous legal standard to the issue of preindictment delay. The defendant challenged the appeal on double jeopardy grounds, arguing that if the appeal were successful it would result in his being retried in violation of *Jenkins*. The Court agreed that if *Jenkins* were still good law, the appeal would be barred, but it concluded that *Jenkins* had been wrongly decided:[275]

> If *Jenkins* is a correct statement of the law, the judgment of the Court of Appeals relying on that decision, as it was bound to do, would in all likelihood have to be affirmed. Yet, though our assessment of the history and meaning of the double jeopardy clause in . . . *Jenkins* . . . occurred only three Terms ago, our vastly increased exposure to the various facets of the double jeopardy clause has now convinced us that *Jenkins* was wrongly decided. It placed an unwarrantedly great emphasis on the defendant's right to have his guilt decided by the first jury empanelled to try him.

This suggests that with respect to a defendant's interest in finality—*viz.*, his interest in having the issue of guilt or innocence swiftly

---

[274] 98 S. Ct. 2187 (1978). Technically, it was unnecessary to overrule *Jenkins* because the particular ruling that was held to be nonappealable there was arguably a factual resolution relating to one of the elements of the offense and, thus, the kind of ruling that remains unappealable under *Scott* in the absence of a prior and valid finding of guilt. Nonetheless, because the Court was rejecting the rationale of *Jenkins*, it may have concluded that it should speak of "overruling."

[275] *Id.* at 2191.

resolved once and for all—acquittals may be no different from mistrials or from retrials following conviction, and that a defendant's interest in avoiding the burdens and anxiety of retrial may be entitled to no greater weight following an erroneous ruling in the defendant's favor than following an erroneous mistrial or erroneous judgment of conviction.

4. *The* Scott *Definition.* Scott afforded a fourth definition: The State may not take an appeal from a ruling terminating a case in a defendant's favor based on facts developed at trial, if the ruling relates to the question of the defendant's factual guilt or innocence. In invoking this rule, the Court drew a distinction between the issue of preindictment delay, which, it said, does not have any bearing on a defendant's " 'criminal culpability,' "[276] and a ruling regarding " 'some or all of the factual elements of the crime charged.' "[277] Specifically, the Court said that if a trial judge ruled in a defendant's favor on a question of entrapment or self-defense, the State would be barred by double jeopardy from appealing the ruling, even if the State could show that the ruling was erroneous.

The foregoing rule finds no support in any of the policies of the Double Jeopardy Clause. The distinction between a defense of insanity and a defense of preindictment delay is that one relates to the defendant's criminal culpability, and the other does not. This suggests that the distinction in finality is based on the fear that an appeal from an erroneous ruling of insanity will somehow lead to the conviction of an innocent defendant. It is difficult to understand how a favorable ruling based on an admittedly erroneous standard of insanity can have bearing on a defendant's innocence, or why trying the defendant under a proper legal standard exposes him to any greater risk of false conviction than he faced at his original trial.[278]

---

[276] 98 S. Ct. at 2197, quoting from *id.* at 2201 (Brennan, J., dissenting).

[277] *Ibid.*, quoting from *Martin Linen*, 430 U.S. at 571.

[278] It might be argued that the trial judge would have reached the same conclusion even under a proper legal standard. But if that were an acceptable argument, there need be no appellate review in any case, criminal or civil. Assume for example that a party to a civil case, or the defendant in a criminal case, takes an appeal from a jury verdict entered under an erroneous instruction of law. It could be said, in response to the appeal, that the jury might well have come to the same decision even under a correct legal standard. And, of course, that is true. But because it can never be determined whether that is what actually happened, the proper disposition is to reverse the ruling and submit it to a new trier of fact under a proper legal instruction. See note 229 *supra*. The same thing is also true when a trial judge in a criminal case makes a ruling in a defendant's favor under an erroneous legal standard. He may have reached the same conclusion

Moreover, the *Scott* rule is inconsistent with other decisions. This can be illustrated by example. Suppose a defendant presents evidence at trial on the issue of insanity and asks the judge to rule in his favor upon what is later determined to be an incorrect legal standard of insanity. The judge could rule on the issue before he submits the case to the jury or afterward. If the judge waits until the jury returns a verdict of guilty and then erroneously rules for the defendant, the State will clearly be allowed to appeal the ruling. The appeal is allowed because the effect of the appeal, if successful, is to reinstate the original verdict of guilty.[279] A contrary rule would also be inconsistent with the existing right of the State to petition the Court to review erroneous rulings by appellate courts in favor of defendants.[280]

If, on the other hand, the trial judge were to grant the defendant's motion before the case goes to the jury, the State has a right to appeal for the reasons offered in *United States v. Sanford*.[281] The defendant in *Sanford* was charged with the federal offense of hunting game in a national park without the government's consent. The first trial ended in a hung jury. Before the second trial commenced, the defendant moved to dismiss the indictment, basing his motion on facts developed at the preceding trial which allegedly showed that the government had consented to his hunting in the national park. The judge granted the motion, and the government appealed. The defendant opposed the appeal, arguing that even if the judge applied an erroneous legal standard to the element of consent, his ruling was final.

The Court ruled against Sanford, holding, implicitly, that the government may appeal an erroneous ruling even if the ruling is based on facts developed at trial regarding an element of the offense.

---

even under a valid standard, but since that can never be known, the proper disposition is to reverse the ruling and see what happens under the legal standard that should have been applied in the first place.

[279] *Wilson*, 420 U.S. at 332.

[280] If the trial judge denies the posttrial ruling on insanity, but the court of appeals grants it, the government clearly has the right to petition the Court to reverse the favorable ruling by the court of appeals. See Forman v. United States, 361 U.S. 416, 426 (1960). If the government can take an appeal from a favorable ruling by the court of appeals, it should also be able to take an appeal from a favorable ruling by the district court. There is no reason why the right of appeal should depend on which court enters the favorable order. See *Wilson*, 420 U.S. at 345.

[281] 429 U.S. 14 (1976).

Sanford is indistinguishable from the insanity hypothetical. Both rulings were based on evidence developed at trial, and both represented a "resolution . . . of [one] of the factual elements of the offense charged." In the Court's language, both rulings were based on grounds related to the defendant's "factual guilt or innocence."[282] If the ruling in *Sanford* was appealable for error, so too should be the ruling on insanity.[283] To be sure, if the hypothetical insanity ruling were reversed on appeal, the prosecutor might be able to correct defects in his case and even draw a more favorable jury the second time around. But that was also true in *Sanford*. And it is true whenever a defendant is retried, including when he is retried following a mistrial. Indeed, as between the two cases, it is harder to justify retrial following a mistrial because a defendant's request for a mistrial is often based on error by the government, while in the insanity hypothetical the motion is based on an erroneous legal standard proferred by the defendant to favor his own cause.

5. *The* Burks *Definition*. The *Burks* rule may be said to be that a defendant cannot be retried following an unreversed ruling that the prosecution failed to introduce sufficient evidence to support a conviction.[284] The defendant in *Burks* was tried by a jury and convicted despite his defense of insanity. After filing a motion for a new trial based on the insufficiency of the evidence, which was denied, the defendant appealed, arguing that his conviction should be reversed for insufficiency of the evidence. The court of appeals agreed that the prosecution had failed to sustain its burden of proof on the issue of insanity, but remanded to the district court to determine whether the defendant should be retried or treated as acquitted. The defendant sought further relief from the Court, arguing that the Double Jeopardy Clause barred the State from retrying him follow-

---

[282] *Scott*, 98 S. Ct. at 2197–98.

[283] The only meaningful difference between *Sanford* and the insanity hypothetical is that the insanity ruling occurred at midtrial and caused the trial to terminate before the case was submitted to the first jury impanelled in the case. But that is an issue of timing, not an issue related to whether the ruling is in the nature of an acquittal. As far as finality is concerned, the two rulings are identical. As for the question of timing, the answer depends on the weight ascribed to the fact that the defendant himself requested that the trial terminate before the case was submitted to the jury. See *Scott*, 98 S. Ct. 2196–98. See also text *infra*, at notes 363–65. It is also true, of course, that the second trial had not yet commenced in *Sanford*. But it should be obvious by now that that has no bearing on whether a ruling is the kind of determination in a defendant's favor that ought to be accorded finality. See Note, note 268 *supra*, at 1836.

[284] 98 S. Ct. at 2141.

ing an unreversed ruling in his favor based on insufficiency of the evidence. The Court agreed:[285]

> [A]n appellate reversal [based on insufficiency of the evidence] means that the government's case was so lacking that it should not have even been *submitted* to the jury. Since we necessarily afford absolute finality to a jury's *verdict* of acquittal—no matter how erroneous its decision—it is difficult to conceive how society has any greater interest in retrying a defendant when, on review, it is decided as a matter of law that the jury could not properly have returned a verdict of guilty.

The Court's analogy between a judicial ruling of insufficiency of the evidence and a jury's verdict of not guilty is highly questionable. A jury's verdict of not guilty is final because it may be a decision by the jury to acquit against the evidence. That explains why a jury's verdict possesses absolute finality and cannot be appealed.[286] The same is not true of a judge's ruling based on the legal insufficiency of the evidence. Among other things, he does not purport to be acquitting the defendant against the evidence.[287] Indeed, that is why a judge's ruling can be reviewed on appeal if the effect is to reinstate a valid finding of guilt.[288]

Moreover, it is an overstatement to say that a defendant can never be retried following an unreversed ruling that the prosecution's evidence was insufficient the first time around. It depends on why the prosecution's evidence was insufficient. The evidence was insufficient in *Burks* because, despite the fullest opportunities to do so, the prosecution simply failed to muster sufficient evidence to convict

---

[285] *Id.* at 2150.

[286] Assume, for example, that before a case is submitted to the jury, the trial judge determines that the evidence of guilt is so overwhelming that no reasonable person could doubt the defendant's guilt. If the jury then finds the defendant not guilty, and the government appeals, it would be possible, at least theoretically, to reinstate the judge's prior finding of guilt. Yet it should be obvious that there could never be such an appeal for the same reason that the trial judge himself could never enter a judgment of conviction on his finding, namely, because the Sixth Amendment precludes a court from directing a verdict against a defendant in a criminal case. See note 234 *supra.* In that sense, a jury verdict of not guilty is more final than a trial judge's ruling, because a jury's verdict can never be appealed if the effect of the appeal is either to retry the defendant or to replace the acquittal with a disposition that is adverse to the defendant. See note 306 *infra.*

[287] See note 248 *supra.*

[288] See, *e.g., Wilson,* 420 U.S. 332.

the first time around.[289] In some cases, however, the evidence is insufficient because the trial judge wrongfully excludes a portion of the prosecution's case. Suppose, for example, that instead of simply dismissing the case for preindictment delay, the judge in *Scott* had first excluded all the prosecution's evidence because of the taint of preindictment delay and then acquitted the defendant for insufficiency of the evidence. Surely, if the State can appeal the judge's erroneous dismissal for preindictment delay, it can also appeal his erroneous acquittal for insufficiency of the evidence, because both rulings are based on precisely the same error.[290] Indeed, in *Burks* the Court emphasized that its decision was limited to the situation in which "the prosecution cannot complain of prejudice [because] it has been given one fair opportunity to offer whatever proof it could assemble."[291] Thus, the most that can be said of the rule in *Burks* is that it precludes retrial following an unreversed ruling of insufficient evidence, where the prosecution has no valid excuse for not having presented sufficient evidence the first time around.[292]

6. *An Unlimited Right to Appeal.* A sixth rule may be put thus: The State may take an appeal from any erroneous ruling of law, unless the error is cured by a subsequent verdict of not guilty by the

---

[289]The Court in *Burks* emphasized that the prosecution was not contending that the trial judge had erroneously excluded evidence which, if admitted, would have cured the insufficiency. 98 S. Ct. at 2144 n.4.

[290] See United States v. Scott, 98 S. Ct. at 2203–04 (Brennan, J., dissenting); see also text *infra*, at notes 354–55.

[291] 98 S. Ct. at 2149. See note 289 *supra*.

[292] This narrow reading of *Burks* is confirmed by *Greene*, 98 S. Ct. at 2151. *Greene* was identical to *Burks*, except that the appellate court appeared to find the government's evidence to be insufficient only because it deemed certain items of that evidence to be inadmissible. In remanding for further determination as to that possibility, the Court specifically reserved the question whether a defendant could be retried following an unreversed finding of insufficiency of the evidence if the government's evidence is insufficient only because the appellate court determined that the certain items must be disregarded. 98 S. Ct. at 2155 n.9. This is an important qualification, because, otherwise, every time a defendant is convicted on the basis of improperly admitted evidence, he might be able to demonstrate on appeal that the valid evidence remaining in the record is insufficient to support a finding of guilt beyond a reasonable doubt. If such a showing were sufficient to bar reprosecution, many of the defendants now being retried under the *Ball* doctrine would suddenly obtain immunity from prosecution. In any event, as long as the prosecution has some excuse of that kind to explain why it did not muster sufficient proof the first time around, the Court may feel that society's interest in law enforcement overrides the defendant's interest in finality. *Cf.* Wright, Federal Practice and Procedure: Criminal § 470, at 270–71 (1969). This analysis suggests that *Burks* is limited to cases in which the government has no excuse for not having mustered sufficient evidence the first time around, and where retrial appears to be nothing more than an effort to get a " 'second bite at the apple.' " 98 S. Ct. at 2150.

trier of fact. This position, which is faintly reflected in a brief by the Solicitor General, would permit the State to take an appeal from any uncured ruling in a defendant's favor.[293] But it is obvious that the Court rejects this position, because it continues to hold that certain rulings remain unappealable even though they are conceded to be erroneous.[294]

Thus, five of the proposed definitions of an acquittal are too broad, while the sixth—which would confine an acquittal to a finding of not guilty by the trier of fact—is too narrow. There is still another possibility—one that appears to be consistent both with the policies of double jeopardy and with the Court's principal decisions. It may be stated as follows:

(1) The State may take an appeal from any erroneous ruling in a defendant's favor if the consequence of the appeal is to reinstate a valid finding of guilt.

(2) The State may also appeal any such ruling in order to retry a defendant, unless retrial would be barred under the independent standards governing retrial following a mistrial.

The first part of this test restates the rule in *Wilson-Jenkins*, and it satisfies the policies of double jeopardy for the reason set forth in those opinions.[295] The second part of the test supplements the first by defining the circumstances under which a defendant can be retried following a ruling in his favor. The virtue of the test is that it reconciles the law governing retrial following an acquittal with the law governing retrial following mistrial, dismissal, and conviction. It recognizes that apart from the authority of the trier of fact to acquit against the evidence, the same principle that governs retrial following an erroneous conviction also governs retrial following a ruling in a

---

[293] See *Wilson*, 420 U.S. at 351 n.19.

[294] See, *e.g.*, *Martin Linen*, 430 U.S. 564; *Fong Foo*, 369 U.S. at 141; see also *Wilson*, 420 U.S. at 351–52.

[295] One might argue that the *Scott* definition is intended to be exclusive and, like a jury verdict of not guilty, absolutely final. If so, one could never appeal such a ruling, even if the consequence of the appeal were to reinstate a valid finding of guilt. But the Court in *Scott* made a point of emphasizing that the *Wilson-Jenkins* rationale had not been "explicitly repudiate[d]." 98 S. Ct. at 2193–94 n.7. Thus, if the government can take an appeal from a "resolution" by a court of appeals "of some or all of the factual elements of the offense charged," Forman v. United States, 361 U.S. 416 (1960), it should also be able to take an appeal from such a "resolution" by the district court, because the level or sequence in which the resolution is made ought to have no bearing on its appealability. See *Wilson*, 420 U.S. at 345. An exception might exist where the trial judge's ruling was based on the kind of assessment of fact that cannot be reviewed by an appellate court on a cold record. See text *infra*, at notes 309–12.

defendant's favor. The standard in each case is the same: One must balance the defendant's interest in finality against society's interest in reprosecution in light of the reasons why the first proceeding failed to result in a valid conviction.

It may be thought that the foregoing rule gives the defendant too little protection against reprosecution, but it gives him precisely as much protection as he now enjoys following a mistrial, dismissal, or erroneous conviction. *Fong Foo v. United States*,[296] for example, is an acquittal case that would have been decided the same way if treated as a mistrial. The defendants in *Fong Foo* were charged with a complicated conspiracy to defraud the government. The trial promised to be "long and complicated." After three preliminary witnesses had testified for the government, and before the prosecution had called its "many" principal witnesses, the judge abruptly concluded that the prosecutor had engaged in improper conduct and that his witnesses were not credible. Without consulting with the defendant or allowing the case to be heard and tried by the jury, the judge directed a verdict of acquittal. The government sought a writ of mandamus to set aside the acquittal and set the case for retrial, but the Court denied mandamus on the ground that retrying the defendant would violate the principles of double jeopardy.

Fong Foo is usually treated as an instance of an acquittal, but the result would have been the same if it had been treated as a mistrial. The defendant was not contending that the trial judge had acquitted him against the evidence, or that the judge's ruling determined that he was actually innocent, or that he was entitled to rely on the erroneous ruling simply because it was favorable to his cause. Rather, his principal grievance was the same as the defendant's in *Downum*, namely, that in the midst of a long and complicated trial, the trial judge had abridged his interest in getting the trial over with once and for all by aborting the proceeding without his consent. Thus, retrial was barred, not because the defendant had in any sense been acquitted, but because the trial judge had acted "irrationally [and] irresponsibly"[297] by denying the defendant his valued right to have his trial completed by the first jury impaneled in the case.

To be sure, if the defendant in *Fong Foo* had been asked whether he wanted the case to terminate with a final acquittal in his favor, he

---

[296] 396 U.S. 141 (1962).

[297] *Washington*, 98 S. Ct. at 835. See note 83 *supra*.

would have said yes. But that is true of the mistrial and dismissal cases as well. If any defendant were asked whether he wanted a dismissal with prejudice or a mistrial with prejudice he, too, would say yes. But to say he wants a mistrial with prejudice is not to say he wants one without prejudice. The same is true of *Fong Foo*. If the defendant there had been told that the acquittal was without prejudice, or that it was up to the appellate courts to decide whether he could be retried, he might well have said that he preferred to continue with the trial. He was never given that opportunity because the trial judge aborted the proceeding without obtaining agreement from the defendant that he would be retried.

The same principle of finality also explains *Burks v. United States*.[298] The prosecution there sought permission to retry the defendant after having had one full, fair, and complete opportunity to prove him guilty beyond a reasonable doubt. The prosecutor could not attribute the "failure of proof"[299] to an erroneous exclusion or admission of evidence, or to an erroneous instruction by the trial judge, or to fraud by the defendant. One must infer, therefore, that he simply wanted "a second bite at the apple,"[300] either to find a more favorable jury, or to correct inexcusable deficiencies in his case. In that event, however, retrial would be barred even in the event of a mistrial. A defendant cannot be retried following a mistrial or following an erroneous conviction if it can be shown that the defect in the original proceeding was deliberately "manipulated" in order to give the prosecutor a second chance to convict.[301] The defendant in *Burks* was entitled to immunity from reprosecution for the same reason. If his interest in finality means anything, it means that the government cannot subject a defendant to the "strain and agony"[302] of a second trial simply in order to "afford the prosecution another opportunity to supply evidence which it failed to muster in the first proceeding."[303]

---

[298] 98 S. Ct. 2141 (1978).

[299] *Id.* at 2149.

[300] *Id.* at 2150.

[301] See note 115 *supra*.

[302] *Scott*, 98 S. Ct. at 2201 (Brennan, J., dissenting).

[303] *Burks*, 98 S. Ct. at 2147. See *Benton*, 395 U.S. at 810 (Harlan, J., dissenting); Hoag v. New Jersey, 356 U.S. 464, 474–75 (Warren, C.J., dissenting). *Burks* is to be distinguished from *Ball*, 163 U.S. 662, where the prosecution retried a defendant whose conviction had been reversed on appeal. There was no showing in *Ball* that the error that caused the conviction to be reversed was deliberately introduced in order to give the prosecutor a "second bite at the apple." Given the difficulty of affording a defendant a completely error-free trial the first time around, the State is "excused" for committing

This also explains the last of the acquittal cases, *United States v. Martin Linen Supply Co.*[304] The case was tried to a jury which became "hopelessly deadlocked" on the question of guilt or innocence. After discharging the jury, the judge entered a judgment of acquittal holding that the federal government had failed to introduce sufficient evidence to support a verdict of guilty. The government appealed, arguing that the acquittal should be reversed and the defendant retried. The government based its appeal on a federal statute that authorized appeals "except . . . where the double jeopardy clause of the United States Constitution prohibits further prosecution."[305] The Court held that the United States Court of Appeals had no statutory jurisdiction to entertain the appeal, because retrying the defendant would violate double jeopardy.

Martin Linen becomes easy to understand when one remembers that the double jeopardy question in the case was not whether the government could take an appeal, but whether it could retry the defendant following an appeal.[306] The answer to the latter question

---

the error and allowed to assert its interest in law enforcement over the defendant's interest in finality. See *Tateo*, 377 U.S. at 466. In *Burks*, on the other hand, the State had no such excuse for retrying the defendant, except its desire to have a "second bite at the apple." See note 126 *supra*.

[304] 430 U.S. 564 (1977). This still leaves two cases to be explained: *Sanabria*, 98 S. Ct. at 2170, and *Finch*, 433 U.S. at 676. For a discussion of *Sanabria*, see text *infra*, at notes 350–67. *Finch* was a bench trial on agreed-upon facts. The trial judge, applying what the government believed to be an incorrect legal standard, found the defendant not guilty on the stipulated facts. The Court held that the government could not appeal the finding, because, if successful, the appeal would result in further proceedings, even though the proceedings might consist of nothing more than the entry of a judgment of conviction by the appellate court applying the proper legal standard on the stipulated facts. *Finch* appears to have since been overruled by *Swisher* v. *Brady* where the Court repudiated the notion that double jeopardy bars a review of a factual record even where it is unnecessary to receive any additional evidence. 98 S. Ct. at 2708.

[305] 430 U.S. at 567, quoting from 18 U.S.C. § 3731.

[306] It is important to distinguish the appeal itself from the disposition following the appeal. The Double Jeopardy Clause is no bar whatever to an appeal provided that the appeal does not result in a retrial or in some adverse consequence to the defendant. Thus, to take the simple case, the Double Jeopardy Clause does not bar the State from taking an appeal from a jury verdict of not guilty in order to obtain a declaratory judgment from the appellate court that the trial judge's rulings were erroneous provided that the appeal does not result in adverse consequences to the defendant. See State v. Gray, 71 Okla. Crim. 309 (1941); see also Comment, *What Constitutes Double Jeopardy?*, 38 J. CRIM. L.C. & P.S. 379, 388 n.50 (1947). In *Martin Linen*, therefore, the double jeopardy question was not simply whether the State could take an appeal, but whether it could retry the defendant following the appeal. The statute, 18 U.S.C. § 3731, prohibits a government appeal in any case in which the disposition would violate double jeopardy. In that respect, the State's statutory right to appeal depends entirely on its constitutional authority to "retry" the defendant following appeal. See note 305 *supra*.

was the same as in *Burks:* The state may not subject a defendant to a second trial after the first trial results in a "failure of proof,"[307] unless it can show some good reason for the failure. In *Martin Linen,* as in *Burks,* the government had no excuse for its failure to mount a successful case the first time around. It simply failed to mount a successful case when it had the chance and, having failed, was not entitled to a "second bite at the apple."

Had the government been allowed to appeal the trial judge's ruling in *Martin Linen,* it might have been able to show that the judge was wrong and that the evidence was sufficient to support a verdict of guilty. Obviously, in that event, retrial would not have been barred, any more than retrial is barred following a hung jury.[308] Thus, the second and more difficult question in *Martin Linen* is, Why was the government not allowed to show that the trial judge's ruling was erroneous? The answer, we think, has nothing to do with law of double jeopardy but with the nature of the trial judge's determination that the government's evidence was insufficient to support a verdict of guilt beyond a reasonable doubt.

When a trial judge finds the government's evidence to be insufficient, he may be ruling as a matter of law that the evidence and inferences therefrom, viewed in the light most favorable to the government, would not support a finding of guilt beyond a reasonable doubt. To that extent, his ruling is freely reviewable on appeal because, by hypothesis, it does not depend on an assessment of credibility or weight of the evidence.[309] On the other hand, he may be ruling as a matter of fact that the government's witnesses, when viewed by him on the witness stand, were not sufficiently credible to sustain a

[307] *Burks,* 98 S. Ct. at 2149.

[308] It is well understood that a defendant can be retried following a hung jury. United States v. Perez, 9 Wheat. 579 (1824). It can be argued, based on *Burks,* that the State should never be allowed to retry a defendant following a hung jury because to do so would give the State a "second bite at the apple" after having tried and failed to muster a sufficient case the first time around. The hung jury can be distinguished from the situation in *Burks.* In *Burks* there was a traditional finding that the government's evidence is insufficient, while in a hung jury situation, the jury is discharged before it can say whether or not the evidence is insufficient. A contrary rule for hung juries would have adverse effects, because judges, knowing that dismissal would confer immunity on the defendant, would be reluctant to discharge juries and might require that they continue to sit beyond the point in which their deliberations are rational. Thus, the rule—that a defendant can be retried following a hung jury—is based in part on the desire to protect the jury from undue "personal suffering" and to prevent the deliberation process from becoming coercive. See *Washington,* 98 S. Ct. at 832 & esp. n.27.

[309] WRIGHT, note 292 *supra,* at §§ 467, 469.

verdict of guilt. To that extent, his ruling is not reviewable on appeal because, like a motion for a new trial for insufficiency of the evidence in a civil case,[310] the ruling depends on observations that an appellate court is incompetent to review on a cold record.

The papers in *Martin Linen* do not reveal which kind of ruling the judge was making. It is possible to conclude, however, that he was making a factual finding of the latter kind, because he emphasized that the case was "the weakest I've ever seen."[311] If so, it may explain why the Court treated the finding as final. The Court may well have concluded that when a federal judge rules on sufficiency of the evidence in a criminal case, he has authority to make some assessment of the credibility of the government's witnesses. If he does, and if he finds the government's evidence insufficient, his ruling will not be subject to further review, not because the Double Jeopardy Clause would bar an appeal, but because the appellate court is simply not in a position, on a cold record, to set aside what is essentially a factual assessment of the government's case.[312]

This explanation of *Martin Linen* has several virtues. For one, it is the only explanation that reconciles *Martin Linen* with the other controlling decisions in the area of double jeopardy.[313] For another, it helps explain some puzzling language in the Court's opinion in *Scott*. In trying to identify the kinds of rulings by a trial judge that are not appealable, the Court in *Scott* distinguished between rulings of "law," and the "resolution" of "issues of fact,"[314] noting that the latter are unappealable because of their bearing on the defendant's "factual guilt or innocence."[315] This distinction is hard to under-

---

[310] WRIGHT & MILLER, FEDERAL PRACTICE AND PROCEDURE: CIVIL § 2819 (1973).

[311] 430 U.S. at 567 n.3.

[312] Conventional wisdom suggests that a trial judge ought not to make a factual assessment of this kind but should view the evidence and inferences in the light most favorable to the government and make a ruling of law of the kind that is reviewable to the same degree by the court of appeals. See *Burks*, 98 S. Ct. at 2150; WRIGHT, note 292 *supra*, § 467 at 259. But see United States v. Melillo, 275 F. Supp. 314, 320 (E.D.N.Y. 1967).

[313] Otherwise *Martin Linen* is inconsistent with *Sanford*, note 281 *supra*. In both cases the judge made his ruling after the original trial had ended and before the next trial was to commence. In both cases the ruling was a "resolution . . . of [one] of the factual elements of the offense charged." 430 U.S. at 571. Yet in *Sanford* the Court held the ruling to be appealable for error. The only difference between the two cases is that in *Martin Linen* the ruling came two months after the original trial ended, while in *Sanford* the ruling came four months afterward. Surely that is a distinction of no constitutional magnitude.

[314] 98 S. Ct. at 2197 n.9.   [315] *Id*. at 2194.

stand because, in a sense, every ruling by a trial judge is a combination of law and fact. Every ruling is a combination of the application of a legal standard to the circumstances of the case.[316] And if the legal standard is erroneous, the resulting ruling, too, is erroneous and is appropriate for review.[317] On the other hand, by "factual" the Court may mean that the ruling is based, in part, on the trial judge's assessment of the credibility or weight of the evidence. In that event, the ruling is not amenable to review because there is nothing for the appellate court to do. That explains why an appeal may not be taken from a trial court's "conclusion that the government [has] not produced sufficient evidence to establish the guilt of the defendant."[318] If the "conclusion" is based on an erroneous legal standard, it can be reviewed.[319] If it is based on the application of a correct legal standard to a factual assessment of credibility, it is not reviewable, certainly where the jury deadlock, too, suggests questions as to the sufficiency of the evidence.[320]

---

[316] *Id.* at 2205 (Brennan, J., dissenting).

[317] See note 278, *supra.*

[318] 98 S. Ct. at 2195.

[319] In *Burks*, 98 S. Ct. 2141 (1978), for example, the court of appeals held the evidence to be insufficient on the ground that the government's witnesses had failed to address certain "precise questions" which the court of appeals required to be addressed in insanity cases. Yet, because the Court explicitly refrained from passing on that part of the case, it can be argued that the court of appeals applied an erroneous standard of sufficiency. See 98 S. Ct. at 2144. Accordingly, if the trial court had found the evidence to be insufficient under that standard, and the Court subsequently determined the standard to be erroneous, it would be appropriate for the Court to review the trial court's finding of insufficiency, because the finding would be based not entirely on a "factual" assessment of the evidence but on the application of an erroneous legal standard to the evidence. That is to be distinguished from *Martin Linen*, where in assessing the sufficiency of the evidence, the trial court applied what appeared to be the correct legal standard of sufficiency.

[320] It remains to be seen whether the *Martin Linen* rule, that no appeal may be taken by the government from a "factual" ruling on insufficiency of the evidence, is limited to cases like *Martin Linen* where the ruling followed a deadlocked jury, or whether it also extends to cases in which the trial judge's ruling follows a verdict of guilty by the jury. *Scott* suggests that all erroneous rulings by a trial judge can be appealed if the only consequence is to reinstate a valid finding of conviction, see 98 S. Ct. at 2193–94 n.7, but it is unclear whether *Scott* meant to include factual rulings that are otherwise unappealable. One could urge that no such ruling is appealable, because the appellate court is simply not in a position to review factual assessments by the trial judge. Alternatively, one could argue that the trial judge's factual assessments can be disregarded in any case in which twelve jurors, having possessed the same opportunity as the trial judge to view demeanor and credibility, disagree with him and find the defendant guilty beyond a reasonable doubt.

D. SUMMARY

Very few rulings by a trial judge, if any, possess the same degree of finality as a jury verdict of not guilty. An acquittal by a jury possesses "absolute finality" and, once entered, cannot be reviewed for any purpose if the consequence is to alter its effect.[321] The same is not true of rulings by the bench that terminate a case in a defendant's favor. Most such rulings can be reviewed even if a consequence is to order that the defendant be retried.

This difference in finality tends to distort the trial process. If, for example, a trial judge wishes to rule in a defendant's favor and yet shield his ruling from review, the system invites him to make his ruling before the case goes to the jury in the hope that the jury will acquit and thereby end the matter. As a result, the judge not only causes an acquittal that might not otherwise occur, but succeeds in guaranteeing that his ruling will never be reviewed. Alternatively, if a conscientious trial judge wishes to preserve an avenue of appeal from his rulings, the system forces him to withhold his rulings until after the jury returns a verdict of guilty. As a result, the judge is not only forced to refrain from entering the ruling that he genuinely believes to be appropriate at the time, but he may cause a defendant to be convicted who would otherwise be acquitted the first time around.[322] These distortions are unfortunate, but they are the inevitable price that must be paid for a system that forecloses interlocutory appeal and that accords "absolute finality"[323] to a jury verdict of not guilty.

IV. APPLICATION OF THE THEORY: TWO ILLUSTRATIONS

The measure of a theory is its usefulness in explaining the data—in this case the decisions of the Supreme Court. The essence of the theory advanced here is that the Double Jeopardy Clause protects three distinct values, each of which is independent of the others and possesses its own respective weight. The theory is useful, we believe, in resolving double jeopardy problems generally, but it is particularly useful in resolving complex cases. We propose to test

---

[321] See note 306 *supra*.

[322] See, *e.g.*, Newman v. State, 148 Tex. Crim. 645, 651–52 (1945), discussed in United States v. Melillo, 275 F. Supp. 314, 319 (E.D.N.Y. 1967).

[323] *Burks*, 98 S. Ct. at 2150.

the theory by applying it to two of the more difficult of the Court's recent double jeopardy cases. The success of the theory may be measured by the degree to which it affords a coherent basis for resolution of these cases.

A. FINALITY AND DOUBLE PUNISHMENT: BROWN V. OHIO

The defendant in *Brown*[324] stole an automobile from East Cleveland, Ohio, on November 29, and was apprehended driving the automobile in Wickliffe, Ohio, on December 8. He was first prosecuted in Wickliffe for the misdemeanor of "joyriding" and given a sentence of thirty days in jail. After serving his sentence, he was returned to East Cleveland where he was convicted of auto theft and given a six-month suspended sentence without credit for the prior thirty days in jail. He challenged his conviction, arguing that the prosecution for auto theft was barred by the Double Jeopardy Clause.

The Supreme Court reversed the conviction for auto theft. The Court proceeded in three steps. First it determined that because joyriding was a lesser-included offense within auto theft, the two statutory offenses were the "same" for purposes of the prohibition against double punishment.[325] It then determined that the offense of joyriding on December 8 and the earlier offense of auto theft on November 29 were also parts of the same offense, noting that "the double jeopardy clause is not such a fragile guarantee that prosecutors can avoid its limitations by the simple expedient of dividing a single crime into a series of temporal or spatial units."[326] Finally, having thus determined that the defendant's actions constituted a single offense for purposes of punishment, the Court concluded that double jeopardy not only barred cumulative sentences, but also barred successive prosecutions, even though the second prosecution in *Brown* was for the greater offense: "Whatever the sequence [of

---

[324] 432 U.S. 161 (1977).

[325] Joyriding is defined as the taking of an automobile without the owner's consent; auto theft is defined as joyriding plus the additional element of intent permanently to deprive the owner of possession. The Court invoked the Blockburger test to determine whether the two offenses were the same for purposes of punishment, concluding that they were the same because, in Blockburger terms, joyriding did not require proof of any fact that was not also required to prove auto theft. For discussion of whether Blockburger should be used as an absolute test or whether it should be used as a presumptive test to determine legislative intent, see text *supra*, at notes 185–92.

[326] 432 U.S. at 169.

prosecution] may be, the Fifth Amendment forbids successive prosecution and cumulative punishment for a greater and lesser included offense."[327]

The Court reached the right decision in *Brown* for the wrong reasons. The Court was wrong to suggest that the two statutory offenses were necessarily the same for purposes of double punishment simply because one was a lesser-included offense within the other. Indeed, the Court's conclusion does not even follow from its premise. The Court recognized as a starting premise that with regard to multiple punishment, "the role of the constitutional guarantee is limited to assuring that the [sentencing] court does not exceed its legislative authorization by imposing multiple punishments for the same offense."[328] Yet nothing prevents a legislature from specifically authorizing the imposition of multiple sentences for both the greater- and lesser-included offense.

Assume, for example, that Ohio wished to punish auto theft at twice the level of joyriding. It could achieve that result in either one of two ways. Having defined the two offenses, it could give auto theft twice the maximum sentence for joyriding and direct that multiple sentences not to be imposed. Or, alternatively, it could provide the same maximum sentence for each offense and direct that the sentence for auto theft be calculated by adding the two sentences together. Surely, if the State has authority to do the former, it also has authority to do the latter.[329] Consequently, since the legislature in *Brown* may have intended that multiple sentences be imposed, the fact that one is a lesser-included offense within the other does not necessarily resolve the issue of double punishment.

Even if the Ohio legislature intended to bar multiple punishment, the Court was wrong to conclude that "[i]f two offenses are the same . . . for purposes of barring consecutive sentences at a single trial, they necessarily will be the same for purposes of barring successive prosecutions."[330] Again, the Court's conclusion does not follow from its premise. The Court assumed that successive prosecu-

---

[327] *Ibid.*

[328] *Id.* at 165.

[329] See Note, note 88 *supra*, 65 YALE L.J. at 364; see also text *supra*, at notes 154–58. Indeed, this conclusion follows from the Court's own recognition that "[t]he legislature remains free under the double jeopardy clause to define crimes and fix punishments." *Brown*, 432 U.S. at 165.

[330] 432 U.S. at 166.

tions are barred where their only purpose is to impose multiple punishment in violation of the Double Jeopardy Clause.[331] But that was not the case in *Brown*. The defendant there was not being prosecuted for the lesser offense after having been fully and completely punished for the greater.[332] He was being prosecuted for the greater offense of auto theft after having been only partially punished for the lesser-included portion of joyriding. Consequently, even assuming that the legislature intended the two offenses to merge for purposes of punishment, the proper disposition (even according to the Court's premise) was not to bar the second prosecution but to allow the second prosecution to proceed with directions that the defendant be given credit on the greater offense for the sentence already served on the lesser.

Nonetheless, although the Court's reasoning was flawed, the result in *Brown* is consistent with the values underlying the Double Jeopardy Clause. The case implicated two separate values: (1) the prohibition against double punishment; and (2) the defendant's interest in finality. When approached in those terms, the decision becomes coherent and even persuasive.

The case raised two issues for double punishment. The first question was whether the State could impose multiple punishments under the two statutes solely for the defendant's act of theft on November 29 and without regard to the defendant's continued use of the auto thereafter. If the State could, then it could also impose multiple punishments for the defendant's extended conduct over the nine-day period because, at the very least, the conduct was a con-

---

[331] Where the judge is forbidden to impose cumulative punishment for two crimes at the end of a single proceeding, the prosecutor is forbidden to strive for the same result in successive proceedings." *Id.* at 166. But there is no logical connection between the prohibition on multiple punishment and the prohibition on multiple trials. If the only constitutional interest at stake is the prohibition on double punishment, it can be fully vindicated at the end of the second trial by barring the imposition of excessive punishment. If the Double Jeopardy Clause also prohibits the second prosecution from even taking place, it must be protecting some interest other than the prohibition on double punishment. The real interest being protected is the defendant's interest in finality. By hypothesis, the State has no legitimate interest whatsoever in subjecting the defendant to the second prosecution. See note 126 *supra*.

[332] *Brown* is to be distinguished in that respect from *Harris*, 433 U.S. 682, where the defendant was first tried and fully punished for the greater offense of felony murder and only then prosecuted for the lesser-included offense of robbery with a firearm. In *Harris*, once it was concluded that the legislature did not intend to impose multiple sentences for the two offenses, it was perfectly appropriate to bar the second prosecution because its only purpose was to seek a penalty that was prohibited by the Double Jeopardy Clause. See note 331 *supra*.

tinuation of his action on November 29. The answer, of course, depends on what the legislature intended. Thus, if the legislature had made it perfectly clear that it intended that the sentence for auto theft be calculated by adding the two sentences together, double jeopardy would be no bar. Since, however, the legislative intent was unclear, and since it is unusual for a legislature to intend multiple punishments for a greater- and lesser-included offense, double jeopardy required that doubts be resolved in favor of lenity in order to avoid imposing multiple punishments where domestic law may have intended only one. In short, while the Court in *Brown* was correct to conclude that the two offenses merged for purposes of punishment, it was not because double jeopardy required that they merge, but because double jeopardy presumed then to merge, absent explicit legislative intent to the contrary.[333]

The second question of double punishment in *Brown* involved defining the unit of prosecution for joyriding. Thus, assuming that joyriding could not be punished separately from auto theft for the theft on November 29, the question was whether the defendant committed a separate offense of joyriding by continuing to use the automobile until December 6. Here the Court was closer to the mark. It recognized that the answer depended on whether the legislature intended to punish joyriding as a separate offense "for each day in which a motor vehicle is operated without the owner's consent."[334] For surely the legislature had the power to do so if it so desired.[335] But, again, since legislative intent was uncertain, and since the two acts of joyriding followed so closely in time, it was constitutionally appropriate to presume that the legislature intended that they be punished as a single unit thereby avoiding the risk of double punishment.

It is true, of course, that the Ohio court below had defined the

---

[333] Indeed, it is puzzling that Mr. Justice Powell would suggest in *Brown* that the Blockburger Rule requires merger, because in *Iannelli*, 420 U.S. at 785 n.17, he recognized the Blockburger Rule to be a presumption for "identifying congressional intent." See text *supra*, at notes 176–96.

[334] 432 U.S. at 169 n.8.

[335] The obvious purpose of such a statute would be to give a defendant an incentive to return the auto to its rightful owner by punishing him for each day he continued operating the auto after the initial theft. See 432 U.S. at 171–72 (Blackmun, J., dissenting). If that is what the legislature intended, there is nothing in the Double Jeopardy Clause to prohibit it. See *Sanabria*, 98 S. Ct. at 2181: "[F]ew, if any, limitations are imposed by the double jeopardy clause on the legislative power to define offenses."

unit of prosecution differently, holding that the defendant had not "shown"[336] that his conduct constituted a single unit of joyriding under Ohio law. But that determination was not binding on the Court. For one thing, instead of putting the burden on the prosecution to show that State law intended multiple units of prosecution, the lower court altered the constitutional presumption by requiring the defendant to show that only a single unit was intended. Furthermore, even if the lower court had stated the presumption correctly, the Court is not bound by its application of the presumption. The question, whether domestic law is sufficiently explicit to override the constitutional presumption in favor of single punishment, is a federal question to be decided and reviewed independently by the federal courts.

The upshot is that the Double Jeopardy Clause prohibited the State from giving the defendant in *Brown* multiple sentences for auto theft on November 29 and joyriding on December 6. But that does not explain why the State was completely barred from prosecuting the defendant for auto theft. At most it suggests that *Brown* should have been decided in the same way as *Jeffers*.

Jeffers, like *Brown*, was prosecuted and punished on a greater offense after having been convicted and punished on a lesser-included offense, the only difference being that Jeffers requested separate trials for the two offenses. Given Jeffers's request for separate trials, the plurality treated the case as if Jeffers had been simultaneously convicted and punished on both offenses and held that, because the legislature did not intend multiple punishment, Jeffers was constitutionally entitled to credit on the greater offense for the sentence he had already received for the lesser. As far as double punishment is concerned, the same analysis governs in *Brown*. Since double punishment is concerned only with the calculation of punishment and not with the sequence in which it is imposed, the State in *Brown* should have been allowed to prosecute the defendant for auto theft provided that it gave him credit for the sentence he had already served for the offense of joyriding.

It follows, therefore, that in barring prosecution for auto theft altogether, the Court in *Brown* was protecting the defendant from something besides double punishment. The obvious candidate is the

---

[336] 432 U.S. at 164.

defendant's interest in " 'finality.' "[337] The successive prosecution subjected the defendant in *Brown* to precisely the same kind of "anxiety and insecurity"[338] a defendant suffers who is retried following a mistrial. It exposed him to the "strain and agony"[339] of facing the "risk of conviction"[340] a second time. Moreover, by splitting the trials, the State was in a position to manipulate the proceedings for its own "tactical advantage."[341] It could use the first prosecution for joyriding as a dry run for the second and more serious prosecution for auto theft, thereby testing for weaknesses in its own case and obtaining a preview of the defendant's evidence. It could also use the second prosecution as a device for shopping for a more severe sentence in the event it was dissatisfied with the sentence the defendant received for joyriding.[342]

To be sure, we have previously concluded that a defendant's interest in finality is relatively soft and can be overridden by a strong and justifiable societal interest to the contrary.[343] But the State had no such interest in *Brown*. The State could not show that the events necessary for prosecution for auto theft had not occurred by the time it prosecuted the defendant for joyriding or that the facts supporting the greater offense were not known or easily discoverable.[344] Nor, since the overlap in evidence between a greater- and a lesser-included offense is practically complete, could the State show any logistical reason for wanting to prosecute the two offenses separately. The only plausible explanation was the State's desire to vest the prosecutors in Wickliffe and East Cleveland with total autonomy regarding prosecution. That interest was not deemed to be sufficient to over-

---

[337] 432 U.S. at 165, quoting from *Jorn*, 400 U.S. at 479 (Harlan, J.).

[338] See note 42 *supra*.

[339] See note 302 *supra*.

[340] See note 45 *supra*.

[341] See note 72 *supra*.

[342] For an example of such abuse, *see* Ciucci v. Illinois, 356 U.S. 571 (1958) (upheld under the Due Process Clause before the Double Jeopardy Clause was held applicable to the States). Presumably *Ciucci* would be decided differently today under the Double Jeopardy Clause. See Comment, note 28 *supra*, at 278.

[343] See text *supra*, at notes 100–28.

[344] 432 U.S. at 169 n.7. In either of these events, the State may be excused from complying with what is otherwise a rule of compulsory joinder. See *Jeffers*, 432 U.S. at 151–52; *Ashe*, 397 U.S. at 453 n.7 (Brennan, J., concurring).

ride a defendant's interest in finality.[345] Accordingly, *Brown* stands for the proposition that double jeopardy not only protects against multiple punishment but also against multiple prosecutions, absent, at least, a substantial State interest in subjecting a defendant to the risks of conviction more than once.[346]

Interestingly, the real significance of *Brown* was overlooked by those who had the greatest interest in noticing it.[347] For the Court has now squarely held that the Double Jeopardy Clause is a constitutional rule of compulsory joinder, at least with respect to greater- and lesser-included offenses for which there is substantial overlap in evidence. It is the first step toward what Mr. Justice Brennan has

---

[345] The Court has held that a State's interest in vesting its State prosecutors with sovereign authority to prosecute without regard to whether the defendant has already been prosecuted for the same offense by a municipal prosecutor is not sufficient to override the defendant's interest in finality. Waller v. Florida, 397 U.S. 387 (1970). *Waller* is to be distinguished from the relationship between other levels of government, where the interest in vesting a prosecutor with sovereign authority to prosecute is sufficient to override the defendant's interest in finality. See *Wheeler*, 98 S. Ct. 1079; Abbate v. United States, 359 U.S. 187 (1959). The cited cases involved retrial following conviction and involved only the defendant's interest in finality. It cannot be assumed that because the dual sovereignty interest is sufficient to override a defendant's interest in finality, that it is also sufficient to override his other double jeopardy interests. On the contrary, while a State may be able to retry a defendant who has been prosecuted and convicted by the federal government, it does not follow that it has the authority to retry a defendant who has been acquitted by the federal government because retrial following acquittal impinges not only upon the defendant's interest in finality but also upon his interest in being acquitted against the evidence. But *cf.* Bartkus v. Illinois, 359 U.S. 121 (1959) (Due Process Clause, rather than the Double Jeopardy Clause, permits a State to retry a defendant who has been acquitted by the federal government). Similarly, the fact that the interest in dual sovereignty justifies successive prosecutions does not mean that it justifies double punishment. The inquiry in that case is whether—in light of the presumption in favor of lenity—the legislature in the second proceeding can be said to have intended that its statutory penalty be added on to whatever sentence a defendant may have already received for his conduct from other sovereignties, or whether it intended its penalty to be exclusive.

[346] See *Jeffers*, 432 U.S. at 151 n.18 (plurality opinion); *Abney* 431 U.S. at 661. Contrary to what the Court says in *Brown*, however, there is no reason to believe that the same definition of offenses applies in both cases, or that offenses which are the same for purposes of the rule against multiple punishment are necessarily the same for purposes of the rule against multiple prosecution. 432 U.S. at 166. Two offenses may be sufficiently related in terms of purpose that the legislature intends them to merge for purposes of punishment, and yet they may be sufficiently distinct in terms of proof that the State should not be required to join them in a single prosecution. Conversely, two offenses may be sufficiently related in terms of proof to require that they be joined, and yet, as in *Iannelli*, the legislature may nonetheless intend that they be punished consecutively.

[347] See 432 U.S. at 170 (Brennan, J., concurring) (advocating that the Court adopt a constitutional rule of compulsory joinder while failing to recognize that the Court's opinion in *Brown* does precisely that); Note, *Double Jeopardy: Multiple Prosecutions Arising from the Same Transaction*, 15 AMER. CRIM. L. REV. 259, 287–88 (1978) (same).

long advocated as the "same transaction" test of compulsory joinder.[348] He takes the position that double jeopardy requires the State, wherever feasible, to join in the initial prosecution all offenses that are factually related to one another. His argument apparently rests on the assumption that where the overlap in evidence is substantial, the State has no sufficient interest in separate trials that would justify the burden that successive prosecution imposes on a defendant's interest in finality. The Court in *Brown* did not explain its decision in those terms, nor did it go as far as Mr. Justice Brennan would go.[349] But the decision cannot be rationally explained on any other terms. If the case was correctly decided, it was because the Court implicitly held that the Double Jeopardy Clause requires the State to join in a single prosecution all offenses that share the same factual core in common, at least where the common factual core is as great as that between joyriding and auto theft.

B. FINALITY AND ACQUITTALS: SANABRIA V. UNITED STATES

The defendant in *Sanabria*[350] was indicted, along with several others, for having conducted an "illegal gambling business" consisting of horsebetting and numbers betting. The government's evidence at trial showed that the defendants were engaged in an illegal gambling business, but the only evidence to "connect" the defendant with that business was evidence that he had engaged in numbers betting. At the close of the evidence, the trial judge granted

---

[348] Thompson v. Oklahoma, 429 U.S. 1053 (1977) (Brennan, J., dissenting from denial of certiorari); *Ashe*, 397 U.S. at 448–60 (Brennan, J., concurring); Abbate v. United States, 359 U.S. 187, 200 (1959) (Brennan, J., concurring).

[349] Mr. Justice Brennan argues that the Double Jeopardy Clause requires the prosecution to join in one proceeding all charges against a defendant "that grow out of a single criminal act, occurrence, episode, or transaction." 397 U.S. at 453–54. It goes without saying, however, that the phrase "same transaction" is not self-defining and that in order to determine whether offense is a part of the "same transaction" one should first identify the reasons why they should be joined. From the defendant's standpoint, on the one hand, he might wish the prosecution to join all offenses of which the prosecution has knowledge in order to conclude his confrontation with society once and for all at a single proceeding. From the State standpoint, on the other hand, it would prefer not to have to join any offenses in a single proceeding. Mr. Justice Brennan presumably means to strike a balance between the defendant's and the State's interests with respect to joinder; the State must join in a single proceeding all offenses which, for the purposes of trial, share a common core of evidentiary facts. The majority in *Brown* is not yet ready to go so far. It reserved the question "whether the repetition of proof required by the successive prosecutions against Brown would otherwise entitle him to the additional protection offered by [compulsory joinder]." 432 U.S. at 166–67 n.6.

[350] 98 S. Ct. 2170 (1978).

the defendant's motion to exclude all evidence of numbers betting on the ground that numbers betting had not been properly alleged in the indictment. Having excluded the evidence, the trial judge then immediately granted a judgment of acquittal on the ground that, without the evidence of numbers betting, there was insufficient evidence to connect the defendant with the business of horsebetting. The government appealed the acquittal, arguing among other things that the acquittal was based on the trial judge's error in excluding the evidence of numbers betting.[351] The Court assumed that the trial judge erred three times in excluding the evidence[352] but dismissed the appeal on the ground that the judge's ruling—that there was insufficient evidence to connect the defendant with the illegal gambling business—was an acquittal that barred reprosecution for the same offense.

The Court, again, reached an arguably correct result for the wrong reason. There is nothing in law or reason that would justify giving a defendant immunity from reprosecution simply because the trial judge made a threefold error in terminating the case in his favor. The trial judge's ruling was certainly no evidence that the defendant was actually innocent. On the contrary, not only were the defendant's alleged accomplices all found guilty, but the trial judge explicitly stated for the record that if the evidence of numbers betting had remained in evidence, it would have sufficed to find the defendant guilty beyond a reasonable doubt.[353]

---

[351] The government argued that the district court's exclusion of the evidence of numbers betting ought to be treated as if the district court had "dismissed" a separate count for numbers betting, thus leaving it open to the government to now retry the defendant for the numbers-betting charge which had been dismissed. The Court rejected the argument. First, the exclusion of evidence was not a dismissal. It was not denominated as such and the government did not treat numbers betting as a separate count in the indictment. Second, regardless of how it had been charged, numbers betting could not be treated as a separate count because the appropriate unit of prosecution under the statute was not numbers betting as opposed to horsebetting, but the combined "business" of numbers betting and horsebetting. In sum, the Court concluded that the trial court's ruling was "an erroneous evidentiary ruling [relating to a single offense] which led to an acquittal for insufficient evidence." 98 S. Ct. at 2181.

[352] The trial judge first erred in assuming that the defendant's involvement in numbers betting (as opposed to his involvement in the "illegal business" as a whole) had to be charged as a separate violation of Massachusetts law. 98 S. Ct. at 2181 n.22. The judge further erred in assuming that numbers betting had to be charged as a violation of § 7 as opposed to § 17 of Mass. Gen. Laws ch. 271. *Id.* at 2177 n.11. Proceeding on these two erroneous assumptions, the trial judge erroneously assumed that the failure to cite § 7 could not be cured by amendment. Id. at 2176 n.8.

[353] *Id.* at 2176.

Nor can *Sanabria* be squared with the Court's prior decisions. The closest parallel is to *Lee v. United States*.[354] The defendant there was tried for theft. At the close of the evidence, the judge stated for the record that the evidence of intent was sufficient to find the defendant guilty beyond a reasonable doubt. Nonetheless, finding that the element of intent had not been properly alleged in the information, the trial judge granted the defendant's motion to dismiss the information. The Court subsequently held that the defendant could be retried following the dismissal, because the judge's ruling was not an acquittal within the meaning of the Double Jeopardy Clause.

Lee is functionally identical to *Sanabria*. In both cases the prosecution introduced sufficient evidence to prove the defendant guilty beyond a reasonable doubt; both cases terminated at the defendant's request because of an error (real or imagined) in the charging paper which had not caused the defendant any actual prejudice but which could not be cured by amendment. Moreover, it was perfectly obvious in both cases that once the "uncharged" evidence was excluded from the government's case, there was insufficient evidence remaining to support a finding of guilt. Thus, the only difference between the two cases is that the trial judge in *Sanabria* took the additional step of actually declaring the remaining evidence to be insufficient—something that could have been readily determined from a casual glance at the record in *Lee*. Surely that additional step is not sufficient to vest the defendant in *Sanabria* with immunity from reprosecution. Surely, if the government was justified in retrying the defendant following a technical failure of proof in *Lee*, it was also justified in retrying the defendant in *Sanabria*.

This conclusion is reinforced by the Court's opinion in *Burks v. United States*.[355] There the Court held that the defendant could not be retried following an unreversed finding that his first trial for the same offense ended in a "failure of proof."[356] But the Court also emphasized that *Burks* was not a case in which "the trial court committed error by excluding prosecution evidence, which, if received, would have rebutted any claim of evidentiary insufficiency,"[357] thus suggesting that the result in *Burks* would have been different if the

[354] 432 U.S. 23 (1977).

[355] 98 S. Ct. 2141 (1978).

[356] *Id.* at 2149.

[357] *Id.* at 2144 n.4.

prosecution had been denied "one fair opportunity to offer whatever proof it could assemble."[358] Yet that was precisely the situation in *Sanabria*. The evidence in *Sanabria* was insufficient, not because of an actual failure of proof but because the trial judge wrongfully excluded probative evidence from the prosecution's case. Thus, if *Burks* was serious in suggesting that the State may retry a defendant following a failure of proof if it can show that it was "prejudice[d]"[359] by the trial court's evidentiary rulings, the State should have been allowed to retry the defendant in *Sanabria*.

This same conclusion also follows from a question the Court reserved in *Greene v. Massey*.[360] *Greene* was identical to *Burks*, except that the lower court may have held the government's evidence insufficient only because the lower court thought certain items of that evidence had to be disregarded for purposes of appeal. Yet in remanding the case for further elucidation of that issue, the Court explicitly reserved the question whether the defendant could be retried if the prosecution could show that the failure of proof was due, not to the prosecution's inability to muster sufficient evidence, but to its good-faith reliance on the trial court's reception of evidence that later turned out to be inadmissible.[361] Yet if it is true that a defendant can be retried following a failure of proof based on an improper admission of prosecution evidence, then, surely, a defendant like Sanabria can be retried where the failure is based on the improper exclusion of prosecution evidence; as between the two, the former is far more problematical than the latter.[362]

This all suggests that *Sanabria* may have been wrongly decided. If the decision was correct, however, it was not because the trial judge's ruling deserved the cloak of absolute finality, but because the trial judge terminated the case at midtrial without obtaining the defendant's consent to be retried. In other words, the proper reference in *Sanabria* was not to jury verdicts of not guilty, but to

---

[358] *Id.* at 2149.

[359] *Ibid.*

[360] 98 S. Ct. 2151 (1978).

[361] *Id.*, at 2155 n.9.

[362] If the State is allowed to retry a defendant following a finding of insufficiency based on the improper admission of evidence, as in *Greene*, the prosecution not only may, but must find and introduce new evidence that it did not introduce at the first trial in order to survive a motion for a directed verdict at the second trial. Thus, the very purpose of the second trial is to give the State an opportunity to muster evidence it did not introduce the first time around. In *Sanabria*, on the other hand, the State is merely seeking an opportunity to introduce the evidence that was wrongfully excluded the first time around.

mistrial cases in which defendants are denied an opportunity to have their cases resolved once and for all by the first jury impaneled in the case. The defendant in *Sanabria* was in a very favorable position at the close of evidence. He had succeeded in persuading the trial court to exclude much, if not all, of the evidence that connected him to the illegal gambling business. If the case had been submitted to the jury, the judge in all likelihood would have instructed the jury to disregard that evidence and the jury, in turn, would have returned a verdict of not guilty. The judge's ruling had the effect of denying the defendant the opportunity to be acquitted by the first jury impaneled in the case without his having consented to be retried.

It is true, of course, that a defendant can be retried following a mistrial if the mistrial is entered at his request. And it is true that the defendant in *Sanabria* asked that the case be terminated at midtrial. But his request for a judgment of acquittal cannot be equated with a request for a mistrial or even with the request in *Lee* for a dismissal. When a defendant requests a mistrial without specifying whether he means a mistrial with prejudice or without prejudice, it is fair to assume that he means without prejudice, because mistrials are rarely based on grounds that are legally inconsistent with reprosecution.[363] The same was true in *Lee*. By requesting a dismissal, the defendant can fairly be presumed to have meant dismissal without prejudice, because the dismissal "was not predicated on any judgment that [he] could never be prosecuted" and because he did not appear to have anything to gain from continuing with the trial.[364] In *Sanabria*, in contrast, the defendant requested a judgment of acquittal,

---

[363] See *Lee*, 432 U.S. at 30. In *Dinitz*, 424 U.S. at 600, for example, the Court presumed that by requesting a mistrial, the defendant either meant a mistrial without prejudice or, at the very least, was willing to allow the issue to be resolved at a future date if the State should choose to try to reprosecute him. This illustrates the importance to the defense of making explicit precisely what kind of mistrial it wants. If the defendant in *Dinitz* had made it explicit that he wanted a mistrial if, but only if, it would be treated as a mistrial with prejudice, and that otherwise he wished to proceed with the first jury, then it could not be said that by requesting a mistrial, he was willing to forego the opportunity to continue with the first jury impaneled in the case. On the other hand, it can be argued that whenever a defendant asks that a case terminate before being submitted to the jury—even when he explicitly relies on the trial judge's assertion that the dismissal is with prejudice—he nonetheless runs the risk of being retried if the appellate court subsequently determines that the trial judge erred in dismissing with prejudice. See *Scott*, 98 S. Ct. at 2187.

[364] 432 U.S. at 30. The trial judge, hearing the case without a jury, stated for the record that the government had proved the defendant guilty beyond a reasonable doubt. *Id.* at 26.

not a dismissal, and the request was based on grounds that did not contemplate further proceedings. The defendant had everything to gain and nothing to lose by going to the jury; it cannot be assumed that by requesting an acquittal, he meant an acquittal without prejudice to his being retried. On the contrary, it must be assumed that he wanted the case to terminate if, and only if, it were certain that he would never be retried and that, otherwise, he wished to proceed with the first jury.[365]

This, in turn, raises the final and most interesting question in the case: If the defendant did not consent to be retried, could the trial have been terminated and the defendant retried without his consent? The answer, of course, depends on the rationale of *Illinois v. Somerville*.[366] In both cases the original trial terminated without a verdict and without the defendant's consent to be retried because of a defect in the indictment (real or apparent) that would have prevented the prosecution from obtaining a valid judgment of conviction. *Somerville* held that the defendant could be retried because the error was not capable of "manipulation." The same may also be true of the error in *Sanabria*, depending on the significance of the fact that the error in *Sanabria* was the judge's, rather than the prosecutor's, and was not raised until after the defendant had presented his evidence.[367] In any event, the finality of the acquittal in *Sanabria* depends on precisely the same considerations that govern the finality of the mistrial in *Somerville*. If *Sanabria* was correctly decided, it was because retrial would have been barred even under *Somerville*. On the other hand, if retrial would not have been barred under *Somerville*, that is, if the defendant in *Sanabria* could have been retried following an erroneous mistrial over his objection, there is no reason why he could not have been retried following an erroneous acquittal at his request.

---

[365] As the Court said in *Sanabria*, "neither petitioner's motion here nor the trial court's rulings contemplated a second trial." 98 S. Ct. at 2184. But see *Scott*, note 363 *supra*, suggesting that a defendant foregoes his interest in finality whenever he requests that a case terminate, even when he bases his request on grounds that do not contemplate a second trial.

[366] 410 U.S. 458 (1973).

[367] The fact that the error occurred after the defendant had revealed and presented the evidence in his defense may be taken into account in assessing a likelihood that the error was a manipulated effort to give the prosecution a preview of the defendant's case. See *Schulhofer*, note 9 *supra*, at 492. For the difference between an error by a prosecutor and an error by a judge, see note 83 *supra*.

V. Conclusion

The moral of this story is that things that look the same may be different, and things that look different may be the same. The Court inclines to assume, for example, that the rule governing retrial following an erroneous conviction is different from the rule for retrial following an erroneous ruling in the defendant's favor because the underlying dispositions are different. Yet the considerations that justify retrial are the same in both cases and the rule, too, should be the same. Conversely, the Court assumes that the rule governing the finality of a jury acquittal is the same as the rule for bench acquittals because both constitute findings that the defendant is not guilty. But since the reasons for according finality to the two findings are different, so, too, are the rules of double jeopardy.

Consider, also, the definition of offenses. The Court assumes that offenses which are the "same" for purposes of the rule against multiple punishment are also the "same" for purposes of the rule against multiple prosecutions. Yet, given the different values that underlie the two rules, one would expect them to be different; and, of course, they should be. So, once again, the answer to the question whether two things are the same or different depends on why one is asked the question.

MARTIN E. MARTY

OF DARTERS AND SCHOOLS AND
CLERGYMEN: THE RELIGION
CLAUSES WORSE CONFOUNDED

The fate of the snail darter, a less than sardine-size fish whose habitat lies exclusively in the waters of a TVA dam site, became of national concern as the United States Supreme Court decided that, pursuant to congressional mandate, work on the nearly completed dam would have to stop in order to preserve this endangered species.[1] There was, on the other hand, almost no public response to two Supreme Court decisions concerned with religion and the First Amendment.[2]

Taken together, the two Religion Clauses cases afford a luxurious opportunity to appraise the thinking of the Court in this controversial area. The occasion is luxurious because neither decision inspired the kind of emotional response that makes for unclear thinking. The *Cathedral Academy* case presented an aspect of the hotly contested issue of financial aid to parochial schools or to the families of students attending such schools. Even the radical separationist watchdog magazine *Church and State* contented itself with

Martin E. Marty is Fairfax M. Cone Distinguished Service Professor at The Divinity School, The University of Chicago.

[1] T.V.A. v. Hill, 98 S. Ct. 2279 (1978).

[2] New York v. Cathedral Academy, 434 U.S. 125 (1977); McDaniel v. Paty, 435 U.S. 618 (1978).

© 1979 by The University of Chicago. 0-226-46431-8/79/1978-0006$01.65

just four lines of comment by Andrew Leigh Gunn, executive director of Americans United: "Once more the majority on the Supreme Court has seen through the camouflage and applied the First-Amendment's church-state separation principle to this crucial religious liberty issue."[3] Most of the religious press ignored the case.

The general press paid slightly more notice to *McDaniel v. Paty*, which dealt with the constitutional rights of an ordained clergyman to hold legislative office. The fact that the State of Tennessee still had a law proscribing such clerical officeholding made it a curiosity.[4] The *McDaniel* decision came in the midst of a presidential administration that gave rise to serious debate about the role of religion—clerical or lay—in the affairs of government. *McDaniel*, however, cannot be described as a major news item or even as one of the more visible Court decisions of the Term.

Citizens are capable of becoming angered over First Amendment decisions in the religion area, as the furor over the famed "school-prayer decisions" made clear.[5] In their wake, about four out of five Americans consistently told polltakers that they disagreed with the Court. Almost as controversial in recent years, at least among academics, was a New Jersey case that spoke to current anxieties. In *Malnak v. Yogi*,[6] a United States district court determined that Transcendental Meditation was tied to a religion and could not be supported as a secular subject in public schools. In contrast with this ruling which dealt with the intrusion of exotic and, to many, disturbing Eastern religions, the 1977 Term Court rulings were concerned with more familiar subjects—Roman Catholics of New York and Baptists of Tennessee.

As already noted,[7] *Church and State* spoke confidently of the Court's application of the First Amendment's church-state separation principle. Certainly this is simplistic in light of the disagreement over both the character of that principle and the question

---

[3] CHURCH & STATE 6 (Jan. 1978).

[4] *Cf.* Epperson v. Arkansas, 393 U.S. 97 (1968), the direct descendant of Scopes v. State, 154 Tenn. 105 (1927) (upholding Tennessee's "monkey law").

[5] Engel v. Vitale, 370 U.S. 421 (1962); School District of Abington Township v. Schempp, 374 U.S. 203 (1963); see Kurland, *The Regents' Prayer Case: "Full of Sound and Fury, Signifying . . ."*, 1962 SUPREME COURT REVIEW 1.

[6] 440 F. Supp. 1284 (D.N.J. 1977).

[7] Text *supra*, at note 3.

whether the Court has discerned and is acting on the basis of any principle of separation. Rather than examine the subject as it has developed over the years,[8] it may be more profitable to analyze and compare the two decisions of the 1977 Term.

The two cases are revealing both because of the lack of concern with which they were greeted and because they seem characteristic of the Court's jurisprudence in the field. They suggest that, while the Court in *Cathedral Academy* was acting consistently with its series of rulings against tax aid for parochial schools since 1971, no other principle of consistency is apparent. The snail darter may be an endangered species, but so also is consistent reasoning about the meaning of the First Amendment. *McDaniel* shows the majority in a defensive posture in its attack on the idea that "religion may not be used as a basis for classification for purposes of governmental action, whether that action be the conferring of rights or privileges or the imposition of duties or obligations."[9] Such an approach, we are told, would be "rigid" and "unitary," and thus "unfaithful to our constitutionally protected tradition of religious liberty."[10] Mr. Justice Brennan, nevertheless, goes on to make use of the "neutrality" principle, but not rigidly.

The general application of a principle may well be thought to be the business of a court in a political society in its movement through history. But if "government may not use religion as a basis of classification for the imposition of duties, penalties, privileges or benefits,"[11] as Mr. Justice Brennan argues it may not, the Court majority made no evident use of the same principle in *Cathedral Academy* and has not done so in its parochial school decisions since 1971. Failure to elucidate a principle is what led lower courts to rule as they did in cases that *Cathedral Academy* overturns. In the New York case, instead of appealing to neutrality or to a ban on the use of religion as a basis for classification, the Court resorts to a different principle: Government should not be too "entangled" in the life of religious institutions.

---

[8] See KURLAND, ED., CHURCH AND STATE: THE SUPREME COURT AND THE FIRST AMENDMENT (1975).

[9] The condemned language is that of KURLAND, RELIGION AND THE LAW 18, 112 (Midway reprint, 1978). It is so identified by Mr. Justice Brennan. 435 U.S. at 639.

[10] 435 U.S. at 638–39.

[11] *Id.* at 639.

I. The Cathedral Academy Case

The story behind the *Cathedral Academy* decision is complex. It derives from efforts by Roman Catholic and other nonpublic schools in New York to come to terms with what they perceive to be a web of entanglements spun by an encroaching civil government with religious institutions. The government intrudes with what they regard as increasingly burdensome and expensive procedures for making educational institutions accountable. The complexity is squared when one reads the Court's deliberations against the background of similar cases since *Everson v. Board of Education*[12] in 1947 and until about 1971. It is clear that both the lower courts in New York and the New York State legislature had busied themselves trying to find a mode of relieving parochial schools of new burdens without running afoul, as they did in the end anyway, of the newer line of the Court's thinking which, in school cases, does use religion as a basis for classification for "the imposition of duties" and penalties. If the scope of governmental supervision were not rapidly increasing and if the Court's reasoning were based on specific and reasonably consistent principles in both school and nonschool cases, the background would be less confusing.

In 1970, the New York legislature passed a law authorizing reimbursement to nonpublic schools for recordkeeping and testing services that were mandated by the State.[13] Public schools by the very nature of their constitution and financing receive such reimbursement. The legislature regarded nonpublic schools sympathetically because of the new burdens placed upon them. But a three-judge federal district court declared the law unconstitutional.[14] It went on to enjoin permanently any payment of funds under the New York law and to extend the ruling even to reimbursement for expenses that had already been incurred by such schools during the second half of the 1971–72 school year when the law was in effect.

The New York legislature responded to the 1972 district court judgment with a remedial statute intended only to reimburse nonpublic schools for the money expended in good faith during the

---

[12] 330 U.S. 1 (1947).

[13] 1970 N.Y. Laws, ch. 138.

[14] Committee for Public Education & Religious Liberty v. Levitt, 342 F. Supp. 439 (S.D.N.Y. 1972), aff'd 413 U.S. 472 (1973).

time that the law was in effect.[15] In the case of religious nonpublic schools—nonreligious nonpublic schools curiously never received mention—the law was designed to deal only with nonreligious expenses incurred by the schools in the latter half of the 1971–72 school year.[16]

It was clear that, although the second statute was restricted to a single payment and took special care to provide nonentangling administrative procedures, it was still substantially congruent with the earlier statute that the three-judge court had nullified. The Supreme Court in *Cathedral Academy* pointed out that the constitutional invalidity that it detected was "in the payment itself, rather than in the process of its administration."[17]

Cathedral Academy, a Roman Catholic school, brought its reimbursement claim under the 1972 law in the New York Court of Claims. That court found the statute in violation of the First and Fourteenth Amendments.[18] But the Court of Claims was reversed by the New York Court of Appeals[19] which relied upon *Lemon v. Kurtzmann I,*[20] and *Lemon v. Kurtzmann II.*[21] *Lemon I* had invalidated a State law providing for reimbursement of nonpublic schools for ongoing specified secular expenses. *Lemon II* allowed reimbursement for expenditures made under the State law prior to invalidation of the statute. Equitable flexibility, the Court said in *Lemon II*, allowed the Court to weigh the "remote possibility of constitutional harm from allowing the State to keep its bargain"[22] against the fact that the schools had relied on State support for expenses incurred for the State-mandated activity.

---

[15] 1972 N.Y. Laws, ch. 996.

[16] The statute authorized reimbursement for "rendering services for examination and inspection in connection with administration, grading and the compiling and reporting of the results of tests and examinations, maintenance of records of pupil enrollment and reporting thereon, maintenance of pupil health records, recording of personnel qualifications and characteristics and the preparation and submission to the state of various other reports required by law or regulation." Quoted at 434 U.S. at 130–31.

[17] 434 U.S. at 131.

[18] 77 Misc.2d 977 (N.Y. Ct. Cl. 1974).

[19] 39 N.Y.2d 1021 (1976). The Court of Appeals actually reversed the Appellate Division decision that had affirmed the Court of Claims. 47 App. Div.2d 390 (3d Dept. 1975).

[20] 403 U.S. 602 (1971).

[21] 411 U.S. 192 (1973).

[22] 434 U.S. at 129.

The Supreme Court found *Lemon II* inapposite in the *Cathedral Academy* case. Because the second New York law was enacted after a federal district court had declared the original statute unconstitutional, the second law also violates the First Amendment "because it will of necessity either have the primary effect of aiding religion . . . or will result in excessive state involvement in religious affairs."[23] The equities, this time, did not support the 1972 law, since such Act itself constituted a "new and independently significant infringement of the First and Fourteenth Amendments."[24]

The Chief Justice and Mr. Justice Rehnquist filed a one-sentence dissenting statement relying on *Lemon II* as a basis for affirmance of the judgment below.[25] Mr. Justice White dissented, as he so frequently has done in First Amendment religious school cases. He, too, needed but a single sentence: "Because the Court continues to misconstrue the First Amendment in a manner that discriminates against religion and is contrary to the fundamental educational needs of the country, I dissent here as I have in *Lemon* . . . ; *Committee for Public Education* v. *Nyquist*, 413 U.S. 756 (1973); *Levitt* v. *Committee for Public Education*, 413 U.S. 472 (1973); *Meek* v. *Pittenger*, 421 U.S. 349 (1975); and *Wolman* v. *Walter*, 433 U.S. 229 (1977)."[26] The first part of his proposition relates to constitutional law, the second to public policy. He is an authoritative voice in the first regard, but it is the legislative branch that is charged with establishing public policy.

The opinion for the Court in *Cathedral Academy*, written by Mr. Justice Stewart, asserted that the 1972 law was condemned by earlier judicial pronouncements because its primary effect would be either to aid religion or because it would result in excessive State involvement, either of which would be in violation of the Establishment Clause. The Court once again raised the banner of entanglement, which it has used increasingly in recent years in an attempt to counter suggestions that the First Amendment calls for simple governmental neutrality in matters of religion. As the Court put it: "The prospect of church and state litigating in court about what does or does not have religious meaning touches the very core of

---

[23] *Id.* at 133.

[24] *Id.* at 134.

[25] *Ibid.*

[26] *Id.* at 134–35.

the constitutional guarantee against religious establishment, and it cannot be dismissed by saying that it will happen only once."[27]

Everyone seemed in agreement that the *Cathedral Academy* case was to be governed by *Lemon II*. What was it then that called for the *Cathedral Academy* case to be disposed of differently than *Lemon II*, which had permitted reimbursement for disbursements made before the statute was invalidated? Apparently the primary problem was that the legislature was deemed in *Cathedral Academy* to have invaded the province of the judiciary. The trial court in dealing with the first statute had enjoined reimbursement for amounts "heretofore or hereafter expended."[28] The supremacy of the judiciary is not to be tampered with lightly:[29]

> The state legislature thus took action inconsistent with the court's order when it passed ch. 996 upon its own determination that, because schools like the Academy had relied to their detriment on the State's promise of payment under ch. 138, the equities of the case demanded retroactive reimbursement. To approve the enactment of ch. 996 would thus expand the reasoning of *Lemon II* to hold that a state legislature may effectively modify a federal court's injunction whenever a balancing of constitutional equities might conceivably have justified the court's granting similar relief in the first place.

One might sympathize with the Court majority here, but as the Court noted, "the dispositive question is whether the payments it authorizes offend the First and Fourteenth Amendments."[30]

The real concern of the Court was that "the aid that [would] be devoted to secular functions [was] not identifiable and separable from aid to sectarian activities."[31] How could the government be assured that payments would truly go only to mandated services? It was said that there was an impermissible risk of religious indoctrination in examinations "prepared by teachers under the authority of religious institutions," that they would "be drafted with an eye, unconsciously or otherwise, to inculcate students in the religious

---

[27] *Id.* at 133.   [29] *Ibid.*

[28] *Id.* at 130.   [30] *Ibid.*

[31] *Id.* at 131, quoting Levitt v. Committee for Public Education, 413 U.S. 472, 480 (1973).

precepts of the sponsoring church."[32] Of course such a risk is present. The course of American history has provided reasons for expressing mistrust of religious schools' ability to segregate their secular impulses. But the Court has consistently paid less attention to the worries of the religious that secular academies are equally unable to segregate their often implicit sets of religious teachings. Thus, a wary Justice Douglas in a concurrence, all but clucked in apparently unconscious condescension: "One can imagine what a religious zealot, as contrasted to a civil libertarian, can do with the Reformation or with the Inquisition" in the classroom.[33] To which Professor Richard E. Morgan responded in sarcasm: "Only libertarians, apparently, are fit teachers to be paid from the common treasury."[34] The risks of intrusion on both sides are real, although the private schools in *Lemon* and *Cathedral Academy* were able to point to numerous structural safeguards that at least reduced the "impermissible" risks and brought them into line with practices taken for granted across the lines separating church and state in American history.

The Court, in *Cathedral Academy*, however, demanded more. Even to check up on whether there might be intrusions across the line of separation would necessarily force a "detailed inquiry into the subtle implications of in-class examinations and other teaching activities [that] would itself constitute a significant encroachment on the protections of the First and Fourteenth Amendments."[35] The Court certainly did not show as much wariness in the school-prayer decisions and did not provide a set of monitors who might make detailed inquiry into the subtle inclinations of public school teachers to teach religion and not "about" religion, as those cases permitted. Nor has it been concerned with such programs as glee club performances which, without surveillance, might be supportive of distinctive religions through the words voiced by public school choirs. The Court invoked the spectre—one that it is not hard to share given current patterns of regulation—of tentacular governmental agencies spying on religious schools and of such

---

[32] 434 U.S. at 131, quoting from Levitt, 413 U.S. at 480.

[33] Lemon v. Kurtzman, 403 U.S. 602, 635–36 (1971).

[34] MORGAN, THE SUPREME COURT AND RELIGION 111 (1972).

[35] 434 U.S. at 132.

schools being diverted from their nobler tasks by the business of "trying to disprove any religious content in various classroom materials."[36] If that is where the burden of proof is to be placed, would the State as a defendant "have to undertake a search for religious meaning" in every classroom examination that it gives? Clearly the demand for such oversight creates an Orwellian content. "The prospect of church and state litigating in court about what does or does not have religious meaning touches the very core of the constitutional guarantee against religious establishment, and it cannot be dismissed by saying it will happen once."[37] Admittedly, if one is to draw the line on entanglement where the Court would draw it, such spectres must be raised. The question is whether the Justices have chosen the proper line.

Mr. Justice White, in his dissent in *Lemon I*, stated that he did not believe that the case had been made that the Pennsylvania nonpublic schools were using the funds in question for religious purposes and that, therefore, the case had to be argued and established on the basis of evidence. However costly such a procedure would be, only the proof thus adduced would afford a basis for constitutional condemnation. But his was a lonely dissenting voice on that score. Until *Cathedral Academy*, *Lemon I* stood as the high-water mark. *Cathedral Academy* has now forbidden even the retroactive one-shot reimbursement found tolerable in *Lemon II*.

In his dissent in *Lemon I*, Mr. Justice White placed reliance on *Board of Education v. Allen*[38] in which he had written the opinion for the Court. *Allen* had pleased what some have come to call the "accommodationists" by allowing public school textbooks to be loaned to private parochial schools, because it allowed for "individual benefit" to students rather than direct support of religious institutions. In *Allen*, Mr. Justice White borrowed some phrases from the Clark opinion in the *Regent's Prayer* case[39] to argue that the concern in all legislation relating to religious nonpublic schools must concentrate on the idea that support for, say, textbooks, must not have as its "purpose and primary effect" either the advancement or inhibition of religion. Mr. Justice White verged here on a concept of general constitutional neutrality which could be logi-

---

[36] *Id.* at 132–33.

[37] *Id.* at 133.

[38] 392 U.S. 236 (1968).

[39] *Schempp*, note 5 *supra*, at 222.

cally congruent with the position of separationists and politically acceptable to accommodationists. But *Allen* proved to have no weight at all in *Lemon I* or in *Leavitt* or in *Cathedral Academy*. It will probably live on only as authority that almost anyone can sue to enjoin public expenditures that might find their way to religious purses.

Cathedral Academy, like *Lemon*, was concerned primarily with the concept of entanglement. The late Donald A. Giannella viewed the outlawing of all public funds for secular aspects of nonpublic elementary and secondary schools—curiously college and university education is regarded differently by the courts—as an invocation of the metaphor of a "high and impregnable" wall of separation,[40] although Chief Justice Burger argued in *Lemon I* that the metaphor might be more appropriately stated in terms of an indistinct and variable barrier with a shape and form dependent on circumstances and particular relationships. Giannella, after setting forth the historical development of First Amendment decisions, walked up to and then backed off from the concept of neutrality, which in some ways is consistent with separationist predilections but otherwise satisfying to accommodationists like Giannella. In the context of the neutrality principle, the equal protection of the laws would be extended to students in religious schools so that they are not discriminated against because they chose such schools—schools ever increasingly burdened with governmental prescriptions. This approach has a bearing on *Cathedral Academy* which ignores the existence of private nonreligious schools. The worries of the Court are all directed to the religious rather than the private aspects of nonpublic schools. The courts decided to rule as they did not because state-mandated recordkeeping could not occur in secular private schools but solely because of possible religious implications. On the grounds of neutrality, whether rigid and unitary or generally, the Court seems to ignore the First Amendment mandate to the courts themselves,[41] since it does use religion as a basis of classification for purposes of governmental action: here imposing obligations on religious schools that nonreligious and public schools need not suffer.

---

[40] Giannella, *Lemon and Tilton: The Bitter and the Sweet of Church-State Entanglement*, 1971 SUPREME COURT REVIEW 147.

[41] *Cf.* Shelley v. Kraemer, 334 U.S. 1 (1948).

On the basis of the neutrality principle, the spectre of inspection by the State and frantic efforts by religious school officials to be seen as pure would be besides the point. The Court, wrote Giannella, evidently shrinks from such an understanding not because it wants for historical grounding or reasoned interpretation of the Religion Clauses. Rather, the Court has been—as perhaps it must be—politically sensitive to the demands of opponents of parochial education. More sympathetically and with respect to a corollary issue that troubles most of those who do not invoke the concept of neutrality, the Court is concerned with burdens placed on those who profess religion, burdens in tension with the Free Exercise Clause. Thus, as Giannella admitted, under a rigid and unitary interpretation of neutrality, "a state would not be free to excuse a Christian Scientist from a vaccination requirement in order to avoid forcing him to do an act contrary to his religious principles."[42] But the Court gives less expression to its concern for what the Free Exercise Clause might mean in the case of a "benevolent neutrality" than it does about being consistent, since 1971, in using religion as a basis for classification for purposes of governmental actions that impose obligations on religious schools. Penalizing private schools that are religious because they are religious extends the First Amendment in the wrong direction, deserts the principle of even "general" neutrality, and applies a line of reasoning inconsistent with that which appeared in *McDaniel v. Paty* less than five months later.

Giannella denied the validity of the entanglement argument in *Lemon I*. "In short, religious and secular expenditures could be segregated on strictly secular accounting procedures. Entanglement through bookkeeping appears to be merely a makeweight argument."[43] As a clear illustration, there is a more far-reaching entanglement in the case of military chaplaincies, but the Court and the public tolerate it.[44] Whether the course of policy taken by the Court will stand it in good stead when it faces future and more emotionally charged issues or when it makes rulings in slightly different cultural contexts, is another question. "The most surprising and disturbing aspect of the Court's opinion in *Lemon* is the absence of any reference to the principle of neutrality, benevolent or other-

---

[42] Giannella, note 40 *supra*, at 153 n.27.

[43] *Id*. at 165–66.   [44] *Id*. at 171.

wise."[45] Only in the dissent did Mr. Justice White come close to taking notice of it. From *Everson* through *Allen*, some view of neutrality was at the base of the Court's decisions in religious school cases, and on that base discussions of policy could prosper. After *Lemon I*, pure separationism on the lines of feared entanglement worked against neutrality.

In *Lemon* I, the Chief Justice tipped his hand when he defined the phrase of the First Amendment "respecting establishment of religion" as governmental action that could constitute "a step that could lead to . . . establishment."[46] This argument from tendency has never been matched with any idea that the Court should also keep in mind tendencies toward neutrality and not only pure separationism. The political approach now in use does allow for flexibility in Court decisions, as the New York Court of Appeals discovered when it sought to apply *Lemon II* to *Cathedral Academy* and found it outdated. Another tip of the political scales might lead a later court to apply *Cathedral Academy*—erroneously.

Some critics of the Court argue cogently that one way to take pressures off the religious issues of the First Amendment would be to appeal less frequently to the Religion Clauses, because "the expression of ideas is properly, if not sufficiently, protected by the speech, press, and association clauses."[47] I should have to venture too far afield to demonstrate in detail the troubles that are present and will complicate the life of the Court in the future now that the role of religion and the definition of religion have become so protean and problematic in American life. The religious dimensions of "secular" teaching are increasingly seen to compromise the neutrality of public schools. The legislatures and the courts will buy only trouble now by needlessly and possibly mischievously overloading the concept of religion. Thus, when Morgan spoke of the "striving toward doctrinal coherence" as "the distinctive, legitimatizing characteristic of the American Supreme Court,"[48] he was pointing to what the Court has been failing to achieve, which can be so readily seen when *Cathedral Academy* is compared with *McDaniel v. Paty*.

---

[45] *Id.* at 185.

[46] 403 U.S. at 612.

[47] MORGAN, note 34 *supra*, at 208.

[48] *Id.* at 209.

II. The Clergyman-Legislator Case

As already noted,[49] Justices Brennan and Marshall took pains, in *McDaniel*, to reject unitary and rigid approaches to the concept of neutrality in relation to the Religion Clauses of the First Amendment. For Mr. Justice Brennan, "rigid conceptions of neutrality have been tempered by constructions upholding religious classifications where necessary to avoid '[a] manifestation of . . . hostility [toward religion] at war with our national tradition as embodied in the First Amendment's guarantee of the free exercise of religion.' "[50] This generally neutral approach at least invokes a principle and does its tempering or compromising on the basis of it. The Court majority, from *Lemon I* through *Cathedral Academy* prefers to eschew principle altogether. It would be pleasant, if unrealistic, to think that *McDaniel* represents a reformation, that its use of a generally neutral concept reflects a "striving toward doctrinal coherence."

How does one explain the disparity between the two decisions of the same Term? The Court's reading of historical situations and the public mind has to be the controlling factor. Evidently the Court regards the parochial school to be residually so strong that it might be regarded as dangerous by large elements of the population. But, in the Tennessee case, the Court seems to have decided—whether with or without proper warrant—that 200 years into the republic the clergy have become sufficiently innocuous or impotent or lackadaisical to be of no threat to anyone in the governmental realm. In the case of the clergy, it seemed safe not to make religion any longer a basis for classification for the imposition of penalties. Some irony may be at play here, since urban Catholic parochial schools have become more secularized and impotent than before. At the same time, in issues having to do with everything from homosexuality to the Equal Rights Amendment to abortion to pornography, lay and especially clerical leadership in many denominations has been more aggressive, always with an eye to having one's own sect prevail in the legislative and judicial arenas.

---

[49] See text *supra*, at notes 9–13.

[50] 435 U.S. at 618, quoting from McCollum v. Board of Education, 333 U.S. 203, 211–12 (1948).

The facts of *McDaniel* are revealing. A Reverend Mr. McDaniel, an ordained Baptist minister in Chattanooga, Tennessee, decided to file as a candidate for delegate to the State constitutional convention. An opponent, Ms. Selma Cash Paty, sued in the chancery court for a declaratory judgment that McDaniel was disqualified because the State constitution prevented ministers from seeking such office.[51] The chancellor, however, held that the governing statute[52] was in conflict with the First and Fourteenth Amendments and therefore invalid. He declared McDaniel eligible to run for the office. McDaniel was overwhelmingly elected and went on to serve at the constitutional convention. Incidentally, the State constitution would have permitted McDaniel to serve in executive or judicial posts but not legislative, a situation that Mr. Justice White in his concurring opinion found to be anomalous.[53] He also commented that forty-nine other states seemed to get along without the protection purportedly afforded Tennessee by its constitutional provision barring clergymen from legislative office.[54]

After the election, the Tennessee Supreme Court reversed the chancellor. It asserted that the disqualification of clergymen from legislative office imposed no burden upon "religious belief."[55] The disqualification hemmed in "religious action" only, and that only "in the lawmaking process of government—where religious action is absolutely prohibited by the establishment clause."[56] The objective of the Tennessee Supreme Court was to minimize divisiveness and counter the tendency to channel political activities along religious lines.

As the United States Supreme Court pointed out, England had disqualified ministers from sitting in the House of Commons—although bishops were a strong faction in the House of Lords:[57]

> In England the practice of excluding clergy from the House of Commons was justified on a variety of grounds: to prevent dual office holding, that is, membership by a minister in both Parliament and Convocation; to insure that the priest or deacon devoted himself to his "sacred calling" rather than to

---

[51] TENN. CONST. Art. IX, § 1.

[52] 1976 Tenn. Pub. Acts, ch. 848, § 4.   [55] *Id.* at 1325.

[53] 435 U.S. at 645.   [56] *Id.* at 621.

[54] *Ibid.*   [57] *Id.* at 622.

"such mundane activities as were appropriate to a member of
the House of Commons"; and to prevent ministers, who after
1533 were subject to the Crown's powers over the benefices of
the clergy, from using membership in Commons to diminish
its independence by increasing the influence of the King and
the nobility. *In re MacManaway* [1951] A.C. 161, 164, 170–71.

Almost by habit, John Locke and Thomas Jefferson concurring,
seven of the new states at first ruled out clergy from such office,
no doubt in an effort to help give a chance of success to the experiment of separating church and state.

James Madison fought such measures of clerical restraint:[58]

> Does not the Exclusion of Ministers of the Gospel as such
> violate a fundamental principle of liberty by punishing a reli-
> gious profession with the privation of a civil right? does it
> [not] violate another article of the plan itself which exempts
> religion from the cognizance of Civil power? does it not vio-
> late justice by at once taking away a right and prohibiting a
> compensation for it? does it not in fine violate impartiality by
> shutting the door against the Ministers of one Religion and
> leaving it open for those of every other? 5 The Writings of
> James Madison 288 (G. Hunt ed. 1904).

The plurality opinion—there was no opinion for the Court[59]—also
quoted the lone cleric who signed the Declaration of Independence,
John Witherspoon, who, with tongue safely in cheek, offered an
amendment to a provision of the sort being challenged in Tennessee:[60]

> No clergyman, of any denomination, shall be capable of
> being elected a member of the Senate or House of Representa-
> tives, because (here insert the grounds of offensive disqualifi-
> cation, which I have not been able to discover) Provided al-
> ways, and it is the true intent and meaning of this part of the
> constitution, that if at any time he shall be completely de-
> prived of the clerical character by those by whom he was in-

---

[58] *Id.* at 624.

[59] The plurality opinion was written by Chief Justice Burger and joined by Justices
Powell, Rehnquist, and Stevens. Mr. Justice Brennan's concurring opinion was joined
by Mr. Justice Marshall. Mr. Justice Stewart and Mr. Justice White each contributed
a concurring opinion. Mr. Justice Blackmun took no part in the decision of the case.

[60] 435 U.S. at 624–25.

vested with it, as by deposition for cursing and swearing, drunkenness or uncleanness, he shall then be fully restored to all privileges of a free citizen; his offense [of being a clergy-man] shall no more be remembered against him; but he may be chosen either to the Senate or House of Representatives, and shall be treated with all the respect due to his *brethren*, the other members of Assembly. 1 A. Stokes [Church and State in the United States] at 624–25.

After this relaxing excursion into history, the Chief Justice set to work to show how the American experiment had succeeded; how the reasons for disqualification had become obsolete; and how well-behaved the clergy had been in civil matters. Tennessee had "failed to demonstrate that its views of the dangers of clergy participation in the political process have not lost whatever validity they may once have enjoyed."[61] The essence of the Tennessee rationale was that ministers in public office would necessarily seek to promote the interests of one sect or thwart the interests of another thus pitting them against each other contrary to the antiestablishment position. That eighteenth-century fear, said the plurality opinion, has little grounding in the facts of contemporary life.

Concurring in the judgment, Mr. Justice White chose not to rely on the First Amendment but preferred to rest on the Equal Protection Clause, thus keeping religion at a distance from the center of the argument. This attempt to shift the decision from the religious sphere squares with the counsel of Professors Morgan and Giannella[62] but carried no weight with any of the other Justices.

The Justices joined in the Burger opinion decided that it was "inapposite" to argue that the Tennessee statute restricted the "freedom to believe," since McDaniel's "status, acts and conduct" were at issue, never his beliefs. On this ground, his free exercise of religion would have to be qualified because he would have to surrender his right to seek legislative office in order to practice religion. The Tennessee court knew that it was restricting religious action, and was, therefore, out of bounds. It was wrong to condition McDaniel's right to the free exercise of his religion on the surrender of his right to seek office.[63]

---

[61] *Id.* at 1329.

[62] *Cf.* KURLAND, note 9 *supra*, at 17.   [63] 435 U.S. at 626.

A valid but not central additional point appeared in a footnote to the Brennan opinion.[64] It is arguable that the Tennessee provision not only discriminates between religion and nonreligion but also discriminates among religions. The State law deprived ministers of faiths that have established and recognizable ministerial offices of rights that members of "nonorthodox humanistic faiths" —and there are others—would continue to hold. Thus, the Tennessee statute employed obsolete concepts of ministry in a day when many clerics, because of ministerial oversupply or their desire to be active largely in the secular world, engage in part-time but ordained "tent-making" ministries after the model of the apostle Paul, who was unquestionably a minister but who supported himself by making tents.

The Tennessee rule further poses a distinction between laity and clergy that is neither tenable in the theology of many religious groups nor visible in their practices. The Tennessee judges pictured the clergy as "those most intensely involved in religion."[65] In fact, lay persons may be more intense than professionals. In the current forums, lay legislators are often more explicit in their desire to impose sectarian views than are clerics. Thus, many Roman Catholics have criticized Congressman Robert Drinan of Massachusetts who, though a Jesuit priest, is allegedly not sufficiently firm in his support of pro-life legislation. At the same time, people like former Congressman John Conlan of Arizona make no secret of support of a "Christian Embassy" in Washington, where the Born Again Protestants would work for the election only of their own kind and the support of legislation congenial to their sects.

McDaniel includes many revealing interpretations of history, but one stands out. The Justices, having condemned rigid and unitary concepts of legal neutrality in religious issues, then invoke neutrality as a guide to decision. Was this because it took less courage to attack Tennessee, the last holdout among fifty states, than to take on the enemies of parochial education? Justices Brennan and Marshall wrote that the Tennessee provision "establishes a religious classification" in this case "governing the eligibility for office . . . which is absolutely prohibited."[66] For this proposition it relied on *Torcaso*

---

[64] *Id*. at 632 n.4.

[65] *Id*. at 636.   [66] *Id*. at 632.

v. Watkins.[67] Yet, in *Cathedral Academy* the Court itself acted on nothing but a "religious classification" in imposing burdens. These Justices went on to quote *Sherbert v. Verner:*[68] "Governmental imposition of such a choice puts the same kind of burden upon the free exercise of religion as would a fine,"[69] a sentence that has some bearing at least on the New York parochial school decision. The opinion goes on to say that the "government generally may not use religion as a basis for classification,"[70] etc., and claimed that Tennessee here establishes a religious classification that has the primary effect of inhibiting religion.

The plurality opinion in *McDaniel* also had no difficulty with the language of neutrality and spoke of "an antiestablishment principle with its command of neutrality."[71] But, in this context, it implied that neutrality had to do chiefly with governmental attitudes toward sects in relation to each other, not to the religious as opposed to the nonreligious private sectors in national life. The quotation from Madison[72] was not warning against nonneutrality but against "discriminating" between religion and nonreligion—as the New York ruling did. Justices Brennan and Marshall returned to the theme once again. "As construed, the exclusion manifests patent hostility toward, not neutrality respecting religion, . . . and in sum, has a primary effect which inhibits religion."[73]

The generally neutral approach—the most consistent that one would expect to get in a pluralistic society where the Court must keep its eye not only on the Constitution but on varying and competitive sets of interests—served the Court well in the Tennessee case, where it found the clergy to be no threat. One wonders whether it would have found a hearing if the Court felt that ministers in legislatures would seek and find the power to pressure for their sectarian views and interests.

To look for a rigid and unitary approach that admits of no exception would be unacceptable to almost all factions on both the "separationist" and "accommodationist" sides of the First Amendment. It is not likely that Kurland will get much of his way, how-

---

[67] 367 U.S. 488 (1961).

[68] 374 U.S. 398 (1963).

[69] 435 U.S. at 633.

[70] *Id.* at 632.

[71] *Id.* at 629.

[72] See text *supra*, at note 58.

[73] 435 U.S. at 636.

ever much it is his thesis that is gnawing at the Court when it is most aware of its inconsistencies. Since it plays such a part in the thinking of the Justices, I should quote Kurland's attempt to integrate the Establishment and Free Exercise Clauses and to minimize apparent tensions or contradictions between them.[74]

> The utilization or application of these clauses in conjunction is difficult. For if the command is that inhibitions not be placed by the state on religious activity, it is equally forbidden that the state confer favors on religious activity. These commands would be impossible of effectuation unless they are read together as creating a doctrine more akin to the reading of the equal protection clause . . . , *i.e.*, they must be read to mean that religion may not be used as a basis for classification for purposes of governmental action, whether that action be the conferring of rights or privileges or the imposition of duties or obligations.

Unitarily and rigidly applied, on the establishment side this approach would alienate all separationists who oppose parochial schools[75] (except for Kurland, who is a separationist who opposes parochial schools but cannot find constitutional grounds for imposing special obligations on them). On the other hand, rigid and unitary action in the zone of free exercise would prohibit legislatures or courts from taking religion into consideration, as in the cases of Christian Scientists and medicine, conscientious objectors and the draft, and the like.

The climate of reasoning in *McDaniel*, however relaxed it may be, thanks to a possible misreading of current historical trends about sectarian involvement with legislation, does demonstrate at least the "striving for coherence" that Richard Morgan found to be distinctive and legitimatizing in the life of the Court. If one wishes to temper or compromise a principle, it is nice to know, as the Tennessee case lets us know, which principle is to be applied only generally and from which one slightly departs in order to

---

[74] KURLAND, note 9 *supra*, at 17–18. Kurland was, of course, cognizant of the difficulties of principled decisions for the Court. "This test is meant to provide a starting point for the solution to problems brought before the Court, not a mechanical answer to them." *Id.* at 112.

[75] See, *e.g.*, Pfeffer, *Religion-Blind Government*, 15 STAN. L. REV. 389 (1963).

deal with policy and interests. In the case of the school decisions, from *Lemon I* through *Cathedral Academy* any principle except fear of entanglement—which is not a principle at all—is as hard to find as is, beyond a single dam site, the endangered and elusive snail darter.

PETER W. SPERLICH

TRIAL BY JURY: IT MAY
HAVE A FUTURE

The ruling of *Ballew v. Georgia*[1] is clear. Juries in state court criminal cases must consist of at least six persons. Five are not enough.
It remains to be seen whether this signifies six as a permanent constitutional minimum or whether it presages a future return to larger
juries. In either case, the slide toward ever-diminishing juries has
been halted. Trial by jury may have a future after all.

No less significant than the constitutional holding was the Court's
utilization of statistical analysis. Here, only two cheers can be
offered. While *Ballew* presents a masterful analysis of empirical
data, it also distorts and ignores the thrust of empirical materials
in order to reaffirm an earlier decision.

I. The Facts

In November 1973, the Paris Art Adult Theatre in Atlanta,
Georgia, showed the motion picture *Behind the Green Door*.

Peter W. Sperlich is Professor of Political Science, University of California at Berkeley.

Author's Note: I should like to thank William Zinn and Coronet Galloway for
their helpful comments, and the Institute of Governmental Studies of the University of
California at Berkeley for technical and financial assistance and unfailing encouragement.

[1] 435 U.S. 223 (1978). Mr. Justice Blackmun announced the judgment, in which all
the Justices concurred on the issue of jury size. Only Mr. Justice Stevens also subscribed
to the Blackmun opinion.

Claude Davis Ballew was the manager of the theatre. On November 9, two Fulton County investigators viewed the film, went to obtain a warrant for the film's seizure, returned to view the film again, seized the film, and arrested the petitioner and a cashier. The very same sequence of events took place again on November 26 and 27. A two-count misdemeanor charge was brought against Ballew for knowingly exhibiting obscene materials in violation of Georgia Code § 26-2101.

The trial took place in the Criminal Court of Fulton County, which court employed five-member juries to try misdemeanor cases. The petitioner requested a jury of twelve, contending that in an obscenity case a jury of five "was constitutionally inadequate to assess the contemporary standards of the community." He also argued that the Sixth and Fourteenth Amendments "required a jury of at least six members in criminal cases."[2] The trial judge denied the motion.

The case was tried before a five-person jury. The jury required only thirty-eight minutes to return a verdict of "guilty" on both counts. The petitioner was sentenced to one year of incarceration and a fine of $1,000 on each count. The sentence provided for concurrent periods of incarceration, which would be suspended upon payment of the fines.

Ballew moved for a new trial. The trial court denied the motion. Ballew took the case to the Georgia Court of Appeals, alleging: (1) insufficient evidence for conviction; (2) First Amendment errors regarding obscenity and jury instructions; (3) illegal seizure of the films; (4) exposure to double jeopardy for being convicted twice for showing the same film; and (5) constitutional insufficiency of the five-person jury under Sixth and Fourteenth Amendment provisions. The court rejected the arguments. "In its consideration of the five-person jury issue, the [Georgia Court of Appeals] noted that *Williams v. Florida* had not established a constitutional minimum number of jurors. Absent a holding by [the Supreme Court] that a five-person jury was constitutionally inadequate, the [Georgia] Court of Appeals considered itself bound by *Sanders v. State*, 234 Ga. 586, 216 S.E.2d 838 (1975), cert. denied, 424 U.S. 931 (1976), where the constitutionality of the five-person jury had

---

[2] *Id.* at 227.

been upheld."[3] Ballew then took his case to the Supreme Court of Georgia, which denied certiorari.

In his petition for certiorari to the United States Supreme Court, Ballew raised three issues: (1) the constitutional sufficiency of a five-person criminal jury; (2) the constitutional sufficiency of the trial court's jury instructions; and (3) the constitutional sufficiency of the obscenity conviction. The Court decided the case solely on the question of jury size and did not reach the other issues. The Court found that State criminal juries of five are constitutionally inadequate.

II. The Minimum Number

In deciding *Ballew v. Georgia*, the Supreme Court did not develop new standards. The decision was secured entirely by reference to the rules and standards developed in *Duncan v. Louisiana*,[4] *Baldwin v. New York*,[5] and *Williams v. Florida*.[6]

The Court noted that in *Duncan* it had applied the Sixth Amendment right of trial by jury in criminal cases to the States through the Fourteenth Amendment "because trial by jury in criminal cases is fundamental to the American scheme of justice."[7] The Court noted further that it had ruled in *Baldwin* that the right of trial by jury applies to all cases in which the maximum penalty is more than six months of incarceration. The right to a jury trial, therefore, "attaches in the present case because the maximum penalty for violating § 26-2101, as it existed at the time of the alleged offense, exceeded six months imprisonment."[8]

The Court then turned to the functional standards laid down in *Williams*.[9] The basic purpose of the jury trial, the Court affirmed, is to prevent oppression by the government. Trial by jury is an "inestimable safeguard against the corrupt or overzealous prosecutor and against the compliant, biased, or eccentric judge."[10] The

---

[3] *Ibid.*

[4] 391 U.S. 145 (1968).

[5] 399 U.S. 66 (1970).

[6] 399 U.S. 78 (1970).

[7] 435 U.S. at 229.

[8] *Ibid.*

[9] Several other cases are relevant to the question of functional standards for trial juries, particularly Colgrove v. Battin, 413 U.S. 149 (1973); Johnson v. Louisiana, 406 U.S. 356 (1972); Apodaca v. Oregon, 406 U.S. 404 (1972).

[10] 435 U.S. at 229. The Court avoided the issue of "jury nullification," *i.e.*, a jury verdict at variance with applicable law. The jury's ability to set aside laws which it

safeguard is secured "by the participation of the community in determinations of guilt and by the application of the common sense
of laymen who, as jurors, consider the case."[11]

The participation of laymen as jurors must satisfy certain requirements and must take place under certain conditions. Of present interest are those requirements which relate to the size of the
jury. In *Williams v. Florida*, the Court had found:[12]

> [T]he essential feature of a jury obviously lies in the interpo-
> sition between the accused and his accuser of the common-
> sense judgment of a group of laymen, and in the community
> participation and shared responsibility that results from that
> group's determination of guilt or innocence. The performance
> of this role is not a function of the particular number of the
> body that makes up the jury. To be sure, the number should
> probably be large enough to promote group deliberation, free
> from outside attempts at intimidation, and to provide a fair
> possibility for obtaining a representative cross-section of the
> community.

The *Williams* Court held that six would do just as well as twelve
for these purposes. "What few experiments have occurred—usually
in the civil area—indicate that there is no discernible difference between the results reached by the two different-sized juries."[13] Mr.
Justice Blackmun in *Ballew* adopted a more forceful language respecting the jury-size requirements. The requirements, however,
remained the same. "Rather than requiring 12 members, then, the
Sixth Amendment mandated a jury only of sufficient size to promote group deliberation, to insulate members from outside intimidation, and to provide a representative cross-section of the community."[14] The opinion expressed some doubt that six would do
just as well as twelve and revealed some misgivings "about the
accuracy of the results achieved by smaller and smaller panels."[15]
In the end, however, *Ballew* "adhered to and reaffirmed" the position taken in *Williams* that six-person juries produce verdicts and

---

deems unjust should be counted as an aspect of the jury's function to prevent oppression
by government.

[11] *Ibid.*

[12] 399 U.S. at 100.   [14] 435 U.S. at 230.

[13] *Id.* at 101.   [15] *Id.* at 234.

protections sufficiently similar to those of twelve-person juries to satisfy all constitutional requirements.[16]

The Court in *Ballew* went beyond *Williams* in that it established a minimum size of six for state criminal juries. In *Williams* the Court had ruled only that a jury of twelve in state criminal trials was neither constitutionally mandated nor functionally required. The jury could be of any size as long as it was able to meet the functional conditions laid down by the Court. The Court explicitly reserved ruling on the constitutionality of state criminal juries smaller than six: "We have no occasion in this case to determine what minimum number can still constitute a 'jury,' but we do not doubt that six is above that minimum."[17] In *Ballew* the Court finally decided what the minimum was to be. To the relief of those who had assumed prior to *Williams* that the constitutional jury in America was the twelve-person common-law jury, the minimum was fixed at no less than six. A criminal jury of six, to be sure, can still be regarded as too small. Several decisions preceding *Ballew*, however, had given rise to considerable anxiety about the Court's plans for the future of the American jury. While *Ballew* is only partially effective in relieving this anxiety, it is a most welcome decision.

III. RECENT JURY CASES

The historical and constitutional development of the jury in England and America is beyond the scope of this essay, as is the unique political importance of the jury in the American colonies

---

[16] *Id.* at 239.

[17] 399 U.S. at 91 n.28. The language of Mr. Justice White, who appeared to look forward to further reductions in jury size, made for considerable difficulty in deciding *Ballew.*

Georgia's brief asserted that: "If six is above the minimum, five cannot be below the minimum. There is no number in between." Brief of Respondent, at p. 4. Mr. Justice Blackmun complained in his opinion that the respondent picked up the White phrase with "absolute literalness" and explained that the Court does "not accept the proposition that by stating the number six was 'above' the constitutional minimum the Court, by implication, held that at least the number five was constitutional. Instead, the Court was holding that six passed constitutional muster but was reserving judgment on *any* number less than six." 435 U.S. at 230–31 n.9.

The flaw in Georgia's argument was not logical but political. The vigorous criticism of *Williams* and the other decisions seems to have made the Court more cautious of its conclusions, at least with regard to the size of State court criminal juries. *Ballew* is more than a clarification of *Williams*; it is a break from the direction set by *Williams*. This is what Georgia did not anticipate when it rested its case wholly on the style and statements of *Williams*.

and the United States.[18] While trial by jury has had its critics in this country as elsewhere, the dominant voices in America have been those that have praised the institution. The Supreme Court often gave such praise. Thus, the Court stated in *Duncan*:[19]

> Those who wrote our constitutions knew from history and experience that it was necessary to protect against unfounded criminal charges brought to eliminate enemies and against judges too responsive to the voice of higher authority. The framers of the constitutions strove to create an independent judiciary but insisted upon further protection against arbitrary action. Providing an accused with the right to be tried by a jury of his peers gave him an inestimable safeguard against the corrupt or overzealous prosecutor and against the compliant, biased, or eccentric judge. If the defendant preferred the common-sense judgment of a jury to the more tutored but perhaps less sympathetic reaction of the single judge, he was to have it.

Together with *Baldwin*,[20] *Duncan* was the last decision by the Court in praise of juries. The counterreformation of the Burger Court in jury matters began only three years later with *Williams v. Florida*. *Williams* followed a period of unusually intense advocacy of jury diminution in the professional journals and a judicial denigration of trial by jury. The abolitionist debate also found reflection in the popular media, sometimes with judicial encouragement.[21]

---

[18] For standard and comprehensive treatments, see DAWSON, A HISTORY OF LAY JUDGES (1960); TOCQUEVILLE, DEMOCRACY IN AMERICA 280 (Bradley ed. 1945); DEVLIN, TRIAL BY JURY (1966); FORSYTH, HISTORY OF TRIAL BY JURY (1878); HOLDSWORTH, A HISTORY OF THE ENGLISH LAW (7th ed. 1956); JOINER, CIVIL JUSTICE AND THE JURY (1962); McCART, TRIAL BY JURY (2d ed. 1965); POLLOCK & MAITLAND, HISTORY OF ENGLISH LAW BEFORE THE REIGN OF EDWARD I (1895). Useful shorter discussions can be found in ABRAHAM, THE JUDICIAL PROCESS 102 (3d ed. 1975); BECKER, COMPARATIVE JUDICIAL POLITICS (1970); BONSIGNORE, ET AL., BEFORE THE LAW 221 (1974); EHRMANN, COMPARATIVE LEGAL CULTURES 95 (1976); Hyman & Tarrant, *Aspects of American Trial Jury History*, in SIMON, THE JURY SYSTEM IN AMERICA 21 (1975); KALVEN & ZEISEL, THE AMERICAN JURY 3 (1966); Van Dyke, *The Jury as a Political Institution*, 3 CENTER MAG. 17 (March 1970); VAN DYKE, JURY SELECTION PROCEDURES ix, 1 (1977). Arguments against jury trials can be found in FRANK, COURTS ON TRIAL (1949); GLEISSER, JURIES AND JUSTICE (1968).

[19] 391 U.S. at 156.

[20] The Court ruled in *Baldwin* that in State proceedings a jury trial was required where the possible penalty exceeded a six-month prison term.

[21] Numerous trial and appellate courts have adopted and supported rules to reduce the size of trial juries and to change the requirements from unanimous to majority verdicts. Often this was done on questionable authority, but with a clear understanding of where

The Supreme Court's contribution to the diminution of the jury can take at least these three forms: (1) restricting the availability of trial by jury to certain types of cases; (2) allowing reductions in the size of juries from the customary twelve to a smaller number; and (3) allowing changes in the rules of jury verdicts from the customary unanimity to a majority decision. The first of these approaches is represented by *McKeiver v. Pennsylvania*,[22] where the Court ruled that there is no constitutional right to a jury trial in the juvenile court system. While *McKeiver* is limited in its direct importance, it does represent a break with the previous tendency of the Court to extend the right to trial by jury.

The second aspect, reduction in size, is represented by *Williams* on the criminal side and by *Colgrove* on the civil. In *Williams v. Florida* the Court ruled that the Constitution does not require a twelve-person jury and, specifically, that States may try a criminal defendant with a jury of six, even if the maximum sentence is life imprisonment.[23] To produce this ruling, the Court arguably had to discard about 700 years of common law and 200 years of American constitutional history. There was no way in which *Williams* could be reconciled with any of the earlier decisions on jury size.[24] *Williams* was a clear break with the past.

---

the Supreme Court seemed to be headed. *Cf.* ZEISEL, SIX MAN JURIES, MAJORITY VERDICTS: WHAT DIFFERENCE DO THEY MAKE? (Occasional Papers from the Law School, The University of Chicago, No. 5, 1972). On the Supreme Court Justices' attitudes, also see LEVY, AGAINST THE LAW (1974), especially at 14–36, and FUNSTON CONSTITUTIONAL COUNTER-REVOLUTION (1977), especially at 344.

As for the popular media, Kevin Starr's column in the San Francisco Examiner (July 10 and 11, 1978) can serve as example. Starr reports that judges have been telling him that "the jury system must bear the blame for both the slowness of the criminal justice system and for the fact that the guilty (frequently the violent guilty) are walking the streets." Starr further reports: "As the jury system now works, it favors the criminal. It's a miracle, in fact, that murderers, rapists, burglars, muggers, and other assorted darlings of misguided social activists, ever do any time behind bars at all." The jury system, Starr has learned from his judicial informants, "is based on one principle and one principle alone—to hell with the public."

[22] 403 U.S. 528 (1971).

[23] While *Williams* specifically addressed itself only to State criminal trials, the implications were broader. "In sweeping language, the Court removed the constitutional obstacles to decreasing the size of federal and state juries in both civil and criminal cases." Zeisel, . . . *And Then There Were None*, 38 U. CHI. L. REV. 710, 712 (1971).

[24] In its earlier decisions, the Court held without exception that the word "jury" in the Sixth Amendment meant a body of twelve. See Thompson v. Utah, 170 U.S. 343 (1898); Maxwell v. Dow, 176 U.S. 581 (1900); Rasmussen v. United States, 197 U.S. 516 (1905); Patton v. United States, 281 U.S. 276 (1930); Capital Traction Co. v. Hof, 174 U.S. 1 (1899) (civil action).

Examining the origins of the twelve-person jury, the Court overcame the force of history by finding that "while sometime in the 14th century the size of the jury at common law came to be fixed generally at 12, that particular feature of the jury system appears to have been a historical accident, unrelated to the great purposes which gave rise to the jury in the first place."[25] The Court took the position that, since it could not discover a rational justification for the development of a jury of twelve out of earlier bodies greatly fluctuating in size, there could not be one.[26] The Court did not understand that the failure to discover something is not proof of its nonexistence.

Having settled the issue of historical origins at least to its own satisfaction, the Court turned to the framers' intent, first raising the question whether "this accidental feature of the jury [a body of twelve] has been immutably codified into our Constitution."[27] Since the Constitution immutably codifies only what the Court says it does, the answer was no. The Court let it be known that its prior decisions were in error in their assumption "that if a given feature existed in a jury at common law in 1789, then it was necessarily preserved in the Constitution."[28] The Court briefly considered the possibility that the framers of the Constitution did not give an exact numerical definition for "jury," because they took for granted that a jury consisted of twelve persons. This possibility, however, was rejected in favor of a declaration that "there is absolutely no indication in 'the intent of the Framers' of an explicit decision to equate the constitutional and common-law [*i.e.*, twelve persons] characteristics of the jury."[29] Critics have argued that the rejected alternative more likely was the correct one.[30] It is not a particularly fruit-

---

[25] 399 U.S. at 89–90. Mr. Justice White delivered the opinion of the Court. The decision was supported by a seven-member majority. Mr. Justice Marshall dissented. Mr. Justice Blackmun did not participate.

[26] "History, however, might have embodied more wisdom than the Court would allow. It might be more than an accident that after centuries of trial and error the size of the jury at common law came to be fixed at twelve. A primary function of the jury was to represent the community as broadly as possible; yet, at the same time, it had to remain a group of manageable size. Twelve might have been and might still be, the upper limit beyond which the difficulty of self-management becomes insuperable under the burdensome condition of a trial. On this view, twelve would be the number that optimizes the jury's two conflicting goals—to represent the community and to remain manageable." Zeisel, note 23 *supra*, at 712.

[27] 399 U.S. at 90.   [28] *Id*. at 92–93.   [29] *Id*. at 99.

[30] See, *e.g.*, Stevens, *Defendant's Right to a Jury Trial: Is Six Enough?* 59 Ky. L.J. 996, 1002–03 (1971).

ful enterprise, however, to argue with the Supreme Court about the intent of the framers. The empirical arena is a more promising field for critical analysis.

Having disposed of the question of the framers' intent and of the historical origins of the jury, the Court in *Williams* turned to its final and decisive focus: functional inquiry. The basic result was the same. The Court concluded that functional considerations also did not require a jury of twelve: "The relevant inquiry, as we see it, must be the function that the particular feature [size] performs and its relation to the purposes of the jury trial. Measured by this standard, the 12-man requirement cannot be regarded as an indispensible component of the Sixth Amendment."[31] The fundamental purpose of the jury trial, the Court noted, was to prevent oppression by the government. But "the performance of this role is not a function of the particular number of the body that makes up the jury."[32]

In *Williams*, the Court rested the constitutionality and empirical validity of the decision on the functional equivalence of twelve- and six-member juries.[33] The Court's examination of the evidence led to the following conclusions:[34]

> What few experiments have occurred—usually in the civil area—indicate that there is *no discernible difference* between the results reached by the two different-sized juries. In short, neither currently available evidence nor theory suggests that the 12-man jury is necessarily more advantageous to the defendant than a jury composed of fewer members.
>
> Similarly, while in theory the number of viewpoints represented on a randomly selected jury ought to increase as the size of the jury increases, in practice the difference between the 12-man and the six-man jury in terms of the cross-section of the community represented seems likely to be *negligible*. ... We conclude, in short, as we began: the fact that the jury at common law was composed of precisely 12 is a historical accident, unnecessary to effect the purposes of the jury system and *wholly without significance* "except to mystics." [Italics added.]

---

[31] 399 U.S. at 99–100.   [32] *Id.* at 100.

[33] *Ballew* treats only with difficulty the functional equivalence basis of *Williams*. Although *Ballew* reaffirms *Williams*, this aspect of the *Williams* opinion was a source of embarrassment, at least to Mr. Justice Blackmun.

[34] 399 U.S. at 101–02.

On what evidence did the Court reach these astonishing conclusions? *Williams* offers six items to substantiate the asserted functional equivalence of twelve- and six-person juries.[35] Inspection revealed that these items were mere collections of opinions and preferences, laced with a few casual observations.[36] Not by any flight of the imagination could they be regarded as substantial evidence.[37]

When *Williams* was decided, to be sure, systematic studies of

---

[35] Wiehl, *The Six Man Jury*, 11 Judge's J. 31 (1972); Tamm, *The Five-Man Civil Jury: A Proposed Constitutional Amendment*, 51 Geo. L.J. 120 (1962); Cronin, *Six-Member Juries in District Courts*, 2 Bost. B.J. 27 (April 1958); Note, *Six-Member Juries Tried in Massachusetts District Court*, 42 J. Am. Jud. Soc. 136 (1958); Note, *New Jersey Experiments with Six-Man Jury*, 9 A.B.A. Bull. 6 (May 1966); Phillips, *A Jury of Six in All Cases*, 30 Conn. B.J. 354 (1956).

[36] Professor Zeisel undertook a careful analysis and found this to be the substance of the citations:

"(1) Judge Wiehl approvingly cites Charles Joiner's *Civil Justice and the Jury*, in which Joiner somewhat disingenuously states that 'it could easily be argued that a six-man jury would deliberate equally as well as one of twelve.' Since Joiner had no evidence for his conclusion, Judge Wiehl also does not have any.

"(2) Judge Tamm presided over condemnation trials in the District of Columbia in which five-man juries are used and found them satisfactory.

"(3) Cronin relates that the Massachusetts legislature had authorized, on an experimental basis, the use of six-member juries in civil cases. . . . The clerk of the court is said to have reported that 'the six-member jury verdicts are about the same as those returned by regular twelve-member juries.' Three lawyers also testified that they could not detect any difference in verdicts, one because 'the panel is drawn from the regular Superior Court panel of jurors,' another because 'there seems to be no particular reason why the size of a finding would be affected by a six-man jury.' All those trials, it seems, were given preferential scheduling to endear them to counsel.

"(4) The Court's fourth cited authority consists of an abbreviated summary of the Massachusetts experiment and concludes that 'the lawyers who use the District Court, as well as the clerk, report that the verdicts are no different than those returned by twelve-member juries.'

"(5) The *ABA Bulletin* contains the statement that 'the Monmouth County Court has experimented with the use of a six-man jury in a civil negligence case.'

"(6) Judge Phillips summarizes the economic advantages derived from the Connecticut law that permits litigants to opt for a six-member jury in civil cases. He advocates the mandatory reduction in jury size, but never mentions the problem of possible differences in verdicts in comparison to the twelve-member jury." Zeisel, note 23 *supra*, at 714–15.

[37] *Williams* generated an extensive critical literature. For examples of the more empirically-oriented criticism, see Beiser & Varrin, *Six-Member Juries in the Federal Courts*, 58 Judicature 424 (1975); Lempert, *Uncovering "Nondiscernible" Differences: Empirical Research and the Jury-Size Cases*, 73 Mich. L. Rev. 643 (1975); Nagel & Neef, *Deductive Modeling to Determine an Optimum Jury Size and Fraction Required to Convict*, 1975 Wash. U.L.Q. 933; Padawer-Singer & Barton, Experimental Study of Decision-Making in the 12- Versus 6-Man Jury under Unanimous Versus Non-Unanimous Decisions, Interim Report, Columbia University (May 1975); Walbert, *The Effect of Jury Size on the Probability of Conviction: An Evaluation of* Williams v. Florida, 22 Case-West. Res. L. Rev. 529 (1971); Saks, *Ignorance of Science Is No Excuse*, 10 Trial 18 (Nov.-Dec. 1974); Zeisel, note 23 *supra*.

actual juries were scarce.[38] But better evidence was available than the items cited by the Court. The Court could have drawn on a fairly large literature of jury simulations, mock jury studies, deductive work, and social-psychological investigations of decision-making and small group behavior.[39] The Court might have requested additional briefs and arguments concerning existing knowledge. A monumental decision such as *Williams* would well have justified the effort.

The second case in which the Court legitimated the new mini-juries was *Colgrove v. Battin*,[40] decided in 1973. The Court ruled that the Seventh Amendment does not require twelve-person juries in civil cases in the federal courts and that six-member federal civil juries meet the Seventh Amendment requirement of trial by jury. *Colgrove* extended the trend set by *Williams*. It did not come as a surprise. While *Williams* explicitly had reserved ruling on the constitutionally required size of civil juries, it delivered clear signals to federal judges.[41] Wick reports that by 1972, fifty-five of the ninety-two federal district courts had already adopted six-member civil jury rules.[42] Since *Colgrove*, most of the remaining federal district courts have begun to employ six-member civil juries.[43]

It was easier politically for the Court to effect the *Colgrove* than the *Williams* diminution. Since some consider the civil jury less im-

---

[38] The scarcity is not wholly due to lack of scholarly interest. Many courts are unwilling to cooperate in jury research, even when the project does not produce any change, disturbance, or delay in the trial proceedings. See Hoffman & Brodley, *Jurors on Trial*, 17 Mo. L. Rev. 235 (1952); BUCKHOUT ET AL., JURY VERDICTS: COMPARISON OF SIX VS. 12 PERSON JURIES AND UNANIMOUS VS. MAJORITY DECISION RULE IN A MURDER TRIAL 5 (1977). Another factor, of course, is the extraordinary reaction of Congress to The University of Chicago study, as part of which observations were made (with everyone's consent) of the deliberating jury. That is now a federal offense. For a description of The University of Chicago study, see Kalven, *A Report on the Jury Project of the University of Chicago Law School*, 24 INS. COUNS. J. 368, 376 (1957). On reactions to the study, see KALVEN & ZEISEL, note 18 *supra*, at *vi–vii*.

[39] Much of this literature has been reviewed and summarized in Lempert, note 37 *supra*.

[40] 413 U.S. 149 (1973). The five-to-four majority opinion was written by Mr. Justice Brennan.

[41] See note 21 *supra*.

[42] Wick, *The Half-filled Jury Box: Is Half a Loaf Better than None?* 2 LITIGATION 11, 13 (Winter 1976).

[43] As of May 9, 1978, eighty of ninety-five federal judicial districts had adopted six-person civil juries. Personal communication from William R. Burchill, Jr., Associate General Counsel, Administrative Office of the United States Courts.

portant, it tends to be less well defended than the criminal jury. Constitutionally, however, *Colgrove* was more difficult to justify. The Sixth Amendment contains no explicit reference to the common law. The Seventh Amendment, however, states: "In Suits at common law . . . the right of trial by jury shall be preserved." But as in *Williams*, the Court was not to be deterred by history or precedent.[44] The Court first determined that the real objective of the Seventh Amendment was to preserve "the substance of the common-law right of trial by jury, as distinguished from mere matters of form or procedure."[45] Second, the Court decided that the size of the jury was a mere matter of form or procedure and that "it cannot be said that 12 members is a substantive aspect of the right of trial by jury."[46] Third, the Court elected, as in *Williams*, to make functional analysis the cornerstone of the decision. The question, said the Court, "comes down to whether jury performance is a function of jury size."[47] The Court ruled that it was not.

What was the empirical evidence offered in support of the *Colgrove* decision? There had been some hope in the scholarly community that the reviews of *Williams*, which had clearly exposed the inadequacy of that "evidence," would persuade the Court to accord a more critical and more responsible treatment to purported empirical materials.[48] The Court, however, would not be educated.[49] The same deficient studies were resurrected for *Colgrove*:[50]

> We had no difficulty reaching the conclusion in *Williams* that a jury of six would guarantee an accused the trial by jury secured by Art. III and the Sixth Amendment. Significantly, our determination that there was "no discernible difference between the results reached by the two different-sized juries" . . . drew largely upon the results of studies of the operations of juries of six in civil cases. Since then, much has been written about the six-member jury, but nothing that persuades us to depart from the conclusion reached in *Williams*.

---

[44] The leading decision on the size of civil juries antecedent to *Colgrove* was Capital Traction Co. v. Hof, 174 U.S. 1 (1899).

[45] 413 U.S. at 156. The Court was quoting from Baltimore & Caroline Line, Inc. v. Redman, 295 U.S. 654, 657 (1935).

[46] 413 U.S. at 157.   [47] *Ibid.*

[48] The Court was aware of at least some of the critical reviews. *Id.* at 159 n.15.

[49] Although Professor Zeisel had pointed out that Joiner had no evidence for his position, see note 36 *supra*, and the Court was aware of this criticism, see 413 U.S. at 159 n.15, *Colgrove* nevertheless noted Joiner's conclusion approvingly. *Ibid.*

[50] *Id.* at 158–59.

The Court also set out to gather new empirical support for its position that twelve- and six-person juries are functionally equivalent: "In addition, four very recent studies have provided empirical evidence of the correctness of the *Williams* conclusion that 'there is no discernible difference between the results reached by the two different-sized juries.' "[51] Unfortunately, the new empirical evidence was no more convincing than the old. While *Colgrove* did not restrict itself to treating simple expressions of belief or preference as proof, its use of empirical studies was uncritical.[52] The studies were greatly flawed.[53] Once again the Court had no competent evidence for its ruling.[54]

This brings the discussion to the third form of judicial jury paring. Not quite three years after *Williams*, the Supreme Court al-

---

[51] *Id.* at 159 n.15. The Court referred to Bermant & Coppock, *Outcomes of Six- and Twelve-Member Jury Trials: An Analysis of 128 Civil Cases in the State of Washington,* 48 Wash. L. Rev. 593 (1973); Inst. Jud. Adm., A Comparison of Six- and Twelve-Member Civil Juries in New Jersey Superior and County Courts (1972); Mills, *Six-Member and Twelve-Member Juries: An Empirical Study of Trial Results,* 6 U. Mich. J.L. Reform 671 (1973); Kessler, *An Empirical Study of Six- and Twelve-Member Jury Decision-Making Processes,* 6 U. Mich. J.L. Reform 713 (1973).

[52] It has been suggested that the Court was "misled" by the four studies cited, Zeisel & Diamond, *"Convincing Empirical Evidence" on the Six-Member Jury,* 41 U. Chi. L. Rev. 281, 282, 292 (1974), and that the Court cannot be expected to have skills necessary for a critical evaluation of empirical materials, Walbert, note 37 *supra,* at 531, n.8. But "the expertise required to spot the major flaws in that empirical research is modest. And the expertise required to know when one is dealing with empirical evidence and when one is dealing with bald assertions is even easier to come by." Saks, note 37 *supra,* at 20; see also Zeisel & Diamond, *supra,* at 281, 292; Wick, note 42 *supra,* at 13, 14.

[53] The major flaws in the studies cited in note 51 *supra,* are easily discerned: (1) Bermant and Coppock compared 128 workmen's compensation trials. The attorneys had the chance to choose larger juries. These requests did not occur at random but reflected the nature of the case (especially complexity and amount in controversy). No valid comparisons can be made; no conclusions about performance equivalence can be drawn. (2) The Institute of Judicial Administration conducted a study in which the litigants had a choice between the twelve- and six-person juries. The Institute's data shows that settlements and verdicts were about three times as large in the twelve-person jury cases as in the six. No valid comparisons are possible; no conclusions can be drawn. (3) Mills used a before/after design to take advantage of Michigan's 1970 shift from twelve- to six-person juries. Unfortunately, other changes also occurred at the same time, *e.g.,* a mediation board was instituted and discovery of insurance limits was permitted. These other changes could not be factored out and the conclusions about verdict equivalency were necessarily invalid. (4) Kessler did a laboratory study using videotaped mock trials and student subjects. The study had numerous serious deficiencies, ranging from wholly one-sided presentations to faulty computations. Thus, contrary to the Court's assertion, there was no "convincing empirical evidence" to support its ruling in *Colgrove.*

[54] For criticism of the *Colgrove* decision and of the studies cited by the Court in support thereof, see Zeisel & Diamond, note 52 *supra;* Diamond, *A Jury Experiment Reanalyzed,* 7 U. Mich. J.L. Reform 520 (1973); see also Lempert, note 37 *supra,* at 644; Saks, note 37 *supra,* at 19; Wick, note 42 *supra,* at 13.

lowed majority decisions to take the place of the traditional unanimity in criminal jury verdicts. *Johnson v. Louisiana*[55] and *Apodaca
v. Oregon*[56] were decided on May 22, 1972. In five-to-four decisions, the Court ruled that majority verdicts in State criminal trials
were constitutionally valid.[57] Specifically, the Court permitted majorities of nine out of twelve in *Johnson* and ten out of twelve in
Apodaca. Majority verdicts for federal criminal trials were averted
only by the constitutional scruples of Mr. Justice Powell, who was
willing to interpret the Sixth Amendment to require unanimous
jury verdicts, even if he was unwilling to extend this requirement
to the States via the Fourteenth Amendment.[58]

The keystone of the *Johnson* and *Apodaca* rulings, once again,
was the assertion of the functional equivalence of juries deliberating under the two different decision rules:[59]

> Our inquiry must focus upon the function served by the jury
> in contemporary society. . . . As we said in *Duncan*, the pur-
> pose of trial by jury is to prevent oppression by the Govern-
> ment by providing a "safeguard against the corrupt or over-
> zealous prosecutor and against the compliant, biased, or eccen-
> tric judge." . . . "Given this purpose, the essential feature of a
> jury obviously lies in the interposition between the accused
> and his accuser of the commonsense judgment of a group of
> laymen. . . ." . . . A requirement of unanimity, however, does
> not materially contribute to the exercise of this commonsense
> judgment. As we said in *Williams*, a jury will come to such a
> judgment as long as it consists of a group of laymen repre-
> sentative of a cross-section of the community who have the
> duty and the opportunity to deliberate, free from outside at-
> tempts at intimidation, on the question of a defendant's guilt.
> In terms of this function we perceive no difference between
> juries required to act unanimously and those permitted to con-
> vict or acquit by votes of 10 to two or 11 to one.

---

[55] 406 U.S. 356 (1972).

[56] 406 U.S. 404 (1972).

[57] While it is idle to speculate about what other types of majorities the Court will
approve, *e.g.*, seven of twelve, it should be noted that the minimally sufficient majority
has not yet been determined. Mr. Justice Blackmun, however, expressed reservations
about seven-to-five majorities in his concurring opinion. 406 U.S. at 366.

[58] *Id*. at 370–71. Mr. Justice White had delivered the majority opinions.

[59] 406 U.S. at 410–11.

The Court's majority did not claim any empirical evidence for its new assertion of functional equivalence. There was none to support its position. In *Johnson* and *Apodaca*, the Court cited no empirical evidence whatsoever. Rather, Mr. Justice White complained that the petitioner (Johnson) did not provide empirical evidence to support his claim that majority-rule deliberations differ from those conducted under the unanimity requirement: [60]

> Appellant offers no evidence that majority jurors simply ignore the reasonable doubts of their colleagues or otherwise act irresponsibly in casting their votes in favor of conviction, and before we alter our own longstanding perceptions about jury behavior and overturn a considered legislative judgment that unanimity is not essential to reasoned jury verdicts, we must have some basis for doing so other than unsupported assumptions.

But surely the Court has been quite willing to base its decisions on "unsupported assumptions," when these assumptions were in accord with the Court's purposes. In *Johnson* and *Apodaca*, in any case, the Court relied upon its "longstanding perceptions about jury behavior." The Court did not reveal how these perceptions were obtained. Given the secrecy of jury deliberations, one is entitled to wonder.

The *Johnson* and *Apodaca* majority invented what Richard Harris called the "doctrine of the conscientious juror."[61]

> We have no grounds for believing that majority jurors, aware of their responsibility and power over the liberty of the defendant, would simply refuse to listen to arguments presented to them in favor of acquittal, terminate discussion, and render a verdict. On the contrary it is far more likely that a juror presenting reasoned argument in favor of acquittal would either have his arguments answered or would carry enough other jurors with him to prevent conviction. A majority will cease discussion and outvote a minority only after reasoned discussion has ceased to have persuasive effect or to serve any

---

[60] 406 U.S. at 362. The Court, it must be noted with concern, has shifted the burden of proof to the petitioner who pleads for his customary rights. The matter had been anticipated: "Sometimes I suspect that the jury issue will go to whichever side does not have the burden of proof." Kalven, *The Dignity of the Civil Jury*, 50 VA. L. REV. 1055, 1074 (1964); see also Lempert, note 37 *supra*, at 698.

[61] Harris, *Trial by Jury*, THE NEW YORKER 117 (Dec. 6, 1972).

other purpose—when a minority, that is, continues to insist upon acquittal without having persuasive reasons in support of its position.[62]

And it never rains on Sundays.[63] The appellant (Johnson) argued that a majority verdict violates the reasonable-doubt standard and, thus, due process of law. The Court responded that the fact that three jurors voted for acquittal does not prove that the nine jurors who voted for conviction had a reasonable doubt.[64] This, of course, is true. However, the response refuses to acknowledge that the reasonable-doubt standard is arguably applicable to the jury as a unit, as well as to each single juror.[65]

The *Johnson* and *Apodaca* decisions generated strong judicial dissent and much scholarly criticism. Justice Douglas (joined by Justices Brennan and Marshall) wrote:[66]

> The plurality approves a procedure which diminishes the reliability of a jury. First, it eliminates the circumstances in which a minority of jurors (a) could have rationally persuaded the entire jury to acquit, or (b) while unable to persuade the majority to acquit, nonetheless could have convinced them to convict only on a lesser-included offense. Second, it permits prosecutors in Oregon and Louisiana to enjoy a conviction-acquittal ratio substantially greater than that ordinarily returned by unanimous juries.
>
> The diminution of verdict reliability flows from the fact that nonunanimous juries need not debate and deliberate as fully as must unanimous juries. As soon as the requisite majority is attained, further consideration is not required either by Oregon or by Louisiana even though the dissident jurors might, if given the chance, be able to convince the majority. Such persuasion does in fact occasionally occur in States where the unanimous verdict applies. . . .

---

[62] 406 U.S. at 361.

[63] Or, as Professor Zeisel put it, in his characteristically gentle manner: "The Court here fails to reckon with the realities of the deliberation process." Zeisel, note 21 *supra*, at 6.

[64] 406 U.S. at 361.

[65] For a detailed discussion of the possible definitions of reasonable doubt, see SAKS, JURY VERDICTS: THE ROLE OF GROUP SIZE AND SOCIAL DECISION RULE 24–27 (1977). For decisions holding that unanimity was constitutionally required, see Andres v. United States, 333 U.S. 740, 748 (1948); Maxwell v. Dow, 176 U.S. 581, 586 (1900); American Publishing Co. v. Fisher, 166 U.S. 464, 468 (1897).

[66] 406 U.S. at 388–90.

It is said that there is no evidence that majority jurors will refuse to listen to dissenters whose votes are unneeded for conviction. Yet human experience teaches that polite and academic conversation is no substitute for the earnest and robust argument necessary to reach unanimity. As mentioned earlier, in Apodaca's case, whatever courtesy dialogue transpired could not have lasted more than 41 minutes. I fail to understand why the Court should lift from the States the burden of justifying so radical a departure from an accepted and applauded tradition and instead demand that these defendants document with empirical evidence what has always been thought to be too obvious for further study.

Justice Douglas showed that the Court did not have to rely on "perceptions" about the functional equivalence of the two verdict rules. There was evidence to demonstrate that the two verdict rules did not produce the same deliberation results. For example:[67]

The new rule also has an impact on cases in which a unanimous jury would have neither voted to acquit nor to convict, but would have deadlocked. In unanimous-jury States, this occurs about 5.6% of the time. Of these deadlocked juries, Kalven and Zeisel say that 56% contain either one, two, or three dissenters. In these latter cases, the majorities favor the prosecution 44% (of the 56%) but the defendant only 12% (of the 56%). Thus, by eliminating these deadlocks, Louisiana wins 44 cases for every 12 that it loses, obtaining in this band of outcomes a substantially more favorable conviction ratio (3.67 to 1) than the unanimous-jury ratio of slightly less than two guilty verdicts for every acquittal. H. Kalven & H. Zeisel, The American Jury 461, 488 (Table 139) (1966).

Zeisel showed in his review of the jury cases that under majority rule provisions in twelve-person juries the jury majority is able simply to disregard the minority position in 85 percent of the relevant cases. "Only in the [15 percent of] cases in which we must expect three or more minority jurors will they be able to influence the verdict."[68] Rule change, Zeisel notes, is even more effective than size reduction in diminishing the jury:[69]

---

[67] Id. at 390–91.

[68] Zeisel, note 23 supra, at 723. The figures assume a minority position held by 10 percent of the population.

[69] Id. at 722.

> The important element to observe is that the abandonment of
> the unanimity rule is but another way of reducing the size of
> the jury. But it is reduction with a vengeance, for a majority
> verdict requirement is far more effective in nullifying the po-
> tency of minority viewpoints than is the outright reduction
> of a jury to a size equivalent to the majority that is allowed to
> agree on a verdict. Minority viewpoints fare better on a jury
> of ten that must be unanimous than on a jury of twelve where
> ten members must agree on a verdict.

Not all the evidence one would wish to have is yet available. This
point, however, is well established: Juries using majority-verdict
rules are not functionally equivalent to juries deciding unanimously in deliberation characteristics or in verdicts.[70]

The decisions from *Williams* to *Apodaca*, as this brief review
will have shown, contain two key elements: (1) the progressive diminution of the American jury and (2) the inept and irresponsible
treatment of empirical evidence. The first element permits several reactions. Some, in good faith, will welcome the trend. Others,
in equally good faith, will regard it as wrong and dangerous. What
some view as needed reforms, others interpret as steps toward
abolition. No division of opinion, however, is possible regarding
the second element: The Court's use of empirical evidence is uniformly dreadful.[71] The Court has chosen to regard as "empirical
evidence" mere statements of personal belief and anecdotal reports
of personal experience. The Court has used empirical studies as
decoration for preconceived decisions rather than as relevant information. The Court has treated data uncritically and has made
inferences from inadequate investigations. The Court has misinterpreted proper evidence.[72] The Court has ignored relevant, easily

---

[70] See the inductive evidence generated by Padawer-Singer & Barton, note 37 *supra*,
and the deductive evidence generated by Nagel & Neef, note 37 *supra*.

[71] Counsel does no better than the Court. "The quality of social science scholarship
displayed in those decisions would not win a passing grade in a high school psychology
class. The briefs presented by opposing counsel were oblivious to well established
social science findings and/or methodological principles, which would have supported
the appellant. In short, the law's confrontation with some relatively simple empirical
questions was simply an embarrassment." Saks, note 37 *supra*, at 18.

[72] Zeisel, *e.g.*, had cause to complain about the Court's use of his findings: "In *Williams*,
the Court cites the studies conducted in connection with *The American Jury* to support
its proposition that 'jurors in the minority on the first ballot are likely to be influenced
by the proportional size of the majority aligned against them.' It is only fair to point
out that the findings are quite different." Zeisel, note 23 *supra*, at 719; see also Zeisel,
Twelve Is Just, 10 TRIAL 13 (Nov.–Dec. 1974); Saks, note 37 *supra*, at 19.

available data. The Court, in other words, has shown itself unwilling and unable to deal adequately and fairly with the scientific
studies and the empirical facts important to its decisions.

IV. FIVE IS NOT ENOUGH

Ballew v. Georgia differs from the *Williams-Johnson* sequence of jury decisions in two important respects: (1) It halts the
jury diminution trend, and (2) it incorporates a new approach to
empirical evidence in jury matters. The first deviation will be welcomed by those who have found themselves in disagreement with
the previous trend. The second deviation will almost uniformly be
welcomed.

The basic facts of *Ballew* have been stated. Mr. Justice Blackmun
tested the constitutionality of the jury in question by the established
functional criteria: Can a five-person State criminal jury fulfill the
constitutionally determined purposes of trial by jury? This is how
he put the issue:[73]

> When the Court in *Williams* permitted the reduction in jury
> size . . . it expressly reserved ruling on the issue whether a
> number smaller than six passed constitutional scrutiny. . . .
> The Court refused to speculate when this so-called "slippery
> slope" would become too steep. We face now, however, the
> two-fold question whether a further reduction in the size of
> the state criminal jury does make the grade too dangerous,
> that is, whether it inhibits the functioning of the jury as an
> institution to a significant degree, and, if so, whether any state
> interest counterbalances and justifies the disruption so as to
> preserve its constitutionality.

Mr. Justice Blackmun noted that the previous jury cases had generated much scholarly work and proceeded to examine the functional issues raised by *Ballew* in light of the evidence generated by
this work.

He noted first that[74]

> recent empirical data suggest that progressively smaller juries
> are less likely to foster effective group deliberation. At some
> point, this decline leads to inaccurate fact-finding and incor-
> rect application of the common sense of the community to the

---

[73] 435 U.S. at 230–31.   [74] *Id.* at 231–32.

facts. Generally, a positive correlation exists between group
size and both the quality of group performance and group
productivity.

Mr. Justice Blackmun secured this statement well by references to
Thomas & Fink, Lempert, and *Saks.*[75] The Justice proceeded to
examine some of the possible reasons for this positive correlation,
noting in particular that "the smaller the group, the less likely it is
to overcome the biases of its members to obtain an accurate result."[76] The examinations and conclusions were accurately based
on *Lempert* and *Kelley & Thibaut.*[77]

Mr. Justice Blackmun then turned to the second issue, finding
that[78]

> the data now raise doubts about the accuracy of the results
> achieved by smaller and smaller panels. Statistical studies sug-
> gest that the risk of convicting an innocent person (Type I
> error) rises as the size of the jury diminishes. Because the risk
> of not convicting a guilty person (Type II error) increases
> with the size of the panel, an optimal jury size can be selected
> as a function of the interaction between the two risks.

The Justice correctly referred to *Nagel & Neef* and *Friedman*[79] to
substantiate the asserted relationships between jury size and the
two error types. The analysis continued: "Another doubt about
progressively smaller juries arises from the increasing inconsistency
that results from the decreases. Saks argued that the 'more a jury
type fosters consistency, the greater will be the proportion of juries
which select the correct (*i.e.,* the same) verdict and the fewer
"errors" will be made.' "[80] In addition to the *Saks* reference, the
Justice also cited *Nagel & Neef, Kalven & Zeisel, Lempert,* and
Walbert[81] in support of the conclusion that the verdicts of smaller

---

[75] Thomas & Fink, *Effects of Group Size,* 60 PSYCH. BULL. 371 (1963); Lempert, note
37 *supra;* Saks, note 37 *supra.*

[76] 435 U.S. at 233.

[77] Lempert, note 37 *supra;* Kelley & Thibaut, *Group Problem Solving,* in 4 LINDZEY &
ARONSON, HANDBOOK OF SOCIAL PSYCHOLOGY c. 29 (2d ed. 1969).

[78] 435 U.S. at 234.

[79] Nagel & Neef, note 37 *supra;* Friedman, *Trial by Jury: Criteria for Convictions, Jury
Size and Type I and Type II Errors,* 27 AM. STAT. 21 (1972).

[80] 435 U.S. at 235.

[81] Nagel & Neef, note 37 *supra;* Kalven & Zeisel, note 18 *supra;* Lempert, note 37
supra; Walbert, note 37 *supra.*

juries are less consistent and less reliable than those of larger juries. The Court correctly interpreted these several scholarly investigations.

Third, Mr. Justice Blackmun found that[82]

> the data suggest that the verdicts of jury deliberation in criminal cases will vary as juries become smaller, and that the variance amounts to an imbalance to the detriment of one side, the defense. Both Lempert and Zeisel found that the number of hung juries would diminish as the panels decreased in size. Zeisel said that the number would be cut in half—from 5% to 2.4% with a decrease from 12 to six members. Both studies emphasized that juries in criminal cases generally hang with only one, or more likely two, jurors remaining unconvinced of guilt. Also, group theory suggests that a person in the minority will adhere to his position more frequently when he has at least one other person supporting his argument. . . . As the numbers diminish below six, even fewer panels would have one member with the minority viewpoint and still fewer would have two. The chance for hung juries would decline accordingly.

The Justice properly anchored his conclusion about the defense-detrimental reduction of jury size in the work of *Lempert, Walbert, Zeisel,* and *Asch.*[83]

The representation of minority groups was the fourth issue considered by Mr. Justice Blackmun. After taking note of the many prior decisions in which it was held that "meaningful community participation cannot be attained with the exclusion of minorities or other identifiable groups from jury service,"[84] the Justice stated that although[85]

> *Williams* concluded that the six-person jury did not fail to represent adequately a cross-section of the community, the opportunity for meaningful and appropriate representation does decrease with the size of the panels. Thus, if a minority group

---

[82] *Id.* at 236.

[83] Lempert, note 37 *supra;* Walbert, note 37 *supra;* Zeisel, note 23 *supra;* Asch, *Effects of Group Pressure upon the Modification and Distortion of Judgments,* in CARTWRIGHT & ZANDER, GROUP DYNAMICS 189 (2d ed. 1960).

[84] 435 U.S. at 236–37.

[85] *Id.* at 237.

constitutes 10% of the community, 53.1% of randomly selected six-member juries could be expected to have no minority representative among their members, and 89% not to
have two. Further reduction in size will erect additional barriers to representation.

The Justice correctly obtained the percentage data from Lempert
and also noted the concurring evidence presented by Saks.

The fifth and final point in Mr. Justice Blackmun's direct review
of the empirical issues raised by *Ballew* regarded certain methodological problems in jury research which tend "to mask differences
in the operation of smaller and larger juries."[86] One of these problems is that many cases handled by the judicial system are quite
clear on points of fact and law and that different decision makers
(*e.g.*, judges, smaller juries, larger juries) will reach similar verdicts.
Mr. Justice Blackmun noted that Lempert's investigation showed a
likely disagreement rate between smaller and larger juries in only 14
percent of the cases. He properly noted that nationwide[87]

> these small percentages will represent a large number of cases.
> And it is with respect to those cases that the jury trial right
> has its greatest value. When the case is close, and the guilt or
> innocence of the defendant is not readily apparent, a properly
> functioning jury system will insure evaluation by the common
> sense of the community and will also tend to insure accurate
> factfinding.

Another masking problem was found in the use of aggregate data
for a showing of "no difference." Aggregate data often hide individual differences. The Justice pointed out that, for example, Kalven and Zeisel[88]

> found that judges held for plaintiffs 56% of the time and that
> juries held for plaintiffs 59%, an insignificant difference. Yet
> case-by-case comparison revealed judge-jury disagreement in
> 22% of the cases. . . . This casts doubt on the conclusion of
> another study that compared the aggregate results of civil

---

[86] *Ibid.* In its recognition of the masking effect, Mr. Justice Blackmun drew upon
Lempert, note 37 *supra;* Nagel & Neef, note 37 *supra;* Walbert, note 37 *supra;* Saks,
note 37 *supra;* and Zeisel & Diamond, note 52 *supra.*

[87] 435 U.S. at 237–38.   [88] *Id.* at 238–39.

cases tried before six-member juries with those of 12-member jury trials. The investigator in that study had claimed support for his hypothesis that damage awards did not vary with the reduction in jury size. Although some might say that figures in the aggregate may have supported this conclusion, a closer view of the cases reveals greater variation in the results of the smaller panels, a standard deviation of $58,335 for the six-member juries, and of $24,834 for the twelve-member juries.

Mr. Justice Blackmun wrote that these studies "lead us to conclude that the purpose and functioning of the jury in a criminal trial is seriously impaired, and to a constitutional degree, by a reduction in size to below six members."[89] With this, the Justice had answered his first question and could turn to Georgia's arguments and in particular to the issue of overriding state interests.

The State of Georgia, as the respondent in the case, presented a number of arguments to show that its criminal jury of five did not violate important Sixth Amendment interests. In addition, Georgia argued for overriding state interest with respect to certain economic issues.

Georgia's Sixth Amendment presentation consisted of five arguments. First, Georgia argued that the Supreme Court had previously approved the five-person jury in *Johnson v. Louisiana*. The Court, of course, had done no such thing: "Because the issue of the constitutionality of the five-member jury was not then before the Court, it did not rule upon it."[90] Second, Georgia argued that its five-member jury was constitutionally sufficient because it is used only in misdemeanor cases. Mr. Justice Blackmun replied:[91]

> The problem with this argument is that the purpose and functions of the jury do not vary significantly with the importance of the crime. In *Baldwin v. New York* . . . the Court held that the right to a jury trial attached in both felony and misdemeanor cases. Only in cases concerning truly petty crimes, where the deprivation of liberty was minimal, did the defendant have no constitutional right to trial by jury. In the present case the possible deprivation of liberty is substantial.

---

[89] *Id.* at 239. The Justice also relied on Faust, *Group versus Individual Problem Solving*, 59 J. Ab. & Soc. Psych. 68 (1959) (per Lempert); Barnlund, *A Comparative Study of Individual, Majority, and Group Judgment*, 58 J. Ab. & Soc. Psych. 55 (1959).

[90] 435 U.S. at 240.   [91] *Ibid.*

The Justice also noted that the mere label of "felony" or "misde-meanor" is not an adequate test for the determination of the issue, since these labels are matters of choice by the States.

Third, Georgia argued that the unanimity rule employed by its five-person juries was sufficient to satisfy the functional standards laid down in the Court's prior decisions. Mr. Justice Blackmun did not agree: "That a five-person jury may return a unanimous decision does not speak to the question whether the group engaged in mean-ingful deliberation, could remember all the important facts and arguments, and truly represented the common sense of the entire community."[92]

Fourth, Georgia argued that its five-person juries adequately rep-resent the community because no particular class is excluded arbi-trarily. This, of course, does not speak to the issue at hand. The requirement of adequate community representation and the prohi-bition of the arbitrary exclusion of cognizable groups are not identi-cal. Any random selection system of jurors will prevent arbitrary exclusions.[93] But if the group selected is too small—say, one person— it certainly cannot satisfy the representation requirement. Mr. Jus-tice Blackmun recognized the irrelevance of Georgia's argument and restated his doubts about the representational abilities of small juries:[94]

> But the data outlined above raise substantial doubt about the ability of juries truly to represent the community as member-ship decreases below six. If the smaller and smaller juries will lack consistency, as the cited studies suggest, then the sense of the community will not be applied equally in like cases. Not only is the representation of racial minorities threatened in such circumstances, but also majority attitude or various mi-nority positions may be misconstrued or misapplied by the smaller groups.

---

[92] *Id.* at 241.

[93] On the use of random selection methods for nondiscriminatory selection of jury panels and jurors, see Sperlich & Jaspovice, *Grand Juries, Grand Jurors, and the Constitu-tion*, 1 HASTINGS CONST. L.Q. 63 (1974); Sperlich & Jaspovice, *Statistical Decision Theory and the Selection of Grand Jurors: Testing for Discrimination in a Single Panel*, 2 HASTINGS CONST. L.Q. 75 (1975); Sperlich & Jaspovice, *Methods for the Analysis of Jury Panel Selections: Testing for Discrimination in a Series of Panels*, 5 HASTINGS CONST. L.Q. —— (1979), and the references in all three studies.

[94] 435 U.S. at 242.

Fifth, Georgia argued that the decline in the size of the jury will not affect the aggregate number of convictions or hung juries. Georgia cited Saks in support of this assertion. The Court recognized that Georgia had used Saks in a highly selective way and pointed out that Saks's overall conclusion was that "[L]arger juries (size twelve) are preferable to smaller juries (six). They produce longer deliberations, more communication, far better community representation, and, possibly, greater verdict reliability (consistency)."[95]

Mr. Justice Blackmun continued: "Far from relieving our concerns, then, the Saks study supports the conclusion that further reduction in jury size threatens Sixth and Fourteenth Amendment interests."[96] Georgia relied on three additional studies to support its contentions. Two of them—*Kessler* and *Mills*[97]—belong to the group of flawed and deficient studies cited by the Court in support of its *Colgrove* decision. Mr. Justice Blackmun recognized the flaws that the *Colgrove* Court had failed to notice and did not accept the two studies as valid evidence. The third additional study fared no better.[98] The Justice noted that it suffered from the same flaw as Kessler's study in that it "presented an extreme set of facts so that none of the panels rendered a guilty verdict."[99] He concluded: "None of these three reports, therefore, convinces us that a reduction in the number of jurors below six will not affect to a constitutional degree the functioning of juries in criminal trials."[100]

Georgia's arguments regarding overriding State interest were cast in economic terms. Georgia claimed that its savings in court time and in financial costs justified the reduction to five.[101] Mr. Justice Blackmun acknowledged that reductions from twelve to six brings substantial reductions in juror fees.[102]

---

[95] Quoted, *ibid*.   [96] *Ibid*.

[97] For a discussion of the two references, see note 53 *supra*.

[98] Davis, *et al.*, *The Decision Processes of 6- and 12-Person Mock Juries Assigned Unanimous and Two-Third Majority Rules*, 32 J. Pers. & Soc. Psych. 1 (1975).

[99] 435 U.S. at 243.   [100] *Ibid*.

[101] Cited in support of this claim are N.J. Criminal Law Revision Commission, Six-Member Juries (1971); Bogue & Fritz, *The Six-Man Jury*, 17 S. Dak. L. Rev. 285 (1972).

[102] 435 U.S. at 244. The Justice relied on Zeisel, note 72 *supra;* Pabst, *Statistical Studies of the Costs of Six-Man versus Twelve-Man Juries*, 14 Wm. & M. L. Rev. 326 (1972), for its estimate of actual savings.

On the other hand, the asserted saving in judicial time is not
so clear. Pabst in his study found little reduction in the time
for voir dire with the six-person jury because many questions
were directed at the veniremen as a group. Total trial time did
not diminish, and court delays and backlogs improved very
little. The point that is to be made, of course, is that a reduction in size from six to five or four or even three would save
the States little. . . . If little is gained by the reduction from
12 to six, less will be gained with a reduction from six to five.

The Justice rejected Georgia's claim, stating that "We find no significant state advantage in reducing the number of jurors from six
to five."

Mr. Justice Blackmun's treatment of the *five-person* issue presents
a gratifying picture. In his analysis of the functional aspects of the
five-member criminal jury, the Justice acted responsibly and competently on valid empirical evidence. The same conclusion emerges
from the examination of his treatment of the economic issues. The
contrast to *Williams* and the other cases discussed earlier could not
be greater.

The reviewer finds little to criticize in the handling of the empirical materials. There are some misstatements of the cited materials.
The Justice said, for example, that Nagel and Neef "tested the average conviction propensity of juries," and that they "found that half
of all 12-person juries would have average conviction propensities
that varied by no more than 20 points."[103] Nagel and Neef, of
course, did not study actual juries but developed a deductive model
of jury behavior. "Tested" and "found" suggest inductive work.
The Justice also used "significant"[104] to describe a point difference
which Nagel and Neef had characterized as "substantial."[105] The
former term has a technical meaning that is not present in the latter.
The Justice also stated that Nagel and Neef "concluded"[106] that the
conviction propensity was 0.677, when, in fact, Nagel and Neef
obtained this figure from *The American Jury*.[107] Somewhat more

---

[103] 435 U.S. at 245.   [105] Nagel & Neef, note 37 *supra*, at 972.

[104] *Ibid.*   [106] 435 U.S. at 235 n.19.

[107] Nagel & Neef, note 37 *supra*, at 951–52. There also are some aspects of the empirical materials of which Mr. Justice Blackmun did not take note—at least, not explicitly. For example, Nagel & Neef's model assumes that the number of guilty defendants per 1,000 defendants is 950. Only with this assumption will the model identify
seven as the jury size minimizing error. Changes in the assumption about the proportion
of guilty defendants alter the "ideal" jury size. If there are fewer than 950 guilty defendants per 1,000 persons brought to trial (a not unlikely proposition!), juries larger

important, the Justice reported that Lempert "concluded that smaller and larger juries could disagree in their verdicts in no more than 14% of the cases."[108] Lempert, however, concluded that his computations produced "a final estimate of 14.1% as the proportion of cases in which jury size has a reasonable probability of affecting jury verdict."[109] Lempert's percentage is a "best estimate," not an absolute upper limit.

Whatever the shifts in terminology and conceptualization, *Ballew* presents an opinion of great learning.[110] A large variety of empirical evidence has been treated with competence and responsibility. While judges, naturally, are more comfortable with the adversary approach to the resolution of matters in dispute, the academic approach to the determination of fact has been given a fair hearing.

The Justice's extensive and competent treatment of empirical evidence is all the more remarkable for the relative paucity of the litigants' briefs, in which the attorneys for Ballew did somewhat better than the attorneys for the State of Georgia.[111] The briefs of the State of Georgia contained but a single reference to materials other than cases and statutes. Georgia resurrected Judge Tamm's *The Five-Man Civil Jury: A Proposed Constitutional Amendment,* of questionable relevance.[112] The Court had relied upon it for *Williams* and had been soundly criticized for it. Georgia enlarged the scope of its evidentiary offerings in oral argument.[113] It clearly did not have much luck in dealing with empirical evidence. It must be

---

than seven will be required to minimize verdict error. The required increases are substantial. If, for example, there were only 900 guilty defendants per 1,000 defendants, the "ideal" jury size would be *twenty-three.* Without attention to these circumstances, there is peril in Mr. Justice Blackmun's reliance on the Nagel-Neff model in support of a jury of fewer than 12 persons. See Nagel & Neef, note 37 *supra,* at 367.

[108] 435 U.S. at 237.   [109] Lembert, note 37 *supra,* at 653.

[110] Mr. Justice Blackmun's undergraduate major in mathematics appears to be a great asset to the Court. He also wrote the excellent Castaneda v. Partida, 430 U.S. 482 (1976), decision on the Texas "key man" system for selecting grand juries. *Castaneda,* like *Ballew,* draws competently on a variety of empirical studies.

[111] Regarding the jury-size issue, the petitioners relied, in their briefs, on Zeisel, *The Waning of the American Jury,* 58 A.B.A.J. 367 (1972); Zeisel & Diamond, note 54 *supra;* KALVEN & ZEISEL, note 18 *supra;* Lempert, note 37 *supra;* Thomas & Fink, note 75 *supra.* In oral argument, the petitioners relied in addition on Padewer-Singer & Barton, note 37 *supra* (personal communication from Robert Eugene Smith of Atlanta, Georgia, attorney for the petitioner).

[112] See notes 35 and 36 *supra.*

[113] Here it referred to Kessler, note 51 *supra;* Mills, note 51 *supra;* Davis, note 98 *supra;* Saks, note 65 *supra.* Mr. Justice Blackmun took the Respondent to task for its selective and distorting reading of the Saks study. 435 U.S. at 242.

admitted, on the other hand, that there seems to be no valid evidence favoring Georgia's position.

V. Six Is Not Enough

Ballew v. Georgia represents one of the better examples of judicial treatment of scientific evidence. Unfortunately, admiration and approval can be extended only to the treatment of empirical data in the analysis of the *five-person* issue. They cannot be given to the handling of the *six-person matter*.

Ballew stopped the diminution of the State criminal jury to five. The Court had excellent functional reasons for halting the decline and was supported in this action by the uniform testimony of a great variety of empirical studies. These studies, however, testified to the deficiencies of six just as much as to the deficiencies of five. The empirical evidence demanded a rejection of Florida's six-person juries just as much as of Georgia's five-person juries. The evidence called for a reversal of *Williams*. The *Williams* six-person issue was, of course, not before the Court. The Court, however, was unwilling to confront the faulty "functional equivalence" arguments with any remedial intent. Indeed, Mr. Justice Blackmun was unwilling even to remain silent on the point. Instead, he included in *Ballew* a gratuitous affirmation of the *Williams* decision: "[W]e adhere to, and re-affirm our holding in *Williams v. Florida*."[114] This unfortunate affirmation required the Justice to misread some of the empirical evidence and greatly blemished an otherwise exemplary opinion.

Referring to the scholarly work generated by *Williams* and the other decisions, Mr. Justice Blackmun stated:[115]

> These writings do not draw or identify a bright line below which the number of jurors would not be able to function as required by the standards enunciated in *Williams*. On the other hand, they raise significant questions about the wisdom and constitutionality of a reduction below six.

These two sentences sharply expose the dilemma and foretell the misreading of the evidence.

The first sentence makes a false claim about *Williams*. It con-

---

[114] *Id.* at 239.

[115] *Id.* at 231–32.

veys the idea that the Court's approach in *Williams* consisted of
the delineation of clear functional standards and a search for the
minimally adequate number of jurors to satisfy these standards,
from which followed the finding that six was above this minimum
number. A reading of *Williams*, however, reveals that this was not
the approach.

There are only two places in *Williams* where anything even resembling a "minimally adequate number" language is employed.
One is found in the text of the decision. It is not a forceful and clear
pronouncement. It is no more than a hedged afterthought:[116]

> The performance of this role is not a function of the particular
> number of the body that makes up the jury. To be sure, the
> number should probably be large enough to promote group
> deliberation, free from outside attempts at intimidation, and
> to provide a fair possibility for obtaining a representative
> cross-section of the community.

The other is found in a footnote and only serves to show that the
Court indeed did not rely upon the "minimally adequate number"
approach: "We have no occasion in this case to determine what
minimum number can still constitute a 'jury,' but we do not doubt
that six is above that minimum."[117]

There are no places in *Williams* where "clear functional standards" are delineated, against which the adequacy of a given jury
size could be tested.[118] To say, for example, that the jury should
be a representative cross-section of the community (as *Williams*
hedgingly does) is not to spell out a clear standard. How can one
know, for instance, that a given jury is representative in terms of
the Court's requirements, or that juries of a given size are likely to
meet or not to meet the cross-section standard? *Williams* does not
say. Nor does *Williams* reveal just what quality of group discussion is required, and how the achievement or lack of achievement
of this quality is to be ascertained. It is eminently clear that the
Court in *Williams* did not approach the question of the constitu-

---

[116] 399 U.S. at 100.

[117] *Id.* at 91 n.28.

[118] Justice Harlan arrived at the same conclusion: "The Court's elaboration of what
is required provides no standard and vexes the meaning of the right to a jury trial in the
federal courts, as well as the state courts, by uncertainty." *Id.* at 126.

tional sufficiency of a criminal jury of six by the "clear functional standards" and "minimally adequate number" route. The evidence is abundant that the approach was that of a "functional comparison," leading to the assertion of the functional equivalence of different-sized juries. The Court, in other words, started with the undisputed constitutional sufficiency of the twelve-person jury, asserted that there were no significant differences between juries of twelve and of six, and, thus, found itself able to announce the constitutional sufficiency of the jury of six. These are the relevant passages:[119]

> But we find little reason to think that these goals are in any meaningful sense less likely to be achieved when the jury numbers six, than when it numbers 12—particularly if the requirement of unanimity is retained. And, certainly the reliability of the jury as a factfinder hardly seems likely to be a function of its size. . . .
>
> What few experiments have occurred—usually in the civil area—indicate that there is no discernible difference between the results reached by the two different-sized juries. . . .
>
> But when the comparison is between 12 and six, the odds of continually "hanging" the jury seem slight, and the numerical difference in the number needed to convict seems unlikely to inure perceptibly to the advantage of either side. . . .
>
> Similarly, while in theory the number of viewpoints represented on a randomly selected jury ought to increase as the size of the jury increases, in practice the difference between the 12-man and the six-man jury in terms of the cross-section of the community represented seems likely to be negligible. . . . the concern that the cross-section will be significantly diminished if the jury is decreased in size from 12 to six seems an unrealistic one.

Returning to the first sentence of the *Ballew* quote,[120] it is clear that it is misleading in its picturing of the *Williams* approach. It is also clear why the scholarly work generated by *Williams* does not draw that "bright line." The scholarly efforts followed the Court's lead. All but one of the studies cited in *Ballew*[121] sought to provide evi-

---

[119] *Id*. at 100–02 and n.47.

[120] Text at note 114 *supra*.   [121] 435 U.S. at 231–32 n.10.

dence on the functional similarity/dissimilarity of six- and twelve-person juries,[122] for this was the question that the Court had posed.

This brings the discussion to the second sentence: "On the other hand, they raise significant questions about the wisdom and constitutionality of a reduction below six." This is so massive a misreading of clear-cut evidence that it can be attributed only to the Court's unwillingness to come to terms with the *Williams* error. With the possible exception of Nagel and Neef's modeling effort, none of the studies cited by Ballew investigated the effect of a possible shift in jury size from six to five.[123] Instead, they dealt with the effects of the *Williams* shift from twelve to six. The focus of these studies was the wisdom and constitutionality of a reduction not below six, *but to six.*

One commentator on *Williams* wrote that "the Court's first step in *Williams* was blemished. But it was needed to permit the *non sequitur* that the jury of six and the jury of twelve are functionally equivalent."[124] The same criticism applies to *Ballew. Ballew* is flawed because the Court was trying to hold on to the clearly false assertion of the functional equivalence of twelve- and six-person juries.[125]

Another commentator concluded that *Williams* was "unconstitutional" by its own standards: "The test laid down in *Williams* indicates that the reduced jury is unconstitutional if the smaller size impairs its performance. Consequently, a correct application of the Court's test would hold that a jury of six persons is unconstitutional."[126] The comment still applies. The empirical evidence is clear. It is likely that sooner or later the Court will have to face the

---

[122] The exception is the deductive modeling study of Nagel & Neef, note 37 *supra*, which provides information about jury sizes from one to fifteen, with a variety of decision rules. The model incorporates a number of assumptions which, though reasonable, will not receive everyone's support. Furthermore, the model is not presently responsive to such issues as jury representativeness, protection from outside intimidation, the law-legitimizing function, and the educational function of the jury. However, if the model were to be used it would draw the type of line sought by *Ballew*, but it would draw it between six and seven. A minimum-adequate size of seven, however, is not supportive of the *Williams* approval of juries of six.

[123] See note 110 *supra*.   [124] Zeisel, note 110 *supra*, at 367.

[125] It should be noted that in deciding *Ballew* the Court moved away from the "functional equivalence" approach and toward the "minimally adequate" standard. The "clear functional standards" to determine what number is minimally adequate, however, are still lacking.

[126] Walbert, note 37 *supra*, at 554.

question of overruling.[127] It is unfortunate that the Court did not avail itself of the *Ballew* opportunity to begin its corrective work.

VI. OBJECTIONS TO "NUMEROLOGY"

Mr. Justice Powell, joined by Justices Burger and Rehnquist, wrote a concurring opinion in *Ballew*. He agreed with Mr. Justice Blackmun that "the line between five- and six-member juries is difficult to justify, but a line has to be drawn somewhere if the substance of jury trial is to be preserved."[128] Mr. Justice Powell, however, did not join the majority opinion because "it assumes full incorporation of the Sixth Amendment by the Fourteenth."[129] Mr. Justice Powell went on:[130]

> Also I have reservations as to the wisdom—as well as the necessity—of MR. JUSTICE BLACKMUN's heavy reliance on numerology derived from statistical studies. Moreover, neither the validity nor the methodology employed by the studies cited was subject to the traditional testing mechanisms of the adversary process. The studies relied on merely represent unexamined findings of persons interested in the jury system.

One hopes that the first sentence of this quote merely served to vent spleen. It is difficult to believe that Mr. Justice Powell would fail to draw a distinction between scientific studies and gross irrationality. He may have wished only to express his personal distaste for numbers.[131]

---

[127] Lempert, note 37 *supra*, at 705–06, asked what the Court might do if and when the evidence became available for proof of the superiority of twelve over six. "While there is no reason to be confident that the Supreme Court would do an about-face on the jury size in question if presented with these . . . results, the question of how the Court should react to such research is an interesting one. . . . Given the Court's functional response to the apparent intent of the framers, if a substantial body of well-conducted research should demonstrate that jury size does affect verdicts in ways that are detrimental to important values, the Court should reconsider its conclusions in *Williams* and *Colgrove*."

[128] 435 U.S. at 245–46.

[129] *Id.* at 246. In Duncan v. Louisiana, 391 U.S. 145 (1968), the Court extended the Sixth Amendment right to trial by jury in criminal proceedings to the States through the Due Process Clause of the Fourteenth Amendment. It has been argued that the Court in *Duncan* overlooked the twelve-person jury requirement in federal criminal cases and that *Williams* was an effort to minimize the effect of *Duncan*. See, *e.g.*, Gibbons, *The New Minijuries: Panacea or Pandora's Box*, 58 A.B.A.J. 594, 595 (1972); Stevens, note 30 *supra*, at 1006.

[130] 435 U.S. at 246.

[131] In light of the fact that Justices Burger and Rehnquist associated themselves with Mr. Justice Powell's expression of ill temper, it is appropriate to quote Mr. Justice Blackmun's response: "We also note that THE CHIEF JUSTICE did not shrink from the

The second and third sentences deserve serious attention. Mr. Justice Powell complains that the studies relied upon by Mr. Justice Blackmun have not been subjected to the traditional testing. It is not clear what Mr. Justice Powell means by this objection. He may mean that these studies were not made part of the trial record and, thus, were not subject to cross-examination. Or he may be arguing that Mr. Justice Blackmun was taking judicial notice of legislative facts without giving proper notice to the parties to permit the litigants to submit written or oral argument on the validity of the studies' methodology, on their relevance, etc. Indeed, ordinarily it is not sufficient merely to assemble the studies that have been published in the scholarly journals. Not only is there no cross-examination, but publication is not evidence of probity. Many journals do not subject their materials to a truly critical review before deciding on publication. Some even will decline to publish critiques that point out the errors in their published materials.[132] But courts do not mind using law review materials in other contexts as support for judicial arguments, even where the references are no more trustworthy.

Mr. Justice Powell's complaint about the failure to subject the *Ballew* studies to the "traditional testing mechanisms of the adversary process" points to a real problem. It is a problem that can be solved within the accepted rules of evidence. But it will require greater cooperation between the law and the scientific disciplines and a willingness on the part of each to invest in a greater understanding of the other.

VII. Conclusion

What, then, of *Ballew v. Georgia?* Mr. Justice Blackmun had set himself a difficult and thankless task and one which, in the last analysis, could not be done: to find juries of five unconstitutional while upholding the constitutionality of juries of six. The evidence that condemns the five-person jury equally condemns the six-person jury. Mr. Justice Blackmun deserves admiration, how-

---

use of empirical data in *Williams* v. *Florida* . . . , when the data were used to support the constitutionality of the six-person criminal jury, or in *Colgrove* v. *Battin* . . . , a decision also joined by Mr. Justice Rehnquist." 435 U.S. at 232 n.10.

[132] *Cf.* Saks, note 65 *supra*, at 54. It is only fair to state that if the Court does not make perfect use of social science, social science does not provide perfect materials for the Court's use.

ever, for his treatment of the empirical data with respect to the five-person issue. This is true all the more since he had to find most of the empirical evidence himself, and since, as the Powell-Burger-Rehnquist opinion shows, his efforts were not uniformly welcomed by his colleagues.

What does *Ballew* mean substantively? Clearly, it means a halt in the slide to ever smaller juries and the firm establishment of the six-person minimum. The reaffirmation of *Williams*, however, undercuts any expectation of an early reversal of that decision and of an increase in the constitutional minimum size of the state criminal jury.

In its treatment of empirical evidence, *Ballew* presents a similarly mixed appearance. The handling of the data, including complex tables and sophisticated statistical concepts, with respect to the five-person issue is excellent. Yet, the empirical side of *Ballew* is flawed because of the Court's desire to preserve *Williams*. The affirmation of *Williams* required the misreading of texts and the skirting of inferences clearly demanded by the data. Nevertheless, the decision gives encouragement to scientific studies of judicial institutions and legal processes. For all its limitations and flaws, *Ballew* is a welcome decision.

MARGARET A. BLANCHARD

THE INSTITUTIONAL PRESS AND
ITS FIRST AMENDMENT PRIVILEGES

The nation's press was given a clear message by the Supreme Court in the 1977 Term. Attempts to find a special protection for the institutional press within the Speech and Press Clauses of the First Amendment will not succeed, the Court said repeatedly as it dealt with a docket in which press claims were heavily represented. The Justices were, in a sense, responding to the argument that has sprung up in recent years that the Court has created, is creating, or will create a unique First Amendment privilege for the institutional press. Legal commentators have been debating the possibility of such a special privilege for several years;[1] critics in the media have been arguing that the Court is depriving the institutional press of

Margaret A. Blanchard is a Lecturer in the School of Journalism at the University of North Carolina at Chapel Hill.

AUTHOR'S NOTE: I thank John E. Semonche for his careful criticism which led to a greater clarification of the issues considered here.

[1] See, e.g., Bezanson, The New Free Press Guarantee, 63 VA. L. REV. 731 (1977); Van Alstyne, The Hazards to the Press of Claiming a "Preferred Position," 28 HASTINGS L.J. 761 (1977); Jaxa-Debicki, Problems in Defining the Institutional Status of the Press, 11 RICHM. L. REV. 177 (1976); Lange, The Speech and Press Clauses, 23 U.C.L.A. L. REV. 77 (1975); Nimmer, Introduction—Is Freedom of the Press a Redundancy: What Does It Add to Freedom of Speech?, 26 HASTINGS L.J. 639 (1975); Stewart, "Or of the Press," 26 HASTINGS L.J. 631 (1975); see also Schwarzlose, For Journalists Only?, COLUMBIA J. REV. 32 (July–Aug. 1977).

the special station in life to which it is constitutionally entitled.[2] This Term the Court has ruled again and again that attempts to find a special privilege for the press were futile, that there is but a single standard for measuring the rights and privileges afforded to press and speech.

Freedom of the press is almost universally measured by the standard of what the general public could do in a like situation. If the public has a right to attend trials,[3] to have access to certain records,[4] or to comment about public officials,[5] so too does the press. If the public must testify at grand jury hearings,[6] may be subject to properly drawn search warrants,[7] or must follow administrative procedures to have access to sources of information,[8] so too must the press. If the protection sought by the press for its activities is not identical with the protection granted the public in a like situation, the Court will be sympathetic if, and only if, a distinct benefit will accrue to the public from such a decision.[9] If the Court sees the press asking not only for a special privilege but for a form of preference which might be harmful to the public, the press claim will be promptly rebuffed.[10]

This standard for determining press rights, which will be detailed below, has its roots deep in Court decisions relating to the press. Historically, this intimate relationship between the press and the public rests on the idea that the press is an extension of speech. Freedom of speech was granted to the individual, as was freedom of the press. That which a person could speak he could print and

---

[2] Lyle Denniston of the *Washington Star* wrote: "Thus the court has erased some of the constitutional illusions that the press has long held about its status. For example, the notion that there was a 'firstness' about the First Amendment's freedom of the press clause, giving the press special status and constitutional priority, was shaken several times during this court term." *High Court Jolts Press's Illusion on Rights*, Washington Star, July 2, 1978, p. A1.

[3] *E.g.*, Sheppard v. Maxwell, 384 U.S. 333 (1966).

[4] *E.g.*, Cox Broadcasting Corp. v. Cohn, 420 U.S. 469 (1975).

[5] *E.g.*, New York Times Co. v. Sullivan, 376 U.S. 254 (1964).

[6] *E.g.*, Branzburg v. Hayes, 408 U.S. 665 (1972).

[7] *E.g.*, Zurcher v. Stanford Daily, 436 U.S. 547 (1978).

[8] *E.g.*, Houchins v. KQED, 98 S. Ct. 2588 (1978).

[9] *E.g.*, New York Times Co. v. United States, 403 U.S. 713 (1971).

[10] *E.g.*, Estes v. Texas, 381 U.S. 532 (1965).

distribute to others. That which a person could not speak with impunity was not protected in print.

In this view of the press as an extension of the individual freedom
to speak, we find one of the more consistent lines of precedent in
the Court's history. Critics with a special interest in expanding the
orbit of the freedom of the institutional press often find little consistency in the Supreme Court's treatment of First Amendment
claims. Instead, to them, rulings are based on whether the Justices
making up the Court at any given time have personal predilections
favorable toward or hostile to the press. A more accurate explanation of the Court's press rulings, however, and one directly consistent with the speech-press relationship, is that press rulings are
intimately tied to society's tolerance, at any given time, of various
forms of communication. A society which wants wide-open debate will often find the Court supportive of that desire. A society
which wishes, for one reason or another, to quiet debate and dissent,
will likewise find help in the Court's rulings on speech and press
issues. As society's tolerance for individual speech—and behavior—
has expanded or contracted, so too has its tolerance of freedom of
the press. Regardless of the condition of society at any given time,
the standard for measuring press claims has remained focused on the
freedom of the individual to speak.

The clarity of this standard is somewhat obscured in the earliest
stages of its development. As the Court began to deal with speech
and press questions, it was necessary to etch into the record the notion that freedom of speech and of the press was an individual
freedom. The evolution of doctrine then moved to establishing the
inseparability of First Amendment freedoms. This meant equating
the terms "speech" and "press" in decision writing and using them
interchangeably with terms such as "opinion," "belief," "discussion," and "expression." Such Court opinions on freedom of the
press often involved a form of printing done by someone who
could be labeled a dissident in society. Thus it is that much of the
doctrine on freedom of the press was set in place by what could
be called the noninstitutional press.[11] The institutional press began

---

[11] Exploration of the rights of individuals and groups to First Amendment protections
of speech and press has been a key factor in the Court's development of the inner and
outer limits of the protections offered by the Amendment. Decisions in noninstitutional
cases, as in Gitlow v. New York, 268 U.S. 652 (1925), have often been claimed later

a sustained campaign for First Amendment protection in the Supreme Court in the late 1930s and early 1940s. The first cases it argued before the Court clustered around an effort to find a proprietary protection for its money-making interests.[12] Almost simultaneously, however, the institutional press began an effort to find protection for the press's role as information gatherer for the public.[13]

Decisions in cases brought by the institutional press were clearly built upon those earlier, noninstitutional cases. One fact stands out in this evolutionary process, however: the standard which the Court has used to determine all such speech and press claims has never changed. That standard has appeared in much bolder relief in the last few years, but it has always been there and has always been used. In determining which requests for First Amendment press protection to grant, the Court seems always to have asked itself: What can the public do in a like situation?

I. The Court Responds to Pleas for Special Protection: The 1977 Term

Years of effort to find a special protection for the institutional press within the First Amendment peaked in the Supreme

---

as keys to the preservation of the development of the protection of the institutional press even though the institutional press played no part in securing the "victory." In other instances, such as Gertz v. Robert Welch, Inc., 418 U.S. 323 (1974), a noninstitutional press claim rebuffed by the Court results in a corresponding contraction of freedom available to the institutional press. Among the Justices of the Supreme Court, Louis D. Brandeis and William O. Douglas have shown the keenest appreciation of the relationship between the noninstitutional and institutional press. See United States ex rel. Milwaukee Social Democratic Publishing Co. v. Burleson, 255 U.S. 407 (1921) (Brandeis, J., dissenting); United States v. Rumely, 345 U.S. 41 (1953) (Douglas, J., concurring).

[12] Efforts here have often focused on the notion held by some that the press is the only business granted specific protection by the Constitution. With this belief, some members of the media establishment argued that the press is thus exempt from business regulations. One of the earliest arguments in the line of cases, Lewis Publishing Co. v. Morgan, 229 U.S. 288 (1913), established the principle that nondiscriminatory regulation did not infringe upon freedom of the press. That line of reasoning has remained intact. Some of the sharpest skirmishes over such alleged protection came when the anti-Roosevelt press challenged New Deal legislation affecting newspapers. E.g., Associated Press v. N.L.R.B., 301 U.S. 103 (1937).

[13] It is with the information gathering and dispersing role of the press that the Court has the most sympathy, and it is here also that the press as public agent concept comes most distinctly to the fore. Even in the days when the Court considered cases involving the press on a non–First Amendment basis this standard was applied. See Holden v. Minnesota, 137 U.S. 483 (1890); United States v. Dickey, 268 U.S. 378 (1925).

Court's 1977 Term, when the Justices left little doubt as to the place that portion of the First Amendment held in the constitutional system. The 1977 docket contained the greatest number of cases seeking protection for the institutional press since the 1973 Term.[14] Seven cases involving the institutional press were present, and several of them included requests from the press for constitutional privileges not available to the ordinary citizen. Beginning in 1975, and with increasing intensity since then, legal commentators have speculated about a possible difference in meaning between the terms "speech" and "press" as contained in the First Amendment. In the 1977 Term the Justices took greater pains than ever before to tell the press that it has no special First Amendment protections beyond that granted to the individual.

That response was made to a myriad of issues although the decisions in which it appeared did not all go against the claimed First Amendment right. The Court rejected attempts to obtain the Nixon tapes for public distribution;[15] refused to exempt newsrooms from search under a valid warrant;[16] rejected claims that F.C.C. rules on cross-ownership of broadcast media by newspapers invaded the First Amendment rights of the newspapers;[17] refused to force open jail doors to the media;[18] and found no objection to the F.C.C.'s proposed sanctions against indecent language over the airwaves.[19] On the other hand, the Court protected corporations' right to free speech on issues before the electorate,[20] and it sanctioned a newspaper's printing of confidential proceedings of a judicial inquiry board.[21] The pivotal point in decision making was equality of treatment of press and individual. The media received no special or preferential treatment.

An attempt by broadcasters to obtain "permission to copy, broad-

---

14 Major media cases in the 1973 Term were: Pell v. Procunier, 417 U.S. 817 (1974); Saxbe v. Washington Post Co., 417 U.S. 843 (1974); Miami Herald Publishing Co. v. Tornillo, 418 U.S. 241 (1974); Gertz v. Robert Welch, Inc., 418 U.S. 323 (1974).

15 Nixon v. Warner Communications, Inc., 435 U.S. 589 (1978).

16 Zurcher v. Stanford Daily, 436 U.S. 547 (1978).

17 F.C.C. v. National Citizens Committee for Broadcasting, 98 S. Ct. 2096 (1978).

18 Houchins v. KQED, 98 S. Ct. 2588 (1978).

19 F.C.C. v. Pacifica Foundation, 98 S. Ct. 3026 (1978).

20 First National Bank of Boston v. Bellotti, 435 U.S. 765 (1978).

21 Landmark Communications, Inc. v. Virginia, 435 U.S. 829 (1978).

cast, and sell to the public portions of the [Nixon] tapes played at [the Haldeman] trial" was the issue in *Nixon v. Warner Communications.*[22] Some twenty-two hours of tape recordings were heard as part of the trial, and printed transcripts of the tapes, although not allowed in evidence, were made available to the media and were disseminated to the public. One objection raised to the copying of the tapes and further distribution of their contents was that such release could prejudice possible appeals made by those convicted. The media countered with the familiar statement that the public had the right to know, meaning, in this instance, that the public had the right to hear the tapes verbatim. The press argued that since the tapes had been entered into evidence in the Haldeman trial, they had become part of the public record and should be available for a wider dissemination. Seven members of the Court joined to reverse a Court of Appeals decision that ordered the release of the tapes to the media. Mr. Chief Justice Burger and Justices Stewart, Blackmun, and Rehnquist joined Mr. Justice Powell in the opinion of the Court.

A significant part of the media's argument was based on *Cox Broadcasting Corp. v. Cohn,*[23] a 1975 decision in which the Court had determined that information made available to the public via a trial could not be kept from further distribution through the media. "Our decision in that case," wrote Mr. Justice Powell, "merely affirmed the right of the press to publish accurately information contained in court records open to the public. Since the press serves as the information-gathering agent of the public, it could not be prevented from reporting what it had learned and what the public was entitled to know."[24] In *Warner Communications*, the Justice continued, the media and the public had both heard the tapes in the courtroom and typed transcripts of the tapes had been made available. To the majority, then, there was "no question of a truncated flow of information to the public."[25] The press was not asking for access to information, said the majority, but for access to the actual tapes "to which the public has never had *physical* access"[26] for broadcasting, reproduction, and sale. Reiterating

---

[22] 435 U.S. at 594.

[23] 420 U.S. 469 (1975).   [25] *Ibid.*

[24] 435 U.S. at 609.   [26] *Ibid.*

once again the general principle that "[t]he First Amendment generally grants the press no right to information about a trial superior to that of the general public,"[27] the Court rejected the media's request.

Mr. Justice Powell, however, did not see the Court's ruling as forever barring access to the tapes. The Presidential Recordings Act empowered the Administrator of General Services to supervise the processing and release of material from the Nixon White House years. "The presence of an alternative means of public access tips the scales in favor of denying release,"[28] he said, adding that the Court should not circumvent the purposes of the act by ordering release of the tapes. Nor would the Court order the Administrator of General Services to speed the way in which material would be made available.

Justices White and Brennan agreed with the judgment of the Court and would have reversed the appeals court determination that the tapes should be given to the media. In an opinion by Justice White, however, the two dissented from the five-man decision to subject the tapes to the long, involved procedure of release by the Administrator of General Services. Although he avoided dealing directly with the issue of media access to the tapes, Mr. Justice White said he would order the lower court to deliver the tapes in question to the Administrator of General Services "forthwith"[29] for processing and release.

Dissenting in separate opinions were Justices Marshall and Stevens. Mr. Justice Marshall said that the Presidential Recordings Act "strongly indicates that the tapes should be released to the public."[30] Mr. Justice Stevens found "the normal presumption in favor of access is strongly reinforced by the special characteristics of this litigation."[31] The "subject [was] of great historical interest," he said, adding that "[f]ull understanding of this matter may affect the future operation of our institutions."[32] Neither of the dissenters seemed any more willing than the majority to entertain requests from the media for a special access to the tapes. Both preferred to see the issues in the case in terms of making the tapes available to the

---

[27] *Ibid.*

[28] *Id.* at 606.

[29] *Id.* at 612.

[30] *Id.* at 613.

[31] *Id.* at 615–16.

[32] *Id.* at 616.

public. From such public availability, apparently, would come any access to the tapes which the media would have.

In *Warner Communications*, the Court would not read into the First Amendment a privilege for the press greater than that of the general public. In *First National Bank of Boston v. Bellotti*,[33] the Court held that where the press was free to advocate points of view in elections there was no valid reason to deny a similar right to corporations. Mr. Justice Powell, speaking for a five-man majority that included Chief Justice Burger and Justices Stewart, Blackmun, and Stevens, based the decisions on the Court's time-honored objective of providing as much information as possible to the people in order to enhance the possibilities for intelligent self-government. Massachusetts had tried to limit corporate participation in discussions of referenda to issues directly and materially affecting the corporation. This, the Court said, amounted "to an impermissible legislative prohibition of speech based on the identity of the interests that spokesmen may represent in public debate over controversial issues and a requirement that the speaker have a sufficiently great interest in the subject to justify communication."[34] Such a scheme "suggests an attempt to give one side of a debatable public question an advantage in expressing its views to the people,"[35] an idea which the majority found offensive. Nor did the Court favor the State's contention that there was a difference between media corporations and nonmedia corporations, with the media corporations automatically allowed to speak and the nonmedia corporations limited. "[T]he press," said Mr. Justice Powell, "does not have a monopoly on either the First Amendment or the ability to enlighten."[36]

Chief Justice Burger seized upon this opportunity to write his longest and most explicit exposition of the meaning of the First Amendment. In the course of that explication, he directly confronted and rejected the contentions of legal commentators who had been seeking a special protection for the press. The Chief Justice equated the freedom of the press to speak on issues with that

---

[33] 435 U.S. 765 (1978).

[34] *Id.* at 784.   [35] *Id.* at 785.

[36] *Id.* at 782. Justices White, Brennan, Marshall, and Rehnquist dissented. Their main dispute with the majority was over the effect unrestricted corporate expenditures in election campaigns would have on the political balance of power. White, J., *id.* at 802; Rehnquist, J., *id.* at 822.

of the public to speak on the same issues. If such freedom was not granted to nonmedia corporations, he asked, how then could it be granted to media corporations?[37] The Chief Justice forcefully rejected the idea that the speech and press guarantees in the First Amendment offered any qualitative difference in protection to media corporations than they provided to nonmedia corporations. In fact, he saw a substantial danger to media corporations if the State law restricting the speech of nonmedia corporations was allowed to remain in force. By using such a "narrow reading of the Press Clause," the Chief Justice said, "government could perhaps impose on nonmedia corporations restrictions not permissible with respect to 'media' enterprises."[38] The problem of differentiating between media and nonmedia corporations under the First Amendment bothered the Chief. He recognized that "[t]he Court has not yet squarely resolved whether the Press Clause confers on the 'institutional press' any freedom from governmental restraint not enjoyed by all others,"[39] but he was ready to say that it conveyed no such privilege. Searching the history of the Clause, he found no suggestion "that the authors contemplated a 'special' or 'institutional' privilege."[40] He added:[41]

---

[37] The Chief Justice, in setting the stage for his concurrence, wrote: "A disquieting aspect of Massachusetts' position is that it may carry the risk of impinging on the First Amendment rights of those who employ the corporate form—as most do—to carry on the business of mass communications, particularly the large media conglomerates. This is so because of the difficulty, and perhaps impossibility, of distinguishing, either as a matter of fact or constitutional law, media corporations from corporations such as the appellants in this case." *Id.* at 796. In an attempt to carry this point further, the Chief Justice added several statements that raised the ire of media corporations: "In terms of 'unfair advantage in the political process' and 'corporate domination of the electoral process,' . . . it could be argued that such media conglomerates as I describe pose a much more realistic threat to valid interests than do appellants and similar entities not regularly concerned with shaping popular opinion on public issues." *Id.* at 796–97. "In terms of Massachusetts' other concern, the interests of minority shareholders, I perceive no basis for saying that the managers and directors of the media conglomerates are more or less sensitive to the views and desires of minority shareholders than are corporate officers generally. Nor can it be said, even if relevant to First Amendment analysis— which it is not—that the former are more virtuous, wise, or restrained in the exercise of corporate power than are the latter. . . . Thus, no factual distinction has been identified as yet that would justify government restraints on the right of appellants to express their views without, at the same time, opening the door to similar restraints upon media conglomerates with their vastly greater influence." *Id.* at 797. The institutional press concluded that the Chief Justice was threatening its right to function.

[38] *Id.* at 798.   [40] *Ibid.*

[39] *Ibid.*   [41] *Id.* at 799–800.

To conclude that the Framers did not intend to limit the freedom of the press to one select group is not necessarily to suggest that the Press Clause is redundant. The Speech Clause standing alone may be viewed as a protection of the liberty to express ideas and beliefs, while the Press Clause focuses specifically on the liberty to disseminate expression broadly and "comprehends every sort of publication which affords a vehicle of information and opinion." . . . Yet there is no fundamental distinction between expression and dissemination. The liberty encompassed by the Press Clause, although complementary to and a natural extension of Speech Clause liberty, merited special mention simply because it had been often the object of official restraints.

There would be problems in determining who would be eligible for an institutional press classification, should one exist. Voicing concern that media corporations, because of increased diversification which makes dissemination of information only a partial occupation, might not be eligible for the protection offered by an institutional press classification, the Chief Justice said, "Because the First Amendment was meant to guarantee freedom to express and communicate ideas, I can see no difference between the right of those who seek to disseminate ideas by way of a newspaper and those who give lectures or speeches and seek to enlarge the audience by publication and wide dissemination."[42] The First Amendment, he concluded, "does not 'belong' to any definable category of persons or entities: it belongs to all who exercise its freedom."[43]

---

[42] *Id.* at 802.

[43] *Ibid.* The media related more to the Chief Justice's opinion than to that of the majority. *Time* termed some of the Chief Justice's discourse as "gratuitous." It added: "Many journalists would readily concede Burger's point that the press possess no special corner on virtue, wisdom or restraint. But he also maintains that a corporation whose principal and openly stated business is publishing news is guaranteed no more protection than any other corporation. Many newsmen—and some constitutional lawyers—would surely dispute that point." *Burger's Blast*, TIME 68 (May 8, 1978).

New York Times columnist Leonard Silk looked at reaction to *First Boston Bank* this way: "Burger's opinion in the Bellotti case has been read in some quarters with alarm as reviving the attack on the 'media' first leveled by Vice President Agnew and later pursued by President Nixon and some of his aides.

"In fact, however, Burger in his Bellotti opinion does not seek to narrow the rights of the press but to broaden the rights of other corporations. If it is all right for newspapers to do something he seems to imply, it is all right for anyone else." *Issue of Media Power Not Addressed*, Raleigh News and Observer, May 29, 1978, p. 4.

Editor & Publisher commented: "Chief Justice Warren Burger's concurring opinion extending First Amendment rights to corporations and corporate advertising was met with 'mixed reviews' by newspaper editors. A few seemed to read something sinister

The key to the Chief's concurrence was the essential identity of speech rights and press rights. The question presented in *Landmark Communications, Inc. v. Virginia*,[44] was whether any preference was to be given to the press to perform its duty as information gatherer for the public. The answer: If the press was filling the public's need for information about government, the Court would look with favor upon its requests for protection. *Landmark Communications* involved the publication of details about the deliberations of a State judicial inquiry commission. The commission's sessions were allegedly confidential, but some of its proceedings had been leaked to the *Virginian Pilot* in Norfolk. The newspaper published the information and Virginia instituted criminal proceedings against the publication for divulging the material. In appealing its conviction to the Supreme Court, Landmark Communications sought no new protection, asked for no special privilege for the press, and rested its case primarily upon the right of the public to have information necessary for intelligent participation in government.

The Court appreciated the limited nature of Landmark's request. The Chief Justice wrote for a unanimous Court that the case presented no "constitutional challenge to a State's power to keep the

---

into his comment that the Constitution grants no special privilege to the institutional press.

"It seems to us that in these final two paragraphs, Justice Burger was saying what newspaper editors have been saying for years. . . ." *Burger's opinion*, May 13, 1978, p. 6.

To the Reporters Committee for Freedom of the Press, the Chief Justice's concurrence "once again indicated his disaffection with the news media—this time in a concurring opinion in the corporate advertising case which amounts to a wide ranging personal essay on the press." *Chief Justice Chides Media on Free Press Editorial Claims*, NEWS MEDIA & THE LAW 41 (July 1978).

Dan Paul, a Miami, Florida, attorney with many media clients, however, sees the Chief Justice's concurrence as a possible boon to First Amendment litigation. He arrived at this conclusion by surveying the cost of legal actions and the "advent of corporate journalism [which] has seen the burgeoning importance of favorable quarterly earnings reports, higher earnings per share, and a strong stock market performance as primary corporate goals." With the Chief Justice's concurrence, says Paul, "there may be hope. If Chief Justice Burger is right in his analysis in the Bellotti case that there is no basis for distinguishing between the managers and directors of media conglomerates and their counterparts in banking and manufacturing corporations, corporate managers of the big newspapers will recognize that the First Amendment is a newspaper's constitutional franchise to do business and will be willing to commit substantial additional resources to defend it against these new attacks in very much the same way Xerox protects its patents." Paul, *Litigation costs growing threat to free press*, EDITOR & PUBLISHER 22 (July 15, 1978).

[44] 435 U.S. 829. Justices Brennan and Powell did not participate.

Commission's proceedings confidential or to punish participants for breach of this mandate"; there was no effort to "argue for any constitutionally compelled right of access for the press to those proceedings"; nor was there any attempt to label State statutes regulating the dissemination of such information "a prior restraint or attempt by the State to censor the news media."[45] The news organization, in its appeal, relied upon the long-accepted Court standard "that truthful reporting about public officials in connection with their public duties is always insulated from the imposition of criminal sanctions by the First Amendment."[46] In looking with favor upon this claim, the Court found that "the publication Virginia seeks to punish under its statute lies near the core of the First Amendment, and the Commonwealth's interests advanced by the imposition of criminal sanctions are insufficient to justify the actual and potential encroachments on freedom of speech and of the press which follow therefrom."[47] The material published by Landmark, the Chief Justice said, "clearly served those interests in public scrutiny and discussion of governmental affairs which the First Amendment was adopted to protect."[48]

The case involved the publication of confidential proceedings of a body charged by law to operate in secrecy. Anyone reading the Court's opinion hoping to find within it a sanction for violating the secrecy of such hearings would be disappointed. The Court recognized the right to publish information which had originated in a closed hearing insofar as someone participating in commission deliberations chose to breach the confidentiality of the hearing room. When this breach occurred and the material became available to a reporter, it could be disseminated without fear of the press's being prosecuted for publication of confidential information. There was, however, a way for the State to protect the deliberations of the judicial inquiry commission, said the Chief Justice, for "much of the risk [of undesired publication] can be eliminated through careful internal procedures to protect the confidentiality of Commission proceedings.[49] The way to maintain the confidentiality of the Commission hearing was to prevent any leaks of information

---

[45] Id. at 837–38.

[46] Id. at 838.   [48] Id. at 839.

[47] Ibid.   [49] Id. at 845.

to the press.[50] In suggesting this method to control information originating in the judicial inquiry commission hearings, the Court was reiterating another well-accepted doctrine which granted the press no special right of access to information for publication.[51]

The decision, however, reflected an admission by the Court of the realities of the situation. Although the Justices found no right for the press to attend such confidential hearings, they did remove what could have developed into a major obstacle to the publication of such material. If details of commission proceedings appeared in print, the Court said, the State must look to prosecute someone other than the newspaper for violating the commission's confidentiality. A participant in the hearings had made the decision to divulge the information, and that person had chosen a representative of the press as the recipient of such information. The realities of life in America made a reporter the logical person to be told about commission proceedings, for in no other way could the public be effectively told of the information which the person responsible for the leak wished to have brought into the open. The Court, then, in this decision, acknowledged the realities of the situation and directed the State's attention to the person who made the information available in the first place.

Of all of the cases heard and decided in the 1977 Term, the one which most clearly identified public responsibilities with press responsibilities and the one which has evoked the most clearly negative reaction from the press was *Zurcher v. Stanford Daily.*[52] The

---

[50] The Court specifically recognized that this question was not present in the *Landmark* case. "The broader question—whether the publication of truthful information withheld by law from the public domain is similarly privileged—was not reached and indeed was explicitly reserved in *Cox.* . . . We need not address all the implications of that question here." *Id.* at 840.

[51] See, *e.g.*, Zemel v. Rusk, 381 U.S. 1 (1965).

[52] 436 U.S. 547 (1978). Mr. Justice Brennan did not participate.
The *Zurcher* decision brought reactions on many fronts. The President asked the Justice Department to look into possible ways to protect the press from searches. *Safeguards Sought for Press*, Washington Post, June 16, 1978, p. A3. A Senate judiciary subcommittee began hearings on the need for such protection. *Panel Opens Drive to Reverse Ruling on Newsroom Searches*, Washington Post, June 23, 1978, p. A6. A House government operations subcommittee began similar hearings. *Newsroom-Search Ruling Already Hurts, Media Testify*, Washington Post, June 27, 1978, p. A5.
Editor & Publisher magazine termed the decision "almost a lethal" blow to the First Amendment and voiced concern about its ramifications to the public. *High Court Shoots Holes in 1st and 4th Amendments*, EDITOR & PUBLISHER 6 (June 10, 1978). For a sampling of editorials responding to *Zurcher*, see *Editorials Lambast Court's Search Ruling, id.* at 7. The Reporters Committee for Freedom of the Press said that "uniformly condemnatory

case was spawned in the turmoil of the early 1970s. A demonstration at Stanford University had resulted in a confrontation with police in which several officers were injured. Present at the melee and taking pictures was a photographer from the *Stanford Daily*. The District Attorney's office procured a warrant and a search of the newspaper's office was conducted to find pictures and negatives taken at the confrontation in the hospital. The newspaper's photographer was the only person on the scene taking pictures, and law enforcement officials obviously felt that the photographs might make it easier to pinpoint those responsible for injuring police. When appealed to the Supreme Court, the case turned on the vulnerability of a newspaper office to search and on the validity of a third-person search warrant, one served on a party not involved in a crime for the sole purpose of obtaining information in that party's possession that might have an impact on a criminal prosecution.

The Court split five to three in its determination that a newsroom was no more exempt from a properly drawn search warrant than was the home or business of any other citizen. Joining Mr. Justice White in the majority were the Chief Justice and Justices Blackmun, Powell, and Rehnquist. "Under existing law," wrote Mr. Justice White, "valid warrants may be issued to search *any* property, whether or not occupied by a third party, at which there is probable cause to believe that fruits, instrumentalities, or evidence of a crime will be found."[53] He acknowledged that the Court had been urged to find that the involvement of First Amendment factors in the case required "a nearly *per se* rule forbidding the search warrant" and that the Court had been told "that searches of newspaper offices for evidence of crime reasonably believed to be on the premises will seriously threaten the ability of the press to gather, analyze, and disseminate news."[54] Answering these arguments, the

---

statements have come from reporters, editors, publishers and broadcasters and from virtually every major news media association." In analyzing the comments, the Reporters Committee said, "Not since the 1971 effort to suppress the Pentagon Papers has the press so vehemently attacked a government action involving the media. Press rhetoric in the *Stanford Daily* case appears to be even more impassioned than in the Pentagon Papers case." *Leading Media Figures Attack Police Raid Ruling*, THE NEWS MEDIA & THE LAW 4 (July 1978). For another collection of comments on the ruling, see Williamson, *Newspaper Editors Rap High Court Search Ruling*, EDITOR & PUBLISHER 9 (June 17, 1978).

[53] 436 U.S. at 554.

[54] *Id.* at 563.

Court referred to the intentions of those who framed the Constitution:[55]

> Aware of the long struggle between Crown and press and
> desiring to curb unjustified official intrusions, the Framers
> took the enormously important step of subjecting searches to
> the test of reasonableness and to the general rule requiring
> search warrants issued by neutral magistrates. They neverthe-
> less did not forbid warrants where the press was involved,
> did not require special showings that subpoenas would be im-
> practical, and did not insist that the owner of the place to be
> searched, if connected with the press, must be shown to be
> implicated in the offense being investigated.

The usual standards for issuance of a warrant, "probable cause,
specificity with respect to the place to be searched and the things
to be seized, and overall reasonableness,"[56] said the majority, would
be sufficient safeguards for the press, as they were for the public.

The majority's determination drew heated dissents from Justices
Stewart, Marshall, and Stevens. Writing for himself and Mr. Justice Marshall, Mr. Justice Stewart said, "It seems to me self-evident
that police searches of newspaper offices burden the freedom of the
press."[57] Not only does a search disrupt the smooth functioning of
a newsroom, but an unannounced search threatens "the possibility
of disclosure of information received from confidential sources, or
of the identity of the sources themselves."[58] He added, "Protection
of those sources is necessary to ensure that the press can fulfill its
constitutionally designated function of informing the public, because important information can often be obtained only by an assurance that the source will not be revealed."[59] From his inspection

---

[55] *Id.* at 565. Mr. Justice Powell, in a concurrence, elaborated on the position of the
framers in this dispute: "If the Framers had believed that the press was entitled to a
special procedure, not available to others, when government authorities required evidence
in its possession, one would have expected the terms of the Fourth Amendment to
reflect that belief. As the opinion of the Court points out, the struggle from which the
Fourth Amendment emerged was that between Crown and press. . . . The Framers
were painfully aware of that history, and their response to it was the Fourth Amendment. . . . Hence, there is every reason to believe that the usual procedures contemplated
by the Fourth Amendment do indeed apply to the press, as to every other person."
Id. at 569.

[56] *Id.* at 565.   [58] *Ibid.*
[57] *Id.* at 571.   [59] *Id.* at 571–72.

of affidavits from leading journalists attached to the case record, Mr. Justice Stewart found "uncontroverted evidence . . . that unannounced police searches of newspaper offices will significantly burden the constitutionally protected function of the press to gather news and report it to the public."[60] He concluded:[61]

> Perhaps as a matter of abstract policy a newspaper office should receive no more protection from unannounced police searches than, say, the office of a doctor or the office of a bank. But we are here to uphold a Constitution. And our Constitution does not explicitly protect the practice of medicine or the business of banking from all abridgment by government. It does explicitly protect the freedom of the press.

Mr. Justice Stewart's comments, obviously, did not convince the majority which felt that there was no magic constitutional shield that could be imposed between the press and a search warrant. But, then, Mr. Justice Stewart had argued much the same point six years earlier in *Branzburg v. Hayes*,[62] with no more success.

Mr. Justice Stevens, in his solo dissent, met the majority on its terms—press rights equal to but no greater than public rights. He found that the decision in *Zurcher* was based on a 1967 opinion which first condoned third-party warrants.[63] The Court's extension of that doctrine threatened "[c]ountless law-abiding citizens—doctors, lawyers, merchants, customers, bystanders—[who] may have documents in their possession that relate to an ongoing criminal investigation."[64] Although the freedom of the press might have been of concern to him, it found no place in his dissent, for Mr. Justice Stevens preferred to attack the ruling that allowed third-party warrants in the first place. Protecting the public from such warrants

---

[60] *Id*. at 574.   [61] *Id*. at 576.

[62] 408 U.S. 665 (1972). In this dissent, Mr. Justice Stewart wrote, "The error in the Court's absolute rejection of First Amendment interests in these cases seems to me to be most profound. For in the name of advancing the administration of justice, the Court's decision, I think, will only impair the achievement of that goal. . . . in my view, the interests protected by the First Amendment are not antagonistic to the administration of justice." *Id*. at 746. In *Branzburg*, he was joined in his dissent by Justices Marshall and Brennan; Justice Douglas dissented alone. In *Zurcher*, Mr. Justice Brennan was not participating, leaving only Mr. Justice Marshall to join the Stewart position. Mr. Justice White wrote for the Court in *Branzburg*, as he did in *Zurcher*. Mr. Justice Powell added a special concurrence in the 1972 decision as he did in 1978. The five-man majority remained unchanged in both decisions.

[63] 436 U.S. at 577.   [64] *Id*. at 579.

seemed to be his first concern; searching for a like protection for the press could come later if that battle then needed to be fought at all.[65]

If the Court was badly divided in its efforts to apply the press-public standard to *Zurcher*, it found unanimity in applying the standard to *F.C.C. v. National Citizens Committee for Broadcasting*.[66] Here, to safeguard the public's need for a diversity of voices, the Court upheld F.C.C. regulations limiting the joint ownership of newspapers and broadcast outlets in the same community.[67] Among the arguments with which the Court had to contend was "that the regulations, though designed to further the First Amendment goal of achieving 'the widest possible dissemination of information from diverse and antagonistic sources,' . . . nevertheless violate the First Amendment rights of newspaper owners."[68] This violation occurs, the Court was told, because "it is inconsistent with the First Amendment to promote diversification by barring a newspaper from owning certain broadcasting stations."[69] For a unanimous Court, Mr. Justice Marshall wrote, "[W]e see nothing in the First Amendment to prevent the Commission from allocating licenses so as to promote the 'public interest' in diversification of the mass communications media."[70] The "purpose and effect" of the regulations, he said, was "to promote free speech, not to restrict

---

[65] One of those commenting on the Court's resolution of *Zurcher* was *New York Times* columnist Anthony Lewis. He found the Court's determination "not so novel or shattering" and said "[i]t is a fundamental mistake . . . for the press to argue that it is entitled to a different and better treatment under the Constitution." Of Mr. Justice Stewart's dissent, he said, his "attempt . . . to put the press in a special constitutional status was labored and unconvincing." The Stevens approach drew the columnist's praise, for, as Lewis said, "the problem needs deeper consideration by the court and others, in a context broader than the press." Lewis, *The Court and the Press*, New York Times, June 8, 1978, p. A27.

[66] Note 17 *supra*. Mr. Justice Brennan did not participate. See Polsby, *FCC v. National Citizens Committee for Broadcasting and the Judicious Uses of Administrative Discretion*, *supra*. This case should also be seen as one of a series of cases in which the Court has been asked to deal with the electronic media. The Justices have never seemed truly comfortable with the position they have accorded to the electronic media within the constitutional system.

[67] The Court allowed existing combinations to remain undisturbed, except in some sixteen instances where the sole daily newspaper published in a community and the sole broadcast outlet providing the community with a clear signal were owned by the same person.

[68] 98 S. Ct. at 2114.

[69] *Ibid.*   [70] *Ibid.*

it."[71] In addition, there was no attempt to discriminate against newspaper owners, said the Court, for "the regulations treat newspaper owners in essentially the same fashion as other owners of the major media of mass communications were already treated under the Commission's multiple ownership rules."[72] Elaborating, the Justice said that "owners of radio stations, television stations, and newspapers alike are now restricted in their ability to acquire licenses for co-located broadcast stations."[73] Consequently, "[t]he regulations are a reasonable means of promoting the public interest in diversified mass communications; thus they do not violate the First Amendment rights of those who will be denied broadcast licenses pursuant to them."[74]

To the Court, this case obviously fell into a line of precedents in which the First Amendment was seen as no bar to the application of general business regulations to media businesses. An added basis for this decision was the Court's repeated statement that the public needed to have access to as much information from as many voices as possible. These two factors made the decision inevitable. To the institutional press, however, no amount of precedent would make palatable the curtailment of their ability to diversify corporate moneys into broadcast facilities in the same community.[75]

All members of the Court participating in *Houchins v. KQED*[76] seemed to agree that press access and public access to information were equal. The Court split badly, however, over whether the public's right to inquire into prison conditions was adequately satisfied by restrictions on jail visitation imposed by a California sheriff.

---

[71] *Id.* at 2115.

[72] *Ibid.*

[73] *Ibid.*

[74] *Id.* at 2115–16.

[75] In viewing the cross-ownership decision, *Editor & Publisher* wondered whether the Court was not indeed regulating the press. "[W]hile the ruling tells publishers no more of them will be able to join the exclusive class of those who own transmitters in their own communities, it is also telling broadcasters they cannot indulge in publishing a newspaper in the same community.

"Isn't that regulating the print media? Under the First Amendment how can anyone be precluded from publishing a newspaper?" *Cross-Ownership Decision,* EDITOR & PUBLISHER 4 (June 17, 1978).

The American Newspaper Publishers Association held its annual meeting before the Court handed down its decision in the cross-ownership case. Its task force on Radio-TV Ownership, however, warned members that should an unfavorable decision appear, "[r]emedial legislative activity may be necessary." *ANPA Task Forces Augment Committee Studies, Vigilance,* EDITOR & PUBLISHER 19 (April 29, 1978).

[76] Note 8 *supra.* Justices Marshall and Blackmun did not participate.

Houchins was the one decision during the 1977 Term in which the Justices clearly faced the press-public equation and for the first time sought to determine the limits on access to information enforceable against both the press and public under the First Amendment.

Houchins began its route to the Supreme Court's docket when the sheriff of Alameda County, California, refused a KQED request to go inside the jail to take pictures. The request was preceded by broadcast reports about poor conditions within the jail. When the sheriff refused the media access, KQED brought suit. The area branches of the National Association for the Advancement of Colored People joined the action charging that Sheriff Houchins[77]

> had violated the First Amendment by refusing to permit media access and failing to provide any effective means by which the public could be informed of conditions prevailing in the Greystone facility or learn of the prisoners' grievances. Public access to such information was essential, they asserted, in order for NAACP members to participate in the public debate on jail conditions in Alameda County. They further asserted that television coverage of the conditions in the cells and facilities was the most effective way of informing the public of prison conditions.

After the complaint was filed, the sheriff announced plans for public tours of the jail which were open to reporters. The tours were limited to certain parts of the facility, no cameras or tape recorders were allowed, and no contact with inmates was permitted. It was this policy that a split Court upheld. Mr. Chief Justice Burger announced the judgment of the Court in which Justices Stewart, White, and Rehnquist joined. Only Justices White and Rehnquist joined the Chief Justice's opinion. Justices Brennan and Powell joined in a dissent written by Mr. Justice Stevens. Two members of the Court, Justices Marshall and Blackmun, did not participate in the case.

The Chief Justice, in his opinion, recognized the importance of public knowledge about prison conditions and the importance of the press in providing needed information. "Beyond question, the role of the media is important," he wrote, for as the " 'eyes and ears'

---

[77] 98 S. Ct. at 2591.

of the public, they can be a powerful and constructive force, contributing to remedial action in the conduct of public business. They have served that function since the beginning of the Republic, but like all other components of our society media representatives are subject to limits."[78] The request by media representatives to have a freer access to the jail, to be able to take cameras and tape recorders inside, and to talk indiscriminately with prisoners was disturbing to the Chief Justice. Underlying this request for special access he found the assumption that there needed to be an investigation of conditions at the jail and that representatives of the media were "the best qualified persons for the task of discovering malfeasance in public institutions."[79] But, said Mr. Chief Justice Burger, "that assumption finds no support in the decisions of this Court or the First Amendment."[80] Investigations of public institutions by media representatives were suspect to the Chief Justice because "[e]ditors and newsmen who inspect a jail may decide to publish or not to publish what information they acquire."[81] Having thus labeled media claims for access to the jail as less than imperative, the Chief Justice found little difficulty in concluding that, since the appropriate legislative body had not mandated opening of the jail to the press and the public, the Court did not derive from the First Amendment the power to impose such a visitation policy:[82]

> Neither the First Amendment nor the Fourteenth Amendment mandates a right of access to government information or sources of information within the government's control. . . . [U]ntil the political branches decree otherwise, as they are free to do, the media has no special right of access to the Alameda County Jail different from or greater than that accorded the public generally.

Mr. Justice Stewart concurred in the Court's judgment in *Houchins* because he agreed "that the preliminary injunction against the petitioner was unwarranted."[83] But, to him, "KQED was entitled to injunctive relief of a more limited scope."[84] He agreed with the basic principle that the First and Fourteenth Amendments "do

---

[78] *Id.* at 2594.

[79] *Id.* at 2596.

[80] *Ibid.*

[81] *Ibid.*

[82] *Id.* at 2597.

[83] *Id.* at 2598.

[84] *Ibid.*

not guarantee the public a right of access to information generated or controlled by government, nor do they guarantee the press any basic right of access superior to that of the public generally."[85] To Mr. Justice Stewart, "The Constitution does no more than assure the public and the press equal access once government has opened its doors."[86] Thus, he found, he could "agree substantially with what the opinion of The Chief Justice has to say on that score."[87] He felt, however, that the Chief Justice was wrong in "applying these abstractions to . . . this case. Whereas he appears to view 'equal access' as meaning access that is identical in all respects, I believe that the concept of equal access must be accorded more flexibility in order to accommodate the practical distinctions between the press and the general public."[88] "When on assignment, a journalist does not tour a jail simply for his own edification. He is there to gather information to be passed on to others, and his mission is protected by the Constitution" because "[o]ur society depends heavily on the press for . . . enlightenment."[89]

To this conclusion, he brought his own philosophy on the place of the press in society:[90]

> That the First Amendment speaks separately of freedom of speech and freedom of the press is no constitutional accident, but an acknowledgment of the critical role played by the press in American society. The Constitution requires sensitivity to that role, and to the special needs of the press in performing it effectively. A person touring Santa Rita jail can grasp its reality with his own eyes and ears. But if a television reporter is to convey the jail's sights and sounds to those who cannot personally visit the place, he must use cameras and sound equipment. In short, terms of access that are reasonably imposed on individual members of the public may, if they impede effective reporting without sufficient justification, be unreasonable as applied to journalists who are there to convey to the general public what the visitors see.

With this in mind, Mr. Justice Stewart found the district court's determinations, that the press should be given access to the jail on a more frequent and flexible basis than the public and that the media

[85] *Ibid.*

[86] *Ibid.*

[87] *Ibid.*

[88] *Ibid.*

[89] *Ibid.*

[90] *Ibid.*

should be allowed to use cameras and recording equipment during their visits, to be "sanctioned by the Constitution and amply supported by the record."[91] He disagreed, however, with the lower court's order to allow reporters into a specific portion of the jail where a prisoner had committed suicide and with its order that reporters be allowed to interview inmates encountered at random. "In both these respects," he said, "the injunction gave the press access to areas and sources of information from which persons on the public tours had been excluded, and thus enlarged the scope of what the Sheriff and Supervisors had opened to public view."[92] Because the lower-court order had "exceeded the requirements of the Constitution,"[93] he agreed that the order must be reversed. "But I would not foreclose the possibility of further relief for KQED on remand. . . . In my view, the availability and scope of future permanent injunctive relief must depend upon the extent of access then permitted the public, and the decree must be framed to accommodate equitably the constitutional role of the press and the institutional requirements of the jail."[94]

In his *Houchins* opinion, Mr. Justice Stewart was not far from the position he had staked out as the writer for the majority in two previous cases involving media requests for access to prisons, *Pell v. Procunier*[95] and *Saxbe v. Washington Post Co.*[96] There he found, for the Court, that certain restrictions imposed by prison authorities on media representatives were counterbalanced by avenues opened to the press to obtain information about the prisons involved. The regulations which his opinions upheld in 1974 limited the face-to-face contact between reporters and prisoners.[97] In *Houchins*, not only was the face-to-face contact between media and prisoners

---

[91] *Id.* at 2599.   [92] *Ibid.*   [93] *Ibid.*

[94] *Ibid.* "[S]ome media lawyers," reported *Broadcasting* magazine, "took solace from a concurring opinion of Justice Potter Stewart in the KQED case. While agreeing generally that the press does not enjoy any greater right of access to information than does the public—and providing the swing vote in the case—Justice Stewart indicated he could be persuaded to support special consideration for the press in some cases." *High Court No Friend of the Media*, BROADCASTING 22–23 (July 10, 1978).

[95] 417 U.S. 817 (1974).   [96] 417 U.S. 843 (1974).

[97] In *Pell*, Mr. Justice Stewart outlined the type of access to the prisons available to the press. "The Department of Corrections regularly conducts public tours through the prisons for the benefit of interested citizens. In addition, newsmen are permitted to visit both the maximum security and minimum security sections of the institutions and to stop and speak about any subject to any inmates they may encounter. If security considerations permit, corrections personnel will step aside to permit such interviews to be confidential. Apart from general access to all parts of the institutions, newsmen are also

limited, but so too were the other avenues for obtaining information and presenting it to the public that were available in the 1974
cases. If the district court had followed Mr. Justice Stewart's 1974
guidelines and not required special arrangements for the press, perhaps the decision in *Houchins* would have gone the other way.

The dissenters, in an opinion by Mr. Justice Stevens, found that
the sheriff's practices regarding tours of the jail were too restrictive
for everyone involved—press and public alike. "[T]he Court," he
wrote, "has never intimated that a nondiscriminatory policy of excluding entirely both the public and the press from access to information about prison conditions would avoid constitutional scrutiny."[98] He added:[99]

> It is not sufficient, therefore, that the channels of communi-
> cations be free of governmental restraints. Without some pro-
> tection for the acquisition of information about the operation
> of public institutions such as prisons by the public at large,
> the process of self-governance contemplated by the Framers
> would be stripped of its substance.
>
> For that reason information-gathering is entitled to some
> measure of constitutional protection. . . . As this Court's de-
> cisions clearly indicate, however, this protection is not for the
> benefit of those who might qualify as representatives of the
> "press" but to insure that the citizens are fully informed re-
> garding matters of public interest and importance.

permitted to enter the prisons to interview inmates selected at random by corrections
officials. By the same token, if a newsman wishes to write a story on a particular prison
program, he is permitted to sit in on group meetings and to interview participants. In
short, members of the press enjoy access to California prisons that is not available to
other members of the public." 417 U.S. at 830–31.

Some members of the press, however, were unhappy with this arrangement. They
wanted to be able to interview inmates which they, not prison authorities, chose. Those
with whom such interviews were requested had been purposely restricted from contact
with the press by institutional personnel. In California, media representatives had been
allowed such interviews until a period of prison violence led to a rule change. The new
regulation, said Mr. Justice Stewart, "did not impose a discrimination against press
access, but merely eliminated a special privilege formerly given to representatives of
the press vis-à-vis members of the public generally." *Id.* at 831.

In the *Saxbe* case, Mr. Justice Stewart found federal restrictions like those imposed
in California equally permissible. Joining the majority in both cases were the Chief
Justice and Justices White, Blackmun, and Rehnquist. Mr. Justice Powell concurred in
part and dissented in part in *Pell* and dissented outright in *Saxbe*. Dissenting in both cases
were Justices Douglas, Brennan, and Marshall. In *Houchins*, the alignment of the Justices
remained virtually the same, with Mr. Justice Stevens replacing Justice Douglas and
with Justices Blackmun and Marshall not participating.

[98] 98 S. Ct. at 2603.

[99] *Id.* at 2606.

To the dissenters, the channels of information were closed to both the press and the public, and that situation needed to be changed.

This same lack of agreement on how best to serve the public was apparent in the final media decision of the Term, *F.C.C. v. Pacifica Foundation.*[100] Here a five-man majority decided that the F.C.C. could inhibit the ability of a radio station to broadcast offensive language under carefully prescribed circumstances. The case involved Pacifica's broadcast of the "Filthy Words" monologue by comedian George Carlin. Mr. Justice Stevens wrote the opinion of the Court in which Mr. Chief Justice Burger and Justices Blackmun, Powell, and Rehnquist joined. The Court held that Carlin could perform the monologue in a variety of circumstances under his right of free speech, but that the F.C.C. could look askance at putting it on the air in the middle of the day. The nature of the broadcast medium which "confronts the citizen, not only in public, but in the privacy of his home, where the individual's right to be let alone plainly outweighs the First Amendment rights of an intruder," had to be considered. "[T]he broadcast audience is constantly tuning in and out," so that "prior warnings cannot completely protect the listener or viewer from unexpected content. To say that one may

---

[100] Note 19 *supra.* Broadcasters found the Court decision in *Pacifica Foundation* unsettling and worried about its implications for other programming because of its emphasis on the nature of the medium and its pervasiveness. As *Broadcasting* magazine said, "A major effort by the broadcasting establishment and allies in related fields to stake out new First Amendment protection for broadcasters shattered last week on a 5-to-4 vote of the Supreme Court." Supporting the *Pacifica* appeal, according to the magazine, were such groups as the National Association of Broadcasters, the commercial and noncommercial networks, the Radio Television News Directors Association, the Motion Picture Association of America, and various citizens' groups. In reporting comment on the decision, the magazine was careful to point out that supporters of the *Pacifica* appeal did not necessarily support the use of language such as that contained in the Carlin monologue over the air. *WBAI Ruling: Supreme Court Saves the Worst for the Last,* BROADCASTING 20 (July 10, 1978).

Washington Star Syndicate columnist James J. Kilpatrick, however, found that "[i]n affirming the action of the Federal Communications Commission in this affair, the Supreme Court may have struck a small but useful blow for good taste and simple decency." He found it "high time . . . that some stuck up for the rights of the enormous majority of our people who find George Carlin's filthy words offensive" and that it was also "high time for zealous libertarians to stop equating the George Carlins of the garbage circuit with Shakespeare, Chaucer and Twain." And he added, "The coverage of the Supreme Court's opinion ought to tell us something. Not a single newspaper, so far as I am advised, has printed the Seven Dirty Words, even though we are in business to answer our readers' reasonable questions. This is a matter of editorial judgment, which is all the FCC has asked the broadcasters to exercise. It is a matter of taste." Kilpatrick, *The Seven Dirty Words Debate and Freedom of the Majority,* Raleigh News and Observer, July 12, 1978, p. 5.

avoid further offense by turning off the radio when he hears inde-
cent language is like saying that the remedy for an assault is to run
away after the first blow."[101] The fact that children have easy access to the medium was also considered important to Mr. Justice
Stevens and, with such considerations as the context in which the
broadcast was made in mind, the F.C.C.'s action was upheld.

In concurring, Mr. Justice Powell said the case turned "on the
unique characteristics of the broadcast media, combined with society's right to protect its children from speech generally agreed
to be inappropriate for their years, and with the interest of unwilling adults in not being assaulted by such offensive speech in their
homes."[102] Any adult who wanted to hear Carlin's monologue, in
Mr. Justice Powell's opinion, was free to purchase a record and
do so.

Responding to the majority's determination, Justices Brennan and
Marshall in dissent accused the Court of deciding "that the degree
of protection the First Amendment affords to protected speech
varies with the social value ascribed to that speech by five Members
of this Court."[103] To Mr. Justice Brennan, the Court had become
more and more willing to suppress expression that a majority of the
sitting Justices found distasteful. Responding to the majority, he
said:[104]

> It is quite evident that I find the Court's attempt to unstitch
> the warp and woof of First Amendment law in an effort to
> reshape its fabric to cover the patently wrong result the Court
> reaches in this case dangerous as well as lamentable. Yet there
> runs throughout the opinions of my Brothers POWELL and
> STEVENS another vein I find equally disturbing: a depressing
> inability to appreciate that in our land of cultural pluralism,
> there are many who think, act, and talk differently from the
> Members of this Court, and who do not share their fragile
> sensibilities. It is only an acute ethnocentric myopia that en-
> ables the Court to approve censorship of communications sole-
> ly because of the words they contain.

---

[101] 98 S. Ct. at 3040.

[102] Id. at 3047.

[103] Ibid. Mr. Justice Stewart wrote an additional dissent in which Justices Brennan,
White, and Marshall joined. Id. at 3055.

[104] Id. at 3054.

The question that the Brennan dissent raises is whether his breth-ren are indeed suffering from "ethnocentric myopia" or whether they are heeding the demands of society for a quieter, less disrup-tive environment. As society itself becomes less willing to tolerate the strident voice, the jarring disruption of life, and, indeed, inde-cent language, the lack of tolerance spills over into law enforce-ment and into the judiciary. Such changes in the social fabric of American life in turn contract the breadth allowed speech and press activities as, in the past, movement of American society in the other direction has expanded speech and press freedoms.

The Court's decisions on speech and press issues last Term defi-nitely indicated such a contraction of freedom of expression, but, as indicated in the decisions above, the Justices forming the majorities did not see their determinations as out of line with the amount of freedom allowed individuals in American society. The Court han-dled seven media cases during the Term, five of which resulted in split decisions. There was one seven-two division, three five-four splits, and one four-three lineup. The number of split decisions in media cases, however, should not be seen as indicative of a frag-mented Court undecided on what approach to take in media cases. All of the Justices basically applied the press-public standard to the cases presented to them in the 1977 Term. The varied responses were due in part to the fact situations presented and in part to the Justices' perceptions of how the public would be allowed to func-tion in a like situation in 1978. Thus the emphasis was on abiding by the wishes of a society tired of antiwar protests and the Watergate furor, on redressing the balance among those able to communicate their points of view to the public, and, perhaps, on showing the press that society expected it to fulfill the same duties and responsi-bilities expected of individuals.

In the divided cases, Mr. Justice Stevens, four out of five times, was willing to allow what could be termed a greater toleration of First Amendment claims, although his dissents in *Warner Commu-nications* and *Zurcher* did not place his views in a First Amendment context. He was with the majority in *First National Bank* and was the opinion writer in *Pacifica Foundation*. Mr. Justice Stevens's ap-pearance in the majority in the last case may be indicative of his willingness to join with other members of the bench in preserving the delicate balance between press and public rights. Chief Justice

Burger was with the majority in all five of the divided cases, drawing the ire of the press for his concurrence in *First National Bank*
and for his opinion in *Houchins*. Both opinions, however, were
based on this press-public balance; the Chief Justice carries this conservative attitude over into his view of the press-public equation.

In three of the four divided cases in which he participated, Mr.
Justice Brennan was among the dissenters. Although Mr. Justice
Marshall appeared among the dissenters in all four of the divided
cases in which he participated, it was Mr. Justice Brennan who most
often took the Court to task for its use of the press-public equation.
While the Court majority was willing to balance press and public
rights almost equally, Mr. Justice Brennan would have chosen the
standard which gave a decided preference to the press. Although
dissents in First Amendment cases have in the past sometimes anticipated future majority positions, Mr. Justice Brennan's dissents have
the ring of the Warren Court about them, and, unless American society changes dramatically, his dissents will not soon return to the
majorities from which they came. By the end of the Term, then, if
the Justices had not, as the Chief Justice said in *First National Bank*,
squarely resolved the question of whether there was a special privilege for the institutional press, they had come very close to answering the query in the negative.[105]

Such wrestling with speech and press questions and such a measuring of speech and press demands in terms of the public's needs
at a certain time and place in American history are not unique to
the Burger Court. Changes in American society bring changes in
the way in which appointees to the High Bench are chosen, and
these new members of the Court bring with them the value systems
of the times which spawned them. In this way dissenters do become
voices of later Court majorities and majorities dwindle into lonely

---

[105] One analyst of the Court's voting patterns in the media cases finds "four of the nine
present justices are more or less on the press' side, constitutionally." That should not be
reassuring he says because "the press is discovering increasingly . . . that it has some definite adversaries on the court, including justices formerly thought to be mainly on its side—
particularly, the chief justice and Justice Byron R. White." He finds "[i]f there is anything like an 'anti-press bloc' on the court, it probably consists of Burger, White and
Justice William H. Rehnquist." The press discovers Justices William J. Brennan and
Thurgood Marshall "voting its way almost predictably" and "can usually get the votes"
of Justices Potter Stewart and John Paul Stevens. "The votes of Justices Harry A.
Blackmun and Lewis F. Powell, Jr. seem to be within reach, but not often enough to
make a certain five-member majority on any given case." Denniston, note 2 *supra*.

voices in opposition. This is not an extraordinary statement about the United States Supreme Court. What is extraordinary is that despite this fluctuation of personnel and political philosophies Justices of a generation ago and Justices of today, Justices of conservative, liberal, or middle-of-the-road political persuasions, and Justices interested in expanding First Amendment rights or interested in contracting them have responded in a consistent manner to the speech and press claims placed before them. In almost every instance, the Court has settled upon the same guideline for decision making that has emerged so clearly this year: the press is, if anything, the information-gathering agent of the public and in that role not only are its rights and privileges defined, but so are its duties and obligations.

II. Tentative Explorations into the Meaning of Freedom of the Press before 1931

Although the Supreme Court did not start using the First Amendment as a vehicle to decide speech- and press-related cases until the early twentieth century, the Justices did have opportunities much earlier to consider the place accorded the press in society. These decisions of the nineteenth and early twentieth centuries laid much-needed groundwork in the areas of determining what was included within the term "press," to whom the freedom of the press belonged, and what regulations could be imposed upon that freedom.

One of the Court's earliest confrontations with the term "press" came in cases brought to contest the regulation of obscenity through limiting its access to the mails. "In excluding various articles from the mails," wrote the Court in *Ex parte Jackson*, "the object of Congress has not been to interfere with the freedom of the press, or with any other rights of the people; but to refuse its facilities for the distribution of matter deemed injurious to the public morals."[106] Some fourteen years later, in 1892, the Court added that so long as "[t]he freedom of communication is not abridged within the intent and meaning of the constitutional provision,"[107] Congress could prohibit materials which it deemed as injurious to

---

[106] 96 U.S. 727, 736 (1878).

[107] *In re* Rapier, 143 U.S. 110, 134–35 (1892).

the public morals from the mails. Through these early decisions, we find set in place the notion that the freedom of the press belongs to the public, that not all activities may claim its protection, and that there are some regulations of it which could be upheld.

As if to substantiate some of these statements, the Court conveyed its understanding of the press in 1897 when it discussed the position held in society by the guarantees of the Bill of Rights. "In incorporating these principles into fundamental law," said the Court, "there was no intention of disregarding the exceptions, which continued to be recognized as if they had been formally expressed."[108] Such a view, the opinion continued, meant "the freedom of speech and of the press . . . does not permit the publication of libels, blasphemous or indecent articles, or other publications injurious to public morals or private reputation."[109] Such a way of interpreting freedom of speech and of the press was very much in line with the predominant opinions of state courts and leading legal commentators of the time.[110]

Also in line with contemporary thought was a Court opinion which indicated that the press could be excluded from an execution without offense to its freedom or its place in society. This challenge to a Minnesota law came not from the press but from the soon-to-be executed prisoner. The Court had little difficulty in upholding the statute which read in part, "no person admitted [to the execution] shall be a newspaper reporter or representative. No account of the details of such execution, beyond the statement of the fact that such convict was on the day in question duly executed according to law, shall be published in any newspaper."[111] The Court found no infringement of the prisoner's "substantial rights" through the "exclusion altogether of reporters or representatives of newspapers."[112] The regulations, said the opinion, were passed by the state legislature "for the public good,"[113] and the rules were allowed to remain in force.

The press was not seeking to have access to the execution in the above case. In fact, the press, in its institutional sense, appeared only

---

[108] Robertson v. Baldwin, 165 U.S. 275, 281 (1897).

[109] *Ibid.*

[110] See, *e.g.*, COOLEY, CONSTITUTIONAL LIMITATIONS 510–70 (6th ed. 1890).

[111] Holden v. Minnesota, 137 U.S. 483, 486 (1890).

[112] *Id.* at 491.   [113] *Ibid.*

sporadically as a party to cases on the Court's docket during these early years. One reason for this, of course, was the fact the Court had not yet interpreted the Fourteenth Amendment to make the First Amendment applicable to the States. The Court did hear a number of press cases, including several libel actions.[114] Much of this early action by the Court is overlooked by historians who search for the evolution of the Court's attitude toward the press only in those few early cases in which the Court was asked to consider a free press claim.

Patterson v. Colorado[115] provided the Court with such a request. A newspaper convicted of contempt of the State's supreme court sought to have the Justices of the United States Supreme Court review the conviction. A majority of the Court refused the request, saying that the Fourteenth Amendment did not provide the means for the Justices to inspect State action in this area. The decision, however, is important for the dissenting opinion of Justice John Marshall Harlan in which he gave eloquent voice to the need for Supreme Court oversight in First Amendment matters:[116]

> I . . . hold that the privileges of free speech and of a free press, belonging to every citizen of the United States, constitute essential parts of every man's liberty, and are protected against violation by that clause of the Fourteenth Amendment forbidding a State to deprive any person of his liberty without due process of law.

He added that he found it "impossible to conceive of liberty, as secured by the Constitution against hostile action, whether by the Nation or by the States, which does not embrace the right to enjoy free speech and the right to have a free press."[117] To Justice Harlan, writing in 1907, freedom of speech and press were individual rights to be protected from all invasion.[118]

---

[114] Libel actions heard by the Court came from both media and nonmedia sources. In the nonmedia area, in particular, the Court established important guidelines which allowed citizens greater latitude for discussing the conduct of public officials. See, *e.g.*, Peck v. Tribune Co., 214 U.S. 185 (1909); White v. Nicholls, 3 How. 266 (1845).

[115] 205 U.S. 454 (1907).   [116] *Id.* at 465.

[117] *Ibid.*

[118] Justice Harlan, in his dissent, indicated a strong disapproval of a standard which would equate the freedom of the press with the public welfare. The Court majority, he said, determined that it "leaves undecided the specific question whether there is to be

Such early indications of the individual nature of freedom of the press did not deter the institutional press from seeking a form of proprietary protection under the First Amendment. In 1913, in *Lewis Publishing Co. v. Morgan*,[119] the institutional press attacked new congressional standards for the maintenance of second-class mailing privileges. The legislation required the disclosure of publication owners, managers, and circulation on a regular basis to postal authorities and within the pages of the publication, and also required that any material inserted in the publication for pay be clearly labeled as an advertisement.[120] Newspaper owners argued that the new requirements were restrictions on the First Amendment's guarantee of freedom of the press. A unanimous Court found little merit in the publishers' argument. If anything, the Court said, the second-class privilege was just that, a privilege granted to newspapers "to secure to the public the benefits to result from 'the wide dissemination of intelligence as to current events.' "[121] A public-policy determination, said the Court, had allowed the newspaper

---

found in the Fourteenth Amendment a prohibition as to the rights of free speech and a free press similar to that in the First. It yet proceeds to say that the main purpose of such constitutional provisions was to prevent all such 'previous restraints' upon publications as had been practiced by other governments, but not to prevent the subsequent punishment of such as may be deemed contrary to the public welfare. I cannot assent to that view, if it be meant that the legislature may impair or abridge the rights of a free press and of free speech whenever it thinks that the public welfare requires that to be done." *Id.* at 464–65.

[119] 299 U.S. 288 (1913). This case brought the American Newspaper Publishers Association (ANPA) before the Court for the first time and began an effort to find proprietary protection for the business interests of newspapers which continues even today. The ANPA is the leading trade organization in the newspaper business. Membership is limited to publishers, meaning those usually connected more with the business side of the newspaper operation than with the informational side. Legislatively and judicially, the ANPA has historically been interested in promoting the financial well-being of the institutional press. EMERY, HISTORY OF THE AMERICAN NEWSPAPER PUBLISHERS ASSOCIATION 114–18 (1950).

[120] The distress of the press with this legislation is apparent in looking at a portion of the Lewis Publishing Co. argument which the Court had inserted in its opinion. The publishing company found the law "neither in form nor substance a law designed to regulate the carriage of the mails but *to regulate journalism.*" "The law in question makes no reference to the mails except that it uses exclusion therefrom *as a means of enforcing this censorship of the press.*" The provision which called for the disclosure of names of owners and managers and circulation figures was termed *"the inquisitorial provision."* The segment of argument included by the Court in the record concluded, "Its [the Post Office's] function is to carry the mails and in such carriage it cannot matter whether *the public* are advised as to the ownership, editorial direction and circulation of a newspaper or not, or whether the matter which it publishes is published for a consideration." 299 U.S. at 298.

[121] *Id.* at 304.

press "to secure to it great pecuniary and other concessions and a wider circulation and consequently a greater sphere of influence."[122] Such a discriminatory base in favor of newspapers for the second-class mailing privilege should not be forgotten, the decision implied, indicating that spurious claims of infringement of First Amendment rights in the business area would find no sympathetic ear among Justices of the Supreme Court.

The Court carried its unwillingness to find a special protection for the press over to a case involving a request for immunity from a contempt of court citation in 1918. *Toledo Newspaper Co. v. United States*,[123] unlike *Patterson*, came up through the federal court system and forced the Court to confront the First Amendment protection. The Court was asked to find the press immune from contempt citations if the subject reported on was of public interest. Such urgings angered the majority of the Court who believed that if such a contention were accepted the press would be allowed "to do wrong with impunity and implies the right to frustrate and defeat the discharge of those governmental duties upon the performance of which the freedom of all, including the press, depends."[124] The freedom of the press, the Court seemed to be saying, was one part of a well-honed society in which all the parts are carefully balanced to prevent any single part from creating chaos. In order to maintain this societal balance, the right of the press to criticize the administration of justice had to be limited. "It suffices to say," the Court concluded, "that, however complete is the right of the press to state public things and discuss them, that right, as every other right enjoyed in human society, is subject to the restraints which separate right from wrong-doing."[125]

By 1918, then, one year before *Schenck v. United States*,[126] the basis of the Court's view of the place of the press in society had been put in position. The right of freedom of the press was granted to individuals, and when that right was exercised by the institutional press it was subject to restraint in the public's interest. This view evolved through cases that involved the media only peripherally, or through cases that did not invoke the First Amendment, or through cases where First Amendment claims were made but not

---

[122] *Id*. at 313–14.

[123] 247 U.S. 402 (1918).

[124] *Id*. at 419.

[125] *Id*. at 419–20.

[126] 249 U.S. 47 (1919).

considered relevant by the Court. When sedition prosecutions of the World War I era forced the Court to explore more deliberately the meaning of the First Amendment, its work was based on these earlier comprehensions.

An understanding of the Justices' view of the role of the press in society would not be significantly advanced by a careful examination of these sedition cases here. *Schenck*, for instance, indicates the complications which this type of case presents. Schenck had published the material which resulted in his conviction. Justice Holmes wrote the Court's opinion in terms of freedom of speech. The use of freedom of speech may indicate that speech was seen as the more important value and thus that term was used. Or freedom of speech may have been used because the noninstitutional character of Schenck's publication may have made it seem more like an extension of an individual's expression than a statement made by the newspaper press. Or the term may have been used because Justice Holmes was imprecise in his language.[127] Regardless of the reason for the use of the word "speech" in these cases where printed materials were before the Court, this word usage was adhered to in several other opinions handed down by the Justices.[128]

As the source of cases came closer to the traditional concept of the word "press"—as when German-language newspapers were involved—the Justices fell to using the terms "speech" and "press" together with no apparent differentiation in meaning. In *Schaefer v. United States*,[129] a case involving such a publication, the Court said "freedom of speech and of the press are elements of liberty." In the same case, Justice Brandeis, in dissent, wrote of the problems the decision would create by "abridging freedom of speech, [and] threaten[ing] freedom of thought and belief."[130]

---

[127] Justice Holmes had a propensity for mixing terms in First Amendment opinions, seeming to favor speech as a generic concept which encompassed press. In United States *ex rel*. Milwaukee Social Democratic Publishing Co. v. Burleson, 255 U.S. 407 (1921), for instance, a case dealing with the removal of second-class mailing privileges from a newspaper, Justice Holmes, in dissent, said that "the use of mails is almost as much a part of free speech as the right to use our tongues." *Id*. at 437. In Gitlow v. New York, 268 U.S. 652 (1925), another case involving the publication of a newspaper and the punishment of its publisher for its contents, Justice Holmes dissented on the grounds that "free speech" should have been sufficient to protect Gitlow and grant him a right to make his views known. *Id*. at 672.

[128] See Frohwerk v. United States, 249 U.S. 204 (1919); Abrams v. United States, 250 U.S. 616 (1919).

[129] 251 U.S. 466, 474 (1920).   [130] *Id*. at 495.

The Court had obviously come to a point in its deliberations on free-speech and free-press issues where the Justices were seeking to enlarge the range of expression eligible for First Amendment protection. Members of the Court began using speech and press synonymously, without discrimination as to the format of the material presented, and used the two words as apparent equivalents with thought, belief, expression, and opinion.

In considering this effort by the Court to expand the range of expression eligible for speech and press protection, one should not assume that the post–World War I years were completely devoid of opportunities to focus on the role of the press in society. The cases heard by the Court, however, centered on the issues raised by the noninstitutional press. The Court's opinions in these cases provided a vital link to its later decisions in institutional press cases, as some of the Justices writing during the era tried to make clear.[131] More common, though, is *Gitlow v. New York*,[132] the 1925 decision which extended the First Amendment to the States via the Fourteenth. Here the reader is told that the First Amendment[133]

> is a fundamental principle, long established, that the freedom of speech and of the press which is secured by the Constitution, does not confer an absolute right to speak or publish, without responsibility, whatever one may choose, or an unrestricted and unbridled license that gives immunity for every possible use of language and prevents the punishment of those who abuse this freedom. . . . Reasonably limited . . . this freedom is an inestimable privilege in a free government; without such limitation, it might become the scourge of the republic.

This opinion, whose offhanded comment about the relationship of the First Amendment to the States later became vital to the development of a protection for the activities of the institutional press, thus carried no ringing tributes about the value of a free press in society. Perhaps it is important that such a substantial change in First Amendment policy should have come in a case which assured that application of the constitutional freedoms of speech and press to

---

[131] See, *e.g.*, United States *ex rel.* Milwaukee Social Democratic Publishing Co. v. Burleson, 255 U.S. 407, 417 (1921) (Brandeis, J., dissenting).

[132] 268 U.S. 652 (1925).

[133] *Id.* at 666–67.

cases arising from the States would not result in an emancipation of the press from its responsibilities.[134]

The institutional press, or at least one small outlet of it, however, did seek protection for information-dispensing activities during these early years and, in 1925, won the right to distribute official public information. The case, *United States v. Dickey*,[135] involved the right to publish personal income tax returns in a newspaper at a time when Congress required that such material be posted in public places, available to all who went to that location to see. The Court, in construing the statute, decided the newspaper could not be stopped from publishing the information so made available. "Information, which everybody is at liberty to acquire," said the Court, "and the acquisition of which Congress seemed especially desirous of facilitating, . . . cannot be regarded otherwise than as public property, to be passed on to others as freely as the possessors of it may choose."[136]

With its decision in *Dickey* protecting the press in its publication of material made available to the public, the Court put in place the final portion of its basic philosophy on freedom of the press. These early cases had seen the Justices state their belief in the fact that freedom of the press was an individual right that could be curtailed in the public interest. The connection between institutional and noninstitutional press rights had been recognized and the Court had begun its exploration of what kinds of activities might qualify for what was now termed freedom of expression. The Courts of later years would take these tentative beginnings, build on them, and sharpen their focus until, ultimately, in 1978 they would emerge as a clear statement of the relationship between the press and the public.

---

[134] The institutional press later reaped the benefits of *Gitlow*. "Although Gitlow went to jail, his case had brought acceptance of a principle of high importance. The confining interpretation of free expression fostered in many states over many decades would now be brought to the scrutiny of the United States Supreme Court," say the authors of a leading undergraduate textbook on mass communications legal problems. NELSON & TEETER, LAW OF MASS COMMUNICATIONS 38 (2d ed. 1973).

The institutional press, however, was not on hand in the courts to fight against the censorship of the nonconformist views put forth by Gitlow. The anarchistic views of Benjamin Gitlow were no more acceptable to the establishment press of the day than they were to the majority of the Court.

[135] 268 U.S. 378 (1925).

[136] *Id.* at 387.

III. An Increased Probing for the Meaning of Freedom of the Press: The 1930s and 1940s

As the Court embarked upon these two decades in which the value of freedom of the press would be probed and explicated, it relied heavily upon the common understandings established in its earlier years of more sporadic decision making on the subject. But even with this background to draw on and even taking account of the Court's work in the post–World War I sedition cases, the Justices needed a vehicle to help the move from this older, more limited method of considering press claims into the modern era. The Court's decision in *Near v. Minnesota*[137] provided that bridge.

Near is generally heralded as the opinion in which the Court recognized that the Blackstonian cornerstone of freedom of the press— freedom from prior restraint—was included in American constitutional law.[138] The principle discussed in *Near* dealt with the right of every "freeman"[139] to make statements without fear of prior restraint. Thus, when the freedom from prior restraint was applied to newspapers, it was based on the individual's freedom from such inhibitions on speech. The extension of this protection to the press found its basis in the role such publications played in putting information before the public. As if to stress the nature of this connection between the individual and the press, the Court pointed out that "liberty of the press, and of speech, is within the liberty safeguarded by the due process clause of the Fourteenth Amendment. . . . It was found impossible to conclude that this essential liberty of the citizen was left unprotected by the general guaranty of fundamental rights of person and property."[140] Although the Court may have considered freedom of the press a fundamental liberty, there is a strong indication throughout the opinion that freedom of the press, its special position under the First and Fourteenth Amend-

---

[137] 283 U.S. 697 (1931).

[138] Nelson & Teeter, note 134 *supra*, at 45.

[139] 283 U.S. at 713–14. The Court quoted Blackstone as follows: " 'The liberty of the press is indeed essential to a free state; but this consists in laying no *previous* restraints upon publications, and not in freedom from censure for criminal matter when published. Every freeman has an undoubted right to lay what sentiments he pleases before the public; to forbid this, is to destroy the freedom of the press; but if he publishes what is improper, mischievous or illegal, he must take the consequence of his own temerity.' " *Ibid.*

[140] *Id.* at 707.

ments notwithstanding, was relative. For, as the Court said, though the press could not be subjected to prior restraints, it could be held responsible for a variety of abuses of its freedom, including prosecutions for libel.[141]

In order to lay the groundwork for extending to the press the individual's freedom from prior restraint, the Court conducted an extensive exploration of the status of speech and press in the States. The majority concluded that, even though the Court was for the first time declaring a State statute unconstitutional under the First Amendment's guarantee of freedom of the press, the decision was very much in tune with the prevailing climate of opinion on the place of speech and press in American society.[142] One other factor in *Near* makes that case important to the development of later Court doctrine regarding First Amendment protection for the press. *Near* marked the first time that the institutional press supported legally and financially a noninstitutional press case before the Supreme Court.[143] Through its efforts here, the institutional press helped to establish firmly the Supreme Court's role in press adjudication.

---

[141] The Court noted here what would become a continuing theme in press-related cases: the problem of the irresponsible exercise of the freedom of the press. The States, Chief Justice Hughes had noted, used libel actions in an attempt to stop some of this irresponsibility. The Chief Justice endorsed this action: "The fact that liberty of the press may be abused by miscreant purveyors of scandal does not make any the less necessary the immunity of the press from previous restraint in dealing with official misconduct. Subsequent punishment for such abuses as may exist is the appropriate remedy, consistent with constitutional privilege." *Id*. at 720.

[142] *Near* included an extensive exploration of the status of speech and press in the States. The Court indicated its approval of State actions to punish contempt of court, *id*. at 715, of State libel laws, *id*., and of State court disapproval of attempted prior restraints, *id*. at 719.

[143] The ANPA's involvement in this case was a direct result of an appeal from J. M. Near and Howard Guilford, editors of the *Saturday Press*, to Colonel Robert R. McCormick, editor and publisher of the *Chicago Tribune*. The *Tribune* had just defeated an effort by the City of Chicago to extract $10 million in libel damages from it because of false stories about the city's financial stability and had become a symbol of press freedom in the Midwest. Colonel McCormick encouraged ANPA participation in the *Near* case. This participation came in the form of a $5,000 contribution to legal fees and in the establishment of a permanent committee on freedom of the press headed by Colonel McCormick. The Colonel's own law firm represented Near, thus adding to McCormick's personal pride when the Court's decision favored Near. Of greater significance, however, was the establishment of that standing committee on freedom of the press. It was through this group that the publisher's organization was put in a stronger position for future intervention in the court cases dealing with press issues. Such involvement continues to this day. See McCORMICK, THE FREEDOM OF THE PRESS 42–52 (1936); EMERY, note 119 *supra*, at 222–23.

A basic belief in the need of the public to hear information about government from a variety of sources characterized the Court's reasoning in *Grosjean v. American Press Co.*,[144] the case in which the Justices overthrew a Louisiana tax scheme aimed at putting certain newspapers out of business. The Court conducted an extensive analysis of the British press system and of that nation's effort to "establish and preserve the right of the English people to full information in respect of the doings or misdoings of their government."[145] The decision in *Grosjean*, the Court stressed, was not intended "to suggest that the owners of newspapers are immune from any of the ordinary forms of taxation for support of the government."[146] But the opinion did give an indication of the Court's feeling about the place of the press in the society of 1936:[147]

> The predominant purpose of the grant of immunity here invoked was to preserve an untrammeled press as a vital source of public information. The newspapers, magazines and other journals of the country, it is safe to say, have shed and continue to shed, more light on the public and business affairs of the nation than any other instrumentality of publicity; and since informed public opinion is the most potent of all restraints upon misgovernment, the suppression or abridgement of that publicity afforded by a free press cannot be regarded as otherwise than with grave concern.

The Court thus seemed to be saying that the press functioned for the public's benefit and that in fulfilling such a role it would find protection, even if such a decision by the Justices also meant providing protection to the press's proprietary interests.

Although the Court would not permit discriminatory taxes to be levied against media businesses, it had no difficulty in finding nondiscriminatory business regulations applicable to the press. This point was made clear one year after *Grosjean* when the Court ordered the Associated Press to reinstate an employee it had fired for union organizing activities. "The business of the Associated Press is not immune to regulation because it is an agency of the press," said the Court.[148] "The publisher of a newspaper has no special immu-

---

[144] 297 U.S. 233 (1936).   [146] *Id.* at 250.

[145] *Id.* at 247.   [147] *Ibid.*

[148] Associated Press v. N.L.R.B., 301 U.S. 103, 132 (1937).

nity from the application of general laws."[149] A publisher must face libel actions, must stand in danger of contempt of court citations, must answer to charges of antitrust violations, and must pay taxes. Consequently, said the Court, the National Labor Relations Board ruling being challenged by the Associated Press fell into the category of laws to which the press generally was subject. Such regulation "in nowise circumscribes the full freedom and liberty of the petitioner to publish the news as it desires."[150] First Amendment arguments did not remove the press from the application of non-discrimnatory regulations in 1937.

The 1940s were important years for the development of an understanding of freedom of the press. The Court's caseload in the area increased significantly, and the Court, with its energies now directed toward the protection of individual liberties, was asked to place many activities under the provisions of the Speech and Press Clauses of the First Amendment. As the Court approached these cases, it undoubtedly had an eye turned toward the world situation in which the communication of ideas was being drastically curtailed in nation after nation. With that in mind, the Court gave careful attention to the minorities seeking a voice in American society, and through this process the Justices further explicated the meaning of the speech and press protections.

A series of cases brought by the Jehovah's Witnesses to secure the right to distribute religious handbills resulted in an early demonstration of how the Roosevelt Court would react to such requests. The Court found municipal restrictions placed on the distribution of such handbills were unacceptable because "[t]he lib-

---

[149] *Ibid.*

[150] *Id.* at 133. Although the Associated Press would not have much luck in the future convincing the Court to grant it a special privilege, it had won one round with the Court in 1918 when the Court found a way to keep the International News Service from pirating the Associated Press's news reports without finding that the news could be copyrighted. Justice Pitney, for a seven-man majority, determined that the individual property interest in news stories was protected " '*until its commercial value as news to the complainant and all its members has passed away.*' " International News Service v. Associated Press, 248 U.S. 215, 245 (1918). Justice Brandeis dissented in the 1918 case, contending that the Court was reaching a conclusion too rapidly. "[W]ith the increasing complexity of society, the public interest tends to become omnipresent; and the problems presented by new demands for justice cease to be simple. Then the creation or recognition by courts of a new private right may work serious injury to the general public, unless the boundaries of the right are definitely established and wisely guarded." *Id.* at 262–63. Here, then, was an early cry against special privilege granted to the press without careful consideration of all factors involved.

erty of the press is not confined to newspapers and periodicals. It necessarily embraces pamphlets and leaflets. These indeed have been historic weapons in the defense of liberty. . . . The press in its historic connotation comprehends every sort of publication which affords a vehicle of information and opinion."[151] Such language may well have marked the first time that the Court consciously referred to the existence of a "press" other than that of the daily newspaper.

Such explorations were necessary in these early days of substantial litigation involving the First Amendment, for the Court was called upon repeatedly to express its views on the relevance of the speech and press guarantees to a variety of activities.[152] Through such discussions, the Justices reaffirmed the personal nature of the Speech and Press Clauses,[153] and they wrote into the Court's record how important they felt it was to remove any roadblocks to effective use of speech and press. For instance, an effort to levy a tax on those who wished to distribute handbills drew the wrath of Chief Justice Stone, writing in dissent in *Jones v. Opelika*.[154] Such a tax had to be invalidated, he protested, for, if it was not, "the cumulative effect of such taxes, in town after town, throughout the country, would be destructive of freedom of the press for all persons except those financially able to distribute their literature without soliciting funds for the support of their cause."[155]

The Court's probe for the outer limits of activities eligible for

---

[151] Lovell v. City of Griffin, 303 U.S. 444 (1938), at 452.

[152] Among the activities seeking and finding some degree of First Amendment protection were union activity, motion pictures, broadcasting, and obscenity. See, *e.g.*, Thornhill v. Alabama, 310 U.S. 88 (1940); United States v. Paramount Pictures, Inc., 334 U.S. 131 (1948); National Broadcasting Co. v. United States, 319 U.S. 190 (1943); Winters v. New York, 333 U.S. 507 (1948).

[153] See, *e.g.*, Schneider v. State, 308 U.S. 147 (1939).

[154] 316 U.S. 584 (1942).

[155] *Id.* at 604. Stone's view was accepted by the majority in a later series of cases. Jones v. Opelika, 319 U.S. 103 (1943); Murdock v. Pennsylvania, 319 U.S. 105 (1943).

Joining Stone in dissent, Justice Murphy found another reason to protect those who sought to distribute information through means other than those provided by the institutional press. "The pamphlet," he wrote, "an historic weapon against oppression, . . . is today the convenient vehicle of those with limited resources because newspaper space and radio time are expensive and the cost of establishing such enterprises great." 316 U.S. at 619.

This problem of the individual finding access to the institutional media has been present in many Court decisions but there has been no solution to it. The Court has indicated that it will not force media outlets to carry information they do not want to carry. See, *e.g.*, Lloyd Corp. v. Tanner, 407 U.S. 551 (1972); Columbia Broadcasting

First Amendment speech and press protection made a significant contribution to the foundation on which future institutional press claims for protection would seek to build. Also of importance to future institutional press litigation were those decisions in which the Court indicated that, in its mind, not only were the freedoms guaranteed in the Speech and Press Clauses inseparable from one another, but so too were they closely joined to the other guarantees housed in the First Amendment.

One such statement on the inseparability of the First Amendment's guarantees came in a case involving a labor union's effort to disseminate information about an organizational drive. Here, the Court found speech, press, and assembly inextricably joined. "It was not by accident or coincidence," said the Court, "that the rights to freedom in speech and press were coupled in a single guaranty with the rights of the people peaceably to assemble and to petition for redress of grievances. All of these, though not identical, are inseparable."[156]

The same thread of inseparability appeared in a case involving the use of minors to distribute religious literature where the Court turned back an attempt to find protection only within the First Amendment's guarantee of freedom of religion. "Appellant does not stand on freedom of the press. Regarding it as secular, she concedes it may be restricted as Massachusetts has done. Hence, she rests squarely on freedom of religion under the First Amendment."[157] To the Court, it was improper to seek "for freedom of conscience a broader protection than for freedom of the mind," because "it may be doubted that any of the great liberties insured by the First Article can be given a higher place than the others. All have preferred position in our basic scheme. . . . All are interwoven there together."[158] There were some differences in the way these rights were exercised, the Court said, but[159]

System v. Democratic Nat'l Committee, 412 U.S. 94 (1973); Miami Herald Publishing Co. v. Tornillo, 418 U.S. 241 (1974). But see Douglas v. City of Jeannette, 319 U.S. 157 (1943).

[156] Thomas v. Collins, 323 U.S. 516, 530 (1945).

[157] Prince v. Massachusetts, 321 U.S. 158, 164 (1944).

[158] Ibid.

[159] Id. at 164–65. While Justice Rutledge, writing for the Court in Prince, may have found the guarantees inseparable, Justice Murphy, writing for the Court in another opinion, was able to find some differences in those same guarantees. In Chaplinsky v. New Hampshire, 315 U.S. 568 (1942), the Court found that Chaplinsky had sought

they have unity in the charter's prime place because they have
unity in their human sources and functionings. Heart and
mind are not identical. Intuitive faith and reasoned judgment
are not the same. Spirit is not always thought. But in the
everyday business of living, secular or otherwise, these variant
aspects of personality find inseparable expression in a thousand
ways. They cannot be altogether parted in law more than
in life.

With such a philosophic framework firmly in place, the Court
faced its first flurry of cases seeking a protection for the institutional press. Cases argued on this basis during the 1940s split almost
evenly between those seeking a proprietary protection and those
seeking a shield for informational functions. Each time that the
argument for exception from business regulation was based on the
First Amendment, the press lost.[160]

In the major proprietary case, *Associated Press v. United States*,[161]
the nation's leading wire service was prosecuted for violating the
antitrust statutes because it limited access to membership and hence
access to its news report. The news agency, which had lost a case
seeking an exemption from business regulation in 1937,[162] was again
rebuffed. Even if news services are essential to the operation of
newspapers, said the Court, the First Amendment did not immunize
them from the operation of laws:[163]

It would be strange indeed, however, if the grave concern for
freedom of the press which prompted adoption of the First
Amendment should be read as a command that the government
was without power to protect that freedom. The First Amend-

protection under the freedoms of speech, press, and worship. Said Justice Murphy,
"[O]nly an attack on the basis of speech is warranted. The spoken, not the written,
word is involved." *Id*. at 571. Such attempts at specificity in the use of terms in First
Amendment cases was uncommon.

[160] The institutional press was also losing proprietary cases brought on non–First
Amendment grounds. See N.L.R.B. v. Express Publishing Co., 312 U.S. 426 (1941);
N.L.R.B. v. Hearst Publications, 322 U.S. 111 (1944).

[161] 326 U.S. 1 (1945). The Court had heard two previous cases involving the media
and antitrust laws and had decided both of them on the basis of whether the violations
charged occurred within interstate commerce, thus bringing them under the law. No
First Amendment protection was claimed in either instance. Both cases involved the
alleged monopolization of advertising. See Blumenstock Bros. Advertising Agency v.
Curtis Publishing Co., 252 U.S. 436 (1920); Indiana Farmer's Guide Publishing Co. v.
Prairie Farmer Publishing Co., 293 U.S. 268 (1934). In the first case, no use of interstate commerce was found. In the second instance, the material was found to be in
interstate commerce and the case was referred back to a lower court for another hearing.

[162] See note 148 *supra*.   [163] 326 U.S. at 20.

ment, far from providing an argument against application of the Sherman Act, here provides powerful reasons to the contrary. That Amendment rests on the assumption that the widest possible dissemination of information from diverse and antagonistic sources is essential to the welfare of the public, and that a free press is a condition of a free society. Surely a command that the government itself shall not impede the free flow of ideas does not afford non-governmental combinations a refuge if they impose restraints upon that constitutionally guaranteed freedom. Freedom to publish means freedom for all and not for some. Freedom to publish is guaranteed by the Constitution, but freedom to combine to keep others from publishing is not. Freedom of the press from governmental interference under the First Amendment does not sanction repression of that freedom by private interests. The First Amendment affords not the slightest support for the contention that a combination to restrain trade in news and views has any constitutional immunity.

In his concurring opinion, Justice Frankfurter stressed that "[t]he interest of the public is to have the flow of news not trammeled by the combined self-interest of those who enjoy a unique constitutional position precisely because of the public dependence on a free press."[164] Once more the Court had made it clear that the main reason for the press's existence was service to the public, and it stressed again its intent to assure that the service was delivered.

Two more business-related cases involving the press appeared on the Roosevelt Court's docket the next year. A First Amendment challenge to the Fair Labor Standards Act in *Mabee v. White Plains Publishing Co.*[165] was rejected. In *Oklahoma Press Publishing Co. v. Walling*,[166] a newspaper had invoked the First Amendment to stave off a subpoena requiring it to turn over its records as part of an investigation into Fair Labor Standards Act violations. The Court noted that "[c]oloring almost all of petitioners' positions, as we understand them, is a primary misconception that the First Amendment knocks out any possible application of the Fair Labor Standards Act to the business of publishing and distributing newspa-

---

[164] *Id.* at 28–29. Certain members of the Associated Press, spurred on by Colonel Robert McCormick, attempted to obtain legislation in Congress to provide an exemption for newspapers to the antitrust legislation. The effort failed. See references to the Mason Bill in EDITOR & PUBLISHER 9 (May 17, 1947); *id.* at 42 (June 28, 1947); *id.* at 51 (July 12, 1947).

[165] 327 U.S. 178 (1946).   [166] 327 U.S. 186 (1946).

pers."[167] The First Amendment, said the opinion, "does not forbid this or other regulation which ends in no restraint upon expression or in any other evil."[168]

Although it was becoming apparent that cases involving the institutional press's attempts to insulate itself from regulation annoyed the Court, cases involving the informational role of the press were much more warmly received. The importance of providing information to the American people was clearly seen as falling within the protection of the First Amendment. The 1940s saw a major attack levied against contempt of court citations by the institutional press, and, by the end of that decade, the ability to report on activities in the courtroom had been greatly expanded.

The leading case involving contempt of court, *Bridges v. California*,[169] centered on a nonmedia contempt citation. Joined in the Court's decision with a similar case involving a citation against a newspaper,[170] the ruling carried significant implications for the press. The Court determined that "liberty of the press" was to be given "the broadest scope that could be countenanced in an orderly society."[171] With that goal in mind, the Court said, public interest demanded that contempt citations be kept at a minimum, for "[i]t must be recognized that public interest is much more likely to be kindled by a controversial event of the day."[172] Since contempt citations "produce their restrictive results at the precise time when public interest in the matters discussed would naturally be at its height," the ban imposed "is likely to fall not only at a crucial time but upon the most important topics of discussion."[173] Upholding such citations, the Court held, would be in direct contradiction of the "prized American privilege to speak one's mind, although not always with perfect good taste, on all public institutions."[174] Because of this need of the public—not of the press—to speak its mind regarding matters pending in court, the contempt power vis-à-vis

---

[167] *Id.* at 192.

[168] *Id.* at 193. For a general overview of press-Court interactions on business-related issues see GERALD, THE PRESS AND THE CONSTITUTION 1931–1947 72–99 (rept. ed. 1968).

[169] 314 U.S. 252 (1941).

[170] The *Bridges* case was joined in the decision with *Times-Mirror Co. v. California.*

[171] 314 U.S. at 265.   [173] *Ibid.*

[172] *Id.* at 268.   [174] *Id.* at 270.

the press was cut back. Press freedom to report was extended through this ruling primarily because such an extension facilitated an identifiable public need for freedom of expression.

Bridges was decided by a five-man majority in 1941. Five years later, in *Pennekamp v. Florida*,[175] the Court was unanimous in overturning a newspaper employee's conviction for contempt. In its opinion, the Court talked of the need to "weigh the right of free speech" against the need of the courts to be free from "coercion and intimidation."[176] "Free discussion of the problems of society is a cardinal principle of Americanism,"[177] noted the Justices as they ruled "that the danger under this record to fair judicial administration has not the clearness and immediacy necessary to close the door of permissible public comment. When that door is closed, it closes all doors behind it."[178] Although *Pennekamp* clearly originated with the institutional press, the implication present in the ruling was that the rights protected were those of the public in general, not those of the press in particular. Justice Frankfurter expanded that point in his concurring opinion. "Without a free press there can be no free society," he wrote.[179] "Freedom of the press, however, is not an end in itself but a means to the end of a free society. The scope and nature of the constitutional protection of freedom of speech must be viewed in that light and in that light applied."[180]

In yet another contempt case, *Craig v. Harney*,[181] the Court overturned the citation. "A trial is a public event," said the Court.[182] "What transpires in the court room is public property. . . . Those who see and hear what transpired may report it with impunity."[183]

---

[175] 328 U.S. 331 (1946).

[176] *Id*. at 346.   [178] *Id*. at 350.

[177] *Ibid*.   [179] *Id*. at 354.

[180] *Id*. at 354–55. Justice Frankfurter used his concurrence to register his concern over the effect press coverage had on trials: "The press does have a right, which is its professional function, to criticize and to advocate. The whole gamut of public affairs is the domain for fearless and critical comment, and not least the administration of justice. But the public function which belongs to the press makes it an obligation of honor to exercise this function only with the fullest sense of responsibility. Without such a lively sense of responsibility a free press may readily become a powerful instrument of injustice." *Id*. at 365. This concern about the role of the press and the maintenance of the sanctity of the judicial system would be repeated in later years by Justice Frankfurter and other members of the Court.

[181] 331 U.S. 367 (1947).

[182] *Id*. at 374.   [183] *Ibid*.

Justice Murphy, in concurring, added, "A free press lies at the heart of our democracy and its preservation is essential to the survival of liberty. Any inroad made on the constitutional protection of a free press tends to undermine the freedom of all men to print and to read the truth."[184]

Once more the theme had appeared that the protection of the rights of all men was the main concern of the Justices in their decision making. The protection of the press simply was a vehicle used to help protect those rights of the public.

IV. ESTABLISHING SOME LIMITS FOR FREEDOM OF THE PRESS:
    THE 1950s AND 1960s

The Court, in the 1930s and 1940s, had explored the topic of freedom of the press repeatedly and had consistently been guided in its decision making by the press-public relationship: that which the public could do, so too could the press do. The Court in the 1950s was guided by the same standard, although, in the face of the Communist scare, the tenor of its decisions often was quite different. This variation in the questions put before the Court and in the Court's interpretation of the rights of the public clearly shows the effect a change in society's tolerance for certain ideas can have on the freedom of speech and of the press.

Epitomizing this changed attitude was the decision in *American Communications Association v. Douds*.[185] The Communist party, the Court said, could be subjected to regulation because, in spite of the First Amendment provisions "that Congress shall make no law abridging the freedom of speech, press or assembly, it has long been established that those freedoms themselves are dependent upon the power of constitutional government to survive . . . [and do] not comprehend the right to speak on any subject at any time."[186] With such an attitude toward the First Amendment freedoms firmly entrenched and with most of the First Amendment cases of the 1950s being brought on speech and association grounds, statements from the Court on the place of freedom of the press in the constitutional system are somewhat hard to find. One place where they may be found, however, is in commentary from certain members of the Court about prosecutions of the noninstitutional press and the ef-

---

[184] *Id.* at 383.

[185] 339 U.S. 382 (1950).   [186] *Id.* at 394.

fect such cases could have both on the institutional press and on the freedom of the public to obtain information.

Congressional investigations of this era provided many opportunities for such comment. One case involved Edward A. Rumely, who was told to produce a list of those to whom he had sold politically oriented books. The Court upheld Rumely's refusal to provide such a list. Justice Douglas, concurring, reminded his colleagues that "[r]espondent represents a segment of the American press," adding that, although there might be some judicial disapproval of Rumely's political philosophy, Rumely was a publisher "who through books and pamphlets seeks to reach the minds and hearts of the American people. He is different in some respects from other publishers. But the differences are minor. Like the publishers of newspapers, magazines, or books, this publisher bids for the minds of men in the marketplace of ideas."[187] Seeing in a congressional attack on Rumely grave implications for all publishers, Justice Douglas said that if the Court did not forcefully stop Congress here[188]

the press would be subjected to harassment that in practical effect might be as serious as censorship. A publisher, compelled to register with the Federal Government, would be subjected to vexatious inquiries. A requirement that a publisher disclose the identity of those who buy his books, pamphlets, or papers is indeed the beginning of surveillance of the press. . . . Once the government can demand of a publisher the names of the purchasers of his publications, the free press as we know it disappears. Then the spectre of a government agent will look over the shoulder of everyone who reads. The purchase of a book or pamphlet today may result in a subpoena tomorrow. Fear of criticism goes with every person into the bookstall. . . . The press and its readers will pay a heavy price in harassment.

---

[187] United States v. Rumely, 345 U.S. 41, 56 (1953).

[188] *Id.* at 57. Justice Douglas would continue his efforts to tie the plight of those brought before Congress on loyalty grounds to the danger decisions against such persons would carry for the institutional press. In Wilkinson v. United States, 365 U.S. 399 (1961), Justice Douglas, in dissent, lectured his brethren: "Criticism of government finds sanctuary in several portions of the First Amendment. It is part of the right of free speech. It embraces freedom of the press. Can editors be summoned before the Committee and be made to account for their editorials denouncing the Committee, its tactics, its practices, its policies?" *Id.* at 425–26. If such an extension to the press occurred, Justice Douglas believed, "[t]he list of editors will be long as is evident from the editorial protests against the Committee's activities." *Id.* at 426. See also Russell v. United States, 369 U.S. 749 (1962).

This was one of Justice Douglas's early attempts to explain how speech and press cases were interrelated and how an incursion on any First Amendment protection could eventually affect all those seeking such protection.

Although politically controversial issues dominated the First Amendment related cases placed before the Court in the 1950s, other press-related issues did, at times, come to the fore, especially as the need to balance two constitutional guarantees in free press–fair trial cases appeared. In the 1940s, based upon the public's need to discuss the administration of justice, a court's ability to use the contempt power against the press had been all but eliminated. The Supreme Court maintained this stance on media-related cases,[189] but the discontent of some members of the Court over press performance at trials could not be subdued for long and it soon surfaced. In *Shepherd v. Florida*,[190] newspapers had printed as facts statements that four Negroes accused of rape by a teenaged girl had confessed. The convictions of the men were reversed *per curiam*, but Justice Jackson found the press's performance so reprehensible that he added a special warning in his concurring opinion. The Justice reminded the press that "[t]his Court has recently gone a long way to disable a trial judge from dealing with press interference with the trial process."[191] But, he said, "[n]ewspapers, in the enjoyment of their constitutional rights, may not deprive accused persons of their right to a fair trial."[192] The message to the press was clear: Americans had been granted the right to a fair trial as well as the right to a free press. The Court was not about to sacrifice one public right in order to allow another right of the public—this one being misused by a few people—to have precedence.

Freedom of the institutional press from business regulations once more was before the Court in the 1950s. In one antitrust suit charging the attempted monopolization of an advertising market, the Court turned away arguments that the prosecution involved prior restraint and restrictions on the medium's freedom of the press, finding that the actions of the newspaper did constitute a violation of the Sherman Act.[193] A similar antitrust conviction of the *New*

---

[189] See, *e.g.*, Maryland v. Baltimore Radio Show, 338 U.S. 912 (1950).

[190] 341 U.S. 50 (1951).

[191] *Id*. at 52.   [192] *Id*. at 53.

[193] Lorain Journal Co. v. United States, 342 U.S. 143 (1951).

Orleans Times-Picayune, however, was reversed by the Court.[194] The Court's opinion in the latter case reflected the Justices' growing concern about the economic condition of the nation's press:[195]

> The daily newspaper, though essential to the effective functioning of our political system, has in recent years suffered drastic economic decline. A vigorous and dauntless press is a chief source of feeding the flow of democratic expression and controversy which maintains the institutions of a free society. . . . By interpreting to the citizen the policies of his government and vigilantly scrutinizing the official conduct of those who administer the state, an independent press stimulates free discussion and focuses public opinion on issues and officials as a potent check on arbitrary action or abuse. . . . Yet today, despite the vital task in our society the press performs, the number of daily newspapers in the United States is at its lowest point since the century's turn.

This 1953 expression of concern about the economic condition of American newspapers would be repeated in later decisions. What would happen, the Court seemed to be asking, if the number of people wanting to say something exceeded the ability of the press to accommodate that expression? How would the decreasing number of newspaper outlets affect the Court's policy of equating press and public rights? In 1953, and in later years, the Court could only speculate about such possibilities.[196]

---

[194] Times-Picayune Publishing Co. v. United States, 345 U.S. 594 (1953).

[195] *Id.* at 602–03. In 1969, the Court found newspaper combinations that, *inter alia*, fixed advertising prices to be *per se* violations of the Sherman Act, and not justified by the failing business excuse. Citizen's Publishing Co. v. United States, 394 U.S. 131 (1969). The application of the law, said the Court, did not violate the First Amendment: "Neither news gathering nor news dissemination is being regulated by the present decree. It deals only with restraints on certain business or commercial practices. The restraints with which the present decree deals comport neither with the antitrust laws nor with the First Amendment." 394 U.S. at 139.

This decision led to an appeal from the media to Congress for relief, and, in 1970, Congress responded by passing the Newspaper Preservation Act. This measure validated joint operating agreements between forty-four newspapers in twenty-two cities. The law allowed these newspapers to continue sharing business, advertising, circulation, and production facilities, while maintaining separate managements and ownerships. See Lewels, *The Newspaper Preservation Act*, FREEDOM OF INFORMATION CENTER REPORT 254 (1971).

The Newspaper Preservation Act is the product of the only successful attempt by the newspaper industry to bypass a Court ruling thus far. Other attempts followed Associated Press v. United States, note 164 *supra;* Branzburg v. Hayes, note 6 *supra;* and Zurcher v. Stanford Daily, note 16 *supra.*

[196] See, *e.g.*, Miami Herald Publishing Co. v. Tornillo, 418 U.S. 241 (1974).

Many years earlier, the Court had discussed the essentially inter-related nature of speech, press, and the public as it rendered decisions involving a variety of efforts to put information before the people. In the 1950s, the Court was asked to draw upon this background to determine if there was a place for obscenity within the constitutional system. The decision in *Roth v. United States*[197] did not bode well for those seeking such protection for obscene materials. "The protection given speech and press," wrote the Court, was "fashioned to assure unfettered interchange of ideas for the bringing about of political and social changes desired by the people."[198] Although this might mean a protection for "[a]ll ideas having even the slightest redeeming social importance," obscenity was not considered in that category, as the Court agreed with the historical view that rejected "obscenity as utterly without redeeming social importance."[199] In another obscenity decision, *Smith v. California*,[200] however, the Court found that the same press-public standard provided protection for disputed literature. The Court, wondering whether a California scienter requirement "may tend to work a substantial restriction on the freedom of speech and of the press,"[201] decided that such a restriction would create constitutional problems because "the bookseller's burden would become the public's burden, for by restricting him the public's access to reading matter would be restricted."[202] Here, then, the need of the public to have an unrestricted access to a variety of information served as the vehicle to allow dissemination of information which some would have suppressed.

As the Court worked to sharpen its identification of speech and press protections with the public's needs and rights, it tended further to blur the distinction between speech and press. In cases dealing with motion pictures, for instance, the Court decided "that expression by means of motion pictures is included within the free

---

[197] 354 U.S. 476 (1957).

[198] *Id.* at 484.   [200] 361 U.S. 147 (1959).

[199] *Ibid.*   [201] *Id.* at 150.

[202] *Id.* at 153. The Court's rulings in the area of obscenity regulation are good examples of the way in which the Justices have repeatedly tried to find a standard for measuring alleged obscenity against the public's needs. *Compare* A Book Named "John Cleland's Memoirs of a Woman of Pleasure" v. Massachusetts, 383 U.S. 413 (1966), *with* Miller v. California, 413 U.S. 15 (1973).

speech and free press guaranty of the First and Fourteenth Amendments."[203] This reliance on the words speech and press equally in a variety of situations and in relation to a variety of media offended some Justices.[204] The Court, however, was obviously firmly entrenched in the belief that the protections offered were identical.

The institutional press as a party to litigation became a major factor in the development of the meaning of First Amendment guarantees in the 1960s. Fact situations presented in cases in which the Justices were asked to provide First Amendment interpretations in this decade were varied, even if the responses were not. An Alabama statute forbidding newspapers to publish editorials on election day urging readers to cast their ballots in a certain way fell, labeled as a prior restraint.[205] "Suppression of the right of the press to praise or to criticize governmental agents and to clamor and contend for or against change . . . muzzles one of the very agencies the Framers of our Constitution thoughtfully and deliberately selected to improve our society and keep it free," said the Court.[206] Justice Douglas, in concurring, put the issue even more

---

[203] Joseph Burstyn, Inc. v. Wilson, 343 U.S. 495, 502 (1952). The Court recognized the problems that came with placing motion pictures within the protection of First Amendment guarantees: "It does not follow that the Constitution requires absolute freedom to exhibit every motion picture of every kind at all times and all places. That much is evident from a series of decisions of this Court with respect to other media of communication of ideas. Nor does it follow that motion pictures are necessarily subject to the precise rules governing any other particular method of expression. Each method tends to present its own peculiar problems. But the basic principles of freedom of speech and the press, like the First Amendment's command, do not vary. Those principles, as they have frequently been enunciated by this Court, make freedom of expression the rule. There is no justification in this case for making an exception to that rule." *Id.* at 502–03.

Justice Douglas continued his efforts to make his brethren understand the interrelated nature of the various media and the need to make First Amendment protections apply equally to them all in a series of motion picture cases. See Superior Films, Inc. v. Dep't of Education, 346 U.S. 587 (1954); Kingsley Int'l Pictures Corp. v. Bd. of Regents, 360 U.S. 684 (1959).

[204] Those Justices most distressed by the imprecision in their colleagues' opinions in the speech and press area were Frankfurter and Jackson. An expression of their views on the matter can be seen in Niemotko v. Maryland, 340 U.S. 268 (1951), and Kunz v. New York, 340 U.S. 290 (1951). Both men were concerned that Court rulings were not giving proper guidance on what the Court considered allowable governmental action in the First Amendment area to lower courts and public officials.

[205] Mills v. Alabama, 384 U.S. 214 (1966).

[206] *Id.* at 219. Significantly, Justice Black defined the press in his opinion: "The Constitution specifically selected the press, which includes not only newspapers, books, and magazines, but also humble leaflets and circulars . . . to play an important role in the discussion of public affairs." *Ibid.*

Some interpretations of this decision ignore Justice Black's inclusion of the non-

succinctly. "We deal here with the rights of free speech and free press in a basic form: the right to express views on matters before the electorate."[207] Again the Court found a protection for the press's role in helping the public make intelligent decisions in the area of self-government.

The measuring of a request from a litigant in a speech and press case against the rights, obligations, duties, and privileges of individuals became quite visible in these years of the Warren Court. The "First Amendment goal of producing an informed public capable of conducting its own affairs"[208] became the reason for requiring broadcasters to carry responses from individuals injured by a personal attack carried over that station. The inability of the general public to visit Cuba to learn " 'at first hand . . . the effects abroad of our Government's policies' "[209] was sufficient to deny that right to visit to one who had argued for a First Amendment right to gather information. The need to remove any "hazard of discouraging the press from exercising the constitutional guarantees"[210] was cited as a reason for allowing an alleged invasion of privacy to go unpunished. In the latter case, however, the Court cautioned that "[t]hose guarantees are not for the benefit of the press so much as for the benefit of all of us. A broadly defined freedom of the press assures the maintenance of our political system and an open society."[211]

Public need again was the key to the development of a libel law interpretation by Supreme Court. In the landmark case, *New York Times Co. v. Sullivan*,[212] a unanimous Court found protection had

institutional press in the list of those publications warranting protection because of their contributions to the discussion of public affairs. With such an exclusion, the decision becomes one giving a special privilege to the newsgathering operation of the institutional press. See Watkins, *Newsgathering and the First Amendment*, 53 JOURNALISM Q. 406 (1976).

[207] 384 U.S. at 221.

[208] Red Lion Broadcasting Co. v. F.C.C., 395 U.S. 367 (1969) at 392.

[209] Zemel v. Rusk, 381 U.S. 1, 16 (1965).

[210] Time, Inc. v. Hill, 385 U.S. 374, 389 (1967).

[211] *Ibid.*

[212] Note 5 *supra*. The decision produced the *New York Times* rule for libel: "The constitutional guarantees require, we think, a federal rule that prohibits a public official from recovering damages from a defamatory falsehood relating to his official conduct unless he proves that the statement was made with 'actual malice'—that is, with knowledge that it was false or with reckless disregard of whether it was false or not." 376 U.S. at 279–80.

to be granted to a libelous advertisement printed in the *New York Times* because "[a]ny other conclusion would discourage newspapers from carrying 'editorial advertisements' of this type, and so might shut off an important outlet for the promulgation of information and ideas by persons who do not themselves have access to publishing facilities—who wish to exercise their freedom of speech even though they are not members of the press."[213] Protection of the "citizen-critic of government" was vital, said the Court, because of "his duty to criticize."[214] This public need to comment on activities related to government thus immunized the press carrying such comment from attack, in this case from a potentially costly libel suit brought by public officials. In concurring, Justice Black pointed out that "[t]hese officials are responsible to the people for the way they perform their duties," consequently, "the people and the press" should be free "to criticize officials and discuss public affairs with impunity."[215]

Although the institutional press was quick to put the decision in *New York Times* to work in defending multiple-libel actions, the role of nonmedia persons in the case must not be underplayed.[216] The advertisement was placed by private citizens who had to convey their message in such a fashion because they had no media outlet of their own. There were also individual, nonmedia defendants

---

[213] *Id.* at 266.

[214] *Id.* at 282.   [215] *Id.* at 296.

[216] "The Supreme Court of the United States handed down a decision in 1964 that added a great new dimension of protection to news media in the field of libel. It said that news media are not liable for defamatory words about the public acts of public officials unless the words are published with malice. It defined the word 'malice' with a rigor and preciseness that had been lacking for centuries and in a way that gave broad protection to a publication. Public officials, it said, must live with the risks of a political system in which there is 'a profound national commitment to the principle that debate on public issues should be uninhibited, robust, and wide-open. . . .' Even the factual error, it said, will not make one liable for libel in words about the public acts of public officials unless malice is present." NELSON & TEETER, note 134 *supra*, at 100.

The role of the civil rights leaders in the action is given in better perspective by Clifton O. Lawhorne. He says, "[T]here was evidence that Alabama was using its libel laws to suppress Negroes and their supporters in the civil rights movement. Sullivan, in suing the *New York Times*, also had sued four of the eighty-four individuals who signed the published advertisement. Interestingly, the only four sued were Alabama Negro clergymen, including Dr. Martin Luther King's chief lieutenant, the Reverend Mr. Ralph D. Abernathy. . . . The entire decision, then, was based on the First Amendment guarantee of free speech and press. The issue was libel, but the foundation was the right to discuss public issues." LAWHORNE, DEFAMATION AND PUBLIC OFFICIALS 219–20 (1971).

in the libel action itself. In fact, the extension, for a time, of this new line of libel doctrine at the Supreme Court level rested on decisions involving nonmedia litigants. Those finding that their comments were protected by the *New York Times* rule included an obstreperous district attorney,[217] a man arrested for disturbing the peace,[218] publishers of a union leaflet,[219] and a teacher criticizing his employers.[220]

Two years passed before the Court, in *Rosenblatt v. Baer*,[221] had an opportunity to apply its new libel standard to another representative of the media. And in this case, the media representative was only a part-time, unpaid employee. Concurring in the Court's decision to protect the newspaper columnist, Justice Douglas spoke of libel, traditionally considered as defamation by printed expression, and asked if "freedom of speech is now the guideline, do State libel laws have any place in our constitutional system, at least when it comes to public issues? If freedom of speech is the guide, why is it restricted to speech addressed to larger public matters?"[222] His goal, of course, was to eliminate all libel actions on the grounds of freedom of speech. Justice Black, who also wished to eliminate all libel laws, commented, "To be faithful to the First Amendment's guarantees, the Court should free private critics of public agents from fear of libel judgments for money just as it has freed critics from fears of pains and penalties inflicted by government."[223] Such a vision of freedom from libel judgments obviously was not limited to an exception for the press only.

The attempt by Justices Black and Douglas to base the elimination of libel prosecutions on the individual's right to criticize government was discussed by the Court in *Curtis Publishing Co. v. Butts*.[224] Here Justice Harlan proclaimed that there should be "some further exploration and clarification of the relationship between libel law and the freedom of speech and press."[225] He added:[226]

---

[217] Garrison v. Louisiana, 379 U.S. 64 (1964).

[218] Henry v. Collins, 380 U.S. 356 (1965).

[219] Linn v. Plant Guard Workers Local 114, 383 U.S. 53 (1966).

[220] Pickering v. Bd. of Education, 391 U.S. 563 (1968).

[221] 383 U.S. 75 (1966).

[222] *Id*. at 90.   [224] 388 U.S. 130 (1967).

[223] *Id*. at 95.   [225] *Id*. at 135.

[226] *Id*. at 148–50. Mr. Justice White continued the nonmedia emphasis in *New York Times* in St. Amant v. Thompson, 390 U.S. 727 (1968), where he stressed, "The stake

The modern history of the guarantee of freedom of speech and press mainly has been one of a search for the outer limits of that right. . . .

It is significant that the guarantee of freedom of speech and press falls between the religious guarantees and the guarantee of the right to petition for redress of grievances in the text of the First Amendment, the principles of which are carried to the States by the Fourteenth Amendment. It partakes of the nature of both, for it is as much a guarantee to individuals of their personal right to make their thoughts public and put them before the community . . . as it is a social necessity required for the "maintenance of our political system and an open society." . . . It is because of the personal nature of this right that we have rejected all manner of prior restraint on publication . . . despite strong arguments that if the material was unprotected the time of suppression was immaterial. . . .The dissemination of the individual's opinions on matters of public interest is, for us, in the historic words of the Declaration of Independence, an "unalienable right" that "governments are instituted among men to secure." History shows us that the Founders were not always convinced that unlimited discussion of public issues would be "for the benefit of all of us" but that they firmly adhered to the proposition that the "true liberty of the press" permitted "every man to publish his opinion."

The rights of the press as defined by the rights of the public became the key to the libel decisions of the 1960s. So too did this combination of press rights with public rights provide the base upon which decisions in the free press–fair trial area were built.

In *Estes v. Texas*[227] the claims of the press for greater access to a trial, including the right to broadcast some of the proceedings, clashed with the right of the defendant to a fair trial. Here, said the Court, the right to a fair trial took precedence. The Court dismissed claims of broadcast journalists that their First Amendment rights were infringed when their camera equipment was excluded from the courtroom, stressing that "reporters of all media, including television, are always present if they wish to be and are plainly free to report whatever occurs in open court through their respective media."[228] In concurring, Chief Justice Warren spoke in terms of a public trial, a right which, he said, was fulfilled "in the con-

---

of the people in public business and the conduct of public officials is so great that neither the defense of truth nor the standard of ordinary care would protect against self-censorship and thus adequately implement First Amendment policies." *Id.* at 731–32.

[227] 381 U.S. 532 (1965).   [228] *Id.* at 541–42.

stitutional sense, when a courtroom has facilities for a reasonable number of the public to observe the proceedings."[229]

The Court, obviously tired of press behavior at trials, had, by the 1960s, heard too many appeals in which trials were claimed to be flawed by publicity. As the Court said in *Sheppard v. Maxwell*, "[a] responsible press has always been regarded as the handmaiden of effective judicial administration. . . . This Court has, therefore, been unwilling to place any direct limitations on the freedom traditionally exercised by the news media."[230] Underlying that statement was the warning that the Court could soon begin looking with greater favor upon efforts by judges to curtail press activities in the courtroom.[231]

Indeed, as the 1960s ended, an impression was generated that the outer limits of public toleration of press activities may well have been reached. The society was changing, the Court's membership was changing, and with those changes was coming a new image of the public's needs against which to measure press freedom.

V. Putting the Press-as-Public-Agent Definition Firmly in Place: The 1970s

For decades the Court's opinions in the area of speech and press had indicated that press rights were limited by the public's rights. In the 1970s, the number of claims made by representatives of the institutional press for a special privilege multiplied, and the

---

[229] *Id.* at 584.   [230] 384 U.S. 333, 350 (1966).

[231] A newspaper editor, writing before *Sheppard* in 1966, summed up the role of the press in the free press–fair trial controversy this way: "The press, when it recognizes its responsibilities, is as essential to truth and justice as are the courts. . . . Yet if the press is completely free, it will not always be fair, just as officers of the law will not always be fair, especially if they are completely free of observation by the press. Editors and lawyers must realize that they both hold a public trust and cannot be guided by business motives alone or personal motives alone. To the extent that the press and bar tolerate injustice, they are both neglecting their trust. Their privileged position under the Constitution obligates them to render more conscientious service to the Bill of Rights than the public demands.

"Ideally, there should be no conflict between the press and the courts. Ideally, the press, through the responsible exercise of its freedom, should promote justice and not injustice. The object of the press is to advance the general welfare. The press speaks to and for the public but should champion the individual.

"Ideally, the courts, through the responsible, unhampered conduct of trials, should produce justice. This is their function. The courts speak to the individual but they should champion the public good.

"But neither the press nor the courts are perfect and neither can function in a vacuum. They are inseparable forums of justice." LOFTON, JUSTICE AND THE PRESS 355 (1966).

Court found it necessary to become far more explicit in pointing out this press-public relationship. Although the press's rights had been equated with public rights for many decades, the decisions of the 1970s carried an extra sting because they often included references to the fact that the growing corporate power of the institutional press threatened the delicate press-public balance that had been created.

One of the clearest statements of judicial concern over the corporate press came in *Buckley v. Valeo*,[232] a decision which, although dealing with the federal financing of political campaigns, had a good deal to say about the role of the press in the political process. The Court noted that the "electorate's increasing dependence on television, radio, and other mass media for news and information has made these expensive modes of communication indispensable instruments of effective political speech."[233] Restrictions on expenditures would limit access to such forms of communication, said the Court, and "would appear to exclude all citizens and groups except candidates, political parties, and the institutional press from any significant use of the most effective modes of communication."[234] The limits placed on contributions in the act, the opinion continued, "do not undermine to any material degree the potential for robust and effective discussion of candidates and campaign issues by individual citizens, associations, the institutional press, candidates, and political parties,"[235] but do limit "all individuals, who are neither candidates nor owners of institutional press facilities, and all groups except for political parties and campaign organizations, from voicing their views 'relative to a clearly identified candidate.' "[236] Although *Buckley* was decided on complex issues and the comments here represent only a small fraction of the entire decision, the Court's repeated use of the term "institutional press" in close conjunction with comments about the power that the institutional press would have under the challenged law carried an ominous ring. The decision which, in effect, removed many of the regulations which would have favored an increase in the power of the institutional press in federal elections, was due perhaps to a concern on the part of the Court that such unchecked

---

[232] 424 U.S. 1 (1976).

[233] *Id.* at 19.

[234] *Id.* at 19–20.

[235] *Id.* at 29.

[236] *Id.* at 40.

power granted to the institutional press was dangerous. Such judicial apprehension may well be reflected in the use of the term "institutional" in referring to the press rather than the more customary words "media" or "press" in the decision.

This 1976 decision with its stress on the institutional press was but one in a line of decisions rendered by the Burger Court which affected the institutional press. Throughout the 1970s, the Justices expressed concern about a press becoming more irresponsible, about a press demanding special privileges, and about the need to bring the press back closer in line with the rights and the needs of the public which it allegedly served.

In the area of libel, for instance, in 1971 a badly divided Court had extended the definition of public official/public figure to include a private individual caught up in a news event. But *Rosenbloom v. Metromedia*[237] carried some words of warning to the press from Mr. Justice White. Writing in a concurring opinion, he said that some of his brethren "seem haunted by fears of self-censorship by the press and of damage judgments which would threaten its financial health. But technology has immeasurably increased the power of the press to do both good and evil. Vast communications combines have been built into profitable ventures."[238] The possibility of damage suits stemming from libel action did not bother Mr. Justice White, who said his interest was not "in protecting the treasuries of communicators but in implementing the First Amendment by insuring that effective communication which is essential to the continued functioning of our free society."[239] He said he was not at all convinced that, in order to further such communication, it was necessary to "fashion a constitutional rule protecting the whole range of damaging falsehoods and so shift the burden from those who publish to those who are injured."[240]

Three years later, *Gertz v. Robert Welch, Inc.*[241] saw the Court

---

[237] 403 U.S. 29 (1971).   [239] *Ibid.*

[238] *Id.* at 60.   [240] *Ibid.*

[241] 418 U.S. 323 (1974). *Gertz*, the first major libel case before the Court in three years, offered the opportunity to clarify some of the issues left clouded in *Rosenbloom*. It involved a suit against an organ of the noninstitutional press, for Gertz was suing Robert Welch, Inc.'s publication, *American Opinion*, the organ of the John Birch Society. Although the case carried the possibility of great significance in libel litigation, no member of the institutional media filed amicus briefs on behalf of Robert Welch. So, even though the Court used its traditional press terminology in its decision and even though the institutional media later complained about the effect of the opinion on them,

move away from the *New York Times* standard in certain libel cases. The Court recognized that "for nearly a decade"[242] it had been trying "to define the proper accommodation between the law of defamation and the freedoms of speech and press protected by the First Amendment."[243] To the Justices, "absolute protection for the communications media requires a total sacrifice of the competing value served by the law of defamation"[244] and the Court would not make that sacrifice. Nor was the Court willing to make all persons public figures: "[T]he communications media are entitled to act on the assumption that public officials and public figures have voluntarily exposed themselves to increased risk of injury from defamatory falsehood concerning them. No such assumption is justified with respect to a private individual."[245] The basic thrust of this

---

the institutional press had no direct input into the arguments which shaped the opinion later criticized. See summary of briefs, 41 L.Ed.2d at 1303–04. *Compare* the lack of support in *Gertz* with the number of amicus briefs filed on behalf of the press in Miami Herald Publishing Co. v. Tornillo, 418 U.S. 241 (1974); briefs 41 L.Ed.2d at 1298–1300. The *Tornillo* briefs came from seven individual newspapers and eight leading professional organizations, including the American Newspaper Publishers Association and the American Society of Newspaper Editors. Both decisions were handed down on the same day.

Writing soon after the decision in *Gertz*, D. Charles Whitney commented, "While the *Tornillo* right-to-reply case grabbed most of the news and editorial attention of the U.S. Supreme Court's June 25 session, a second decision that day probably will have a far greater impact on the day-to-day workings of the American press. The subject was libel." Whitney, *Libel: New Ground Rules for an Old Ball Game*, The Quill 22 (August 1974). Critics termed the result reached in *Gertz* "revolutionary" in the way in which it allowed each state to "establish its own standard less stringent than the *New York Times* standard where the plaintiff is a private individual." Phelps & Hamilton, Libel 191 (rev. ed. 1978). As Whitney concluded, "It is, nevertheless, abundantly clear that, barring any major reversal by the Supreme Court, the law of libel is alive, regardless of whether it is well." Whitney, *supra*, at 25.

The Court may not have finished its revolutionizing of the law of libel. In the 1977 Term it agreed to hear Herbert v. Lando, 435 U.S. 922 (1978), a case in which the reporter's state of mind as he approaches a story is at issue.

[242] 418 U.S. at 325.

[243] *Ibid.*   [244] *Id.* at 341.

[245] *Id.* at 345. Mr. Justice White, although in dissent, was still sympathetic to the need to develop a way for private individuals to recover damages for libel actions. He felt the press could afford such suits: "The press today is vigorous and robust. To me, it is quite incredible to suggest that threats of libel suits from private citizens are causing the press to refrain from publishing the truth. I know of no hard facts to support that proposition, and the Court furnishes none.

"The communications industry has increasingly become concentrated in a few powerful hands operating very lucrative businesses reaching across the Nation and into almost every home. Neither the industry as a whole nor its individual components are easily intimidated, and we are fortunate that they are not. Requiring them to pay for the occasional damage they do to private reputation will play no substantial part in their future performance or existence." *Id.* at 390–91.

opinion carried over into the 1976 decision in *Time, Inc. v. Firestone*,[246] but the foundation of the enunciated doctrine of libel could be traced back over a century into State court decisions that clearly drew the line of permissible comment when it came to private persons, or, for that matter, the private character of public persons. Concern for the private individual was once again being expressed in judicial decisions, and the balance was tipping away from the press.

The clearest indication of the Burger Court's dedication to the press-public relationship came in a series of cases in which reporters asked the Justices to find First Amendment protections for newsgathering.[247] In only one of these instances, that involving the publication of the Pentagon Papers, could the press claim anything resembling a judicial sanction for its assertion of First Amendment privilege. So deeply engrained in American constitutional tradition had the principle of freedom from prior restraint on expression become that when *New York Times Co. v. United States*[248] appeared

---

[246] 424 U.S. 448 (1976).

[247] The increased efforts by media representatives to obtain access to information was matched, to a certain degree, by those outside the media seeking access to those same media in order to advocate certain ideas not finding representation within the establishment press. This access movement has as its father Jerome Barron. Barron, *Access to the Press—a New First Amendment Right*, 80 HARV. L. REV. 1641 [1967], and the movement rose and fell in one Court case, Miami Herald Publishing Co. v. Tornillo, 418 U.S. 241 (1974), in which the Court invalidated a Florida law which required newspapers to provide space for candidates to reply to critical editorials. A precursor of this decision, Columbia Broadcasting System v. Democratic National Committee, 412 U.S. 94 (1973), held that television stations could not be forced to carry editorial advertisements advocating an end to the Vietnam War and other such topics.

These two cases present side issues to the overall development of the press as an agent of the public. The cases could be seen as the Court once more simply upholding the idea that the imposition of prior restraint by forcing media to carry certain information was impermissible. But it could also be said that since the Court would not permit an individual to be forced to say something which he did not want to say, West Virginia Board of Education v. Barnette, 319 U.S. 624 (1943), it needed only to extrapolate from that base and find such a protection for the media as well.

[248] 403 U.S. 713 (1971). Commentary by media representatives on the Pentagon Papers decision focused on the lack of outright support for the right to print such classified material, on the lack of guidelines for use should such a case present itself again in the future, and on how a slight change in Court personnel could alter the decision. See Landau, *Free at Last, at Least*, THE QUILL 7 (August 1971); Pember, *The 'Pentagon Papers' Decision: More Questions than Answers*, 48 JOURNALISM Q. 403 (1971); *The First Amendment on Trial*, COLUMBIA J. REV. (Sept./Oct. 1971).

In an editorial comment, the *Columbia Journalism Review* compared the Court's reaction to the *New York Times*'s appeals in *Sullivan* (labeled by them as *Times I*) and in *Pentagon Papers* (*Times II*). "The differing subject matter of the two cases provides the most telling contrast. Constitutional scholars have pointed out that the decision in

on the Court's docket in 1971 the Court's brief *per curiam* decision rested solely on that proposition.[249] The separate opinions filed by each of the Justices sitting on the case indicated that if the government had presented its argument more forcefully or in a different way it might have justified a ban on publication. Out of the welter of decisions, one comment by Mr. Justice Blackmun was seized upon as indicative of a hostility to the press. Writing in dissent, he said, "The First Amendment, after all, is only one part of an entire Constitution. . . . Each provision of the Constitution is important, and I cannot subscribe to a doctrine of unlimited absolutism for the First Amendment at the cost of downgrading other provisions."[250] The comment itself was not out of line with the feeling expressed by a variety of Justices over the years about the place of the press in society. As it appeared in this decision, it was indicative of the Court's increased willingness to make forceful and open statements about the proper place of the press.

When representatives of the institutional press sought, in *Branzburg v. Hayes*,[251] to keep reporters from having to testify in grand jury hearings and thus, through such testimony, to reveal their

---

Times I was intimately connected with the substance of the issue; that is, the Court advocated the widest possible freedom of discussion in part because the subject of discussion was the civil rights movement. The hesitancy in *Times II* must be taken as reflecting an uncertainty about providing the same kind of charter for subjects that have been considerably restricted in this and other countries—foreign policy, military policy, and ideology." The editors also said that "*Times I* came at a climax of the struggle for civil equality" and "*Times II* fell at the end of a decade of contention over the claims of national security on news organizations." The events of the 1960s had forced "the news media into an ever more open recognition that their own definitions of national welfare and public need could not always coincide with those of administrations in power. The publication of the Pentagon documents was an ultimate recognition that the divergence had reached a point where what the Government defined as necessary concealment was seen, with equal fervor, by the media as crying out for revelation." *The Foggy Landmark*, COLUMBIA J. REV. 3 (Sept./Oct. 1971).

[249] 403 U.S. at 714.

[250] *Id.* at 761. Some critics in the media joined Mr. Justice Blackmun with Chief Justice Burger as those who "showed remarkably little sensitivity to the importance of a free press." Pember, note 248 *supra*, at 403, 411. The assessment was based in part on Mr. Justice Blackmun's comment cited above and in part on his comments in his opinion about what he considered to be the rapidity with which the case was brought before the Court. 403 U.S. at 760–61.

[251] 408 U.S. 665 (1972). The Court had heard at least one earlier case in which a newsman had attempted to find a constitutional protection for his sources. In Burdick v. United States, 236 U.S. 79 (1915), the Court dealt with a newsman's attempt to use the Fifth Amendment as a shield to protect his sources of information about an ongoing criminal investigation. The Fifth Amendment claim was upheld. See Blanchard, *The Fifth Amendment Privilege of Newsman George Burdick*, 55 JOURNALISM Q. 39 (1978).

sources of information, the Court rejected the claimed privilege. The Justices agreed that freedom of speech, press, and assembly was vital to the country's welfare and that news gathering most likely qualified for some First Amendment protection, for "without some protection for seeking out the news, freedom of the press could be eviscerated."[252] But the Court would not accept the reporter's contention that the names of news sources must be kept secret and that reporters were exempt from grand jury appearances designed to ferret out those names:[253]

> The sole issue before us is the obligation of reporters to respond to grand jury subpoenas as other citizens do and to answer questions relevant to an investigation into the commission of crime. Citizens generally are not constitutionally immune from grand jury subpoenas; and neither the First Amendment nor any other constitutional provision protects the average citizen from disclosing to a grand jury information that he has received in confidence. The claim is, however, that reporters are exempt from these obligations because if forced to respond to subpoenas and identify their sources or disclose other confidences, their informants will refuse or be reluctant to furnish newsworthy information in the future. This asserted burden on news gathering is said to make compelled testimony from newsmen constitutionally suspect and to require a privileged position for them.

The argument found no support among the majority, just as a claim to a "constitutional right of special access to information not available to the public generally"[254] had not won adherents in the past. Even though the news-gathering process might be hampered, said the majority, the press was generally excluded from a variety of potential news-making activities such as "grand jury proceedings, our own conferences, the meetings of other official bodies gathered in executive session, and the meetings of private organizations. Newsmen have no constitutional right of access to scenes of crime or disaster when the general public is excluded."[255] The Court considered these to be legitimate exclusions of newsmen; the requirement that newsmen testify before grand juries was not seen as an extraordinary burden on freedom of the press.

---

[252] 408 U.S. at 681.

[253] Id. at 682.

[254] Id. at 684.

[255] Id. at 684–85.

The Court clearly wanted to keep reporters from finding within the First Amendment a way to withhold information about a crime from the appropriate authorities. "Although stealing documents or private wiretapping could provide newsworthy information, neither reporter nor source is immune from conviction for such conduct, whatever the impact on the flow of news,"[256] said the Court. Newsmen had alleged that the government was harassing them through the issuance of unnecessary subpoenas, but the Court did not find that issue present in *Branzburg*. And although the majority recognized that reporting techniques had changed over the years and that now confidential sources of information were more important, no special privilege for reporters tapping such sources was to be created. Sooner or later, if the Court established such a privilege, it would become[257]

> necessary to define those categories of newsmen who qualified for the privilege, a questionable procedure in light of traditional doctrine that liberty of the press is the right of the lonely pamphleteer who uses carbon paper or a mimeograph just as much as of the large metropolitan publisher who utilizes the latest photocomposition methods. . . . The informative function asserted by representatives of the organized press is also performed by lecturers, political pollsters, novelists, academic researchers, and dramatists. Almost any author may quite accurately assert that he is contributing to the flow of infor-

---

[256] *Id.* at 691.

[257] *Id.* at 704–05. Critics of the *Branzburg* decision in the media labeled it as the beginning of restrictions on freedom of the press. "When the Supreme Court decided on June 29 to deny reporters a constitutional right to refuse to disclose news sources before grand juries, the majority brought to an evident end a period that had seen the court encouraging—even leading—the press into a larger vision of its role in society. The Warren Court's decisions of the 1960s . . . had been made in the name of wider freedom to gather, publish, and comment on news. The early Burger Court had defended that freedom, somewhat ambiguously, in the narrow decision on the Pentagon Papers. The new court majority . . . has shown now that the narrowing view of the First Amendment implied in parts of the Pentagon Papers opinion should have been seen as a warning that the Court was intent on recovering some of the privileges it had conceded to the press." *A Costly Decision*, COLUMBIA J. REV. 2 (Sept./Oct. 1972). See also *Beyond 'Caldwell,'* *id.* at 18.
The Court's decision in *Branzburg* led to unsuccessful efforts in Congress to create a national shield law to protect journalist's sources. See *Newsmen's Privilege: Hearings before the Subcommittee on Constitutional Rights of the Committee on the Judiciary*, U.S. Senate, 93rd Cong., 1st Sess. (1973); *Newsmen's Privilege: Hearings before Subcommittee No. 3 of the Committee on the Judiciary*, House of Representatives, 92nd Cong., 2nd Sess. (1972); *Newsmen's Privilege: Hearings before Subcommittee No. 3 of the Committee on the Judiciary*, House of Representatives, 93rd Cong., 1st Sess. (1973).

mation to the public, that he relies on confidential sources of information, and that these sources will be silenced if he is forced to make disclosures before a grand jury.

Although the dissenters stressed that the protection of a newsman's source was inextricably intertwined with the protection of dissemination of the news, the majority opinion prevailed in its linkage of the testimonial responsibilities of reporters to the testimonial responsibilities of the public at large. The Court clearly told the representatives of the press that they had a duty to participate in legal proceedings just as any other citizen did. But, would the Court continue to see the reporter's access to information about public affairs as equal to that granted the people? Or, would the Court adopt an amended view, one which saw the press as a conduit, providing information for the public, and thus grant its representatives greater access to information? That was the question posed in two 1974 cases. The resolution of those issues further extended the press-public identity in First Amendment practice.

In *Pell v. Procunier*,[258] reporters sought the Court's support for their request to interview certain prisoners, contending that a prisoner's loss of liberty should have no effect on the First Amendment rights of the press and that "members of the press have a constitutional right to interview any inmate who is willing to speak to them. . . . [T]hey rely on their right to gather news without governmental interference, which media plaintiffs assert includes a right of access to sources of what is regarded as noteworthy information."[259] The Court rejected that claim:[260]

> [N]ewsmen have no constitutional right of access to prisons or their inmates beyond that afforded the general public.
> The First and Fourteenth Amendments bar government from interfering in any way with a free press. The Constitution does not, however, require government to accord the press special access to information not shared by members of the public generally. It is one thing to say that a journalist is free to seek out sources of information not available to members of the general public, that he is entitled to some protection of those sources, . . . and that government cannot restrain publication of news emanating from such sources. . . . It is quite

---

[258] 417 U.S. 817 (1974).

[259] *Id.* at 829–30.   [260] *Id.* at 834–35.

another thing to suggest that the Constitution imposes upon government the affirmative duty to make available to journalists sources of information not available to members of the public generally. That proposition finds no support in the words of the Constitution or in any decision of this Court.

Mr. Justice Powell, concurring in part and dissenting in part, thought "California's absolute ban against prisoner-press interviews impermissibly restrains the ability of the press to perform its constitutionally established function of informing the people on the conduct of their government."[261] Justice Douglas, in dissent, said the reporter-public comparison made by the majority was not valid because the average citizen "is most unlikely to inform himself about the operation of the prison system by requesting an interview with a particular inmate with whom he has no prior relationship. He is likely instead, in a society which values a free press, to rely upon the media for information."[262]

The Court majority, however, was committed to the press-public equation and used that guideline to uphold simliar regulations by federal prison authorities in *Saxbe v. Washington Post Co.*[263] Here, Mr. Justice Powell attacked the majority's equating of the press with the public, finding it too restrictive. He agreed "that neither any news organization nor any reporters as individuals have constitutional rights superior to those enjoyed by ordinary citizens. The guarantees of the First Amendment broadly secure the rights of every citizen; they do not create special privileges for particular groups or individuals."[264] To him this meant that journalists had no special immunity from governmental regulation, "[b]ut I cannot follow the Court in concluding that *any* governmental restriction on press access to information, so long as it is non-discriminatory, falls outside the purview of First Amendment concern."[265] At some point, he believed, restraints on access to news sources "may so undermine the function of the First Amendment that it is both appropriate and necessary to require the government to justify such regulations in terms more compelling than discretionary authority and administrative convenience."[266] He insisted:[267]

---

[261] *Id.* at 835.

[262] *Id.* at 841.

[263] 417 U.S. 843 (1974).

[264] *Id.* at 857.

[265] *Ibid.*

[266] *Id.* at 860.

[267] *Id.* at 862–63.

What is at stake here is the societal function of the First
Amendment in preserving free public discussion of governmental affairs. No aspect of that constitutional guarantee is
more rightly treasured than its protection of the ability of our
people through free and open debate to consider and resolve
their own destiny. . . . It embodies our Nation's commitment
to popular self-determination and our abiding faith that the
surest course for developing sound national policy lies in a free
exchange of views on public issues. And debate must not only
be unfettered; it must also be informed. For that reason this
Court has repeatedly stated that First Amendment concerns
encompass receipt of information and ideas as well as the right
of free expression. . . . An informed public depends on accurate
and effective reporting by the news media. No individual can
obtain for himself the information needed for the intelligent
discharge of his political responsibilities. For most citizens the
prospect of personal familiarity with newsworthy events is
hopelessly unrealistic. In seeking out the news the press therefore acts as an agent of the public at large. It is the means
by which the people receive that free flow of information and
ideas essential to intelligent self-government. By enabling the
public to assert meaningful control over the political process,
the press performs a crucial function in effecting the societal
purpose of the First Amendment.

Mr. Justice Powell's theory that the press should serve as an agent
for the public at large with somewhat greater abilities to obtain
information than allowed the public was not accepted by the Court
majority in 1974 and has not been accepted since then. Indeed,
some of those with whom Mr. Justice Powell was contending might
well have considered their opinion, which gave the press an access
to information equal to that allowed the public, as meeting the demands of the Powell model. In any event, the notion of press rights
equal to and no broader than the rights of the general public had
been a part of the First Amendment decision-making process for
decades. The fact that society was becoming more complex, one
basis underlying the Powell plea for a more expansive interpretation
of the press's role, has not yet been persuasive to a majority of the
Court.

The more limited interpretation of the press as an agent of the
public, however, was sufficient to invalidate a Georgia law prohibiting the printing of rape victims' names in 1975. In *Cox Broadcasting Corp. v. Cohen*, the Court focused its attention on "whether

the State may impose sanctions on the accurate publication of the name of a rape victim obtained from public records—more specifically, from judicial records which are maintained in connection with a public prosecution which themselves are open to public inspection."[268] In holding that such a State law could not stand, the Court once more explored the role of the press in relation to the general public, conceding that [269]

> in a society in which each individual has but limited time resources with which to observe at first hand the operations of his government, he relies necessarily upon the press to bring him in convenient form the facts of those operations. Great responsibility is accordingly placed upon the news media to report fully and accurately the proceedings of government, and official records and documents open to the public are the basic data of governmental operations. Without the information provided by the press most of us and many of our representatives would be unable to vote intelligently or to register opinions on the administration of government generally. With respect to judicial proceedings in particular, the function of the press serves to guarantee the fairness of trials and to bring to bear the beneficial effects of public scrutiny upon the administration of justice.

Public records, said the Court, are "of interest to those concerned with the administration of government, and a public benefit is performed by the reporting of the true contents of the records by the media. The freedom of the press to publish that information appears to us to be of critical importance to our type of government."[270] Because the records were public and would have been available to anyone taking the trouble to go to the courthouse to see them, the press had the right to publish the information contained in them.

This same approach to reporting judicial affairs carried over into the Court's hearing of cases involving gag rules. These judicial orders restricting the publication of certain details of a trial emerged in the 1970s as trial courts, responding to the Supreme Court's decision in *Sheppard*, sought to accept responsibility for safeguarding the judicial process. In 1976 the first gag-rule case to reach the Court, *Nebraska Press Association v. Stuart*, found the Justices

---

[268] 420 U.S. 469, 491 (1975).

[269] *Id*. at 491–92.   [270] *Id*. at 495.

saying that "the barriers to prior restraint remain high and the presumption against its use continues intact."[271] In this particular instance, the Court found "that, with respect to the order entered in
this case prohibiting reporting or commentary on judicial proceedings held in public, the barriers have not been overcome."[272] The
Court added, "To the extent that it [the gag order] prohibited publication based on information gained from other sources, we conclude that the heavy burden imposed as a condition to securing a
prior restraint was not met."[273]

Similar comments about the way in which information was obtained are found in the Court's *per curiam* decision in *Oklahoma
Publishing Co. v. District Court*[274] in 1977. In overturning that gag
rule, the Court said, "There is no evidence that petitioner acquired
the information unlawfully or even without the State's implicit approval. The name and picture of the juvenile here were were 'publicly revealed in connection with the prosecution of a crime' much
as the name of the rape victim in *Cox Broadcasting*."[275] These two
gag-rule cases seem to indicate a continuation of a line of thinking
made clear in *Cox Broadcasting*. If the information has, in some
way, been made available to the public, the press may have access
to it for further dissemination. If the courts can keep the information from becoming so available, then, most likely, the press can be
deprived of it as well.[276]

If it can be said that the press-public equation may, in the case
of coverage of trials, lead to some restrictions on the press, it must
also be pointed out that the press-public equation has led to at least

---

[271] 427 U.S. 539, 570 (1976).

[272] *Id.* at 570.   [274] 430 U.S. 308 (1977).

[273] *Ibid.*   [275] *Id.* at 311.

[276] This possibility of curtailing access to trial proceedings has caused some concern
among the working press. See Denniston, *What Next for Burger's Nebraska Loophole?*
THE QUILL 24 (May 1977).

There is some indication that the Court may approve actions by a judge to suppress
bench conference transcripts, exhibits, and judge-juror communications. The Court
refused to consider an appeal of such actions by the judge in the bribery trial of former
Senator Edward Gurney. Miami Herald Publishing Co. v. Krentzman, 435 U.S. 968
(1978). And the Court did agree in its 1977 Term to hear arguments whether a judge
may seal pretrial proceedings and records if he feels that disclosure of the information
from hearing may prejudice a trial. Gannett Co. v. DePasquale, 435 U.S. 1006 (1978).

For a discussion of Miami Herald Publishing Co., see *Gurney Trial Secrecy Order Upheld*, NEWS MEDIA & THE LAW 20 (July 1978); for a discussion of *Gannett Co.*, see
High Court to Review Pretrial Secrecy, id. at 16.

one significant expansion in the press's right to function. That expansion has occurred in the area of commercial speech, where the Court has held that "[a]dvertising is not . . . stripped of all First Amendment protection. The relationship of speech to the marketplace of products or services does not make it valueless in the marketplace of ideas."[277] Thus the Court opened an entirely new area of litigation, the end of which is not in sight.[278] This new opening in First Amendment protection benefits both the individual and the press.[279]

In almost every media-related case handled by the Burger Court prior to the 1977 Term, the press-public equation had been applied and, based upon the Justices' assessment of the press's rights and the rights of the public, the decision was made. It had taken many years and many decisions on a variety of speech and press topics made by several courts and dozens of Justices to reach the point where the press-public standard could emerge with such clarity. For even though the standard was there, it seemed to lay just beneath the surface of decisions as if waiting for the right combination of circumstances to make it apparent to all concerned. That combination of circumstances—cases, Justices, and expectations of the public—coalesced in the 1977 Term, bringing the press-as-public-agent concept into bold relief.

VI. Conclusion

By the end of the 1977 Term, the idea that the role of the press in society was to serve as an agent of the public—extending the

---

[277] Bigelow v. Virginia, 421 U.S. 809, 826 (1975).

[278] See Va. Pharmacy Bd. v. Va. Consumer Council, 425 U.S. 35 (1976); Linmark Assocs., Inc., v. Township of Willingboro, 431 U.S. 85 (1977); Bates v. State Bar of Arizona, 433 U.S. 350 (1977). But see Pittsburgh Press Co. v. Human Relations Comm'n, 413 U.S. 376 (1973).

[279] This development of a commercial speech doctrine could well be seen as a victory for the proprietary interests of the press, for such an extension of the First Amendment would work to increase advertising revenues. There are two problems, however. First to reach Bigelow, the Court had to decide Pittsburgh Press Co. v. Human Relations Commission, 413 U.S. 376 (1973), a decision which, in the tradition of earlier proprietary opinions, held that the "institutional viability," id. at 382, of the press was not threatened by a requirement that it remove gender-oriented headings over classified advertisements. Secondly, Bigelow once more involved a noninstitutional form of media seeking to advertise for an abortion clinic, a topic the institutional media usually would avoid. It might also be suggested that media advertising coffers are not going to be significantly enriched by advertisements from pharmacists, lawyers, and the like.

public's ability to speak and providing the public with information needed for self-government—was not only well established in First Amendment decisions but made increasingly evident in Court opinions. It had become obvious that the Court was convinced of the validity of its decades of precedent in this area and that there would be no new privilege for the institutional press created within the First Amendment. For, no matter how large the majority in any particular case, or what issues the case presented, the guideline for decision making remained the question of what the public could do in a like situation.

The presence of this press-public equation is of great importance to the institutional press. It should show the institutional press that rather than insisting upon a special protection its interests can best be advanced by widening the protection for the individual to speak and, for that matter, finding a greater latitude for the public to act. The value of this approach has already been proved repeatedly in efforts to obtain open-meetings laws on State and national levels. The purpose of such laws, press lobbyists say, is to allow the public to see how government functions firsthand. For those of the public unable to attend such meetings, the press stands in as its representative. The right to attend governmental meetings is granted to the public, but the press benefits.

It will be difficult for the institutional press to accept such an interpretation of the First Amendment's Speech and Press Clauses. For although there is a certain degree of intellectual agreement on the idea that the press's rights are equal to and no greater than those of the public, emotionally, there is often the feeling that the word "press" in the First Amendment should have a special, talismanic meaning for the organized press.

The equating of the press with the public does carry problems for the institutional press. For one thing, it obviously means that the institutional press must pay less attention to proprietary claims. Persistent requests for exceptions from nondiscriminatory business regulations based on the First Amendment have won no Court approval for years, and the repeated advancing of such claims can only diminish the Court's tolerance for press claims in general. The institutional press must shift its focus in efforts to find protection for the information-gathering aspect of its operation. Cases will have to be built more and more on the basis of what the public can or should be allowed to do in like situations. The Court has already set some targets for argument in this area. For instance, Mr. Justice Powell's comments in *Saxbe* about how the growing complexity of society has made the press a vital element in providing the information the public needs for effective self-government could be built upon. And, even if the Court decides to maintain a strict press-public equation as far as access to news is concerned, Mr. Justice Stewart, in *Houchins*, has indicated there might be viability in the argument that to make such access absolutely equal the media, in many instances, must be allowed to use the tools of their trade. How successful such an effort will be in a society which has implicitly accepted restrictions on the individual's and press's right of action is unknown, but it is in such a course that the press's best hope lies.

The institutional press will also have to take greater cognizance of what is happening to the noninstitutional press in its cases before the Court. It can no longer be doubted that rulings in the area of the noninstitutional press carry direct implications for cases brought by the institutional press. The history of free-press litigation is adorned by monuments to this proposition: Benjamin Gitlow and the extension of the Fourteenth Amendment to the States; the scandal-monger Near and the validation of the concept of no prior restraint; the magazine of the John Birch Society and the restriction of the freedom from libel actions. In many instances, the noninstitutional press has been left alone to fight its battles with members of the institutional press too little concerned with the precedential implications of such decisions. As the Justices have indicated time and time again, freedom of the press belongs to everyone who would put his views before the public. It is time that such inclusiveness be recognized by the institutional press.

The institutional press should also pay careful attention to the areas which concern the Court in media cases. There has been repeated mention in decisions about the decreasing number of newspaper outlets in America and the forming of those remaining newspapers into corporate structures which do not serve the needs of the people. Repeatedly the Court has commented about a lack of responsibility on the part of the media in its reporting of various events, with a particular emphasis on the relationship between reports of trials and the fair administration of justice. The Court also has not determined just what place broadcasting should be accorded in the hierarchy of First Amendment values. Nor has it resolved the touchy issue of how those without a media outlet of their own can put their views before the public.

These concerns appear repeatedly in Supreme Court decisions, as, indeed, they have in the writings of major critics of media activities both from within and without the industry.[280] The only difference between media critics off the bench and those on it is that the critics on the bench may find that the interests of the public have been so offended by a certain action of the press that it cannot be allowed to continue. The Court comes perilously close to such a move in its rulings relating to free press–fair trial.

All in all, the argument for a special press privilege is of dubious value at best and dangerous at worst. Any further clinging to this faulty notion of an institutional privilege could prove that the press is only self-righteous, an attitude that could cost the press the only real chance it has to increase its freedom.

---

[280] See, *e.g.*, LIEBLING, THE PRESS (1961); BAGDIKIAN, THE EFFETE CONSPIRACY AND OTHER CRIMES OF THE PRESS (1972); THE COMMISSION ON FREEDOM OF THE PRESS, A FREE AND RESPONSIBLE PRESS (1947).

WARREN F. SCHWARTZ

ZENITH RADIO CORP. v. UNITED STATES: COUNTERVAILING DUTIES AND THE REGULATION OF INTERNATIONAL TRADE

I. Introduction

Japan levies a tax on certain goods which is remitted if the goods are exported. The issue before the Court in the *Zenith* case[1] was whether remission of the tax constituted the payment of a "bounty or grant" within the meaning of the American countervailing duty statute which authorizes the imposition of a duty on importation into the United States equal to the "net amount of [the] bounty or grant."[2] In holding that it did not, the Court sided with

Warren F. Schwartz is Doherty Professor of Law, the University of Virginia School of Law and Visiting Professor of Law, Georgetown University Law Center.

AUTHOR'S NOTE: I should like to thank Janet Garvey for her research assistance.

[1] Zenith Radio Corp. v. United States, 98 S. Ct. 2441 (1978).

[2] 19 U.S.C. § 1303 (1976). The statute provides as follows: "Levy of countervailing duties (a) (1) Whenever any country, dependency, colony, province, or other political subdivision of government, person, partnership, association, cartel, or corporation, shall pay or bestow, directly or indirectly, any bounty or grant upon the manufacture or production or export of any article or merchandise manufactured or produced in such country, dependency, colony, province, or other political subdivision of government, then upon the importation of such article or merchandise into the United States, whether the same shall be imported directly from the country of production or otherwise, and whether such article or merchandise is imported in the same condition as when exported from the country of production or has been changed in condition by remanufacture or otherwise, there shall be levied and paid, in all such cases, in addition to any duties otherwise imposed, a duty equal to the net amount of such bounty or grant, however the same be paid or bestowed."

the Treasury Department and against an American competitor of Japanese produced television sets.

From a result-oriented perspective the decision is a desirable one. First, because I do not believe that a duty to nullify the effect of a "subsidy" paid in the country of exportation should ever be levied in the country of importation, I am pleased with any decision that restricts the scope of the countervailing duty statute. Second, I am content (although somewhat uneasy) with the choice of the Treasury Department as the agency which determines whether a countervailing duty should be levied. The practical effect of the Court's decision is to vest virtually unlimited discretion in the Treasury.

Unhappily, however, I am unsure whether the reasons which move me to prefer the result reached by the Court are legitimate grounds for the Court's decision. Moreover, since the reasons are not developed in the opinion, I do not know what role they actually played. Finally, and, perhaps most significantly, I am uncertain whether the Court should have stated these concerns candidly in its opinion—if indeed they were regarded as important.

I begin with a discussion of the Court's reasoning, then develop my own analysis, and, finally, turn to the question of what approach the Court should have adopted.

II. The Opinion

The Court's opinion is made up of five parts. First, the Court attempts to demonstrate that a remission of an indirect tax (such as an excise tax) was specifically intended not to be a bounty or grant in the original enactment of the statute.[3] Second, the Court reasons, even if the legislative history did not establish such a specific intent, the position taken by the Treasury was still a reasonable one and was "in accordance with the shared assumptions of the day as to fairness and economic effect of that practice."[4] Third, the Court believes that if subsequent reenactment of the original statute can not be characterized as congressional acquiescence in Treasury practice, neither does it constitute disapproval of such practice.[5] Fourth, the Court stresses deference to the Treasury with respect to its resolution of the questions and uncertainties among scholars as to the pre-

---

[3] 98 S. Ct. at 2445–48.

[4] *Id.* at 2448.   [5] *Id.* at 2448–49.

cise effect of the remission.[6] Finally, the Court distinguishes such of
its earlier decisions, which seem contrary to Treasury practice.[7]

I have no quarrel with much of what the Court says. The statute
which preceded the 1897 statute (from which present law origi-
nates) was concerned with excessive remissions.[8] The 1897 statute,
in its original version, was expressly limited to the problem of excessive remissions.[9] The purpose of the subsequent language which
had exempted nonexcessive remission is obscure and some members
of Congress apparently thought no change was made in this regard.[10] The view, that there should be no countervailing duty
levied when an indirect tax is remitted at the border, is one which
was widely held at the time.[11] Nor has Congress ever explicitly

---

[6] *Id.* at 2449.   [7] *Id.* at 2449–51.

[8] Tariff Act of 1894, ¶ 182½, 28 STAT. 521. The situation was, however, less clear
than the Court indicates. This act imposed an additional import duty, on a variety of
sugar products "which are imported from or the product of any country which . . . pays,
directly or indirectly, a bounty on the export thereof." The additional duty did not,
however, vary with the amount of the bounty. The statute further provided that the
importer "may be relieved from this additional duty . . . in case said importer produces
a certificate of said Government that no indirect bounty has been received upon said sugar
in excess of the tax collected upon the beet or cane from which it was produced, and that
no direct bounty has been or shall be paid." It is not absolutely clear that the exception
covered all remissions. The import duty was imposed on a number of sugar products.
Presumably the reference to "sugar" in the exception was intended to extend to all of
these. It would also appear, however, from the literal language of the statute that if a
tax had been imposed on one of the products rather than the "beet or cane from which it
was produced" the exception would not have controlled and an import duty would have
been levied. Finally, the existence of the exception suggests that, in its absence, a remission would constitute a bounty.

[9] 30 STAT. 1634 (1897). This provision, like the 1894 statute, was limited to sugar
products. The duty was fixed at the amount by which the bounty (undefined in the
statute) was in "excess of any tax collected . . . upon such exported article, or upon the
beet or cane from which it was produced."

[10] The provision with respect to sugar was replaced by the general statute which is the
predecessor of the present version. Tariff Act of 1897, § 5, 30 STAT. 205. This contains
no mention of the previous payment of tax, see note 2 *supra*. Arguably, then, since a remission was considered to be a bounty and the express reference to prior payment of tax
as reducing the amount of bounty was omitted, the full remission constituted a bounty.
There are scattered remarks in the Congressional Record which suggest, however, that
individual congressmen assumed that the tax would be only on excessive remissions. See
30 CONG. REC. 1646, 1650, 1674, 1680, 1719, 1721, 1722 (1897). The point was one
upon which the debate never really focused and there is no unambiguous statement that
the change in language was without substantive effect.

[11] It is, of course, difficult to know what was the intellectual tradition of the times and
how much of it was shared by Congress. It is true (as the Court says) that David Ricardo,
writing in 1822, and Adam Smith, writing in 1776, had taken the view that drawbacks
of excise taxes upon exportation were unobjectionable. See 98 S. Ct. at 2448. Adam
Smith, however, is not really very convincing. He argues: "To allow the merchant to

disapproved of Treasury practice.[12] And the leading Court precedent is distinguishable because the facts indicate that a payment in addition to the remission of the tax was made at the border.[13]

What the Court fails to deal with, however, are two crucial and related matters. First, in the years preceding the enactment of the Trade Act of 1974[14] (the most recent reenactment of the controlling statute), the forces favoring imposition of a countervailing duty in response to the remission of taxes at the border had been vigorously attacking the Treasury position on grounds of both policy and precedent.[15] The question had become extremely significant with the emergence of the value added tax as a principal revenue device in the European Economic Community.[16] As a matter of policy, it was contended that the assumption that remitting taxes at the border had no impact on exports was simply wrong and that the practice had important effects on international trade.[17] The prece-

---

draw back upon exportation, either the whole or a part of whatever excise or inland duty is imposed upon domestic industry, can never occasion the exportation of a greater quantity of goods than would have been exported had no duty been imposed. Such encouragements do not tend to turn towards any particular employment a greater share of the capital of the country than would go to that employment of its own accord, but only to hinder the duty from driving away any part of that share to other employments. They tend not to overturn that balance which naturally establishes itself among all the various employments of the society: but to hinder it from being overturned by the duty." AN INQUIRY INTO THE NATURAL CAUSES OF THE WEALTH OF NATIONS, BOOK FOUR chap. 4, p. 1 (1776). Smith apparently is focusing on the allocative effect of having the excise tax in the first place. The drawback obviously nullifies the effect of the excise tax in allocating resources which are and are not subject to the tax. But if the excise tax remains on domestic goods and is removed from exported goods then the allocation of resources between those two classes is affected.

    [12] Congress did, however, refuse to pass legislation sought by the Treasury specifically approving its practice. See Petitioner's Brief 20.

    [13] Downs v. United States, 187 U.S. 496 (1903).

    [14] P. L. 93–618, 88 STAT. 1978 (1975) (codified in large part at 19 U.S.C. § 2101). Subsequent references will be to the sections of the Act.

    [15] See Marks & Malgrem, Negotiating Nontariff Distortions of Trade, 7 L. & POLICY IN INT'L BUS. 327, 351 (1975).

    [16] See VON STEINAECKER, DOMESTIC TAXATION AND FOREIGN TRADE, THE UNITED STATES- EUROPEAN BORDER TAX DISPUTE (1973).

    [17] See Marks & Malgrem, note 15 supra; DAM, THE GATT: LAW AND INTERNATIONAL ECONOMIC ORGANIZATION 214 (1970). If the tax is a "general" one, changes in the exchange rate of the currency of the two countries and the wage rate in the exporting country may tend to nullify any subsidy effect. See Brief of Ford Motor Company as Amicus Curiae at 18. How general is general enough and how the changes will nullify the effect are much debated issues of considerable complexity. In any event, the tax involved in the Zenith case was not a general one.

dents which supported this position were old Court cases.[18] They did not contain the modern "incidence" analysis on which the policy arguments were based, but they did support the result which the protectionist forces were seeking. The attack on the Treasury position raised serious theoretical questions as to the appropriate definition of the term "bounty or grant."

The second important phenomenon which was ignored by the Court was the congressional response in enacting the Trade Reform Act of 1974 to these attacks on Treasury practice. This response had two aspects. First, Congress refused to choose between the language of the earlier Court cases and Treasury practice.[19] Indeed in Senate and House Reports accompanying a related provision of the statute, it is expressly stated that enactment of that provision did not constitute approval or disapproval of Treasury practice in not imposing countervailing duties for nonexcessive remissions of tax at the border.[20] It thus seems clear that as a matter of congressional intent the question was left open.

More importantly, perhaps, Congress removed two procedural

---

[18] Downs v. United States, note 13 *supra;* see also Nicholas & Co. v. United States, 249 U.S. 34 (1919).

[19] There is no reference to the conflict in the reports accompanying the Trade Reform Act of 1974. However, in United States v. Hammond Lead, 440 F.2d 1024 (Ct. Cust. & Pat. App. 1971), the Court had held that it lacked jurisdiction of an appeal by an American competitor from a failure of Treasury to levy a countervailing duty. An important reason for the Court's conclusion was the conflict between what it characterized as the "dicta" in the decided cases which formulated an extremely extensive definition of the terms "bounty or grant" and the much more restricted conception utilized by the Treasury. *Id.* at 1030. The Court went on to say, referring to the closely analogous provision under United States law for remitting import duties on inputs into products which were then exported, "We do not think it too much to say that if a foreign country adopted a law exactly like . . . [the American law remitting the import duty on export] and if a foreign product on which drawback was paid under that law came to the United States . . . the trial court [which had sustained jurisdiction and relied on the precedents to hold that a countervailing duty had to be imposed] would be compelled by the logic of its opinion and the authorities it cites, to assess countervailing duties." *Ibid.* In concluding that it had no jurisdiction, the Court then asserted: "Congress is, of course well aware of these problems, and it would seem it elects to rely on executive discretion to avoid making the United States ridiculous by penalizing imports from foreign countries which have taken reasonable action, action our own government takes or counsels." *Id.* at 1031. The method employed by Congress to rely on executive discretion, as conceived by the Court, that of precluding judicial review where the conflict between the precedents and the practice would have to be confronted, was overruled when jurisdiction was conferred. See text at note 21 *infra.* As to further evidence of congressional awareness of the conflict, see Petitioner's Brief 22–23.

[20] H.R. REP. No. 93–571, 93d Cong., 1st Sess. 69 (1973); S. REP. No. 93-1298, 93d Cong., 2d Sess. 172 (1974).

barriers which had prevented the forces which had been urging a reversal of Treasury policy from gaining a judicial decision on the merits of their contention. First, the Treasury had disposed of complaints by American competitors that a countervailing duty should be imposed because of the remission of a tax on exportation simply by failing to take any formal action.[21] The statute was amended to require formal disposition within a stated time.[22] Second, American competitors had been held not to have the right to judicial review of a refusal by the Treasury to impose a countervailing duty.[23] The statute was amended to confer that right.[24]

Thus the congressional action which preceded the decision in *Zenith* can be characterized in two relevant ways which the Court chose to ignore: First, the objections to Treasury practice were credited by Congress, at least to the extent of refusing unambiguous legislative authorization for it. Second, by compelling formal disposition by the Treasury and conferring the right to judicial review, the courts were placed in the position of having to address the troublesome issue. Arguably, Congress acknowledged that the objections to Treasury practice were substantial and chose the courts as the institutions to deal with them.

This action of Congress severely impugns the Court's rationale. Even if Congress had a clear preference for the result reached by the Treasury when it passed the 1887 statute[25] that preference was apparently absent when the statute was reenacted in 1975. Similarly, the facts that the Treasury acted in accordance with prevailing theoretical views at the time and that Congress did not expressly dis-

---

[21] The Senate Committee Report states: "The Committee has been concerned over the past years that the Treasury Department has used the absence of time limits to stretch out or even shelve countervailing duty investigations for reasons which have nothing to do with the clear and mandatory nature of the countervailing duty law." S. REP. No. 93–1298, 93d Cong., 1st Sess. 183 (1973). The complaint in the *Zenith* case was one on which Treasury had long refused to take action. The complaint to the Treasury was filed in 1970 and not acted on until 1976 when the Trade Reform Act of 1974 compelled formal disposition. Petitioner's Brief 4.

[22] Sections 331(a) and (d) of the Trade Reform Act of 1974, 19 U.S.C. §§ 1303a(3) and (4) (1976).

[23] See note 19 *supra*.

[24] Section 331(b), 19 U.S.C. § 1516(d) (1976).

[25] The Court says: "Although the congressional debates did not focus sharply on the meaning of the word 'bounty' what evidence there is suggests that the term was not intended to encompass the nonexcessive remission of an indirect tax." 98 S. Ct. at 2446.

approve of its practice lose much of their persuasive force when viewed against the background of the congressional mandate, which is implicit in the procedural changes to reopen the question; the disclaimer of any definitive substantive position in the 1975 re-enactment; and the more recent scholarship which suggests that remission at the border, contrary to the conclusion advanced by earlier work, could affect materially the quantity of exports.[26] Finally, giving complete deference to the Treasury in assessing the relevant effects is a dubious way of addressing the merits in light of the apparent congressional desire to secure a judicial response to the basic substantive question.

The opinion is particularly disingenuous in raising and then avoiding any consideration of the crucial policy issues. The Court says:[27]

> Aside from the contention . . . that the Department's construction is inconsistent with this Court's decisions, petitioner's sole argument is that the Department's position is premised on false economic assumptions that should be rejected by the courts. In particular, petitioner points to "modern" economic theory suggesting that remission of indirect taxes may create an incentive to export in some circumstances, and to recent criticism of the GATT rules as favoring producers in countries that rely more heavily on indirect than on direct taxes. But, even assuming that these arguments are at all relevant in view of the legislative history of the 1897 provision and the long-standing administrative construction of the statute, they do not demonstrate the unreasonableness of the Secretary's current position. Even "modern" economists do not agree on the ultimate economic effect of remitting indirect taxes, and—given the present state of economic knowledge—it may be difficult, if not impossible, to measure the precise effect in any particular case. . . . More fundamentally, as the Senate Committee with responsibility in this area recently stated, "the issues involved in applying the countervailing duty law are complex, and . . . internationally, there is [a] lack of any satisfactory agreement on what constitutes a fair, as opposed to an 'unfair,' subsidy." . . . In this situation, it is not the task of the judiciary to substitute its views as to fairness and economic effect for those of the Secretary.

---

[26] See authorities cited note 17 *supra*.

[27] 98 S. Ct. at 2449.

As I indicated above, the events surrounding the 1975 reenactment make it difficult for the Court to rely on either "the legislative
history of the 1897 statute" or the "longstanding administrative
construction" as reasons for avoiding the merits of the controversy.
Its efforts to avoid "modern" economic theory are equally unpersuasive. The opinion refers to the difficulty of measuring the "precise effect in any particular case" of a remission of taxes at the
border. But it confuses the magnitude of the likely effects with
their direction. If everything else is held constant, remitting a tax
at the border is likely to increase the amount of exports. The magnitude of the effect is, however, very difficult to determine. How
great the effect should be before some legal response is appropriate
and what considerations other than the isolated impact of the remission should be deemed relevant are questions which are much
in dispute. Yet the Court cannot avoid taking sides by characterizing economic analysis as offering no guidance as to what the consequences of the practice are likely to be.

Thus the Court's treatment of the issue is unpersuasive in that it
avoids decision on grounds which seem at odds with congressional
intent and incorporates an exaggerated sense of indeterminacy
concerning the relevant factual consequences of the practice in
issue. As such, the opinion is intellectually unsatisfying. But, as I
have stated before, one may nevertheless approve its result. To understand why this is so it is necessary first to consider what the
Court would have encountered if it had addressed the merits.

III. Subsidies and Countervailing Duties

I believe that no convincing case can be made for having a
countervailing duty law.[28] The notion that a country, to improve
its own welfare or to enhance efficiency throughout the world,
should nullify the effect of foreign subsidization is based upon fundamental misconceptions about the origins and effects of the actions
of national governments which affect international trade. To say
that such laws cannot be justified on the asserted grounds of overall
national or international welfare does not, of course, imply that we

---

[28] I have argued this at length before. See Schwartz & Harper, *The Regulation of
Subsidies Affecting International Trade*, 70 Mich. L. Rev. 831 (1972). For a contrary view
recommending a selective approach, see Barcelo, *Subsidies and Countervailing Duties—
Analysis and a Proposal*, 9 L. & Policy in Int'l Bus. 779 (1977).

necessarily should not have them nor does it suggest surprise that we, in fact, do have them. In the field of international trade (and elsewhere) there are important provisions which are asserted to be efficiency enhancing but whose real *raison d'être* is the distribution of wealth they effect. If costs can be imposed on foreign firms, or the quantity of the goods they can sell in the United States can be limited, domestic competitors will derive benefits in the form of higher prices and more sales. If a distributional theory justifying these benefits is accepted then there can be no quarrel with them. Surely the pursuit of these benefits forms an important part of the explanation of why the laws are enacted.

Although the competition of foreign firms which benefit from subsidies is characterized as "unfair" by those advocating such laws, no explanation of why the competition is unfair is offered.[29] It may be thought to be obvious from the fact that a benefit which leads to competitive advantage is conferred. But firms throughout the world are subject to a wide range of governmentally imposed costs and receive a great variety of governmentally conferred benefits both of which affect their behavior. A coherent theory of "fairness" would have to define a standard by which the net of these costs and benefits is to be judged. I know of no way of doing this and am unaware of any effort to develop such a standard by those support- ing countervailing duty laws. In any event, considerations of na- tional and international efficiency are usually advanced to justify the imposition of countervailing duties.[30] I now turn to these.

I begin with the extreme case where the justification for imposing a countervailing duty is presumably the strongest. Suppose a coun- try decides to increase its exports and provides a large cash payment for each unit exported. It is plain that consumers in the country to which the goods are exported are unambiguously better off. If the subsidy leads to greater sales it is because a portion of it is passed on to consumers in the form of lower prices. The importing country as a whole is also better off. The domestic resources previously used to manufacture the goods which are now imported are shifted to their next highest valued use. Since that value is by definition great-

---

[29] The Court, see text at note 27 *supra*, refers to the lack of "any satisfactory agree- ment on what constitutes a fair, as opposed to an 'unfair' subsidy."

[30] The Court relied upon the rationale of avoiding double taxation as justifying re- mission of taxes at the border. 98 S. Ct. at 2448.

er than the cost of the imported goods (or else they would not be imported) the country as a whole is richer by the amount of the difference.

Undoubtedly, American competitors of the foreign firm receiving the subsidy are worse off. But so are all firms which are undersold by competitors. What is necessary to justify government intervention is a reason why this harm should be prevented. The reason usually advanced is that the payment of the subsidy "distorts" the "true" costs of the foreign firm and thus leads to a misallocation of resources. This argument, however, is unpersuasive.

First, in a hypothetical case, a country decides to make a payment to increase its exports. For such a decision to be rational, it must be believed that the amount of money received for the goods in the absence of the subsidy understates the social value of the goods to the country from which they emanate. Thus there is too little incentive to produce the goods. When private transactions do not take account of all costs and benefits so that the incentive structure does not yield the socially desirable outcome an "externality" is said to exist. To assure that these externalities are taken into account is one of the principal roles of governments. A variety of explanations could justify export subsidization on externality grounds. "Pioneer" exporting firms may generate information about the market abroad which is disseminated throughout the country of export—much of it without the receipt of payment equal to its value. The pioneer firm may create consumer acceptance which extends to products of other manufacturers in the industry or indeed to all products emanating from the country. If externalities of this kind exist and government intervention leads to the production of a more "efficient" quantity of goods and services than would be produced in the absence of governmental action then, by definition, there can be no objection on efficiency grounds to the payment of the subsidy.

Of course, the foreign country could make a mistake and pay "too much" subsidy. It is not clear, however, even in principle, what it means to say that a "mistake" was made. Given the theoretical and practical difficulties of assessing how the foreign government has determined that a given quantity of externalities exist, it is quite uncertain what we mean by "getting it right."[31] In

---

[31] For a fuller exposition of my difficulties see Schwartz & Harper, note 28 *supra*, at 851.

any event, having another country either assume that the country of export always gets it entirely "wrong"—the approach of the present law—or trying to determine the magnitude of the mistake made by the country of origin seems unwise indeed. This is so especially because the costs of error in dealing with the externalities are largely borne by the country paying the subsidy. There may be a diminution in international efficiency but that is because the country of export (if it does make a mistake) has misallocated its own resources. The importing country is plainly ahead to the extent that the subsidy is passed on to its consumers.

The second basic difficulty in justifying the imposition of countervailing duties on efficiency grounds is that it is not plain what yardstick should be used for deciding whether a subsidy has been paid. Take even my simple case of a direct cash payment for every unit exported. Suppose larger cash payments per unit exported are being paid on other goods which require similar resources for their production. Or assume that the domestic consumption of certain goods is subsidized in the same amount that is paid on export. What emerges, as more complications are added, is that the production and consumption of goods are subject to an enormously complex array of governmental measures which either increase or decrease the private costs and benefits of the people making the consumption and production decisions. The likely direction of change in the allocation of resources, if one governmental measure is introduced and everything else is held constant, can be predicted. But whether the overall effect of governmental action is more or less "neutral" before or after the change is a question of extraordinary complexity.

Furthermore, neutrality in the sense that it is employed in the analysis of subsidies may be the wrong end to pursue. The concept postulates firms and individuals having various skills and preferences with respect to resources without regard to government. It is, however, plain for reasons that cannot be explored at length, that some of the "gains of trade" which lead to efficient specialization in production and consumption cannot be realized in the absence of government intervention.[32] The costs and benefits generated by a country's efforts to deal with the interdependencies that will not be taken into account in private transactions are as important an ele-

---

[32] It is fundamentally because of the "prisoner's dilemma." See Luce & Raiffa, Games and Decisions 95 (1957).

ment in defining international efficiency as those manifested in private market transactions.

What all this means is that the price at which a good is offered in a foreign market is the product of private and public efforts to achieve efficiency in the country of origin. Efficient allocation of the world's resources requires that all of these costs be taken into account—not only those which are manifested in private transactions.

I thus believe that the notion of neutrality which underlies the efficiency case for nullifying foreign subsidization is undefinable in terms which can be implemented in any workable legal scheme. It is moreover, not a goal worth pursuing. Finally, if it is both desirable and attainable, it is the country granting the alleged subsidy which has the incentives and the means for achieving it.

IV. The Subsidy in the Zenith Case and the Court's Response to It

The controversy reflected in the *Zenith* case reveals all of the difficulties which are encountered in fashioning a coherent approach to defining the term "bounty or grant" in the American statute. Whether remission is viewed as a subsidy depends crucially on one's point of comparison.

Since the tax is collected on goods which are domestically consumed, but not on exports, remission is likely to make export sales more profitable and domestic sales less profitable thus leading to an increase in the allocation of resources to export sales and a consequent increase in the export of goods subject to the tax.[33] But, as the Court correctly points out, goods which are exported may also be taxed in the country of destination.[34] Thus, if exported goods are taxed both at home and abroad and domestic goods only at home (at the same rate as exported goods), then the result will be to make domestic sales relatively more profitable and effect the allocation of resources in the direction of the domestic market. One might counteract this tendency by "remitting" at the border, not the amount of the domestic tax which has been collected, but rather

---

[33] Ford Motor Company, as Amicus Curiae, urged that the practice could in principle stimulate exports and that the case should be remanded to determine the actual effects of remitting the tax.

[34] 98 S. Ct. at 2448.

the amount of the foreign tax which will be levied. If this were done then both domestic and foreign sales would be taxed at the rate prevailing in the home market. Of course, what the foreign government probably wishes to do is to tax consumption not production, and to tax domestic and foreign sales at the same rate would defeat this goal. Yet, economic theory makes it plain that if you impose varying monetary consequences on different types of consumption, it will affect the demand for the types of goods and consequently the allocation of resources to the production and distribution of the goods. And thus the circle is completed.

V. The Appropriate Judicial Approach

If the Court had been candid about the position in which Congress had apparently placed it, it would have had to face two related, uncomfortable facts: (1) Congress wanted the courts to resolve the troublesome substantive issues and (2) Congress had provided no significant guidance as to how it wished them resolved. Three responses were possible. The Court could have held that since the statute contained no criteria of decision it was an unconstitutional delegation of legislative power.[35] Alternatively the Court could itself have formulated the requisite standard. Finally, the Court could have done what it ended up doing—confer unlimited discretion on the Treasury. My basic difficulty is that what the Court did was both sensible and questionable.

When I say that the approach of the Court was "sensible" I am expressing my own tentative views as to the best we can do in regulating international trade. Congress (and legislatures around the world) are extremely responsive to the demand of domestic interests for protection from international competition. The Trade Reform Act of 1974, by far the most significant American statute regulating international trade, embodies protectionist notions in the limitations imposed on the power conferred on the executive to reduce American trade barriers as part of multinational negotiations to liberalize international trade;[36] restrictions on imports and adjustment assistance available to industries, firms, workers, and commu-

---

[35] For a discussion of this little used doctrine see Mashaw & Merrill, Introduction to the American Public Law System 191 (1975).

[36] Section 101(b) (1).

nities adversely affected by international trade;[37] the ban on price discrimination contained in the antidumping laws;[38] and the countervailing duty statute involved in the present case.[39] In my view, none of these is justified by any notion of the overall national interest.

The liberality of the benefits conferred on domestic interests by this legislation was the result of a complex and protracted struggle. Those advocating free trade were forced to grant protection in order to secure the authority necessary for the United States to participate in the international negotiations designed to reduce national trade barriers. One method which was utilized in achieving the agreement necessary for passage of the legislation was a division of responsibility for implementation among the Congress, the executive, and the courts. A common technique is that the statute confers a potentially significant degree of protection on domestic interests and places on the executive the responsibility for reducing it in the "national interest."[40] There are two ways to look at this phenomenon. Conceivably, Congress as a whole intends only that degree of protection which ultimately emerges after the limiting exercise of discretion by the executive. It does not, however, wish to take political responsibility for mitigating the extremity of the protectionist position in the interests of the overall national interest in international trade. It does appear that protectionist concerns, which are geographically concentrated and of great significance to the people affected, will be brought to bear more intensely upon the congressman originating from the area than upon the President who is elected nationally and is traditionally regarded as responsible for international affairs. A congressman who cannot resist the protectionist pressures but understands the value of international trade may find appealing the solution of passing a "tough" statute but allowing executive mitigation of its severity. The alternative expla-

---

[37] Title II, §§ 2021–74.

[38] Section 321.   [39] Section 331.

[40] *E.g.*, with respect to import relief, that is some species of tariff or quantitative restriction, the President is directed, after receiving a recommendation from the Tariff Commission that the industry is qualified for relief under the statute, to "provide import relief . . . unless he determines that provision of such relief is not in the national economic interest of the United States. . . ." § 202(a) (1) (A). The President may also invoke a wide variety of measures in providing relief and need not conform to the Tariff Commission recommendation. § 203.

nation would view the result simply as conferring discretion on an agency, which the various rivals expect to behave in a particular way—subject, of course, to their continuing efforts to affect the outcome.

Something of this kind may have occurred with respect to countervailing duties—but in a fashion that makes the determination of a correct judicial response very difficult. To begin with, as far as I know, no serious effort to repeal the countervailing duty statute has ever been made. More specifically, earlier efforts to have Congress approve the Treasury position concerning nonexcessive remission of taxes at the border had led to naught.[41] The direction of legislative change in the 1975 enactment was plainly toward more extensive application of the countervailing duty statute and related provisions concerning foreign subsidization. In addition to the changes forcing formal Treasury disposition and conferring the right to judicial review to which I have previously referred, executive discretion in suspending the imposition of countervailing duties was severely limited,[42] the coverage of the statute was extended to goods which were not subject to import duties,[43] and another method for deterring foreign subsidization by the threat of retaliatory action by the executive[44] was added.

Similarly, the chance, granted in 1975, to urge the courts that Treasury practice was wrong can be viewed as one of several concessions made to the protectionist forces. Whatever probability was assigned to the Court's overturning Treasury practice, it was one of the "benefits" conferred in the overall compromise essential to the passage of the legislation. If this was the case, the Court was, in effect, being asked to act as an extension of the political process. Presumably, the costs to Congress of resolving the issue one way or the other were too high. Stated in different terms, the political forces were in equilibrium when Congress declined to resolve the issue but directed the courts to do so.

---

[41] Petitioner's Brief 20.

[42] Section 331(d). Imposition of the countervailing duty may be suspended only when the Treasury is prepared to make certain specified findings including that "the imposition of the . . . duty would be likely to seriously jeopardize the satisfactory completion of . . . negotiations [concerning nontariff trade barriers]." See Petitioner's Brief 32.

[43] See SEN. REP. note 20 *supra*, at 185.

[44] Section 301.

The Court may have been moved to reach the result it did because it refused to play the role envisaged for it by Congress. Moreover, the Treasury may be the institution best suited for performing the role. It is an agency which is more "political" than the courts, but less subject to parochial pressures than the Congress.

My conclusions do not, however, resolve the Court's dilemma. The most extreme statement of the problem is that Congress and the Court took irreconcilable views of the appropriate institutional role for each to play. A candid approach required the Court either to address the merits to a degree it apparently regarded as inappropriate or to articulate a basis for adhering to its own conception of its role which could be assimilated into doctrine applicable to the generality of cases of this kind with which it has to deal. Both of these alternatives were understandably troublesome. The other possibility, the one actually used, is to manipulate the conception of congressional intent to serve the Court's own purposes in defining the scope of judicial review. This is, however, subject to the objection of lack of candor.

It is disappointing how often analysis takes us back to the same old questions. I have argued elsewhere that courts should articulate the reasons which really explain the results reached.[45] The obvious advantage of this approach is that it facilitates critical evaluation. We seem, however, to derive some satisfaction from opinions that read as if the result followed inexorably from the articulated premises. Particularly, where the concerns which move the Court are difficult to generalize and systematize into doctrine, there may be a place for superficial orderliness combined with sensitivity to political reality. Yet I remain unconvinced that, in the long term, this is a desirable approach to the exercise of judicial power.

---

[45] Schwartz & McCormack, *The Justiciability of Legal Objections to the American Military Effort in Vietnam*, 46 Tex. L. Rev. 1033 (1968).

EDMUND W. KITCH

CLARA ANN BOWLER

THE FACTS OF MUNN v. ILLINOIS

The purpose of this article is to resolve factual issues raised but not
answered in *Munn v. Illinois*,[1] in the hope that the commercial and
political context of the litigation will illuminate the case. In *Munn*,
the Supreme Court held constitutional a statute of the State of Illinois setting the maximum price that elevators located in Chicago[2]
could charge for transfer and thirty days storage of grain.[3] The
majority and minority opinions revealed a fundamental difference
in their characterizations of the elevator business. Justice Waite,
writing for the Court, characterized the elevators as common carriers, relying on an assortment of precedents relating to common

Edmund W. Kitch is Professor of Law, The University of Chicago.
Clara Ann Bowler is Research Project Specialist, Law and Economics Program,
The University of Chicago.

AUTHORS' NOTE: Support for our research was provided by the Law and Economics
Program, The University of Chicago Law School; Donald A. Balasa, Esq., assisted in
the early phases of the research.

[1] 94 U.S. 113 (1877), affirming 69 Ill. 80 (1873).

[2] The statute, Warehouse Act of 1871, § 2, 1871 Ill. Laws at 762; § 15, *id*. at 769,
applied to elevators located in a city with a population at of least 100,000. Chicago was
then the only city in Illinois with a population over 100,000.

[3] The maximum price for this service was 2¢ a bushel. § 15, *id*. at 769. The statute
also set the ceiling at 1/2¢ a bushel for each additional fifteen days for storage. See
table 1.

© 1979 by The University of Chicago. 0-226-46431-8/79/1978-0005$02.42

carriers, millers, ferrymen, innkeepers, wharfingers, bakers, cart-men, and hackney coachmen. "Certainly," he wrote, "if any business can be clothed 'with a public interest, . . .' this has been. It may not be made so by the operation of . . . this statute, but it is by the facts."[4] The dissent characterized the elevators simply as private businesses. Justice Field thought the elevator owners were like tailors and shoemakers. "The defendants," he wrote, "were no more public warehousemen . . . than the merchant who sells his merchandise to the public and is a public merchant, or the blacksmith who shoes horses for the public is a public blacksmith."[5]

The dissent argued, in functional terms appealing to the modern ear, that characterization of the elevator business as "affected with a public interest" made no difference, for a restriction on price was still an effective taking of the elevator property:[6]

> [T]he doctrine of this court, that, whenever one's property is used in such a manner as to affect the community at large, it becomes by that fact clothed with a public interest . . . appear[s] to me to destroy, for all useful purposes, the efficacy of the constitutional guaranty. All that is beneficial in property arises from its use, and the fruits of that use; and whatever deprives a person of them deprives him of all that is desirable or valuable in the title and possession.

How did the elevators operate? Did the regulation, in fact, deprive the elevator owners of any value? These factual questions were posed but not answered by the opinions in *Munn* because the record upon which the case came to the Court afforded no basis on which to answer them.

The case was tried after the Chicago fire[7] upon a short and un-

---

[4] 94 U.S. at 132.

[5] *Id.* at 138.

[6] *Id.* at 141.

[7] "[W]e instructed the State's Attorney of the county of Cook, as early as September, 1871, to commence proceedings under the warehouse act against the delinquent warehousemen. Chas. H. Reed, Esq., pursuant to our instruction, promptly commenced an action to test the validity of the law; but owing to the great fire, October 8, 1871, and the total destruction of all the papers on file, and the consequent interruption of legal business, as also the delay produced by the absence of the counsel for defendants, the case failed to come to a final hearing until the 6th of July, 1872, and resulted in a verdict of 'guilty,' and a fine of one hundred dollars was assessed." ILLINOIS R.R. & W'HS. COMM'N, ANNUAL REPORT 11–12 (1872) (hereinafter 1872 ANNUAL REPORT).

informative stipulation of facts,[8] the inadequacies of which provided the opening for the elevator operators' arguments. The Court
relied only on a long quotation from the elevator brief designed to
show the role of the elevators in interstate commerce[9] but used in
the opinion to show the public character of the business.

I. QUESTIONS AND ANSWERS

Questions: Were the elevators in fact operated as common
carriers or private businesses? Were they held open to all on uniform terms or were they operated on an individually negotiated
contract basis?

Answer: The elevators were operated as adjuncts of the railroads,
obligated to take all grain tendered to them by the railroads. A
shipper of grain to Chicago had no effective choice of the elevator
in which his grain would be placed. The elevators were every bit
as much common carriers as the railroads were. They were almost
all built on railroad land and operated under contracts with the
railroads which governed their prices and conditions of service.
They offered their services to the public at a fixed price, regularly
published in the newspapers early each year.

The Munn and Scott elevator involved in the case, the "Northwestern," stood on land leased from the Northwestern Railroad.
In *Chicago & Northwestern R.R. v. People ex. rel. Hempstead,*[10]
the Northwestern had unsuccessfully argued that the clause in the
lease requiring it to prefer the Munn and Scott elevator justified
its refusal to deliver to another elevator. The decision was cited
and argued in the State's brief:[11]

> The judicial reports of Illinois, furnish ample evidence of the
> tendency of the managers of railway companies and propri-

---

[8] In summary, the stipulation was that the defendants did business as the Northwestern
Elevator and charged rates as agreed upon and published by the warehousemen, higher
than the rate specified by the statute; that the elevator received, stored, and mixed
grain in bulk without having taken out a license as required by the statute; and that
Chicago had more than 100,000 inhabitants. Brief for the State of Illinois, pp. 8–10,
reprinted in 7 KURLAND & CASPER, eds., LANDMARK BRIEFS AND ARGUMENTS OF THE
SUPREME COURT OF THE UNITED STATES: CONSTITUTIONAL LAW 605–07 (1975) (hereinafter LANDMARK BRIEFS).

[9] 94 U.S. at 130–31, quoting from brief for Munn and Scott at pp. 11–12, LANDMARK
BRIEFS at 493–94.

[10] 56 Ill. 365 (1870).

[11] Brief, pp. 41–42, 7 LANDMARK BRIEFS at 638–39.

etors of grain elevators and warehouses to enter into combinations to secure a monopoly of the storage of grain, and to
compel shippers from the interior to consign their grain to
such warehouses in Chicago, for storage, as may suit the purposes of the managers of the railways and warehouses.

Question: The Court says that the elevators formed a "virtual
monopoly" and implies that this supports the regulation. Were the
elevators in fact a "monopoly"?

Answer: The elevator price in Chicago was set by concerted
action of the owners and was stable for years (see table 1). The
factual stipulation on which the *Munn* case was tried stated that
the elevators "received, as a compensation, the rates of storage
which had been, from year to year, agreed upon and established
by the different elevators and warehouses in the City of Chicago."[12]
It was not a purpose of the statute to undermine this collusive pricing, for the statute explicitly provided a procedure for uniform
price setting.[13]

Whether or not this collusive pricing reflected an economic monopoly is doubtful, but it is clear that whatever competition existed
did not take place on the price terms. The elevators did not compete directly with each other. Rather, competition was between
different railroads, and the position of each elevator was determined
by the position of the railroads with which it was affiliated. The
profitability of each elevator was determined, in turn, by the rental
terms under the lease from the railroad.

Question: Did the price set in the statute diminish the value of
the elevator property?

Answer: The statute may have had a slight but quite minimal
impact on the value of the leasehold interests of the elevator operators. The statute lowered the economic price by extending the
initial storage term from twenty to thirty days, the two cent per
bushel charge remaining the same. This made little difference to
the elevators because almost all grain was in storage less than twenty days.

The factual stipulation in the case was silent on the subject of
the impact of the rate maximum on the value of the property, or of

---

[12] 94 U.S. at 131, quoting brief, p. 8, 7 LANDMARK BRIEFS at 605.

[13] § 15, 1871 Ill. Laws at 769. The section required the warehousemen to publish
their rates for the year in the first week of January.

its reasonableness or unreasonableness. The only question before the Court was whether a legislative rate maximum, in the absence of any proof or offer of proof of its unreasonableness, was unconstitutional. The elevator argument was a simple argument about the absence of legislative power to set any price.

The railroad lessors could offset any reduction in the value of their elevator land by raising their rail rates, since the important competitive price was the sum of rail and transfer charges. The Chicago fire occurred shortly after the statute was passed, and the new statute was not even mentioned in connection with the rapid replacement of elevator facilities destroyed by the fire.[14] Under the statute, the elevators could have converted to private operation (storing grain they had purchased) and avoided its application,[15] but they did not.

Question: Does the background of the legislation in *Munn* support a view that a legislature is a responsible price-setting body? How did the legislature set the price?

Answer: The legislature changed the price term from two cents for transfer and twenty days storage to two cents for transfer and thirty days storage, a small downward shift in the price in a deflationary period.[16] All parties active in the legislative debate had an interest in insuring adequate transfer and storage facilities at Chicago. There was no participant in the legislative process whose objective was to hobble Chicago as a transfer point. The fact that the legislation was State legislation rather than federal assured that this was so. St. Louis had a hostile interest which it had carried to the courts and Congress in a campaign to stop the railroads from crossing the Mississippi into Iowa.[17] Although there were elevator

---

[14] Twenty-two percent of the Chicago capacity was destroyed. CHICAGO BOARD OF TRADE, ANNUAL REPORT 47 (1871).

[15] The elevators could operate privately by purchasing the grain for storage. See note 102 *infra.* The warehousemen stored substantial amounts of their own grain at the time of the passage of the act. See Central Elevator Co. v. People, 174 Ill. 203 (1898).

[16] The basic national policy from 1866 to 1879 was to raise the value of the dollar to that value in gold that had prevailed prior to the greenback issues of the Civil War. This policy was adopted in 1866, and the pre–Civil War parity was attained in 1879. See FRIEDMAN & SCHWARTZ, A MONETARY HISTORY OF THE UNITED STATES 1867–1960 15–88 (1963).

[17] Absent railroad bridges across the Mississippi, grain from Iowa and other points west of the river would have found the river route relatively more convenient. Charles Taylor described the efforts of St. Louis to stop the first bridge at some length: "The river towns, led by St. Louis, continued the agitation for the removal of the Rock Island

TABLE 1

CHICAGO TRANSFER AND STORAGE RATES PER BUSHEL OF GRAIN, 1855–1890

Year	Rate	Rate for 20 Days in Store (¢)	Rate for 30 Days in Store (¢)	Source	Other Evidence
1855	2¢ for 15 days; winter store up to 4¢	?	4	Contract between Sturges & Burlingame and the Ill. Central R.R. (June 14, 1855)	1853 Board of Trade suggested 1¢ for 30 days, ¼¢ for additional 10 days. See LEE, at 58. 1849 Farmer's Ass'n suggested 1¢ for 30 days. See LEE, at 2.
1857	1¢ for 15 days	?	4	LEE, at 99	St. Louis warehouses were ¼¢ for 30 days, but the handling charges could be as high as 7¢ per bushel. The Chicago handling expenses were only 1½¢ per per bushel because of the elevator system. LEE, at 99
1859–65 (spring)	2¢ for 20 days, ½¢ for additional 10 days; winter store up to 4¢	2	2½	Chicago Tribune, Feb. 14, 1866; LEE, at 124	...
1865 (autumn)	2¢ for 10 days, ½¢ for additional 10 days; winter store up to 4¢	2	3	Chicago Tribune, Feb. 14, 1866; LEE, at 124	...
1866	2¢ for 20 days, ½¢ for additional 5 days; winter store up to 4¢	2	3	LEE, at 120; Chicago Tribune, Feb. 14, 1866; Daily Commercial Letter, April 6, 1866	1866 combine contract with the Northwestern R.R. set maximum of 2¢ for 20 days. See LEE, at 120
1868*	2¢ for 20 days, ½¢ for additional 5 days; winter store up to 4¢	2	3	Chicago Commercial Express, Jan. 6, 1869 at 15 (at Cornell University Library)	The storage price on Toledo and Oswego was dropped to 1¢ in 1869. Chicago Tribune, June 8, 1869. National Board of Trade estimated an average change of 2¼¢ per bushel for 1869. See LEE
1870	2¢ for 20 days, ½¢ for additional 5 days; winter store up to 4¢; "heated grain," 1¢ for each 5 days	2	3	1 TAYLOR, at 397	Iowa Elevator offered to store grain at 1¢ for 20 days and ½¢ for add. 10 days. 1 TAYLOR, at 400

* The rate of transfer and storage from the canal was 1.5¢ for 10 days and .5¢ for each 10 days thereafter. This rate was the same as from rail unless the owner shipped within 10 days, in which case it was lower. The rate from teams was 3¢ for 20 days and .5¢ for each 10 days thereafter. Chicago Commercial Express, Jan. 6, 1869 at 15; CHICAGO BOARD OF TRADE, ANNUAL REPORTS 1871–75.

TABLE 1 (*Continued*)

Year	Rate	Rate for 20 Days in Store (¢)	Rate for 30 Days in Store (¢)	Source	Other Evidence
1871*	2¢ for 20 days, $\frac{1}{2}$¢ for additional 5 days	2	3	CHICAGO BOARD OF TRADE, ANNUAL REPORT 1870, at 44	1871 Ill. Laws 769 provided for a ceiling of 2¢ for 30 days and $\frac{1}{2}$¢ for add. 15 days; 20 days=2¢, 30 days=2¢
1872–77* (published rate)	2¢ for 20 days, $\frac{1}{2}$¢ for 10 additional days	2	$2\frac{1}{2}$	CHICAGO BOARD OF TRADE ANNUAL REPORT 1871, at 47; *id.* 1872 at 44; *id.* 1873 at 56; *id.* 1874 at 56; *id.* 1875 at 55; *id.* 1876 at 61	Hough Elevator offered storage at 2¢ for 30 days, $\frac{1}{2}$¢ for additional 15 days (or statutory rate) in winter 1872. (The other elevators continued to defy the statutory rate until 1878.) Chicago Tribune, Dec. 7, 1872. Armour and Dole's contract with the Chicago Burlington and Quincy R.R. (Oct. 10, 1873) referred to "current" rate and set a floor of $1\frac{1}{4}$¢ per bushel
1878–85 (published and statutory)	$1\frac{1}{4}$¢ for 10 days, $\frac{1}{2}$¢ for additional 10 days	$1\frac{3}{4}$	$2\frac{1}{4}$	1877 Ill. Laws 170 (Statutory rates remained the same until repealed by Act of July 11, 1955, 1955 Ill. Laws 1561). CHICAGO BOARD OF TRADE, ANNUAL REPORT, 1877 at 71; *id.* 1878 at 65; *id.* 1879 at 71; *id.* 1880 at 72	Armour and Dole's contract of Oct. 10, 1873 with the $1\frac{1}{4}$¢ per bushel floor is extended to another elevator. Contract between Armour and Dole and the Chicago, R.R. (April 15, 1879). Contract between Buckingham and Ill. Central R.R. (Oct. 1, 1881) specified "current lawful rate" but not below 1¢ for 10 days unless specified by law
1886	$\frac{3}{4}$¢ for 10 days, $\frac{1}{2}$¢ for additional 10 days	$1\frac{1}{4}$	$1\frac{3}{4}$	LEE, at 310.	Memorandum for the Chicago, B. & Q. R.R. (June 23, 1886) discussed the possibility that the rate might fall below $\frac{1}{4}$¢ per bushel
1888	$\frac{3}{4}$¢ for 10 days, $\frac{1}{4}$¢ for additional 10 days	1	$1\frac{1}{4}$	LEE, at 311	...
1890	$\frac{3}{4}$¢ for 10 days, $\frac{3}{8}$¢ for additional 10 days	$1\frac{1}{8}$	$1\frac{1}{2}$	LEE, at 318 (Chicago Board of Trade agreement)	...

facilities on the Illinois side of the river in East St. Louis,[18] the existing records do not suggest that their representatives played any role in the drive to regulate the Chicago elevators.[19]

Question: What were the political interests that led to the regulation upheld in *Munn?*[20]

Answer: The desire of the Chicago Board of Trade to impose an inspection system on the Chicago elevators led to the regulation in *Munn.*[21] The price term entered the statute as a cosmetic adjunct to this program and became the focus of the case as a matter of litigation strategy. By the course of events, the elevators were forced to accede to an inspection system even before the *Munn* case was decided.

II. The Chicago Elevator System

The statute that was the subject of litigation in *Munn* must be understood in the larger context of the dominance of Chicago

---

Railroad bridge, on the ground that it was dangerous to navigation, and in May a committee of the House of Representatives at Washington reported favorably a bill for this purpose. Whether or not, sectional prejudice inspired the committee, as charged by the "Press," cannot be known; but the bill failed to pass. Later in the year Judge Lowe issued a temporary injunction, restraining the bridge company from making necessary repairs to the bridge, but refused to make the injunction permanent. An attempt to burn the bridge was made about the first of October. Most of the money for the war on the bridge was contributed by the St. Louis Chamber of Commerce, which announced in November that they had $5,000 in hand for this purpose, and tried unsuccessfully to induce the City Council of St. Louis to appropriate an equal sum towards the fund of $12,000.00 which they estimated would be sufficient to accomplish their purpose."
1 Charles H. Taylor, History of the Board of Trade of the City of Chicago 240–41 (1917) (hereinafter Taylor). (This volume is in scarce supply. A copy may be found in Regenstein Library, University of Chicago.)

[18] The first grain elevator in East St. Louis was established in 1867. History of St. Clair County, Illinois 305 (1881).

[19] Mr. Underwood, delegate from St. Clair County (which includes East St. Louis) spoke against the constitutional article. See Debates and Proceedings of the Constitutional Convention in the State of Illinois, 1869–70 1628 (microfiche ed.). Another delegate successfully spoke against the application of the weighing obligation in § 4 to river traffic. *Id.* at 1700.

[20] The Court itself seemed uncertain of the reason for the regulation: "We also are not permitted to overlook the fact that, for some reason, the people of Illinois, when they revised their Constitution in 1870, saw fit to make it the duty of the general assembly to pass laws . . . [relating to grain elevators] . . . This indicates very clearly that during the twenty years in which this peculiar business had been assuming its present 'immense proportions,' something had occurred which led the whole body of the people to suppose that remedies such as are usually employed to prevent abuses by virtual monopolies might not be inappropriate here." 94 U.S. at 132.

[21] The role of the Chicago Board of Trade in obtaining the regulation is described in Woodman, *Chicago Businessmen and the 'Granger' Laws,* 36 Agricultural Hist. 16 (1962).

as a transfer point between western rail and lake traffic for grain destined to Atlantic ports.[22] That dominance existed in the period 1860–80 (see table 2). In the earlier period Chicago was less important than the Mississippi river system through St. Louis and New Orleans. In the later period, Chicago was increasingly bypassed by through rail cars moving from the shipment point directly to eastern ports.[23] But in the period relevant to *Munn*, the Chicago elevators were dominant. They faced competition from the river and from lake transfer at Milwaukee and Toledo[24] but enjoyed a comparative locational advantage for most of the important grain-growing areas, particularly in Illinois and Iowa.

The elevators involved in the case are now gone but once were a prominent feature of the city,[25] standing along the banks of the Chicago River in what is now the downtown business area. Their function was to transfer grain brought to Chicago by western railroads to lake vessels for shipment to the east, with further transfer at Buffalo to Erie canal boats to the port of New York.

The development of these transfer elevators presented problems for the legal system. The operation began simply enough. Prior to the opening of the Michigan-Illinois canal in 1848, farmers would bring their grain to Chicago in bags on carts and either sell it at or place it in a warehouse of their choice.[26] This model of identifiable batches of grain, stored at the warehouse of the shipper's choice, hung on in the political debate long after economic reality had brought about a different system of business. That system arose from the need to gain maximum advantage from mechanized elevator facilities for the handling of grain.[27] These required two

---

[22] The evolution of transportation routes in the upper Mississippi Valley in the nineteenth century is discussed in MILLER, RAILROADS AND THE GRANGER LAWS 3–23 (1971).

[23] "By 1867, however, the rail routes had captured 38 per cent of this traffic and 'the elimination of the Erie Canal as an important factor in the transportation of grain was clearly indicated.' " 2 F.T.C., GRAIN TRADE 63 (1920).

[24] Lee, *The Historical Significance of the Chicago Grain Elevator System*, 11 AGRICULTURAL HIST. 16, 17 (1937).

[25] *Id.* at 19.

[26] *Ibid.*; 2 PIERCE, A HISTORY OF CHICAGO 82–83 (1940).

[27] A detailed account of the development of the Chicago grain elevators can be found in Lee, *History of the Chicago Grain Elevator Industry 1840–1890* (1938) (Ph.D. dissertation in Harvard University Library) (hereinafter LEE). Volume 1 of TAYLOR, note 17 *supra*, contains an unsystematic, but valuable, account of the development of the grain trade in Chicago. See also the discussion of grain elevators in GOLDSTEIN, MARKETING: A FARMER'S PROBLEM (1928); 2 PIERCE, note 26 *supra*, at 77–88 (1940).

TABLE 2

CHICAGO GRAIN RECEIPTS 1859–1890

Years	U.S. Production Wheat, Corn & Oats (Million Bushels)	Chicago Receipts (Million Bushels)	Percent Receipts Increase Over Previous Period	Percentage of Total U.S. Production Received in Chicago (Million Bushels)	U.S. Production Wheat (Million Bushels)	Chicago Receipts (Million Bushels)	Percentage of Total U.S. Production Wheat Received in Chicago
1859.............	1,029	15		1.5	173	8	4.6
1866–70.........	1,270	52		4.1	234	15	6.4
1871–75.........	1,521	78	50	5.1	307	21	6.8
1876–80.........	2,434	105	35	4.3	423	23	5.4
1881–85.........	2,786	112	6	4.0	473	20	4.2
1886–90.........	3,111	139	24	4.5	476	17	3.6

SOURCES.—CHICAGO BOARD OF TRADE, ANNUAL REPORT 1895, at 20; STATISTICAL ABSTRACT OF THE UNITED STATES 512 (1976).

NOTE.—The value of wheat per bushel is higher than for other grains. For example, no. 2 spring wheat sold for $1.23¼ per bushel the week of July 1, 1871; no. 2 corn sold for 52¼¢ per bushel for the same week and oats were sold for 46¾¢. Chicago Board of Trade, Annual Report 1871, at 59, 62.

things: (1) the right of the elevator owner to mix grain within the elevator to avoid the costs of maintaining separate identifiable batches; and (2) the right of the carrier to organize delivery so as to minimize its costs by reducing the unloading time. This was important for the railroads who wished to remove their cars from the physically small Chicago terminal area as quickly as possible and return them to the west.[28]

The elevator managers or "warehousemen" obtained the right to mix grain under the terms of their warehouse receipts.[29] Mixing meant that grain was received and delivered from the elevators by general grade, and the question whether the grain was properly graded upon receipt and delivery was a source of constant friction between the elevator men and their customers.[30]

Prior to 1864, the railroads generally followed the practice of delivery to the consignee designated by the shipper.[31] In that year the Northwestern, and probably other railroads, adopted a rule reserving the right to select the terminal elevator on grain to Chicago.[32] This was met by a statute in 1865 declaring the right of the consignor to select the delivery point.[33] The railroads persisted in their assertion of the right to select the receiving elevator.[34] This

---

[28] The Northwestern justified its preference contract of 1866 on the grounds that "the . . . switching of cars, parts of the same train, to different warehouses, and the great delay in unloading the same consequent thereon may be avoided and the cars be returned sooner to the service of the public." Petition for Mandamus 10, Chicago & Nw. R.R. Co. v. People ex rel. Hempstead, 56 Ill. 365 (1870) (copy supplied by the Clerk of the Illinois Supreme Court). The complexities of switching from the Galena Division to the Illinois Elevator, described 56 Ill. at 374–75, persuaded the court that delivery from the Galena Division was not required. CHICAGO BOARD OF TRADE & MERCANTILE ASS'N JOINT COMMITTEE REPORT ON THE RAILWAY AND WAREHOUSE MONOPOLIES 8–9 (1866) (University of Chicago Library).

[29] This right was affirmed by the Illinois Supreme Court in Low v. Martin, 18 Ill. 286 (1857), and by § 6 of the Warehouse Act of 1867, 1867 Ill. Laws at 178.

[30] 2 PIERCE, note 26 supra, at 82–83; TAYLOR, at 225–449, passim.

[31] LEE, at 137–38. The railroads had been able to influence the choice of a receiving elevator and had used it as an incentive to encourage the erection of new elevators on railroad lands. For example, an early elevator lease states that the railroad agrees to furnish the elevator operators with "all the grain business for elevating and storage which may be subject to its control and which it can properly bring to them." Contract between the Illinois Central R.R. Co. and Solomon Sturges & R. B. Buckingham (June 14, 1855) (Newberry Library, Chicago, Ill.).

[32] Chicago & Nw. R.R. Co. v. People ex rel. Hempstead, 56 Ill. 365 (1870).

[33] Act of Feb. 14, 1865, §1, 1865 Ill. Laws at 75.

[34] Vincent v. Chicago & Alton R.R. Co., 49 Ill. 33 (1868).

led to more legislation[35] and a series of Illinois Supreme Court decisions generally adverse to the position of the railroads.[36] Nonetheless, there never was any "spot market" competition among the elevators for grain delivered by railroad.[37]

The warehousemen in Chicago are identified in table 3. They seem to have been coordinated, and in 1866 those receiving from Northwestern, Burlington & Quincy, and Chicago & Alton secretly combined their ownership.[38] Ira Y. Munn was the managing partner of this combine and of his own elevator. He was prominent in Board of Trade activities throughout the late fifties and sixties and served a term as president of the board in 1860.[39]

The general members of the Chicago Board of Trade were importantly involved in the legislation leading to *Munn*. They acted in two capacities: as speculators in the emerging cash and futures market of the board and as commission merchants for the shippers. In the latter capacity they would hold the elevator receipt and make arrangements for the shipment by lake vessel and delivery of grain from the elevator. These two functions brought the general members of the Board of Trade into conflict with the warehousemen. The conflict preoccupied Board of Trade politics in the years following the Civil War. In their position as commission merchants,

---

[35] "It shall be unlawful for any railroad or railway company to deliver any grain into any warehouse, other than that into which it is consigned, without consent of the owner or consignor thereof." Warehouse Act of 1867, § 22, 1867 Ill. Laws at 181.

[36] Vincent v. Chicago & Alton R.R. Co., 49 Ill. 33 (1868) (§ 22 of the Warehouse Act of 1867 upheld); People ex rel. Hempstead v. Chicago & Alton R.R. Co., 55 Ill. 95 (1870) (railroad cannot be compelled to deliver grain to a warehouse beyond its line); Chicago & Nw. R.R. Co. v. People ex rel. Hempstead, 56 Ill. 365 (1870) (exclusive contracts with warehousemen have no effect against the R.R.'s duty to deliver to consignee designated by shipper); People ex rel. Harmon Spruance v. Chicago & Nw. R.R. Co., 57 Ill. 436 (1870) (railroad cannot be compelled to permit individuals to connect sidetracks extending its line for delivery of grain).

[37] This was because elevator charges remained uniform throughout the period. See table 1. The exclusive contracts between the railroads and the elevator operators were only slightly modified. The railroad "hereby agrees so far as it may lawfully do to furnish during the continuance of this lease . . . to [the elevator operators] . . . for storage, delivering and shipment . . . all the grain business which may come over its Road into Chicago and be subject to its Control and which it may properly and lawfully deliver to them." Contract between the Chicago, Burlington & Quincy R.R. Co. and Armour & Dole Co. (October 10, 1873) (Newberry Library, Chicago, Ill.).

[38] See table 3. The secret agreement was raised as a defense by the Northwestern in Chicago & Nw. R.R. Co. v. People ex rel. Hempstead, 56 Ill. 365, 374 (1870). A copy of the written agreement appears in the Petition for Mandamus, p. 8. The details of the combined ownership were revealed by Ira Munn at his bankruptcy trial in November 1872. His testimony is reported in the Chicago Tribune, November 26, 28, 1872.

[39] TAYLOR, at 266, 307, 354, 361, 367.

the nonelevator members wanted a uniform system of inspection on grains entering and leaving the elevators. This they obtained from the elevator operators by agreement in 1857.[40] In their position as speculators they wanted more: the power to inspect the contents of the elevators. This the warehousemen resisted, and to get it the Board of Trade turned to the State legislature. The 1871 legislation that provided interior inspection also contained the rate section litigated in *Munn*.

The demand for inspection on storage and delivery is easy to understand. It was too costly for each commission merchant to inspect each of his shipments. Absent some system of inspection, the elevator operator would have an incentive to grade and measure down on storage and to grade and measure up on delivery.[41] If there had been competition between the elevators, the elevator with a superior record of honesty in inspection would gain business. The integration between the railroads and the elevators weakened this competition, although the contracts between the railroads and the elevators show that the railroads were concerned about the inspection practices of their terminal elevators. This inspection system was operated by the Board of Trade until the statute of 1871, which set up a state inspection system.

The Board of Trade membership, however, also wanted inspection of the interiors of the elevators. This the warehousemen resisted. The general membership was concerned about interior inspection because of the role of the elevators in futures trading on the board. Futures contracts could be honored by delivery of a "regular" warehouse receipt for the required amount of grain. Only warehouses located in Chicago were "regular."[42] Indeed, it was the

---

[40] *Id.* at 227–28, 242–43, 257.

[41] After the institution of systematic state inspection, the existence of these practices became obvious. Triolus Tyndale, the Warehouse Registrar, commented in 1874 that: "The practice of accumulating a considerable surplus of grain in the course of a year or even a less period of time, continues in certain of the elevators. These 'surpluses' are claimed by the warehousemen as their property, and sold to their own account. They say that in cases where there is a shortage instead of a surplus they have to make it good; which stands to reason. Only somehow the few shortages that occur are remarkably unimportant in amount compared to the surpluses; and since some warehouse firms, doing a very large business, never claim any surplus, it must be quite possible to avoid its occurrence to any considerable extent." ILLINOIS R.R. & W'HS. COMM'N, ANNUAL REPORT 42 (1874).

[42] It seems to have been understood throughout the period that the grain delivered on a futures contract had to be located at Chicago, but this was not codified in the rules of the Board of Trade. The first formal rules governing futures delivery were adopted in

TABLE 3

WHO WERE "THE WAREHOUSE MEN"?

Warehouse	Proprietors	Share in Combine (1866–71)	Receive From	Capacity (Bushels) December 1870	Capacity (Bushels) December 1871
City Elevator	$\frac{5}{16}$ Munn and Scott, Armour (1872) $\frac{3}{16}$ Wheeler $\frac{1}{8}$ Armour $\frac{1}{8}$ Munger (from "old man Taylor") $\frac{1}{8}$ McKay $\frac{1}{8}$ Smith and Dunlap* $\frac{1}{8}$ Armour (1872)	125 shares City + Union	Chicago, Nw. R.R.; canal	1,250,000	1,200,000
Union Elevator	Same as City, $\frac{5}{16}$ Armour (1872)		Chicago & Alton R.R.; canal	700,000	700,000
Northwestern Elevator	$\frac{1}{4}$ Dunlap* $\frac{3}{4}$ Munn and Scott $\frac{1}{4}$ Smith and Dunlap (1872)* $\frac{1}{2}$ Armour (1872)	125 shares Nw. + Munn and Scott's	Chicago, Nw. R.R.; canal	600,000	600,000
Munn and Scott's	Munn and Scott, Armour (1872)	150 shares Galena + Wheeler and Munger + Armour	Canal	200,000	200,000
Galena	Munger, Wheeler		Chicago Nw. R.R., Galena Div. and canal	500,000	800,000
Wheeler and Munger [Hiram Wheeler's]	Munger, Wheeler		Same as Galena	500,000	None||
Munger and Armour's	Munger, Wheeler		Same as Galena	600,000	None||
Chicago B. & Q.R.R. Elevator A	Armour, Dole under leases from Chicago B. & Q.R.R. (1860) (1862) (1864) (1873)		Chicago B. & Q.R.R.	1,250,000	1,250,000
Chicago B. & Q.R.R. Elevator B	Same as Elevator A		Chicago B. & Q.R.R.	850,000	850,000
Total combine capacity				6,450,000	

SOURCES.—EDWARDS, [Merchants'] CHICAGO CENSUS REPORT 1871, at 1234; ILLINOIS R.R. & WHS. COMM'N, ANNUAL REPORT 1872, at 35; 1 TAYLOR, HISTORY OF THE BOARD OF TRADE OF THE CITY OF CHICAGO (1917); testimony of Ira Munn as reported by Chicago Tribune, Nov. 26 & 28, 1872.
* Former managers of Chicago Northwestern R.R.
\|\| Destroyed by fire of September, 1871.

TABLE 3 (*Continued*)

Warehouse	Proprietors	Share in Combine (1866–71)	Receive From	Capacity (Bushels) December 1870	Capacity (Bushels) December 1871
Air Line........	Munger, Wheeler	None	?	None	800,000
Illinois........	Hempstead† ¼ Armour and Munger (1872) ¼ Wheeler (1872) ¼ Buckingham (1872) ¼ Munn and Scott (1872) Wheeler (1872)	None	Canal	200,000	200,000
Central Elevator A..	Sturges & Burlingame under lease from Illinois Central R.R. (1855); Sturges A. Buckingham (1857); J. & E. Buckingham (1866) (1876)	None	Ill. Central R.R.; canal	700,000	Under construction‖
Central Elevator B..	Same as Elevator A	None	Ill. Central R.R.; canal	1,600,000	1,600,000
Rock Island Elevator A..	Flint, Thompson (lease from Chicago Rock Island R.R.?)	None	Chicago, R.I. & P.R.R.; canal	750,000	750,000
Rock Island Elevator B..	Same as Elevator A	None	Chicago, R.I. & P.R.R.; canal	1,250,000	1,250,000
Iowa..........	Mather and Newberry Wheeler (1862) Spruance,‡ Preston (1865) seized by Hugh Mayer (1872) Burned down Aug. 1872	None	Canal	300,000	300,000
Lunt's.........	S.P. Lunt	None	Canal	80,000	None‖
National.......	Vincent Nelson	None	Chicago & Alton R.R.; canal	250,000	Under construction‖
Hough's........	Hough§	None	?	None	Under construction

Total "independent" capacity..5,130,000

† Confrontation with Chicago Nw. R.R. over delivery 1870–72.
‡ Undercut storage rate agreement in 1870.
§ Reduced winter storage rates Nov. 1872; raised rates to "those charged by other elevators" in 1873.

327

concentration in Chicago of a large stock of grain in the normal course of business that gave it a comparative advantage as a trading center. But traders on the Chicago Board of Trade had to worry not only about worldwide long-run demand and supply conditions for grain, but also about short-run demand and supply conditions in Chicago. This was particularly true as the contracts approached the end of their term and the time for offsetting grain movements from other grain storage points shrank.

The history of the Board of Trade for the period recounts repeated efforts to "corner" the market.[43] Toward the end of a contract period a group would attempt to obtain control of all the grain then in store in Chicago and to force those who held contracts obligating them to make delivery of grain to obtain the receipts necessary to satisfy their obligations at a gain to the perpetrators of the corner. Most of these attempts seemed to fail as the victims of the corner rushed to obtain supplies from Milwaukee or more distant points.[44] These corners were a nuisance to the commission merchants because they tended to hold grain in store in Chicago and slow the rate at which grain could move through the transfer point.[45]

Under a state statute passed at the behest of the general membership in 1867, the elevators were required to post weekly the amount of grain in store.[46] But it was widely claimed in the *Chicago Tribune* and elsewhere that these reports were false and that the warehousemen issued false reports to benefit their own speculations. It was also alleged in the *Tribune* that the elevators issued or left outstanding receipts on grain not in store.[47] A statute passed in 1851 had required that receipts be issued only for property actually received into store but failed to provide that receipts must be can-

---

1865. TAYLOR, at 331. CHICAGO BOARD OF TRADE, RULES, REGULATIONS AND BY-LAWS ADOPTED OCT. 13, 1865 (1865). The first rule mentioning "regular" warehouse receipts dates from September 25, 1875. "All deliveries upon grain contracts . . . shall be made by tender of regular warehouse receipts, which receipts shall have been registered by an officer duly appointed for that purpose." General Rule XXIV, § 1, CHICAGO BOARD OF TRADE, ANNUAL REPORT, app. at xlvi (1877).

[43] See discussions of "corners," in GOLDSTEIN, note 27 *supra*, at 127–28; and 2 GRAIN TRADE 110 (1900). The Chicago grain "corners" of the period are described by TAYLOR, at 370–72 (1868), 383–84 (1869), 425–26 (1871), 452–55, 456–60 (1872).

[44] TAYLOR, at 425–26.

[45] 1872 ANNUAL REPORT at 32.

[46] Warehouse Act of 1867, § 5, 1867 Ill. Laws at 178.

[47] TAYLOR, at 398; Chicago Tribune, March 2, 1870; see also LEE, at 159–60, 170.

celled when the property was delivered out.[48] By having more receipts outstanding than he had grain in store, a warehouseman could borrow money while collecting for the storage of the non-existent grain. Both claimed improprieties were to prove true.

The key to the position of the elevators was their contracts with the railroads. Copies of a number of these contracts still exist.[49] They had these features in common: (1) A lease by the railroad of land to a lessee who would agree to erect an elevator. (2) A right in the lessee to charge for storage and transfer, limited by a most favored railroad principle, itself limited by a floor. The floors were in the range of one and one quarter cents.[50] (3) A commitment by the railroad to deliver the grain arriving over its line to the lessee's warehouses, as long as the lessee provided service satisfactory to the railroad. (4) A commitment by the lessee to give priority to grain tendered from the railroad. (5) Rights of inspection on the part of the railroad. (6) A rent provision, variously computed.

The extent of this contractual integration raises the question of why the railroads did not operate the elevators themselves. The earliest elevators in Chicago antedated the railroads who constructed side lines and switches to accommodate them. Some of the elevators built during the 1850s were operated directly by railroads for a short time.[51] The elevators were important to the railroads because inadequate or inefficient transfer facilities would affect the railroad's operations and competitive position throughout its territory. One answer is that elevator operations were beyond railroad charter powers, and there is some contemporary dictum,[52] including dictum in *Munn*,[53] to support this view. Guy Lee concludes that the

---

[48] Act of Jan. 28, 1851, § 1, 1851 Ill. Laws at 9.

[49] See table 4.

[50] *Ibid.*   [51] LEE, at 50–51.

[52] "It would obviously be impossible for the companies to unload and store this grain at their ordinary freight depots, to be there held, unmixed with other grain, subject to the order of the consignees, without incurring great additional expense, and they would hardly claim the right, under their charters, to erect elevators of their own, for the purpose of adding the business of commission merchants to that of common carriers." Vincent v. Chicago & Alton R.R. Co., 49 Ill. 33, 39 (1868). The Rock Island & LaSalle R.R. Co. was prohibited from engaging in the warehouse business in Chicago by its charter. 1851 Ill. Priv. Laws 47, 49–50. The Rock Island built and leased for operation a large elevator in 1856. LEE, at 51.

[53] "The railways have found it impracticable to own such elevators, and public policy forbids the transaction of such business by the carrier." 94 U.S. at 131. This is a quote from the elevator brief designed to suggest that the railroads and the warehousemen were quite separate.

TABLE 4

ELEVATOR CONTRACTS

Date	Railroad	Lessee	Floor on Most Favored Railroad Clause	Preference in Favor of Lessee	Preference in Favor of Railroad	Railroad Right to Inspect	Rent ($)
June 14, 1855....	Ill. Central	Sturges & Burlingame	¼¢	Yes	No	No	5,000 per annum
August 10, 1866.	Northwestern R.R.	Munn & Scott	None	Yes	Yes	Yes	25,000 per annum
October 10, 1873.	Chicago Burlington & Quincy	Armour Dole & Co. (Elevators A, B, & C)	1¼¢	Yes	Yes	Yes	9,000 per annum
April 15, 1879.....	Chicago Burlington & Quincy	Armour Dole & Co. (Elevator D)	1¼¢	Yes	Yes	Yes	½ of Elevator earnings
October 1, 1881..	Ill. Central	Ebenezer Buckingham	1¢	Yes	Yes	No	15,000 per annum
August 1, 1886...	Chicago Burlington & Quincy	Dole & Company	None*	Yes	Yes	Yes	Elevator earnings 88,000 to elevator,† 65,000 to R.R.,† remainder split between elevator and R.R.

SOURCES.—The 1866 Northwestern R.R. contract is quoted in Petition for Mandamus, at 8–14, Chicago Nw. R.R. Co. v. People ex rel. Hempstead, 56 Ill. 365 (1870). Manuscript copies of the other contracts are available at the Newberry Library, Chicago, Ill.

* ¾¢ for first ten days and ⅜¢ thereafter suggested in memorandum of June 23, 1886; no floor appears in the contract.

† 6 percent interest on capital investments in new equipment.

independent operators were able to engage in the related grain trading and merchandising activities more effectively than the railroads.[54]

The other question is why the railroads tolerated the formation
of a combine in elevator transfer services. The answer lies, we
think, in the inability of the railroads to gain the right to control
the delivery point. They asserted this right in 1864, an assertion
that led to a series of cases from which they won only the right to
refuse delivery to elevators off their lines.[55] The existence of a uniform elevator transfer price, however, effectively mooted the issue.
As long as all the elevators charged the same price, the consignor
had no incentive to specify a particular elevator and the railroads
were left free to arrange deliveries in accordance with their operating needs. If this resulted in high profitability to the elevators, the
railroads could get this back through the rental term. Whether the
railroads did so cannot be determined. The sizable gap between
the rate actually charged and the floor on the most favored railroad
clause suggests that they did not.[56] On the other hand, a favorable
price term generated service competition, and the railroads may
have been most concerned about the reliability and quality of the
service at their terminal elevators—particularly during the busy and
crucial late summer and early fall months.[57]

There was one episode of elevator price competition in the period. In 1870 Harmon Spruance, proprietor of the small Iowa elevator and cut off from railroad delivery by the Northwestern, of-

---

[54] LEE, at 50–54, 205 n.63.

[55] See n. 36 *supra*.

[56] It was widely believed that the elevators were very profitable and the business laid
the foundations for the major Chicago fortunes of Armour and Buckingham. Guy Lee
explored the issue at length, including a review of the income tax returns from Chicago
during the Civil War, which were public documents. He could reach no clear conclusion.
LEE, at 124–28.

[57] Another explanation, occasionally suggested at the time, was that the leases were
benefits to friends of corporate management. Solomon Sturges, holder of the Illinois
Central lease in the 1850s (see table 4) had a cousin in the management of the railroad.
LEE, at 52. Smith and Dunlap, who had an interest in Northwestern elevators, had
previously been connected with the Northwestern railroad. No further evidence of this
suggestion exists. Munn, who as a ruined man at the receiver's hearings seems to have
been willing to testify freely, did not suggest the existence of such factors. Chicago
Tribune, November 26, 28, 1872. The Committee Report of 1866 stated about "an alleged complicity on the part of railroad officials with the management of grain elevators,"
that "on this point we can produce no proof aside" from the denials of the "gentlemen"
involved. CHICAGO BOARD OF TRADE & MERCANTILE ASSOCIATION, note 28 *supra*, at 9.

fered a rate of one cent.[58] The railroad continued to refuse to deliver and the elevator was seized by force by Hugh "Meagher" [Maher] in March 1872,[59] probably under the terms of his lease with Spruance. Maher was to be associated with Munn and Scott in the wheat corner in July and August of that year.

Another small elevator, the Illinois, succeeded in getting the Illinois Supreme Court in 1870 to rule that the Northwestern Railroad had to deliver to them from its Wisconsin and Milwaukee divisions. The Illinois Elevator appeal was linked to another order to deliver from the Galena division, which the Court reversed.[60] The case was remanded, and in 1872 the Northwestern sent an engine onto the switch when the Rock Island attempted to deliver thirty cars. The Rock Island was not cowed. It sent two engines to the scene, forced the Northwestern engine off the switch, and completed the delivery. Hempstead renewed his suit, but the whole matter was settled by the sale of the Illinois Elevator to the Munn and Scott combine.[61]

The Board of Trade, too, had an interest in a uniform storage charge. The development of standardized trading on the board required the development of uniform terms. The payment of storage charges was the obligation of the person presenting the warehouse receipt for delivery, and thus the value of the receipt would be affected by the rate of storage.[62] If the rates of storage differed, then it would complicate calculation of the value of the "regular"

---

[58] TAYLOR, at 400. The elevator was constructed by Maher and Newberry in 1862. They leased it to Hiram Wheeler who constructed a track from the Northwestern railroad line to the warehouse. In 1865 Wheeler abandoned the elevator and removed the switch. Spruance leased the elevator in 1869 and sued the Northwestern to allow him to construct a new switch. The Northwestern refused because of its exclusive cortract with Wheeler's large elevator. The Illinois Supreme Court held that Spruance could not compel the Northwestern to permit him to build a switch because the right to make the connection was personal to Maher and Newberry, the original owners. People ex rel. Spruance v. Chicago & Nw. R.R. Co., 57 Ill. 436 (1870).

[59] Hugh "Meagher" must be Hugh Maher of Maher & Newberry, the original owners. Taylor also reports that in the course of the seizure, the occupants, including a newly appointed state grain inspector, were "thrown out into the mud." TAYLOR, at 451.

[60] Chicago & Nw. R.R. Co. v. People ex rel. Hempstead, 56 Ill. 365 (1870).

[61] TAYLOR, at 451.

[62] Under the 1865 Rules, the grain would be held for three days after delivery of the receipts to the buyer without extra storage on the warehouse receipts. CHICAGO BOARD OF TRADE, ACT OF INCORPORATION, RULES, REGULATIONS AND BY-LAWS, GENERAL RULE XII, at 15 (1865). In 1869 the grace period was increased to five days. CHICAGO BOARD OF TRADE, ANNUAL REPORT 164 (1869).

receipts used to meet the contract obligations. A uniform rate of storage made all receipts comparable. Never once did the general membership of the Board of Trade complain about the uniformity of storage charges.[63]

With this background, the events leading to the legislation of 1871 can be briefly sketched. The board organized an inspection system in 1857.[64] The system was at first operated by members. A full-time chief inspector was appointed in 1865.[65] The elevator owners agreed to inspection on delivery from rail cars and later on delivery from canal boats. The inspection system was paid for by a fee. The definition of grades and the fairness and reliability of the inspection presented recurrent problems that need not be recounted here. The grain crop of each season had different characteristics, and adjustments were made in the grading systems to accomodate these differences.

The Board of Trade first turned to the legislature for assistance in 1867. No explanation survives as to why the board, in spite of the near unanimity of its membership, found it necessary to turn to the legislature for assistance. Proposals were repeatedly made that the Board of Trade refuse to accept for delivery on futures contracts warehouse receipts coming from elevators that did not accept the inspection and receipt registration systems desired by the board.[66] We think the answer is that the Board of Trade could not conduct futures trading without the elevators, and the united front of the warehousemen made it impossible for the board, acting alone, to impose the condition. Ironically, the inspection and registration systems were actually implemented in 1873 not as the result of legal process but because the banks, concerned about the security of the receipts in the wake of the Iowa elevator fire, insisted on it.

In 1867 two bills were introduced and the Board of Trade was split. One, the Eastman bill, was supported by the general membership. The other, the Ward bill, was regarded as the "elevator" bill and was supported by some of the directors of the board.[67] The Eastman bill passed, but in a weakened form. The law did require elevator owners to cancel receipts on delivery of grain, thus closing

---

[63] Agitation for competitive rates appeared to originate with the Chicago Tribune. LEE, at 205.

[64] TAYLOR, at 227–28.

[65] *Id.* at 241–42.

[66] See, *e.g.*, *id.* at 398.

[67] *Id.* at 349–52.

the loophole in the 1851 law.[68] It required railroads to deliver to the consignee.[69] Provisions to compel railroads to build switch connections to elevators and the lack of any enforcement mechanism were noted omissions. The bill also made no provision for interior inspection of the elevators. The bill as passed was particularly obnoxious to the Board of Trade because it contained a provision making futures trading a gambling crime.[70] It was widely believed that these sections were inserted at the behest of the warehousemen. This provision led to a notable arrest of leading members of the board on the floor, but the matter was not carried to conviction.[71] The provision did not affect the ongoing futures trading and the sections were repealed in 1869.[72]

The debates of the constitutional convention of 1870 make it clear that the act of 1867 was not regarded as adequate. Numerous petitions, including one from over 700 Chicago businessmen,[73] were received by the convention, complaining of overissues of receipts by warehousemen and short weights in delivery by railroads. During consideration of an article providing that elevators be made subject to inspection by inspectors of the Board of Trade, the owners of the grain, and the owners of the receipts, the chairman of the committee reported that:[74]

> The *Chicago Tribune* tells us that the Board of Trade and the grain dealers of Chicago tried to have grain receipts registered, tried to have some of these safeguards that we propose to put in this article adopted by the elevator owners, but that they refused . . . until the article was reported; . . . [and then] the elevator owners . . . agreed to demands of the Board of Trade, provided the article should be withdrawn.

The article was popular in the convention and, when put to a separate ratification vote, passed easily. The only objection made with any frequency was that the subject matter was legislative in character and inappropriate to a constitution.[75] The only sustained

---

[68] Warehouse Act of 1867, § 11, 1867 Ill. Laws at 179–80.

[69] § 22, 1867 Ill. Laws at 181–82.

[70] §§ 17, 18, 19 and 20, 1867 Ill. Laws at 181.

[71] Taylor, at 352–53.

[72] *Ibid.*; 1869 Ill. Laws at 410.   [74] *Id.* at 1623.

[73] Debates, note 19 *supra*, at 654.   [75] *Id.* at 1622–34.

and vehement opposition came from delegate Turner of Freeport, who, somewhat colorfully, asserted that this was "the grain gamblers article" and proceeded to attack futures traders as "leeches upon commerce and the community, that suck the life blood out of the farmers and dealers in grain, without contributing anything towards the general wealth or production of the country."[76] He claimed that the article had been prepared at the behest of speculators smarting from recent losses and urged the convention to have nothing to do with the whole business.

The constitutional article contained seven sections.[77] The first declared all elevators where grain is stored for a compensation to be public warehouses. The second required a weekly statement of the Chicago elevators of grain in store and warehouse receipts outstanding. The third gave the holder of a receipt the power to examine the property stored. The fourth required railroads to weigh grain on shipment. The fifth required railroads to deliver to the consignee. The sixth and seventh instructed the General Assembly to pass laws to prevent the issue of fraudulent warehouse receipts and for the inspection of grain.

With the passage of the new constitution in 1870, implementing legislation was in order. The Board of Trade proposed a bill in December that left inspection in the Board of Trade but empowered its inspectors to make interior inspections.[78] This bill was modified in the legislature to provide for State-appointed inspectors, a change which the Board of Trade found difficult to resist amid charges that its own chief inspector had been corrupted.[79]

The elevators resisted interior inspection after the bill was passed.[80] They refused to take out the license required by the statute on the grounds that the price provision made the statute unconstitutional. The litigation began. In August 1873, however, the Iowa elevator burned, and in the settlement process it became clear that the receipts outstanding exceeded the grain in store by 165,000 bushels—this in an elevator with total nominal capacity of 300,000 bushels.[81] The insurance companies refused to

---

[76] Id. at 1623.

[77] ILL. CONST. 1870, art. 13.

[78] Chicago Tribune, Dec. 28, 1870.

[79] TAYLOR, at 405–10.

[80] Warehouse Act of 1871, 1871 Ill. Laws at 762.

[81] TAYLOR, at 456–57; Chicago Tribune, Aug. 23, 1872. The proprietor of the Iowa elevator, Hugh Maher, was indicted by the local grand jury on the petition of the state inspectors. 1872 ANNUAL REPORT, at 15–16, 144–45.

pay any losses beyond that on grain actually in store. This event created pressure for interior inspection and registration, particularly from the banks that had been accepting the warehouse receipts as security.[82]

All the warehousemen but one consented to a state investigation of the amount of grain in store.[83] Munn and Scott requested a delay in the inspection of the elevator they managed in order to "collect the grain in as few bins as would be sufficient to hold it, so that the quantity could be more readily and accurately ascertained.[84] The inspectors agreed, and when the inspection was made the grain was found in good order. But it shortly became known—perhaps from employees who had done the work[85]—that Munn and Scott had used the time to erect false bottoms in their bins to conceal the short fall between the grain in storage and receipts outstanding.[86] Munn and Scott sold out to George Armour,[87] who made good on the outstanding receipts.

The trouble become known when George Armour and Company cautioned against accepting Munn and Scott receipts unless they had been endorsed by Armour and Company. Munn and Scott and Maher, the operator of the Iowa elevator, were said to be involved in a large corner on wheat about the time the Iowa elevator fire occurred. The corner collapsed on August 19, speeding Munn and Scott's financial decline.[88] Munn's testimony at the receiver's hearing strongly suggests that he had been in serious financial difficulty since at least 1868.[89] Maher was indicted.[90] Munn and Scott

---

[82] Lee describes the use of warehouse receipts as collateral for bank loans. LEE, at 177–79; 1872 ANNUAL REPORT, at 15, 41; Woodman, note 21 *supra*, at 24.

[83] 1872 ANNUAL REPORT, at 16; TAYLOR, at 457.

[84] 1872 ANNUAL REPORT, at 16.

[85] Chicago Tribune, Nov. 20, 1872.

[86] *Ibid.*; TAYLOR, at 466. The Railroad and Warehouse Commission noted it in their annual report. 1872 ANNUAL REPORT, at 16.

[87] Reportedly for a consideration of ten dollars. LEE, at 267; TAYLOR, at 460, 466. Munn and Scott remained in the litigation because the appeal was from a fine against them personally. As a practical matter, they may not have controlled the litigation after 1872.

[88] TAYLOR, at 458.

[89] Chicago Tribune, Nov. 26, 28, 1872. In March 1873, it was revealed that Munn and Scott had mortaged their elevators to Jesse Hoyt, a New York commission merchant for $450,000 ($500,000 according to Lee). Hoyt persisted in his attempts to collect from Armour until the Munn and Scott properties were sold, by court order, to Munger and Wheeler, another big elevator firm. Chicago Tribune, March 2, 1873; LEE, at 268.

[90] 1872 ANNUAL REPORT, at 144–45.

were expelled from the Board of Trade and later arrested when it appeared they might leave town before the receivership had been settled.[91]

The matter of rates played a decidedly secondary role in the agitation about the warehouse question. At the outset of the Civil War, the closing of the Mississippi route congested the lake route and led to political agitation about prices, which may have been in part a form of covert opposition to the interests supporting the war.[92] The problems seem to have greatly abated by 1863, but in 1865 the Chicago elevators posted new transfer charges which lowered the initial storage term to ten days, and then in the fall of 1865 announced a unilateral increase in the rates of storage on the grain then in store.[93] The elevator men defended this increase on the grounds that the grain was in bad condition and would be difficult to carry through the winter. It created a considerable ruckus and the increase was withdrawn,[94] but the event must have brought to the attention of the general membership in the board the power the elevator men held over the grain trade.

In a pamphlet addressed to the public, a committee of the Board of Trade reviewed the question of storage charges. The committee said:[95]

> Of the second charge—extravagant and arbitrary rates of storage adopted by the warehousemen—it is but proper to say that, with but one exception, no change has been made in the rates of storage on railroad grain for the past 10 years. . . . While we think the rates of storage of grain in this city are quite high enough, we cannot regard them as exorbitant as compared with other points, there being no extra charge for labor of shoveling, running over when necessary to preserve it, or any extras. . . . We trust, however, that elevator proprietors will, the coming season, change their time of first storage back to 20 days instead of 10 as now, even though to balance such concession, they are obliged to shorten the time on the half-cent accumulation afterward.

The rates were in fact so reduced.

---

[91] TAYLOR, at 467; Chicago Tribune, Dec. 13, 1872.

[92] LEE, at 136–40.

[93] Chicago Tribune, Feb. 14, 1866; Well's Commercial Express and Western Produce Reporter, Oct. 30, 1865 (daily ed.).

[94] Chicago Board of Trade and Mercantile Association, note 28 supra, at 8.

[95] Id. at 7–8.

The law of 1867 required the warehousemen to meet and announce a price in January, the price to act as a ceiling for the whole
year.[96] This provision was similar to statutory price posting requirements applicable to ferries.[97] Doubtless the events of 1865 had suggested the utility of limiting the power of the elevator operators to
spring sudden changes on grain then in store or in transit, after the
owners had already committed themselves to storage. The debates
of the constitutional convention of 1869–70 are free of any mention of the rate question. The draft bill of the Board of Trade in
1870 contains a section restating the notice requirement and further
providing that the rate agreed upon could not exceed two cents
for transfer and twenty days storage—the rate urged by the Board
of Trade Committee in 1866 and then in force.[98] The law that
passed extended the initial storage period to thirty days.[99]

Observers agreed that the effect of this change was small. The
Tribune observed on November 22, 1872, that income from the
"extra storage . . . amounts to very little except during the winter
months." Lee estimated that only one-twelfth of the grain remained in store beyond twenty days.[100] Inspection of the weekly
storage received and shipped tables in the Board of Trade annual
reports (for years after interior inspection began) suggests that under a strict first-in, first-out basis, grain would have been in store
during the summer months for about thirty days. Interpretation
of the statistics is clouded by the fact that a significant part of the
grain in store was owned by the elevator operator. It was recognized at the time that the rate provision of the law could be avoided
if the elevators were operated as private warehouses[101] (*i.e.*, if the
elevators were used to store grain owned by the elevator owner
rather than the public), and indeed by the end of the century most
Chicago elevator capacity was operated on a private basis.[102]

---

[96] § 5, 1867 Ill. Laws at 178.

[97] An Act to provide for the establishment of Ferries, etc., Feb. 12, 1827, § 6, Ill.
Rev. Laws at 305 (1833). The function of this type of regulation is discussed in Kitch,
Isaacson, & Kasper, *The Regulation of Taxicabs in Chicago*, 14 J. LAW & ECON. 285,
305–09 (1971).

[98] Reprinted in the Chicago Tribune, Dec. 28, 1870.

[99] § 15, 1871 Ill. Laws at 769.

[100] LEE, at 126. The Illinois Central contract of 1855, note 31 *supra*, stated that the
usual time was 15 days.

[101] TAYLOR, at 411.

[102] After 1885, Chicago elevator operators began to combine public warehousing with
private grain buying on a large scale. The operators' grain was mixed with the public

Aside from a brief period of compliance by one elevator in 1872,[103] the elevators did not comply with the statutory rate until the Supreme Court *Munn* decision in 1877.[104] That year the legislature lowered the statutory rate, over the feeble objection of the warehousemen.[105] Chicago as a transfer point was by that time facing intense competition from through shipments. In 1876 the directors of the Illinois Central observed that:[106]

> Up to a recent period, Chicago held the control of the Grain Traffic. The cost of taking a bushel of grain from Chicago to New York for several successive years was from 22 to 30 cents. As water communication was cheapened, rates by rail have been reduced in greater ratio. Last season, grain was carried by water at an average of $9\frac{1}{2}$¢ per bushel from Chicago to New York. In face of this extremely low rate, nearly one half of the grain was sent direct from local stations in Illinois to the East by railroad. Chicago has ceased, for the present at least, to be the great enterpot [*sic*] for the grain products of the country West and South of it. Since 1872, the rates for grain to Chicago from local stations on our line have been reduced from twenty to thirty percent.

III. CONCLUSION

This research speaks to the need to develop a more complete history of the development of American economic regulation prior to the Interstate Commerce Act of 1887,[107] and to problems

---

grain, but accumulated no storage fees. The Illinois Supreme Court in 1898 ruled that mixing public and private grain was a violation of the Warehouse Act of 1871. Central Elevator Co. v. People, 174 Ill. 203 (1898). Prior to the decision, the legislature attempted to amend the Warehouse Act of 1871 in order to exonerate the elevator operators. 1897 Ill. Laws at 300. In Hannah v. People, 198 Ill. 77 (1902), the Supreme Court held the 1897 amendment to be in violation of the state constitution and reaffirmed the decision in *Central Elevator*. Thereafter Chicago elevators were required to store their private grain in separate bins. The result was that elevator operators began to reorganize on a private basis in order to avoid the separate storage requirement. In 1899, 75 percent of the grain entering Chicago went into private rather than public elevators. By 1917, the percentage of private grain had increased to 80 percent. 2 GRAIN TRADE 96–103.

[103] The newly constructed Hough elevator. TAYLOR, at 467; Chicago Tribune, Dec. 7, 1872.

[104] TAYLOR, at 547.

[105] 1877 Ill. Laws at 169. The warehousemen unsuccessfully lobbied for the old rate in 1874. LEE, at 229.

[106] LEE, at 270.

[107] MILLER, note 22 *supra*, contains much useful material, particularly for the period 1870–80.

in the economic theory of cartels. The elevator price-fixing conspiracy is one of the rare reported cases of a stable price fix and is,
interestingly enough, explainable on plausible efficiency grounds.
The purpose of this essay is, however, somewhat more limited. It
is to use the factual background to illuminate the Court's opinion
in *Munn* and to place the case in better historical perspective.

The factual background is useful in understanding two important aspects of the opinion. The first is the significance of Chief
Justice Waite's statement that "this is a power which may be abused;
but that is no argument against its existence. For protection against
abuses by legislatures the people must resort to the polls, not to the
courts."[108] This dictum is sometimes carelessly read by the modern
reader as a holding.[109] Second is the scope of the concept "affected
with a public interest."

The suggestion that the only relief for abuse is through the polls
can be read as a statement intended to preclude any judicial review and thus inconsistent with later cases, particularly *Smythe v.
Ames*.[110] There is an alternative reading. As the reader can by now
well understand, a major problem in the argument of the elevator
case was how to persuade the Court that the power exercised by the
legislature was harmful. The solution adopted in the briefs was to
argue that if the power was conceded, then it might be abused by
raising the price:[111]

> If this power is sustained, the legislature may, by another act,
> declare that every such warehouseman may charge and receive
> five cents for every bushel of grain received. . . . The legis-
> lature of Illinois is to-day in the control of the producing
> classes, but another time it may be within the management of
> the warehousemen and carriers. Once admit this power and
> there will be no protection of the people from each other.

As the student of modern regulation knows, the hypothetical was
to prove prophetic. But it must have struck the Court as odd, for

---

[108] 94 U.S. at 134.

[109] See, *e.g.*, BOIES & VERKUIL, PUBLIC CONTROL OF BUSINESS 103 (1977).

[110] 169 U.S. 466 (1898). William Jennings Bryan argued this passage to the Court (*id.*
at 487), but the Court ignored it. The decision affirmed a decree invalidating certain
railroad rates established by the Nebraska board of transportation as a violation of the
Due Process Clause.

[111] Brief for Plaintiff in Error (Goudy), 22; 7 LANDMARK BRIEFS 504.

how could the small number of warehousemen capture the legislature from the farmers? The passage in the opinion that points to the vote as the solution can be read as a common-sense response to this argument.

The central analytic flaw in the opinion is the failure to connect the copiously cited precedents, most of them relating to common carriers, to the elevator business. This failure lays the basis for the interpretation of *Munn* offered by a commentator like Commons. He explained:[112]

> The majority introduced a new principle of law, as charged by the minority, in order to sustain the power of the Illinois legislature to fix the prices for handling and storage of grain, and to compel the owners to furnish service at those prices. This was, in effect, the principle that it was *economic conditions* and *not a special grant of sovereignty* that determined the right of the sovereign to regulate prices. The Munn Case was not the case of a railway depending on a public franchise, but of a private business. These warehouses, without a special grant of sovereign power, had become strategic centers for control of the prices of grain shipped from the Northwest, by the mere fact of location, character of the business, and power to withhold service. The majority, recognizing this economic fact, held that property lost its strictly private character and became "clothed with a public interest when used in a manner to make it of public consequence and affect the community at large." Thus the *fact* of economic power over the public in withholding service and thus fixing prices need not proceed from a sovereign grant of a privilege, but proceeds, in this case, from the circumstance that the public had come to depend on the use of the owner's private property, and that therefore the owner had employed his property, not merely to his own use and enjoyment, but had devoted it to use by the public. To that extent he must submit to be controlled by the public.

This way of reading the case was, of course, subsequently adopted by the Court itself in *Nebbia v. New York*,[113] and it is now accepted doctrine that all economic activity is subject to regulation because it is important, *i.e.,* "affected with a public interest."

---

[112] COMMONS, LEGAL FOUNDATIONS OF CAPITALISM 33 (1924).

[113] 291 U.S. 502, 532–34 (1934).

For half a century *Munn* was not so understood, and it is difficult to believe that Waite, writing in 1877, intended to lay the constitutional foundation for pervasive economic regulation, even in dictum. But that leaves the question, why did Waite write an opinion that left unanswered the question, how were the elevators affected with a public interest?

One possible answer is that Waite simply assumed that, given the nature of the elevators, the answer was obvious. That response is unsatisfactory because the dissent and the elevator brief[114] specifically raise the issue. Perhaps Waite thought it best to magisterially ignore the dissent. It would not be the first time that a dissent has been left to give unintended focus to a majority opinion.

Another answer is that the material at hand to establish the link between the elevators and the railroads raised difficult procedural issues. The Court might have taken judicial notice of the *Hempstead* case, but not of the facts reported there. A remand for a factual hearing on the nature of the elevator business, or a holding that the warehouses had failed to discharge some burden of proof, would have been an indecisive and highly technical outcome to decisions in the public eye and long under consideration.[115] Silence may have seemed the wiser course.

One more answer is that Waite introduced the ambiguity, not because he foresaw the expansion of the doctrine, but because it served his rhetorical strategy in what have come to be known as the Granger cases. *Munn* was before the Court alongside cases involving statutes regulating railroad rates.[116] Although *Munn* was before the Court at the same time and involved related issues, it was neither the difficult nor the important case. After the decision, John N. Jewett, a warehouse attorney of florid style, wrote the Court:[117]

---

[114] Brief for Plaintiff in Error (Goudy), 42–48; 7 LANDMARK BRIEFS 524–30.

[115] More than a year passed between argument and decision. MILLER, note 22 *supra*, at 187.

[116] Chicago, Burlington, & Quincy R.R. v. Iowa, 94 U.S. 155 (1877); Peik v. Chicago & Nw. R.R., 94 U.S. 164 (1877); Chicago, Milwaukee, & St. Paul R.R. v. Ackley, 94 U.S. 179 (1877); Winona & St. Peter R.R. v. Blake, 94 U.S. 180 (1877); Stone v. Wisconsin, 94 U.S. 181 (1877). The decisions were all announced together and the opinions were all written by Waite. The legislation involved in *Munn* was unconnected to the Granger Movement.

[117] Brief for Rehearing, 5; 7 LANDMARK BRIEFS 661.

> The prominent position given by your Honors to this cause in the decision of a series of cases, involving to the last degree the existence of private rights in and over the wealth and industry of the country, whenever they come in contact with a public use or convenience, was as unexpected as it was unsought for by the plaintiffs in error and their counsel. . . . The case is thus made to assume an importance altogether disproportionate to the pecuniary interests directly involved in it.

The central issue in the railroad cases was whether the State charters had given the railroads the power to set their prices. The railroads principally relied on charter clauses giving them the power to establish the rules and regulations governing their business. Waite chose *Munn* as the lead opinion, and the rhetorical strategy was as follows. First, establish the proposition that the elevators, which have no charter, are subject to price regulation. That is the *Munn* opinion. Its length, and the extensive, arcane, and seemingly learned citations make it the focus of the decisions. Second, show that the railroads are no different. "Railroad companies," wrote Waite, "are carriers for hire . . . [and] under . . . *Munn* subject to legislative control as to their rates of fare and freight, unless protected by their charters."[118] Such special protection he could not find. The reader, exhausted by the excessive length of *Munn*, welcomes the brief and casual railroad opinions which dispose of the more difficult issues. In this context, it suited Waite's purpose to leave ambiguous the scope of "affected with a public interest," for the implicit theme of justification for the railroad decisions was: why shouldn't the railroads be treated like everyone else?

---

[118] Chicago, Burlington, & Quincy R.R. v. Iowa, 94 U.S. 155, 161 (1877).

ANTONIN SCALIA

VERMONT YANKEE: THE APA, THE D.C. CIRCUIT, AND THE SUPREME COURT

Vermont Yankee Nuclear Power Corp. v. Natural Resources Defense Council[1] produced what, in an era of judicial activism, is a remarkably self-denying opinion, abjuring judicial responsibility for the development of federal administrative procedure except in the relatively narrow area where requirements are imposed by the Due Process Clause. Whether the abjuration is real rather than apparent, and whether realistically it can be followed, are issues of major importance in administrative law. From a broader perspective, the case brings into question the ability of the Supreme Court to establish coherent principles of law in an area which has been largely the province of the United States Court of Appeals for the District of Columbia Circuit (D.C. Circuit). More precisely, it brings into question the willingness of the D.C. Circuit to be guided by the Supreme Court. Finally, the case suggests both the need for a major revision of the Administrative Procedure Act and the impossibility of any successful revision so long as current assumptions about the purposes of such legislation are retained. That is to say, it suggests

Antonin Scalia is Professor of Law, The University of Chicago.

[1] 435 U.S. 519 (1978). The same opinion also disposed of *Consumers Power Co. v. Aeschliman*. Those portions concerned with the *Consumers Power* case will be addressed only briefly. See text *infra*, at notes 121–25.

the indissoluble link between procedure and power, which must determine where and how procedures are made.

I. The Administrative Procedure Act

Taking advantage, it has been suggested, of the bureaucracy's preoccupation with World War II, in 1946 the legal community, led by the American Bar Association, secured legislation designed "to achieve relative uniformity in the administrative machinery of the Federal Government."[2] The Administrative Procedure Act (APA)[3] established two basic forms of rulemaking procedure—so-called formal and informal rulemaking. The former, set forth in §§ 556–57 of the Code, is a judicialized, trial-type procedure very similar to that used in courts. Generally speaking it has the following features: (1) The proceeding is presided over by an administrative law judge, a distinctive type of federal official established by the Act, with extraordinary insulation from agency direction and control.[4] (2) Evidence is presented through witnesses, who are then subject to cross-examination by opposing parties. (3) The exclusive basis for the decision is the "record" produced in this trial-type process. (4) The initial decision is rendered by the administrative law judge, though, of course, with opportunity for review within the agency.

The other procedural form, "informal" or § 553 rulemaking, was one of the major innovations introduced by the APA, and it won fulsome praise from the experts.[5] It prescribes a simple procedure to assure receipt and consideration of public comments before regulations are finally adopted. The agency must publish a notice of proposed rulemaking, which contains either the substantive terms of the

---

[2] Introduction, Attorney General's Manual on the Administrative Procedure Act 5 (1947).

[3] Act of June 11, 1946, 60 Stat. 237, now codified as 5 U.S.C. §§ 551–52, 553–59, 701–06, 1305, 3105, 3344, 5362, 7521. References herein will be to the United States Code.

[4] 5 U.S.C. §§ 3105, 5362, 7521.

[5] Often cited with approval is Prof. K. C. Davis's assessment that the informal rulemaking procedure "is one of the greatest inventions of modern government." 1 Davis Administrative Law Treatise § 6.15, at 283 (Supp. 1970). See, e.g., Auerbach, *Informal Rulemaking: A Proposed Relationship between Administrative Procedures and Judicial Review*, 72 N.W. L. Rev. 15, 21 (1977).

proposed rule or simply a description of the subjects and issues involved. It must then receive and consider written comments from interested persons. Finally, in promulgating the rule the agency must set forth "a concise general statement" of its "basis and purpose."[6] There is no prescription of oral proceedings, much less cross-examination; no requirement for an administrative law judge; no limitation of agency deliberation to any closed "record."

Under the structure of the APA, the normally applicable requirements were to be those for informal rulemaking. The formal procedures were mandated only when triggered by language in the particular substantive statute under which the rulemaking is conducted, *i.e.*, when the rules are "required by statute to be made on the record after opportunity for an agency hearing."[7] The inappropriateness of the judicialized procedures for the sort of quasi-legislative activity generally understood by the term "rulemaking" should be obvious. But the APA's idiosyncratic definition of the term[8] embraces many activities, including particularized ratemaking, for which such procedures would be conventional enough. The formal rulemaking provisions have in fact been applied to very few programs of general rulemaking, where they have had predictably inefficient results.[9]

The APA permitted (though it did not mandate)—and in practice the agencies have employed—a whole spectrum of rulemaking procedures between the simple "notice-and-comment" requirements of APA informal rulemaking and the grand judicial magnificence of APA formal rulemaking. It has been common, for example, to allow interested persons to present oral comments to the agency itself, or to an official of the agency, at a public hearing.[10] Some agencies have employed public panel discussions to explore the issues.[11] And occasionally, even cross-examination on particular points has been al-

---

[6] 5 U.S.C. § 553(c).

[7] *Ibid.*

[8] 5 U.S.C. § 551(4), (5).

[9] The definitive study is Hamilton, *Procedures for the Adoption of Rules of General Applicability: The Need for Procedural Innovation in Administrative Rulemaking*, 60 CAL. L. REV. 1276 (1972).

[10] The APA specifically envisions (though it does not require) use of this optional procedure. 5 U.S.C. § 553(c).

[11] The FCC uses panel discussions with some frequency. See, *e.g.*, Second Report and Order on Network Program Exclusivity Protection, 54 F.C.C.2d 229, 230 (1975); Children's Television Report and Policy Statement, 50 F.C.C.2d 1, 2 (1974).

lowed.[12] But insofar as the text of the APA is concerned, the choice within this available spectrum of possible procedures was left to each agency, unless formal rulemaking was statutorily required.

II. THE DEVELOPMENT OF JUDICIALLY IMPOSED "HYBRID" PROCEDURES

The history of the APA's informal rulemaking provisions, at least since the mid-1960s, has been characterized by the imposition of additional procedural requirements mandated neither by statute nor by the Constitution, but crafted by the courts, with greater or lesser reliance upon the substantive statutes involved. This development can be traced most easily in the opinions of the Court of Appeals for the District of Columbia Circuit, which—because it handles the vast majority of significant rulemaking appeals—has been the leader in the process. For present purposes the particular added requirement I shall focus upon is adjudicatory-type hearing procedures that result in so-called hybrid rulemaking.

In 1966, in the *American Airlines* "blocked space service" case,[13] the D.C. Circuit wrote: "This Court has indicated its readiness to lay down procedural requirements deemed inherent in the very concept of fair hearing for certain classes of cases, even though no such requirements had been specified by Congress."[14] The assertion of such a power was dictum, since the Court rejected the contention that adjudicatory procedures should have been used in the case before it. Moreover, while the Court's language was broad enough to include general rulemaking, the case before it involved particularized ratemaking, or perhaps even licensing,[15] and the cases cited in support of

---

[12] See, *e.g.*, In re California Water & Telephone Co., 35 FED. REG. 6987, 6988 (1970) (FCC).

[13] American Airlines, Inc. v. CAB, 359 F.2d 624 (D.C. Cir. 1966). Except as otherwise indicated, all of the D.C. Circuit cases that I shall discuss were decided by three-judge panels. Generally, I make no attempt to identify or distinguish among the various panels; their handiwork will be attributed to the Court as a whole. Not only is this theoretically accurate (by virtue of the doctrine of delegation), but in fact the basic developments discussed here have, on one occasion or another, received the explicit support of most of the Court's members.

[14] *Id.* at 632.

[15] The ultimate issue in the case was the CAB's determination that American Airlines could not permit customers to "block" or reserve cargo space on a regular basis at rates lower than those charged for individual shipments. While the issue arose in the context of a tariff case, the Board's decision amounted to a determination that the airline could not compete for bulk cargo business. American plausibly argued that it amounted to an amendment of its certificate which would require §§ 556–57 procedures. Rulemaking

its asserted power involved adjudication.[16] With respect to agency
action of that sort (as opposed to general rulemaking), the Constitution itself might require procedures beyond those "specified by Congress."[17] And the Court's opinion can easily be read as saying no
more than that. The dictum in *American Airlines* is repeatedly invoked, however, in later rulemaking cases.[18]

In the 1969 *Marine Space Enclosures* case,[19] the D.C. Circuit again
claimed a general power to determine procedural requirements—or
again seemed to do so. "[W]hether brief and oral argument are sufficient depends on the nature of the issues."[20] "Ordinarily, . . . antitrust issues do not lend themselves to [such] disposition."[21] Once
again, however, the language used was dictum, for the Court decided to "refrain at this juncture from specifying that our remand
order requires an evidentiary hearing."[22] Once again the case before
the Court involved particularized rulemaking or adjudication[23] and,
in addition, contained a statutory requirement for "notice and hearing,"[24] so that the Court's broad language could be construed as
merely an interpretation of what that legislative phrase required.
Nevertheless, *Marine Space Enclosures* is later cited as exemplify-
ing a more general judicial authority to determine procedures.[25]

---

was involved in the case because the policy determination applied in the tariff proceeding
—that only all-cargo carriers would be permitted to provide "blocked space service"—
had been adopted by rule.

[16] Gonzalez v. Freeman, 334 F.2d 570 (D.C. Cir. 1964); Pollack v. Simonson, 350
F.2d 740 (D.C. Cir. 1965). The second did not even involve the Administrative Procedure Act.

[17] *Compare* Londoner v. Denver, 210 U.S. 373 (1908), *with* Bi-Metallic Investment
Co. v. Colorado, 239 U.S. 441 (1915).

[18] *E.g.*, Portland Cement Ass'n v. Ruckelshaus, 486 F.2d 275, 400 n.95 (D.C. Cir.
1973).

[19] Marine Space Enclosures, Inc. v. FMC, 420 F.2d 577 (D.C. Cir. 1969).

[20] *Id.* at 589 n.36.

[21] *Id.* at 589. The two sentences quoted in text are a small portion of the court's discussion of the procedural issue, *id.* at 589–90.

[22] *Id.* at 590.

[23] The case involved a contract for the construction and maintenance of maritime
passenger terminal facilities in the port of New York City, and a companion contract between carriers and the Port Authority for use of the facilities. These contracts required
FMC approval under § 15 of the Shipping Act of 1916, 46 U.S.C. § 814. Such approval
would appear to be licensing under 5 U.S.C. § 551 (8) & (9), which is adjudication under
5 U.S.C. § 551(6) & (7). The APA's definition of rulemaking, however, overlaps that
of licensing to some indeterminate extent. See the last clause of 5 U.S.C. § 551(4).

[24] 46 U.S.C. § 814.

[25] Walter Holm & Co. v. Hardin, 449 F.2d 1009, 1015 (D.C. Cir. 1971).

In 1971, the Court finally produced a holding that adjudicatory procedures (oral hearing and cross-examination) were required. The language of *Walter Holm & Co. v. Hardin*[26] was quite expansive. For example: "This is not an area that may rightly be approached in terms of absolute rigidity of requirement. . . . [I]t is not the case that all administrative actions legitimately denominated regulations are ipso facto freed from any need for oral hearings."[27] The case involved, however, a strange combination of § 553 rulemaking and a marketing order under § 8(c) of the Agricultural Marketing Agreement Act of 1937.[28] And the opinion was tantalizingly ambiguous as to whether it was judicially supplementing the legislative requirements for the former (which would be a step of major consequence) or merely defining the legislative requirements for the latter (which would be of small importance). Once again, the case is later cited as though applicable to rulemaking generally.[29]

The 1973 *International Harvester* case[30] contained an even more extensive discussion of the need for adjudicatory hearing procedures, including the following assertions: "Whether particular attributes of forensic presentation are not only salutary but also mandatory must . . . depend on circumstances. . . . [A] right of cross-examination . . . might well extend to particular cases of need, on critical points where the general procedure proved inadequate to probe 'soft' and sensitive subjects and witnesses."[31] The requirement of adjudicatory procedures here was not dictum, but it might fairly be described as a second-level, vague, and exceedingly strange holding. The Court declined to reverse the agency for its failure to provide adjudicatory procedures. It did, after reversing for other reasons, impose a requirement of "reasonable cross-examination" on remand[32]—leaving the precise issues or witnesses as to which such requirement might become operative completely unspecified. *Inter-*

---

[26] *Ibid.*   [27] *Id.* at 1015.   [28] 7 U.S.C. § 608c.

[29] *E.g.*, Kennecott Copper Corp. v. EPA, 462 F.2d 846, 850 n.18 (D.C. Cir. 1972).

[30] International Harvester Co. v. Ruckelshaus, 478 F.2d 615 (D.C. Cir. 1973).

[31] *Id.* at 631.

[32] *Id.* at 649. According to the majority, the reason cross-examination could appropriately be dispensed with in the original proceeding was the sixty-day time limit which the statute imposed for the Administrator's decision, plus the fact that a sufficiently precise request for cross-examination had not been made. *Id.* at 624, 631. Judge Bazelon's dissent found reliance upon the time limit to excuse adjudicatory procedures with respect to the original proceedings, but not with respect to the remand, a "bit of judicial legerdemain." *Id.* at 652.

national Harvester actually involved adjudication rather than rule-making,[33] though as usual the D.C. Circuit did not inquire into this detail. Moreover, the statute in question contained a special require-ment for "public hearing,"[34] and the opinion can be read as merely an interpretation of that provision. It is later cited, however, as though applicable to rulemaking in general.[35]

The *Mobil Oil* case,[36] later the same year, finally set aside general rulemaking (*viz.*, the Federal Power Commission's establishment of nationwide rates for natural gas) for failure to employ adjudicatory procedures. The opinion relied heavily upon the fact that the appli-cable statute provided a "substantial evidence" test for judicial re-view.[37] It said, *inter alia*, that "Informal comments simply cannot create a record that satisfies the substantial evidence test. . . . [I]t is adversary procedural devices which permit testing and elucidation that raise information from the level of mere inconsistent data to evidence 'substantial' enough to support rates."[38] The inadequacy of the hearing procedures, however, was not the sole, ultimate ground for the judgment. It was part (though perhaps not all) of the basis for the separate conclusion that "we cannot find here in the whole record the substantial evidence necessary to sustain the Com-mission's action."[39] Additional bases for that conclusion, or perhaps entirely separate grounds of decision, included "the lack of fair no-tice"[40] and the fact that "the question as to why mandatory rates . . . are now necessary was never faced squarely, certainly it was never articulated."[41]

Two more D.C. Circuit opinions must be mentioned. In the 1973 *Friends of the Earth* case,[42] the issue of required adjudicatory proce-dures did not affect the outcome and had not even been raised by the parties. Nonetheless, Judge Bazelon described (Judge Leven-

---

[33] The case involved the EPA's denial of an application (provided for by statute) for a one-year suspension of 1975 exhaust emission standards established by the agency Such suspension would appear to be a "statutory exemption or other form of permission," making it licensing under the definitions of 5 U.S.C. § 551(8) & (9), and therefore adjudication under the definitions of § 551(6) & (7).

[34] 42 U.S.C. § 1857f-1(b) (5) (C).

[35] *E.g.*, O'Donnell v. Shaffer, 491 F.2d 59, 62 n.19 (D.C. Cir. 1974).

[36] Mobil Oil Corp. v. FPC, 483 F.2d 1238 (D.C. Cir. 1973).

[37] 15 U.S.C. § 717r(b).

[38] 483 F.2d at 1260.   [40] *Id.* at 1263.

[39] *Id.* at 1264.   [41] *Id.* at 1264.

[42] Friends of the Earth v. AEC, 485 F.2d 1031 (D.C. Cir. 1973).

thal charged that he "discourse[d] on")[43] his concept of the judiciary's responsibility to assure within the agencies "a framework for principled decision-making"—which, he asserted, at least where there is "a possibility of imminent danger to life and health," would "ideally include the clash of opposing expert views in a setting involving some right of cross-examination, in the absence of unusual circumstances or emergency conditions."[44] Judge Leventhal's counter dictum asserted that this went too far. "[O]ral presentations in rulemaking, however desirable, are not generally required, and . . . such requirements as may be evolving apply to crucial issues where alternative procedures are not adequate."[45] Both opinions were devoid of any suggestion that the Court's responsibility for guiding this "evolution" depended upon some explicit authorization in the particular statute, such as the "substantial evidence" review provision in *Mobil Oil*.

The next year, in another dictum, the D.C. Circuit emphasized the same point. In *O'Donnell v. Shaffer*,[46] the Court upheld the Federal Aviation Administration's use of § 553 procedures to establish a rule that commercial airlines could not use pilots older than sixty years of age. Although in the particular case the procedures were found adequate, the Court observed:[47]

> The fact that an agency action falls into the traditional category of "rulemaking" does not, of course, mean that traditional procedures are automatically adequate. This Court has long recognized that basic considerations of fairness may dictate procedural requirements not specified by Congress. Oral submissions may be required even in legislative-type proceedings, and cross-examination may be necessary if critical issues cannot be otherwise resolved.

III. VERMONT YANKEE IN THE COURT OF APPEALS

The principal issue in *Vermont Yankee*[48] was the validity of a rule adopted by the Atomic Energy Commission assigning a series

---

[43] *Id.* at 1035. The panel was made up only of Judges Bazelon and Leventhal.

[44] *Id.* at 1032–33.   [46] 491 F.2d 59 (D.C. Cir. 1974).

[45] *Id.* at 1035.   [47] *Id.* at 62.

[48] The Court of Appeals opinion in *Vermont Yankee* is under the name of Natural Resources Defense Council, Inc. v. NRC, 547 F.2d 633 (D.C. Cir. 1976).

of numerical values to the environmental effects of the nuclear fuel cycle, which would thereafter be factored into the cost-benefit analyses in licensing proceedings for individual reactors. Those assigned values amounted to a determination that the environmental effects were "insignificant."[49] It was essentially that determination that the environmentalist petitioners were seeking to overturn in the Court of Appeals. The rulemaking procedures used by the Commission had included oral comment, but not discovery or cross-examination. The Court of Appeals characterized as the "primary argument" of the petitioners the assertion that:

> the decision to preclude "discovery or cross-examination" denied them a meaningful opportunity to participate in the proceedings guaranteed by due process. They do not question the Commission's authority to proceed by informal rulemaking, as opposed to adjudication. They rely instead on the line of cases indicating that in particular circumstances procedures in excess of the bare minima prescribed by the Administrative Procedure Act, 5 U.S.C. § 553, may be required.[50]

The crucial factual issue in the case was the adequacy of existing high-level waste disposal techniques. The only supporting evidence on this point was a 20-page statement by the director of the Commission's Division of Waste Management and Transportation, which statement had been read during the oral hearings and was subsequently incorporated into the Environmental Survey published after the comment period. On several important points it was strikingly devoid of detail and constituted little more than "conclusory reassurances."[51] Although, in the Court's view, "the vagueness of the presentation regarding waste disposal made detailed criticism of its specifics impossible," the petitioners had offered "a number of more general comments concerning the Commission's approach," including failure to distinguish between design objectives and performance objectives, failure to consider actual experience with waste disposal, and the unjustified assumption that organized human supervision necessary to continued maintenance of the proposed disposal tech-

---

[49] Id. at 642.

[50] Id. at 643, citing, inter alia, Mobil Oil, International Harvester, Walter Holm & Co., and American Airlines, all discussed above.

[51] Id. at 649.

niques would be available "in perpetuity."[52] The Commission's statement of basis and purpose for the rule did not respond specifically to any of these objections.

The Court of Appeals set aside the portions of the rule pertaining to waste disposal and reprocessing issues. Upon remand, the agency was expected to conform to the following judicial mandate.[53]

> Many procedural devices for creating a genuine dialogue on these issues were available to the agency—including informal conferences between intervenors and staff, document discovery, interrogatories, technical advisory committees comprised of outside experts with differing perspectives, limited cross-examination, funding independent research by intervenors, detailed annotation of technical reports, surveys of existing literature, memoranda explaining methodology. We do not presume to intrude on the agency's province by dictating to it which, if any, of these devices it must adopt to flesh out the record. It may be that no combination of the procedures mentioned above will prove adequate, and the agency will be required to develop new procedures to accomplish the innovative task of implementing NEPA through rulemaking. On the other hand, the procedures the agency adopted in this case, if administered in a more sensitive, deliberate manner, might suffice. Whatever techniques the Commission adopts, before it promulgates a rule limiting further consideration of waste disposal and reprocessing issues, it must in one way or another generate a record in which the factual issues are fully developed.

To understand the Supreme Court's subsequent action in this case, it is important to appreciate that the Court of Appeals' opinion sometimes intertwines two bases of decision which conceptually may be quite distinct: (1) the inadequacy of the agency's procedures; and (2) the inadequacy of the record to support the agency decision. The two bases may be merged, if one chooses to regard certain evidence as inherently unreliable unless it has been subjected to particular procedural tests, such as cross-examination. The suggestions of such an approach were evident in the *Mobil Oil* case, there facilitated, or perhaps prompted, by the "substantial evidence" review provision on which the Court chose to rely. In *Vermont*

---

[52] *Id.* at 651–52.   [53] *Id.* at 653–54.

Yankee, even though operating without the "substantial evidence" pretext, the Court of Appeals—in at least some portions of the opinion—appears to adopt the same merged approach.[54] On the other hand, other portions of the opinion seem to take a strictly procedural approach—such as the Court's identification of the petitioners' primary argument, quoted above, and its ensuing assertion that "[t]hus, we are called upon to decide whether the procedures provided by the agency were sufficient to ventilate the issues."[55] The two concurrences also interpret the majority opinion as imposing procedural requirements.

It is also important, in order to appreciate the import of the Supreme Court's action, to note that the Court of Appeals' remand was based not only upon the absence of adversary hearing procedures (and the inadequacy of record which that produced) but also upon the absence of Commission response to the objections raised below by the petitioners. The D.C. Circuit said:[56]

> Since a reviewing court is incapable of making a penetrating analysis of highly scientific or technical subject matter on its own, it must depend on the agency's expertise, as reflected in the statement of basis and purpose, to organize the record, to distill the major issues which were ventilated and to articulate its reasoning with regard to each of them.
>
> An agency need not respond to frivolous or repetitive comment it receives. However, where apparently significant information has been brought to its attention, or substantial issues of policy or gaps in its reasoning raised, the statement of basis and purpose must indicate why the agency decided the criticisms were invalid. Boilerplate generalities brushing aside detailed criticism on the basis of agency "judgment" or "exper-

---

[54] See, *e.g.*, the following passage: "In substantial part, the materials uncritically relied on by the Commission in promulgating this rule consist of extremely vague assurances by agency personnel that problems as yet unsolved will be solved. That is an insufficient record to sustain a rule limiting consideration of the environmental effects of nuclear waste disposal to the numerical values in Table S-3. . . . Not only were the generalities relied on in this case not subject to rigorous probing—in any form—but when apparently substantial criticisms were brought to the Commission's attention, it simply ignored them, or brushed them aside without answer. Without a thorough exploration of the problems involved in waste disposal, including past mistakes, and a forthright assessment of the uncertainties and differences in expert opinion, this type of agency action cannot pass muster as reasoned decisionmaking." *Id.* at 653.

[55] *Id.* at 643. In virtually all its opinions in this area the D.C. Circuit insists that the agency "ventilate the issues."

[56] *Id.* at 646.

tise" avail nothing; what is required is a reasoned response in which the agency points to particulars in the record which, when coupled with its reservoir of expertise, support its resolution of the controversy.

IV. THE SUPREME COURT OPINION

Were it not for the above-described history of D.C. Circuit lawmaking in this field, it would have been surprising that the Supreme Court accepted jurisdiction and reviewed the *Vermont Yankee* case. The essential meaning of the opinion below was unclear. Indeed, the first step in the Supreme Court's analysis had to be a determination whether the basis of decision was inadequacy of procedures or inadequacy of record support. (The Supreme Court concluded that it was the former.[57]) Moreover, the remand order had mandated no specific additional procedures—indeed, it had not clearly ordered any additional procedure beyond what the agency had already provided—so that the issue was presented in a particularly amorphous and generalized form. Finally, there had been subsequent developments before the agency. A new interim rule had been issued and applied to the *Vermont Yankee* proceeding and proceedings had been commenced for a new permanent rule, which the agency indicated it would pursue regardless of the outcome of the pending case. It would seem that all this would normally have sufficed, as one of the environmental respondents on appeal indeed urged,[58] to produce a dismissal for mootness.

However, none of the earlier cases discussed above, by which the D.C. Circuit had developed the principle of judicial supplementation of APA rulemaking, would have afforded the Supreme Court a much better vehicle for review. In its purest form, the principle is expressed only as dictum. When it appears as a holding it is an alternative holding, closely tied to the requirements of a particular statute or merged with the notion of inadequate record support for the agency determination. All these factors not only make Supreme Court review difficult or impossible, they render application for certiorari unlikely. In fact, in *Vermont Yankee* itself the United States opposed the application for certiorari, arguing that the decision below did not present the procedural issue but had been based on the inadequacy of the record, that the discussion concerning the procedures which

---

[57] 435 U.S. at 539–42.   [58] *Id.* at 535–37 n.14.

might be followed on remand was "simply dicta," and that in any event review would be premature until the Court of Appeals should disapprove specific procedures used by the agency upon remand.[59] (The Nuclear Regulatory Commission, it should be noted, did not share these views.[60])

Another factor tending to discourage the seeking of Supreme Court review is that in most of these cases the "hybrid" hearing procedures were imposed (or suggested) instead of the full-blown §§ 556–57 procedures which private parties had argued should apply. The *Mobil Oil* case, for example, in which the government did not seek certiorari, noted that "the defect we find in the Commission's procedures . . . could be remedied by according the procedure described under sections 556 and 557 of the APA, but such complete adjudicatory procedures are not required."[61] In other words, in most of these cases appeal of rulings on the added procedures would have exposed the agencies to risk of even greater restriction, and it might have been the better part of valor (to mix a metaphor) to settle for a half a loaf.

One can understand, then, why the Supreme Court accepted a petition for certiorari which even the Solicitor General recommended be denied. Review of this issue had already been too long delayed.[62]

After completing the necessary task of deciding what the Court of Appeals had decided, the Supreme Court's opinion addressed the basic issue whether hybrid rulemaking procedures could be required. It acknowledged that when, in rulemaking, "a very small number of persons are 'exceptionally affected, in each case upon individual grounds,'" the constitutional requirements of due process may in

---

[59] Brief for the United States and the NRC, pp. 9–10.

[60] *Id.* at pp. 5–9. The Brief takes the unusual course of setting forth the opposing positions of the United States and the Commission, leaving it to the Court to choose between them.

[61] *Mobil Oil Corp.*, 483 F.2d at 1262.

[62] The Supreme Court's opinion did not explicitly acknowledge any stretching of the technical requirements for review, but it is interesting that its first response to the mootness objection was as follows: "As we read the opinion of the Court of Appeals, its view that reviewing courts may in the absence of special circumstances justifying such a course of action impose additional procedural requirements on agency action raises questions of such significance in this area of the law as to warrant our granting certiorari and deciding the case. Since the vast majority of challenges to administrative agency action are brought to the Court of Appeals for the District of Columbia Circuit, the decision of that court in this case will serve as precedent for many more proceedings for judicial review of agency actions than would the decision of another Court of Appeals." 435 U.S. at 537 n.14.

some circumstances demand additional procedures.[63] And it further acknowledged the possibility (though it did not decide) that "a totally unjustified departure from well settled agency procedures of long standing might require judicial correction."[64] It continued:[65]

> But this much is absolutely clear. Absent constitutional constraints or extremely compelling circumstances "the administrative agencies 'should be free to fashion their own rules of procedure and to pursue methods of inquiry capable of permitting them to discharge their multitudinous duties.' "

The Court specifically rejected the argument which it attributed to respondent Natural Resources Defense Council (but which was merely a paraphrase of the position of the D.C. Circuit) that § 553 of the APA "merely establishes lower procedural bounds and that a court may routinely require more than the minimum when an agency's proposed rule addresses complex or technical factual issues or 'Issues of Great Public Import.' "[66] There was, it said, "little doubt that Congress intended that the discretion of the *agencies* and not that of the courts was to be exercised in determining when extra procedural devices should be employed."[67] As practical considerations supporting the same result, the Court noted that any judicial effort to devise "perfectly tailored" procedures for each proceeding would be unpredictable in its outcome, compelling the agencies to adopt full adjudicatory procedures if affirmance is to be absolutely assured. The same result would follow, it noted, from the fact that the courts' determination of the "best" procedure, unlike the agencies', would be made with the benefit of hindsight.[68]

The Court addressed, and rejected, the argument that in the present case the applicability of NEPA required additional procedures. "[W]e search in vain for something in NEPA which would mandate such a result."[69]

---

[63] *Id*. at 542, quoting from *Florida East Coast R. Co.*, 410 U.S. at 245; which in turn was quoting from *Bi-Metallic Investment Co.*, 239 U.S. at 446.

[64] 435 U.S. at 542.

[65] 435 U.S. at 543, quoting from FCC v. Schreiber, 381 U.S. 279, 290 (1965), which in turn was quoting from FCC v. Pottsville Broadcasting Co., 309 U.S. 134, 143 (1940).

[66] 435 U.S. at 545.

[67] *Id*. at 546.

[68] *Id*. at 546–47.

[69] *Id*. at 548.

Despite its earlier finding that procedural inadequacy had been the basis of the decision below, the Court acknowledged "intimations in the majority opinion which suggest that the judges who joined it likewise may have thought the administrative proceedings an insufficient basis upon which to predicate the rule in question."[70] Accordingly, instead of reversing the Court remanded "so that the Court of Appeals may review the rule as the Administrative Procedure Act provides."[71]

V. INTERPRETATION OF THE OPINION

As important as the issue of supplemental hearing procedures in informal rulemaking may be, that is not all the *Vermont Yankee* case was about. Rather, that issue was—and was treated by the Court as—one facet of the much more fundamental question of the status of the APA as the basic charter of judicially enforceable administrative procedure. The opinions of the D.C. Circuit dealing with rulemaking hearing procedures were merely one manifestation of that court's progressive evisceration of the APA. It does not go too far to say that the D.C. Circuit was in the process of replacing the rudimentary procedural mandates of the Act—not only as to rulemaking hearing procedures, but as to adjudicatory hearing procedures,[72] nonhearing aspects of the administrative process,[73] and judicial review—with a much more elaborate, "evolving," court-made scheme approvingly described by one commentator as an "ever-growing common law."[74] This process was not only neither initiated nor approved by the Supreme Court; it was clearly contrary to the tenor of the Supreme Court decisions in the field. The conflict between the positions of the two courts can be exemplified by comparing the following statements by the Supreme Court on various aspects of administrative procedure, and subsequent positions taken by the D.C. Circuit.

---

[70] *Id.* at 549.

[71] *Ibid.*

[72] See Marine Space Enclosures, Inc. v. FMC, 420 F.2d 577, 590 (D.C. Cir. 1969); Cooper Labs, Inc. v. FDA, 501 F.2d 772, 793 (D.C. Cir. 1974) (Leventhal, J. dissenting).

[73] See text *infra*, at notes 144–54.

[74] 1 Davis, ADMINISTRATIVE LAW TREATISE 610 (2d ed. 1978).

SCOPE OF JUDICIAL REVIEW

The Supreme Court, March 1971:[75]

> But the existence of judicial review is only the start: the stan-
> dard for review must also be determined. For that we must
> look to § 706 of the Administrative Procedure Act. . . . In
> certain narrow, specifically limited situations, the agency ac-
> tion is to be set aside if the action was not supported by "sub-
> stantial evidence." . . . Review under the substantial-evidence
> test is authorized only when the agency action is taken pur-
> suant to a rulemaking provision of the Administrative Proce-
> dure Act itself, 5 U.S.C. § 553 . . . , or when the agency action
> is based on a public adjudicatory hearing. See 5 U.S.C. §§ 556,
> 557. . . . The [agency action in this case] was plainly not an
> exercise of a rulemaking function. . . . And the only hearing
> that is required by either the Administrative Procedure Act
> or the statutes regulating the [applicable area] is a public hear-
> ing conducted by local officials. . . . The hearing is nonadju-
> dicatory, quasi-legislative in nature. It is not designed to pro-
> duce a record that is to be the basis of agency action—the basic
> requirement for substantial-evidence review.

The D.C. Circuit, December 1971:[76]

> In many cases, it is unnecessary, and even unwise, to classify
> a given proceeding as either adjudicatory or rulemaking. . . .
> [O]bsession with attempts to place agency action in the proper
> category may often obscure the real issue. . . .
> The next question which arises concerns our scope of review.
>
> We . . . conclude that the nature of that inquiry depends
> not on whether the Commission has issued a rule or an adju-
> dicatory order, but on the nature of the record presented to
> us for review. . . .
>
> Application of no simple formula can avoid the process of
> judgment. In every case, the object of review is to determine
> whether a reasoned conclusion from the record as a whole
> could support the premise on which the Commission's action
> rests. The substantial evidence test is essentially an application
> of this general principle to a particular kind of record, but, in
> all cases, reasoned conclusions are the hallmark of regularity.
> The foregoing makes it unnecessary for us to determine

---

[75] Citizens to Preserve Overton Park v. Volpe, 401 U.S. 402, 413–15 (1971).

[76] City of Chicago v. FPC, 458 F.2d 731, 739, 741, 743–45 (D.C. Cir. 1971).

whether an evidentiary hearing was required in this case [*i.e.*, whether §§ 556–57 apply], for the scope of our review does not turn on the answer to that question.

RULEMAKING PROCEDURES IN GENERAL

The Supreme Court, June 1972:[77]

Because the proceedings under review were an exercise of legislative rulemaking power rather than adjudicatory hearings as in [cases decided on due process grounds], and because [the substantive statute] does not require a determination "on the record," the provisions of 5 U.S.C. §§ 556 and 557 were inapplicable.

This proceeding, therefore, was governed by the provisions of 5 U.S.C. § 553 of the Administrative Procedure Act.... The "Findings and Conclusions" embodied in the Commission's report fully comply with these requirements, and nothing more was required by the Administrative Procedure Act.

We conclude that the Commission's action in promulgating these rules was substantively authorized by [the applicable substantive law] and procedurally acceptable under the Administrative Procedure Act. The judgment of the District Court must therefore be *Reversed*.

The D.C. Circuit, July 1973:[78]

We conclude that the FPC need not employ the precise procedures set forth in sections 556 and 557 of the APA. It does not follow, however, that the Commission may proceed with only the guidance of the less rigorous standards of section 553. The Commission's position assumes that there are only two permissible forms of procedures cognizable under the APA, that the two are mutually exclusive, and that their existence precludes the use of any other procedures that lie between them. This rigid interpretation of what is permitted and required under the APA is inaccurate. . . .

The entire thrust of our opinion in *City of Chicago v. FPC* was that artificial distinctions based upon the language of the APA should be avoided in determining what procedure should be followed. . . .

[That] opinion also emphasized that strict adherence to the

---

[77] United States v. Allegheny-Ludlum Steel Corp., 406 U.S. 742, 757–58 (1972).

[78] *Mobil Oil Corp.*, 483 F.2d at 1251–52, 1262.

explicit dictates of the APA was not the primary test of the appropriateness of a particular type of procedure. . . .

[W]e pin nothing on categorization by "rule-making" or "adjudication," nor by "formal" or "informal," . . . . What is important and decisive is the essential quality of the proceeding under review.

TREATMENT OF FACTUAL ISSUES IN RULEMAKING

The Supreme Court, January 1973:[79]

Here, the [effects of the agency's action] were applicable across the board to all the common carriers by railroad subject to the Interstate Commerce Act. No effort was made to single out any particular railroad for special consideration based on its own peculiar circumstances. . . . Though the Commission obviously relied on factual inferences as a basis for its order, the source of these factual inferences was apparent to anyone who read the order. . . . The factual inferences were used in the formulation of a basically legislative-type judgment, for prospective application only, rather than in adjudicating a particular set of disputed facts.

The Commission's [nonadjudicatory, written] procedure satisfied both the provisions of . . . the Interstate Commerce Act and of the Administrative Procedure Act, and were not inconsistent with prior decisions of this Court. We, therefore, reverse the judgment of the District Court.

The D.C. Circuit, February 1973:[80]

[I]n a situation where "general policy" is the focal question, a legislative-type hearing is appropriate.

A complication is presented by the case before us in that the general policy questions became interfused with relatively specific technical issues. . . .

We distinguish between the assertion of a broad right of cross-examination . . . and a claim of a need for cross-examination . . . on a subject of critical importance which could not be adequately ventilated under the general procedures. . . .

[A] right of cross-examination . . . might well extend to particular cases of need, on critical points where the general procedure proved inadequate to probe "soft" and sensitive subjects and witnesses.

---

[79] United States v. Florida East Coast Ry., 410 U.S. 224, 245–46 (1973).

[80] *International Harvester*, 478 F.2d at 630–31.

While the Court of Appeals had not, of course, contravened any holding of the Supreme Court, it had been, to put it mildly, a remarkably ineffective instrument for implementing the underlying principles of interpretation which the Supreme Court opinions quite clearly expressed. During the period here under consideration, the Supreme Court's opinions dealing with administrative procedure were characterized by meticulous reference to the text and the "technicalities" of the APA. In 1972, with the *Allegheny-Ludlum* case, it was obvious to the perceptive observer—and in 1973, with the *Florida East Coast* case, it became obvious even to the obtuse— that the Supreme Court regarded the APA as a sort of superstatute, or subconstitution, in the field of administrative process: a basic framework that was not lightly to be supplanted or embellished, not even by other legislative enactments, much less by a continually evolving judge-made common law not based upon constitutional prescriptions or rooted in the language of the APA itself. Nor was this a particularly new tack for the Supreme Court. The 1950 *Wong Yang Sung* case[81] was a plain and indeed striking abnegation by the Supreme Court of further judicial involvement in the task of "designing" procedures, even where the foundation of the judiciary's authority was not merely "common-law" oversight of administrative procedures but the text of the Constitution itself. That case held, in effect, that once the courts found that due process required a record hearing, the precise characteristics of that hearing were to be determined not by the courts but by the APA.

By contrast, the D.C. Circuit had, in its own words in *American Airlines*, "indicated its readiness to lay down procedural requirements . . . even though no such requirements had been specified by Congress."[82] It had done this by resort to an arsenal of justifications, including "the very concept of fair hearing for certain classes of cases";[83] the generalized necessity of rendering "the judicial review which Congress has thought it important to provide . . . meaningful";[84] appeal to particular provisions[85]—or even the general im-

---

[81] Wong Yang Sung v. McGrath, 339 U.S. 33 (1950).

[82] *American Airlines*, 359 F.2d at 632.   [83] *Ibid.*

[84] Automotive Parts & Accessories Ass'n v. Boyd, 407 F.2d 330, 338 (D.C. Cir. 1968); see also *Portland Cement Ass'n*, 486 F.2d at 393.

[85] Public Service Comm'n for State of New York v. FPC, 487 F.2d 1043, 1069 (D.C. Cir. 1973); *Mobil Oil Corp.*, 483 F.2d at 1259–60.

port[86]—of the substantive statute in question; the need to avoid "a seed bed for the weed of industry domination";[87] and even those ultimate weapons of judicial authority, "basic considerations of fairness"[88] and "the interest of justice."[89]

The clearest, as well as the most recent, Supreme Court contradiction of the D.C. Circuit's approach was the *Florida East Coast* case. That involved § 1(14)(a) of the Interstate Commerce Act,[90] which authorized the Interstate Commerce Commission to act in the area at issue "after hearing." The Supreme Court held: (1) that this provision did not trigger §§ 556–57 of the APA, and (2) that it did not, in and of itself, impose any procedural requirements over and above those of the APA. The inhospitable reception which the D.C. Circuit gave the Supreme Court's opinion is plain from the description, written less than a month later in the *International Harvester* case, of the Supreme Court's holding:[91]

> The provision of 5 U.S.C. § 556(d) which gives the opportunity for cross-examination as a matter of right, would only be automatically applicable if "rules are required by statute to be made on the record after opportunity for an agency hearing." . . . Without the precise words "on the record," § 556 does not automatically apply.

Of course the limiting word "automatically," which does not appear in the Supreme Court's opinion, intimates that there are situations in which the requirements of § 556 apply, not automatically, but as determined by the circumstances—thus validating the D.C. Circuit's dictum later in its opinion that "a right of cross-examination . . . might well extend to particular cases of need,"[92] and its requirement of "reasonable cross-examination" on remand.[93]

In fact, however, *Florida East Coast* not only opposed the triggering of full §§ 556–57 requirements for rulemaking; it just as clearly

---

[86] *Natural Resources Defense Council*, 547 F.2d at 645, 654.

[87] *Walter Holm & Co.*, 449 F.2d at 1016.

[88] *O'Donnell*, 491 F.2d at 62.

[89] *Kennecott Copper Corp.*, 462 F.2d at 850.

[90] 49 U.S.C. § 1(14)(a).

[91] *International Harvester*, 478 F.2d at 630 n.48.

[92] *Id.* at 631.   [93] *Id.* at 649.

disfavored piecemeal, "nonautomatic" supplementation of the basic
§ 553 procedures. More than twice as much of the Supreme Court's
opinion was devoted to the latter point as to the former, in the context of examining the appellees' contention that "the Commission
procedure . . . fell short of that mandated by the 'hearing' requirement of § 1(14)(a) [of the Interstate Commerce Act], even though
it may have satisfied § 553 of the Administrative Procedure Act."[94]
The Supreme Court held:[95]

> Under these circumstances, confronted with a grant of sub-
> stantive authority made after the Administrative Procedure Act
> was enacted [in fact, that authority had only been *amended*
> post-APA, but the Court considered that sufficient], we think
> that reference to that Act, in which Congress devoted itself
> exclusively to questions such as the nature and scope of hear-
> ings, is a satisfactory basis for determining what is meant by
> the term "hearing" used in another statute. Turning to that
> Act, we are convinced that the term "hearing" as used therein
> does not necessarily embrace either the right to present evi-
> dence orally and to cross-examine opposing witnesses, or the
> right to present oral argument to the agency's decisionmaker.

The Court also rejected the contention that the situation was
changed by that provision of the Interstate Commerce Act requiring
the Commission to "give consideration" to certain factors.[96]

The statement that *Florida East Coast* speaks to the conditions
under which § 556(d) "automatically" applies is the sort of crabbed
interpretation one might expect to find in a litigant's brief, or in a
subsequent decision by the Supreme Court itself seeking to retreat
from its earlier position, or even (according to the practices common-law lawyers have come to accept) in a decision by a lower
court interpreting a judicially disfavored statute. But its application
by a lower court to a decision of the Supreme Court rendered only
a month earlier surely is (or should be) extraordinary.[97]

---

[94] 410 U.S. at 238.   [95] *Id.* at 240.   [96] *Id.* at 235.

[97] For a later D.C. Circuit opinion limiting the scope of *Florida East Coast* to the requirement of "adjudicatory procedures" as distinguished from the requirement that the
decision be made "on the record," see *Public Service Comm'n for State of New York*, 487
F.2d at 1069; see also *Mobil Oil Corp.*, 483 F.2d at 1260–61.

The assertion (to make it explicit) that the D.C. Circuit was deliberately rejecting
the Supreme Court's guidance is supported by law-review criticism authored by one of
that court's own members. In 1974, Judge Skelly Wright wrote: "[S]everal lower court

The D.C. Circuit's subsequent holdings had honored the underlying philosophy of *Florida East Coast* as little as did its *International Harvester* dictum. The Supreme Court had in that case refused to permit the statutory requirement of a "hearing" to augment the APA by even so much as the need for oral presentations. In *International Harvester* the D.C. Circuit found a requirement of "public hearing" to demand not merely oral presentation but even "a right of cross-examination . . . on critical points."[98] In *Mobil Oil* it deduced a requirement of "adversary, adjudicative-type procedures"[99] from a provision which stated that "the finding of the Commission as to the facts, if supported by substantial evidence, shall be conclusive."[100] And in *Vermont Yankee* it derived extra-APA requirements from (in part) no more than a judicially discerned though textually unidentified "feature of the statutory context created by NEPA."[101]

It is important to appreciate that, however little support the D.C. Circuit's approach to the APA could find in the opinions of the Supreme Court, it was fast becoming an accepted part of administrative law theory and practice. Not only did the agencies, for obvious reasons, design their procedures with the D.C. Circuit's philosophy in mind, but the academic community had, by and large, accepted and validated the development.[102] It was no longer regarded as a

---

decisions, both before and after [*Allegheny-Ludlum* and *Florida East Coast*], including a few in my own court, have demonstrated a clear reluctance to heed what I regard as the Supreme Court's message in [those] cases. . . . I would like to register a small note of concern. Consider first the APA's text which, barring constitutional problems or clear evidence of congressional intent in the agency's own statute, seems to allow agencies considerable leeway in the adoption of appropriate rulemaking procedures. The ringing message of the *Florida East Coast* and *Allegheny-Ludlum* cases, to me, is that this leeway, where it exists, must not be obstructed merely because appellate judges sense, with hindsight and on an *ad hoc* basis, that a better system of factual and policy resolution might have been used." Wright, *Court of Appeals Review of Federal Regulatory Agency Rulemaking*, 26 ADMIN. L. REV. 199, 206–07 (1974). One does not find such a strong defense of the integrity of the APA in Judge Wright's opinions, where he goes further than some of his brethren in imposing supplemental procedural requirements. *Compare* Home Box Office, Inc. v. FCC, 567 F.2d 9 (D.C. Cir. 1977) (Wright, J.) *with* Action for Children's Television v. FCC, 564 F.2d 458, 468–78 (D.C. Cir. 1977) (Tamm, J.).

98 478 F.2d at 631.   99 483 F.2d at 1259.

100 *Id.* at 1257–58 n.68. The great weight placed upon the "substantial evidence" test in *Mobil Oil* is particularly curious in light of the D.C. Circuit's minimization of the distinction between "substantial evidence" and "arbitrary or capricious" review two years earlier, in *City of Chicago*, 458 F.2d at 744.

101 547 F.2d at 645.

102 See, *e.g.*, DAVIS, ADMINISTRATIVE LAW OF THE SEVENTIES §§ 6.01, 6.01-2, 6.01-3, 6.01-5 (1976); Williams, *"Hybrid Rulemaking" under the Administrative Procedure Act:*

contradiction in terms but was entirely comprehensible and acceptable to write of "on-the-record section 553 proceedings,"[103] or of
"Hybrid Rulemaking under the Administrative Procedure Act."[104]
And—perhaps most irreversible of all—the students of administrative
law and recent law school graduates on the staffs of the congressional committees had begun to embody this new learning in legislation. Thus, the procedural provisions of the FTC Improvement Act
applicable to (what it calls) "informal hearing[s]"[105] conducted "in
accordance with section 553"[106] read as though they were composed
by the D.C. Circuit with some assistance from Prof. K. C. Davis.[107]
The chairman of the FTC could plausibly describe those complicated procedures as 'basic Administrative Procedure Act notice-
and-comment rulemaking, and . . . informal hearing."[108] And the
director of the FTC's Bureau of Consumer Protection could say
(more conservatively): "I view them less as a radical departure
from Section 553 than as a harbinger of how Section 553 will ultimately be interpreted in its application to other agencies' rules

---

A Legal and Empirical Analysis, 42 U. Chi. L. Rev. 401 (1975); Verkuil, *Judicial Review
of Informal Rulemaking*, 60 Va. L. Rev. 185, 234–42, 244–49 (1974). The members of
the D.C. Circuit themselves contributed to the scholarly literature validating the new
procedure. See, *e.g.*, Wright, *New Judicial Requisites for Informal Rulemaking*, 29 Admin.
L. Rev. 59 (1977); Leventhal, *Environmental Decisionmaking and the Role of the Courts*,
122 U. Pa. L. Rev. 509, 536–41 (1974). Even those scholars who expressed skepticism
as to the desirability of the evolution did not dispute that it was established law. See, *e.g.*,
Nathanson, *Probing the Mind of the Administrator: Hearing Variations and Standards of
Judicial Review under the Administrative Procedure Act and Other Federal Statutes*, 75
Colum. L. Rev. 721 (1975); Auerbach, *Informal Rule Making: A Proposed Relationship
Between Administrative Procedures and Judicial Review*, 72 Nw. U. L. Rev. 15 (1977). To
my knowledge, the only authority so rash as to mount a full-scale attack upon the
legitimacy (as opposed to the desirability) of the new law was the *Harvard Law Review*.
Note, *The Judicial Role in Defining Procedural Requirements for Agency Rulemaking*,
87 Harv. L. Rev. 782 (1974).

[103] Auerbach, note 102 *supra*, at 60.   [105] 15 U.S.C. § 57a(b)(3). (c).

[104] Williams, note 102 *supra*.   [106] 15 U.S.C. § 57a(b) (1976).

[107] These provisions require an oral hearing; a verbatim transcript; an opportunity for
all interested persons to make oral submissions, and to make rebuttal submissions and
conduct cross-examination with respect to "disputed issues of material fact"; and
"substantial evidence" judicial review. I do not mean to suggest that legislative variation
from the APA—in the FTC Improvement Act and other statutes—would not have occurred without the D.C. Circuit's encouragement. There are independent causes of the
phenomenon, which will be discussed below. My only point here is that the D.C. Circuit's
philosophy has "stimulated" legislative thinking in particular directions (see Davis, note
74 *supra*, at 145) causing a "discernible consensus" to emerge (*id.* at 481).

[108] Address of Hon. Lewis A. Engman to ABA Section of Antitrust Law, April 11,
1975, reprinted in 44 Antitrust L. J. 161, 164 (1975).

similar in nature and scope to the FTC's trade regulation rules."[109] In other words, by the time *Vermont Yankee* was presented to the Supreme Court, the D.C. Circuit's "flexible" procedural requirements, uninhibited by the "rigidities" of the APA, were well on their way to becoming a common law of administrative procedure.[110]

The foregoing history sheds further light on the Supreme Court's readiness to accept what must be considered a confused case for review. It also explains some unusual aspects of the text of the Court's decision. The opinion begins like a chapter from a textbook on federal administrative law:[111]

> In 1946, Congress enacted the Administrative Procedure Act, which as we have noted elsewhere was not only "a new, basic and comprehensive regulation of procedures in many agencies," *Wong Yang Sung* v. *McGrath*, 339 U.S. 33 (1950), but was also a legislative enactment which settled "long-continued and hard-fought contentions, enacts a formula upon which opposing social and political forces have come to rest." *Id.* at 40. . . . Interpreting [§ 553] of the Act in *United States* v. *Allegheny-Ludlum Steel Corp.*, 406 U.S. 742 (1972), and *United States* v. *Florida East Coast Railroad Co.*, 410 U.S. 224 (1973), we held that generally speaking this section of the Act established the maximum procedural requirements which Congress was willing to have the courts impose upon agencies in conducting rulemaking procedures. Agencies are free to grant additional procedural rights in the exercise of their discretion, but reviewing courts are generally not free to impose them if the agencies have not chosen to grant them. . . .
>
> Even apart from the Administrative Procedure Act this Court has for more than four decades emphasized that the formulation of procedures was basically to be left within the discretion of the agencies to which Congress had confided the responsibility for substantive judgments. . . .
>
> It is in the light of this background of statutory and decisional

---

[109] Address of J. Thomas Rosch to ABA Section of Antitrust Law, August 11, 1975, reprinted in 44 ANTITRUST L. J. 515, 552 (1975).

[110] For decisions of other Circuits adopting the principles developed by the D.C. Circuit, see, *e.g.*, Natural Resources Defense Council v. NRC, 539 F.2d 824 (2d Cir. 1976), vacated and remanded for consideration of mootness *sub nom.* Allied-General Nuclear Services v. Natural Resources Defense Council, 434 U.S. 1030 (1978); Appalachian Power Co. v. EPA, 477 F.2d 495, 503 (4th Cir. 1973); Duquesne Light Co. v. EPA, 481 F.2d 1, 5–6 (3d Cir. 1973) (dictum). *Contra:* Buckeye Power, Inc. v. EPA, 481 F.2d 162, 172–73 (6th Cir. 1973).

[111] 435 U.S. at 523–25.

law that we granted certiorari to review two judgments of the
Court of Appeals for the District of Columbia Circuit because
of our concern that they had seriously misread or misapplied
this statutory and decisional law cautioning reviewing courts
against engrafting their own notions of proper procedures upon agencies entrusted with substantive functions by Congress.

In that opening passage, and throughout, the opinion is full of the
exasperated tone of one not explaining a new point of law but un-
necessarily reiterating an old one:

> But this much is absolutely clear. . . .[112] Indeed, our cases
> could hardly be more explicit in this regard. . . .[113] We have
> continually repeated this theme through the years. . . .[114] We
> have ... previously shown that our decisions reject this view.[115]
> We have before observed . . . . In fact, just two terms ago we
> emphasized . . . .[116] We have made it abundantly clear before
> that . . . .[117]

Of course the immediate objects of this finger wagging were the
respondents, but they were obviously only surrogates for the creator
of the positions they espoused, the D.C. Court of Appeals. Lest that
subtlety go unnoticed, the Court spiced its opinion with some direct
criticisms of the action below—and indeed even of the general tendencies of the court below—that are extraordinary in their sharpness:

> This sort of Monday morning quarterbacking [engaged in by
> the court below] not only encourages but almost compels the
> agency to conduct all rulemaking proceedings with the full
> panoply of procedural devices normally associated only with
> adjudicatory hearings. . . .[118]
>
> In sum, this sort of unwarranted judicial examination of per-
> ceived procedural shortcomings of a rulemaking proceeding
> can do nothing but seriously interfere with that process pre-
> scribed by Congress. . . .[119]
>
> We accordingly remand so that the Court of Appeals may
> review the rule as the Administrative Procedure Act provides.
> . . . The Court should engage in this kind of review and not

---

[112] *Id*. at 543.

[113] *Id*. at 544.

[114] *Ibid*.

[115] *Id*. at 545.

[116] *Id*. at 548.

[117] *Id*. at 549.

[118] *Id*. at 547.

[119] *Id*. at 548.

stray beyond the judicial province to explore the procedural
format or to impose upon the agency its own notion of which
procedures are "best" or most likely to further some vague,
undefined public good.[120]

The Court's pique is even more clearly expressed in that portion
of the opinion dealing with the *Consumers Power* case—whose issues
were related to those in *Vermont Yankee* principally because they
involved the same court of appeals and exemplified the same penchant for judicial embellishment of statutorily prescribed procedures, contrary (as the prologue of the opinion suggested) to the
settlement which "opposing social and political forces have come
to"[121] in the APA; and perhaps (as the last paragraph of the opinion
suggests)[122] because they display the same more general proclivity
toward judicial lawgiving:

> In sum, to characterize the actions of the Commission as
> "arbitrary or capricious" [as the court of appeals had done]
> . . . is to deprive those words of any meaning.[123]
>
> This surely is, as respondent Consumers Power claims, "judi-
> cial intervention run riot."[124]
>
> To say that the Court of Appeals' final reason for remanding
> is insubstantial at best is a gross understatement. . . . [The
> court's action] borders on the Kafkaesque. . . . The funda-
> mental policy questions appropriately resolved in Congress and
> in the state legislatures are *not* [emphasis in original] subject
> to reexamination in the federal courts under the guise of judi-
> cial review of agency action. . . . Administrative decisions
> should be set aside in this context, as in every other, only for
> substantial procedural or substantive reasons as mandated by
> statute, . . . not simply because the court is unhappy with the
> result reached.[125]

What is most impressive is that all seven of the Justices who sat in
the case (Justices Blackmun and Powell did not participate) not
only agreed with the judgment but joined in the extremely sharp
opinion. There were no separate concurrences. One suspects that the
Court felt, as an institution, that its authority had been flouted.

---

[120] *Id.* at 549.   [122] *Id.* at 557–58.

[121] *Id.* at 523.   [123] *Id.* at 554.

[124] *Id.* at 557, quoting Brief for Petitioner in No. 76-528, at p. 37.

[125] 435 U.S. at 557–58.

The issue most starkly presented by the *Vermont Yankee* case and the decade or so of case law leading up to it is the proper functioning of a court of appeals in a hierarchical judicial system. It is surely disturbing that a fundamentally erroneous approach to important issues of administrative law—profoundly affecting not merely the relationship between the courts and the agencies but the relationship between those two and the legislature as well—should have taken such deep root within the courts, the agencies, the law schools, and even the legislature itself before being corrected by the Supreme Court. Never mind that the Court of Appeals should have known that it was proceeding in a direction not desired by the Supreme Court. That is secondary to the question of how the error could have gone so long uncorrected, so that even now that the Supreme Court has spoken with unquestionable clarity, a prominent commentator feels able to dismiss its views as "largely one of those rare opinions in which a unanimous Supreme Court speaks with little or no authority."[126]

Part of the blame, I suppose, must rest upon the agency lawyers—who should read the opinions of the Supreme Court at least as closely as they do those of the D.C. Circuit. Realistically, however, the pressures to do otherwise are enormous. As a practical matter, the D.C. Circuit is something of a resident manager, and the Supreme Court an absentee landlord. It is the Court of Appeals that must be satisfied, on a day-to-day basis, and the costs of incurring its disapproval are high in terms of delay and uncertainty in agency programs. In the area here under discussion, it would almost always be preferable, in the individual case, to provide the additional procedures which one had reason to believe the Court of Appeals would require, rather than to gamble on Supreme Court review. Even when obtained, that comes at the expense of a year's delay—followed, if one loses, by a recommencement of proceedings at the agency level. Ironically, it is precisely when the agency has most need of expedition that it also has the most incentive to provide the most cumbersome procedures which the Court of Appeals (though not the Supreme Court) may require.

Of course one might expect some agencies to take the long view and, by intentionally disappointing the Court of Appeals' expectations, to seek long-term relief from the Supreme Court at the expense

---

[126] DAVIS, note 74 *supra*, at 616.

of inordinate delay in the proceedings immediately pending. Such long-range thinking is not, however, common in the federal executive. The management incentives are against it. Most policy-level officials expect to be judged (by the Congress and the Administration), not on the basis of what will happen five or even three years hence, but on the basis of how the agency's immediate programs are being implemented. Indeed, most of them probably hope they will have gone on to bigger and better things three years hence, whereupon their short-term sacrifice will redound to someone else's long-term credit. Another factor encouraging the same shortsightedness is the fragmentation of major regulatory authority within the Executive Branch. It would be one thing for a President who had responsibility for all regulatory proceedings to decide that a chance of improving the whole is worth a delay in a particular program of the FTC. It is quite different for an independent chairman of the FTC to make that decision. In any event, I am unaware of any pre-litigation planning within the agencies (much less among them) designed to do anything but meet, rather than place in issue, the demands of the D.C. Circuit.

But I think the most important factor leading to the *de facto* unreviewability of the D.C. Circuit's positions is the failure of that Court itself to facilitate review, even when the most fundamental issues are at stake. Or to put the point more critically: The pattern of dicta, alternate holdings, and confused holdings out of which the D.C. Circuit's principle of APA hybrid rulemaking so clearly and authoritatively emerged had the effect, if not the purpose, of assuring compliance below while avoiding accountability above. The practice is not alien to the D.C. Circuit in other fields as well.[127] Surely

---

[127] See, *e.g.*, MCI Telecommunications Corp. v. FCC, 561 F.2d 365 (D.C. Cir. 1977), mandamus issued, 580 F.2d 590 (D.C. Cir. 1978), in which "[a]s a final and somewhat collateral point," the Court advised the FCC that the FCC had not, although it thought it had, in an earlier rulemaking "determined that the public interest would be served by creating an AT&T monopoly in the interstate MTS [long-distance message telephone service] field"; and that "nowhere in that decision can justification be found for continuing or propagating [such] a monopoly"; so that "it may not properly draw any inferences about the public interest from the bare fact that another carrier's proposed services would compete in that field." 561 F.2d at 379, 380. That point was not expressed as the basis for reversing the agency action in question, and was therefore clearly not appealable—though it was clearly of much greater importance than the point which was made the basis for the decision; and though it was a virtual certainty that the agency would (as it in fact did) accommodate the Court's dictum on remand.

Perhaps the most egregious of the genre is United States v. Ehrlichman, 546 F.2d 910 (D.C. Cir. 1976), in which two of the three-judge panel, in an extraordinary seven-page

when new principles of law as far-reaching as those here discussed are pressed upon the agencies, sound operation of the system demands that, at least at an early date, they be expressed in a form that enables—indeed, invites—Supreme Court review. Repeated dicta, holdings which merely replicate other independent grounds of decision, or pronouncements so carefully obscured that the Solicitor General and the General Counsel of the NRC cannot agree upon the basis of the decision, will not suffice. The unreviewable decision is of course not a judicial technique invented by the D.C. Circuit, and it may be regarded as good clean fun in the ordinary tort case before a court of common pleas. But surely at the level of judicial responsibility here involved, and with respect to the legal questions of national consequence at issue, the societal cost is too high.[128]

While the D.C. Circuit could profit from more attention to the art of being an inferior court, perhaps the Solicitor General's Office could

---

concurrence devoted entirely to a point which, they conceded, "it is not necessary to pass on," 546 F.2d at 933, set forth their view that warrantless physical entries not incident to electronic surveillance—even when conducted by presidential authorization for counterespionage or foreign intelligence purposes—are unlawful. The two judges chose to set forth this view as an unappealable dictum, despite the Justice Department's statement that the contrary "is and has long been the Department's view," 546 F.2d at 935; despite the prospect (which they must have seen) that any federal official thereafter acting upon the Department's view would—because of impairment of a good faith defense—run a risk of prosecution under 18 U.S.C. § 241 and an even more serious risk of civil liability under Bivens v. Six Unknown Named Agents, 403 U.S. 388 (1971); and despite the fact that they could (since they were a majority of the panel) have avoided placing law enforcement officials in this quandary and (perhaps) erroneously obstructing activities important to the national security, by simply making this point the basis of the decision. Praising the court's opinion (which is two-thirds theirs) as "prudentially" avoiding the unnecessary issue, the concurrers defeat the whole purpose of that prudence by reaching the issue in their separate (but nonetheless majority) opinion, and in fact add to the imprudence of reaching the issue the outrage of reaching it in a deliberately unappealable fashion. It must be noted that one of the two concurring judges was not a D.C. Circuit Judge. The same cannot be said of the plurality opinion in Zweibon v. Mitchell, 516 F.2d 594 (D.C. Cir. 1975), decided *en banc*, which gave similar treatment to a similar issue.

[128] These same devices that inhibit Supreme Court review facilitate the development of inconsistency among the various panels of the D.C. Circuit itself. *Compare Mobil Oil Corp.*, 483 F.2d 1238, *with* American Public Gas Ass'n v. FPC, 567 F.2d 1016, 1064–67 (D.C. Cir. 1977) (the latter case disagrees with the alternate holding of the former that the "substantial evidence" review requirement of the Natural Gas Act mandates adversary procedures). *Compare* Action for Children's Television ["ACT"] v. FCC, 564 F.2d 458, 474–78 (D.C. Cir. 1977), *with* United States Lines, Inc. v. FMC, 584 F.2d 519 (D.C. Cir. 1978). (Chief Judge Wright's opinion in *United States Lines*, in an alternate holding, contradicts an extensive dictum in *ACT*, which in turn discussed and contradicted a still earlier opinion of Chief Judge Wright. The *United States Lines* opinion, evidently displaying a new-found appreciation for the distinction between holding and dictum, does not even accord *ACT* the dignity of a citation.)

do with a bit more attention to reality. There was probably no single controverted issue of administrative law as important—and as needful of early Supreme Court resolution—as the D.C. Circuit's approach to the APA, clearly exemplified in its *Vermont Yankee* opinion. Under the circumstances, the clouded question whether the actual holding turned on that issue was a relative detail. The Solicitor General's Office prides itself, and rightly so, upon fastidious attention to the technical aspects of the lawyer's craft; and surely that includes appreciation of the distinction between holding and dictum, and precise identification of the basis for a decision. One wonders, however, whether in the age of the legislative opinion, intentionally designed to say and to impose much more than it holds, a somewhat lesser attention to those factors in selecting cases for certiorari might not be justified. Indeed, one wonders whether it might not be in order to seek an expansion of the generally accepted function of the writ of certiorari to embrace review of a lower-court opinion on an important point of law, even where not essential to the judgment, if (1) the issue is fit for review, in that it involves a purely legal point on which the position of the lower court has been definitively stated, and (2) the court's position requires an immediate and significant change in conduct, with serious consequences attached to noncompliance. These conditions, it may be noted, merely paraphrase the Supreme Court's conditions for preenforcement review of agency action, set forth in the *Abbott Laboratories* case.[129] It is surely ironic that our judicial system has managed to develop a system of review for definitive administrative statements of intent, but not for functionally similar pronouncements by the courts themselves. Of course the expansion of certiorari I have peevishly suggested will not work, because—unlike the situation with respect to review of preenforcement agency action—there is no assurance that any of the parties to the case will have an interest in defending a Court of Appeals' dictum. The Court of Appeals could hardly be asked to defend its own position, if only for the reason that it would be likely to expend an inordinate amount of time in doing so. And the appointment of an *advocatus dicti* is unthinkable. It should be no surprise that our adversary system is unable to adjust to a judicial practice that is simply foreign to its nature. One can only hope for an elevation of the

---

[129] Abbott Laboratories v. Gardner, 387 U.S. 136 (1967).

standards of practice of the D.C. Circuit, and perhaps a lowering of standards by the Solicitor General to meet them halfway.

VI. The APA as Magna Carta of Administrative Procedure

While the Supreme Court was correct in *Vermont Yankee* to chide the D.C. Circuit for failure to follow its guidance concerning the central role of the APA, the question remains whether that guidance itself is substantively correct. The opening passage of the opinion ("In 1946, Congress enacted the Administrative Procedure Act"), redolent of the opening passage of the Gospel of St. John ("In the beginning was the Word"), characterizes an approach that attributes to the APA a fundamentality which, it seems to me, the statute can no longer bear.

A. POST-APA CHANGES IN UNDERLYING ADMINISTRATIVE LAW

It may indeed be true, as the Court said (quoting a 1950 case), that the Act "settled 'long-continued and hard-fought contentions, and enact[ed] a formula upon which opposing social and political forces have come to rest.' "[130] But if they have remained at rest since 1946, the landscape has moved beneath them. The APA is of course not remotely a self-contained statute, but assumes an entire underlying jurisprudence and practice—which have in the interim drastically altered, as reflected in the decisions of the Supreme Court itself.

Consider two categories of massive post-APA change in the particular area of informal rulemaking:

1. Not until 1956 was it established that an agency charged with issuing and denying licenses in adjudicatory hearings could establish generic disqualifying factors in informal rulemaking, thereby avoiding adversarial procedures on those issues.[131] Not until 1968 was it

---

[130] 435 U.S. at 523.

[131] United States v. Storer Broadcasting Co., 351 U.S. 192 (1956). This is the first case in which the Supreme Court addressed the point, and is generally regarded as establishing the broad proposition. See Robinson & Gellhorn, The Administrative Process 188 (1974). In fact, however, the Court seems to have approved the practice *sub silentio* in National Broadcasting Co. v. United States, 319 U.S. 190 (1943). This suggests a point worth emphasizing: In this and later examples I am not asserting that the judicial decisions necessarily "changed the law." Perhaps they did, and perhaps they did

established that a major rate-making agency (the FPC) had implicit authority to fix rates on an areawide basis rather than company by company,[132] enabling the avoidance of constitutional and statutory requirements for an adjudicatory hearing.[133] And not until 1973 was it judicially determined that the FTC, one of the oldest of the regulatory agencies, had authority to prohibit unfair trade practices by rule, as opposed to operating exclusively through individual "cease-and-desist" proceedings.[134]

Decisions such as these have facilitated what is perhaps the most notable development in federal government administration during the past two decades: "The contrivance of more expeditious administrative methods"[135]—that is, the constant and accelerating flight away from individualized, adjudicatory proceedings to generalized disposition through rulemaking.[136] "The increased use of rulemaking has changed the whole structure of administrative law, for as recently as the early 1960's it was generally assumed that any significant regulatory scheme would rely to a considerable extent on trial-type hearings."[137] Those trained in administrative law in the sixties or seventies are repeatedly struck by the apparent absurdity of objections raised by more experienced lawyers when decision-making techniques that are perfectly common in new areas of regulation are applied to some ancient regulatory field. Indignant protests of "lack

---

not. What they do represent cumulatively, however, is a radically altered agency (and perhaps public) perception of what the law permits, and a willingness on the part of the courts to accommodate that perception. For later cases involving other agencies that have applied the *Storer* principle to their own licensing programs, see FPC v. Texaco, Inc., 377 U.S. 33 (1964); Weinberger v. Hynson, Westcott & Dunning, Inc., 412 U.S. 609 (1973) (FDA); American Airlines, Inc. v. CAB, note 13 *supra* (CAB).

[132] Permian Basin Area Rate Cases, 390 U.S. 747 (1968).

[133] See, *e.g.*, Shell Oil Co. v. FPC, 520 F.2d 1061, 1074–76 (1975). See note 17 *supra*. It may be constitutionally necessary, however, to provide the opportunity for individual variance from area-wide rates. See *Permian Basin*, 390 U.S. at 770.

[134] National Petroleum Refiners Ass'n v. FTC, 482 F.2d 672 (D.C. Cir. 1973). The FTC had not attempted to issue such a rule until 1963, 28 FED. REG. 10900 (Oct. 11, 1963). For the Commission's first formal justification of such rulemaking authority, see the Statement of Basis and Purpose accompanying promulgation of the cigarette advertising rules, 29 FED. REG. 8325, July 2, 1964.

[135] *Permian Basin*, 390 U.S. at 777.

[136] See Pedersen, *Formal Records and Informal Rulemaking*, 85 YALE L. J. 38, 39–44 (1975). For indication that the trend can be expected to continue, see, *e.g.*, *Recommendation III* (7), in REPORT OF THE CAB ADVISORY COMMITTEE ON PROCEDURAL REFORM 13 (1975).

[137] Pedersen, note 136 *supra*, at 38–39.

of due process" are common. The explanation is that in such fields, and to such practitioners, the drastic alteration of the old "settlement" wrought by the expansion of rulemaking is most apparent.

2. Another post-APA development of monumental importance was the establishment in 1967 of the principle that rules could be challenged in court directly rather than merely in the context of an adjudicatory enforcement proceeding against a particular individual,[138] combined with the doctrine (clearly enunciated in 1973) that "the focal point for judicial review should be the administrative record already in existence, not some new record made initially in the reviewing court."[139] By reason of these holdings—and of a large number of new statutes which explicitly provided for direct court-of-appeals review of rulemaking—the validity of rules was increasingly decided on briefs in a court of appeals, or before a district court which could take no new evidence.[140]

The cumulative effect of these developments was that by the mid-1970s vast numbers of issues of the sort which in 1946 would have been resolved in a formal adjudicatory context before the agency, or even in an adjudicatory judicial proceeding, were being resolved in informal rulemaking and informal adjudication; that the courts were expected to provide, in the words of one of the Supreme Court's more expansive descriptions (which it probably now regrets), "a thorough, probing, in-depth review"[141] of that agency action, but

---

[138] Abbott Laboratories v. Gardner, 387 U.S. 136 (1967). Here again, earlier cases had pointed in the same direction, *e.g.*, Columbia Broadcasting System v. United States, 316 U.S. 407 (1943), but had been regarded as setting forth the exception rather than the rule. Thus, the three dissenters in *Abbott Labs* could say that "The Court, by today's decisions . . . , has opened Pandora's box." 387 U.S. at 176.

[139] Camp v. Pitts, 411 U.S. 138, 142 (1973). This case involved licensing rather than rulemaking, but there was no reason its pronouncement would not apply to the latter as well.

[140] See Pedersen, note 136 *supra*, at 50; Nathanson, note 102 *supra*, at 755–56. The scope of the change becomes apparent when one realizes that as late as 1950 the D.C. Circuit declined to interpret a provision for direct court-of-appeals review of FPC "orders" to include FPC regulations, because "an appellate court has no intelligible basis for decision unless a subordinate tribunal has made a record fully encompassing the issues." United Gas Pipe Line Co. v. FPC, 181 F.2d 796, 799 (D.C. Cir. 1950). See Currie & Goodman, *Judicial Review of Federal Administrative Action: Quest for the Optimum Forum*, 75 COLUM. L. REV. 1, 39–41 (1975); *Citizens to Preserve Overton Park*, 401 U.S. at 415.

[141] *Citizens to Preserve Overton Park*, 401 U.S. at 415. The adoption of stricter standards for judicial review of the factual basis of rules may itself be considered a reaction to the transfer of traditionally adjudicated issues to rulemaking. I think it goes too far to say that in 1946 "the universal assumption was that, just as Congress need not provide

taking the agency record as it was and without conducting any additional evidentiary proceedings.[142] In these changed circumstances the D.C. Circuit's imposition of cross-examination requirements in rulemaking was merely a continued application of adjudicatory procedures to issues which extra-APA developments had wrenched out of their 1946 adjudicatory context. Realistically it should be regarded as an affirmation, rather than a repudiation, of the 1946 "settlement."[143]

The principal focus of this article—because it was the focus of *Vermont Yankee*—has been those revisions to the original APA which the D.C. Circuit fashioned in the area of required hearing procedures. It fashioned other revisions as well, which may be mentioned briefly because they appear even more clearly as adjustments to changed circumstances, designed to preserve rather than destroy the status quo of procedural treatment.

The APA requires that "the agency shall incorporate in the rules adopted a concise general statement of their basis and purpose."[144] There is no doubt that the burden meant to be imposed by this provision was minimal.[145] The 1947 Attorney General's Manual on the Administrative Procedure Act, which has been treated by the Su-

---

factual support for enactments, an agency need not develop factual materials in support of rules." 1 DAVIS, note 74 *supra*, at 498. See, *e.g.*, National Broadcasting Co. v. United States, 319 U.S. 190, 224 (1943): "Our duty is at an end when we find that the [rulemaking] action of the Commission was based upon findings supported by evidence, and was made pursuant to authority granted by Congress." Still, there is no doubt that the intensiveness of judicial review of the factual basis for rules increased enormously. No court reviewing a rule in 1946 would have conceived of saying (as the D.C. Circuit said in 1973) that "the court and agency are in a kind of partnership relationship." Portland Cement Ass'n v. Ruckelshaus, 486 F.2d 375, 394 (D.C. Cir. 1973); see also Kennecott Copper Corp. v. EPA, 462 F.2d 846, 848–49 (D.C. Cir. 1972). To which statement it is fair to append Judge Friendly's observation that "there is little doubt who is considered to be the senior partner." Friendly, *"Some Kind of Hearing,"* 123 U. PA. L. REV. 1267, 1311 n.221 (1975). It may well be, however, that this development is less a consequence of the shift of formerly adjudicated issues into rulemaking than of a general increase in the importance of the judiciary relative to the other two branches. But see Polsby, *F.C.C. v. National Citizens Committee for Broadcasting and the Judicious Uses of Administrative Discretion, supra.*

[142] Camp v. Pitts, *supra* note 139. See also *Citizens to Preserve Overton Park*, 401 U.S. at 415.

[143] I mean this to be merely a statement of fact, and not an expression of approbation for the D.C. Circuit's rejection of Supreme Court guidance—except to the extent that *tout comprendre c'est tout pardonner.*

[144] 5 U.S.C. § 553(c).

[145] See, *e.g.*, 1 DAVIS, note 74 *supra*, at 496–98.

preme Court as a "contemporaneous interpretation" entitled to "some deference . . . because of the role played by the Department of Justice in drafting the legislation,"[146] described the simplicity of the provision as follows:[147]

> [F]indings of fact and conclusions of law are not necessary. Nor is there required an elaborate analysis of the rules or of the considerations upon which the rules were issued. Rather, the statement is intended to advise the public of the general basis and purpose of the rules.

In his testimony on the proposed provision, the Attorney General had described it as serving "much the same function as the whereas clauses which are now customarily found in the preambles of Executive Orders."[148]

The following quotation demonstrates the fate of this provision in the D.C. Circuit:[149]

> [I]t is appropriate for us . . . to caution against an overly literal reading of the statutory terms "concise" and "general." These adjectives must be accommodated to the realities of judicial scrutiny, which do not contemplate that the court itself will, by a laborious examination of the record, formulate in the first instance the significant issues faced by the agency and articulate the rationale of their resolution. We do not expect the agency to discuss every item or opinion included in the submissions made to it in informal rulemaking. We do expect that, if the judicial review which Congress has thought it important to provide is to be meaningful, the "concise general statement of . . . basis and purpose" mandated by Section 4 [now § 553] will enable us to see what major issues of policy were ventilated by the informal proceedings and why the agency reacted to them as it did.

Thus, in its application to a particular case, the new § 553 works as follows:[150]

---

[146] 435 U.S. at 546.

[147] ATTORNEY GENERAL'S MANUAL ON THE ADMINISTRATIVE PROCEDURE ACT 32 (1947).

[148] ADMINISTRATIVE PROCEDURE ACT, LEGISLATIVE HISTORY, S. Doc. No. 248, 79th Cong., 2d Sess. 225 (1946).

[149] *Automotive Parts & Accessories Ass'n,* 407 F.2d at 338.

[150] United States v. Nova Scotia Food Prods. Corp., 568 F.2d 240, 253 (2d Cir. 1977).

[T]he comment that to apply the proposed [FDA food processing] requirements to whitefish would destroy the commercial product was neither discussed nor answered. We think that to sanction silence in the face of such vital questions would be to make the statutory requirement of a "concise general statement" less than an adequate safeguard against arbitrary decision-making. . . .

What we are entitled to at all events is a careful identification by the Secretary, when his proposed standards are challenged, of the reasons why he chooses to follow one course rather than another. Where that choice purports to be based on the existence of certain determinable facts, the Secretary must, in form as well as in substance, find those facts from evidence in the record. . . .

Another prominent area of APA interpretation concerns the requirement for publication of the material the agency will consider. All the Act requires in this regard is publication (in the notice of rulemaking) of "either the terms or substance of the proposed rule or a description of the subjects and issues involved."[151] Consider, however, what the courts have imposed beyond this:

We find a critical defect in the decision-making process . . . in the inability of petitioners to obtain—in timely fashion—the test results and procedures . . . which formed a partial basis for the [decision] adopted. . . . It is not consonant with the purpose of a rulemaking proceeding to promulgate rules on the basis of inadequate data, or on data that, critical degree [*sic*], is known only to the agency.[152]

When the basis for a proposed rule is a scientific decision, the scientific material which is believed to support the rule should be exposed to the view of interested parties for their comment. . . . To suppress meaningful comment by failure to disclose the basic data relied upon is akin to rejecting comment altogether. . . . [W]e conclude that the failure to disclose to interested persons the scientific data upon which the FDA relied was procedurally erroneous.[153]

There is to my mind no doubt that both of these instances represent a distortion of the original text of the APA.[154] But, in light of

---

[151] 5 U.S.C. § 553 (b) (3).

[152] *Portland Cement Ass'n*, 486 F.2d at 392, 393.

[153] *Nova Scotia Food Prods. Corp.*, 568 F.2d at 252.

[154] As to the former, see text *supra*, at notes 145–48. As to the latter, the justification plausibly adduced for the requirement that the agency publish in advance the data upon

the massive transferral of adjudicatory issues to rulemaking, and the requirement for "record-only" judicial review, do they represent an overturning of the APA's original "settlement"? In 1946, a decision to which a factual or scientific determination was central would ordinarily have been examined in an adjudicatory context, initially before the agency or later before a court. Even if the most costly elements of that context (oral hearing and cross-examination) are to be abandoned, much at least will be preserved if the adversary testing, and the necessity of reasoned selection between the adversary positions, are retained. And this, I take it, is the purpose of the textual distortions just discussed.

In sum, there seems to me little to be said for the Supreme Court's assumption that its *Vermont Yankee* opinion represents a firm adherence to the "settlement" of the APA. That is so only if one considers the APA's abstract principles rather than the concrete dispositions it was expected to produce and, then, only if one considers those principles in isolation from related assumptions which the Supreme Court itself has since drastically altered. It is ironic but true that the D.C. Circuit's irreverent approach to the text of the APA[155] served to render the nature of agency resolution of particular issues, and the nature of judicial review, closer to what was the expectation in 1946. The Court was, in a sense, restoring the balance which the Supreme Court's consistent approval of "the contrivance of more expeditious administrative methods" had upset. I think it more than coincidental that a high proportion of the D.C. Circuit cases impos-

---

which it intends to rely is that without such publication the "opportunity to participate in the rule making through submission of written data, views, or arguments," guaranteed by § 553, would be meaningless. The "opportunity," the argument runs. must mean a "realistic opportunity." But surely the opportunity to comment is not utterly worthless without advance knowledge of the agency's data. And if knowledge of the agency's own data is absolutely essential for a "realistic opportunity" to participate, why is not knowledge of the data to be introduced by other participants (and upon which the agency may rely in the final rule) equally essential—so that the APA would require rebuttal comments? Surely what constitutes a "realistic opportunity" to participate is a matter of judgment. And the Congress made its judgment clear when it specifically required advance publication of only "the terms or substance of the proposed rule or a description of the subjects and issues involved." 5 U.S.C. § 553(b)(3). Or, to put the point another way, if the mere requirement of an "opportunity to participate" was, as the argument suggests, sufficient in itself to require by implication publication of agency data, it would *a fortiori* have been sufficient to require publication of "a description of the subjects and issues involved"—so that the language of § 553(b)(3) would have been superfluous. It is quite clear that that is all the Congress thought it essential for the agency to disclose.

[155] *E.g.*: "[I]n many cases, it is unnecessary, and even unwise, to classify a given proceeding as either adjudicatory or rulemaking." *City of Chicago*, 458 F.2d at 739.

ing extra-APA requirements involved precisely instances in which agencies had sought to transfer traditionally adjudicated issues into rulemaking.[156]

I do not mean to denigrate the philosophy of judicial restraint and of strict judicial adherence to statutory text which the Court's opinion in *Vermont Yankee* displays. It is a philosophy that I share. One must be realistic, however, about what it achieves, and about how far one wishes to carry it. When the legislative mandate leaves to the agencies (as earlier Supreme Court opinions said the APA did) broad freedom to alter the underlying realities of administrative practice, then strict adherence to the statute will permit a distortion, rather than enforce an observance, of the original legislative compromise.[157] And the problem is even greater if one regards the alteration of realities as not merely the product of the agencies but as at least equally the product of the Supreme Court itself, which changed the understood "common law" of administrative procedure and judicial review.[158] On that view of things, one might plausibly assert that the courts had a positive obligation to "reinterpret" the statute, in order to prevent their own actions from subverting its basic intent. In other words, a rapidly evolving court-made law (such as we have seen with respect to administrative law over the past two decades) is not conducive to—if it is compatible with—stability of interpretation of related statutes.

B. NATAL DEFECTS OF THE APA

Apart from the fact that the legal firmament underlying the APA has drastically altered, there is an entirely independent reason why that Act cannot serve as the judicially untouchable foundation for administrative procedure envisioned by *Vermont Yankee*. It was an unstable and incomplete foundation to begin with.

Consider, first, the central conceptual distinction of the statute, upon which application of virtually all its procedural provisions de-

---

[156] See *American Airlines*, note 13 *supra*; *Walter Holm & Co.*, note 26 *supra*; *City of Chicago*, note 76 *supra*; *Mobil Oil Co.*, note 36 *supra*; *Public Service Comm'n for State of New York*, note 85 *supra*; *O'Donnell v. Shaffer*, note 46 *supra*.

[157] Of course this assumes, as I think correct, that the 1946 Congress did not contemplate such agency use of their freedom—if, indeed, it even realized that the freedom existed, and assuming that the freedom did exist, *i.e.*, that it is not the result of judicial "changes" in the law.

[158] See note 131 *supra*.

pends, the distinction between rulemaking and adjudication. Rulemaking is defined as the "process for formulating, amending, or
repealing a rule";[159] adjudication as the "process for the formulation
of an order."[160] This throws us back upon the definitions of "rule"
and "order." The latter is almost entirely uninformative, saying in
effect that "orders" are all final dispositions that are not "rules"—
"but including licensing."[161] Thus, we fall back ultimately upon the
definition of "rule." This is (omitting the specific examples recited)
"an agency statement of general or particular applicability and future effect designed to implement, interpret, or prescribe law or
policy or describing the organization, procedure, or practice requirements of an agency."[162] Since *every* statement is of either general or particular applicability, and since *everything* an agency does
is "designed to implement, interpret, or prescribe law or policy,
etc.," the only limiting (that is to say, defining) part of the definition
is "agency statement of . . . future effect." This is of course absurd.
It means, for example, that an EPA directive that a particular company must, in order to comply with existing law and regulations,
install particular emission-control equipment at a particular factory
is a rule rather than an order; that the proceeding looking to its issuance is rulemaking rather than adjudication; and that therefore—
even if, despite the relative inflexibility displayed in *Florida East
Coast*,[163] it is held to be formal rulemaking, so that most of the procedural requirements of §§ 556 and 557 apply—at the very least the
crucial separation-of-functions provision directed only to adjudication is inapplicable. Such an analysis produces a categorization which
is so contrary to the common understanding of what constitutes rulemaking, and practical results so antithetical to what the APA was
clearly designed to achieve, that it is generally acknowledged that
the only responsible judicial attitude toward this central APA definition is one of benign disregard.[164]

A major gap in the APA, which has become of increasing importance over the years but was already a major mistake when the Act
was adopted, is its total exclusion of interpretative rules from any
required procedures. This exclusion was apparently based in part
upon the assumption that " 'interpretative' rules—as merely inter-

---

[159] 5 U.S.C. § 551(5).
[160] 5 U.S.C. § 551(7).
[161] 5 U.S.C. § 551(6).

[162] 5 U.S.C. § 551(4).
[163] See text *supra*, at note 90.
[164] See DAVIS, note 74 *supra*, at 3–7.

pretations of statutory provisions—are subject to plenary judicial review."[165] On this assumption, what the agency might do in interpretative rulemaking was relatively unimportant, since the courts would ultimately decide the issue according to their own lights. Unfortunately, even in 1946 this was not so. As the Report of the Attorney General's Committee on Administrative Procedure correctly observed in 1941:[166]

> Even on questions of law [judicial] judgment seems not to be compelled. The question of statutory interpretation might be approached by the court de novo and given the answer which the court thinks to be the "right interpretation." Or the court might approach it, somewhat as a question of fact, to ascertain, not the "right interpretation," but only whether the administrative interpretation has substantial support. Certain standards of interpretation guide in that direction. Thus, where the statute is reasonably susceptible of more than one interpretation, the court may accept that of the administrative body. Again, the administrative interpretation is to be given weight—not merely as the opinion of some men or even of a lower tribunal, but as the opinion of the body especially familiar with the problems dealt with by the statute and burdened with the duty of enforcing it. This may be particularly significant when the legislation deals with complex matters calling for expert knowledge and judgment.

In other words, an interpretative rule under a statute which contains vague legislative standards and which applies to a highly technical area of activity is likely to have near-conclusive effect. The need for public notice and comment prior to the adoption of such an interpretative rule is indistinguishable from the need in the case of "legislative" rulemaking. Any procedural framework which seeks to impose a clear dividing line between the two is irrational and invites judicial disregard. The courts' tendency to replace the APA's legislative-interpretative distinction with a judicially created "substantial-impact test"[167] was entirely predictable.

Another major gap in the APA is its failure to provide any mini-

---

[165] Senate Judiciary Committee Print of June, 1945, reprinted in ADMINISTRATIVE PROCEDURE ACT, LEGISLATIVE HISTORY, S. Doc. No. 248, 79th Cong., 2d Sess. 18, 1946.

[166] FINAL REPORT OF THE ATTORNEY GENERAL'S COMMITTEE ON ADMINISTRATIVE PROCEDURE 90–91 (1941).

[167] See American Bancorp., Inc. v. Board of Governors of the Federal Reserve System, 509 F.2d 29, 33 (8th Cir. 1974). But see Shell Oil Co. v. FPC, 491 F.2d 82, 87–88 (5th Cir. 1974).

mum structured procedures whatever for an entire category of
agency activity. As we have seen, the Act establishes structured procedures for rulemaking required by statute to be conducted on the
record (formal rulemaking); for rulemaking not required by statute
to be conducted on the record (informal rulemaking); and for adjudication required by statute to be conducted on the record (formal
adjudication). What is left is adjudication not required by statute to
be conducted on the record (informal adjudication)—and for this
no structured procedures whatever, not even the minimal notice-
and-comment established for informal rulemaking, are required by
the APA.[168] To be sure, in extreme cases the Constitution itself may
require an "on-the-record" hearing, whereupon (under the Supreme
Court's interpretation of the APA expressed in *Wong Yang Sung*[169])
the matter becomes formal adjudication and the full magnificence
of §§ 556–57 applies. Absent such transmutation, however, the APA
establishes no requirements whatever. Since informal adjudication
undoubtedly constitutes the vast majority of agency actions,[170] it is
quite simply inconceivable that—confronted by a total vacuum in
the APA—the courts will abstain from developing a "common law"
of procedures in this area. Even if the Supreme Court persists in its
Vermont Yankee abnegation of such a power, it can achieve the
same result by simply finding a whole spectrum of "due process"
requirements for less than an "on-the-record" hearing.[171] Either
way, the APA could no longer realistically be viewed as occupying
the field.

Consider, for example, the agency action involved in the D.C.

---

[168] This is not to say that none of the protections of the Act extend to informal adjudication. Section 555, for example, guarantees the right to be accompanied by counsel when
compelled to appear in person, the right to procure a transcript of evidence presented, and
the right to receive prompt notice of denial of a written application "made in connection
with any agency preceeding." 5 U.S.C. § 555; see also §§ 552(a)(1), 558. Perhaps most
important of all, informal adjudication, like other forms of agency action, can be set
aside by the courts as "arbitrary, capricious, an abuse of discretion, or otherwise not in
accordance with law." 5 U.S.C. § 706(2)(A). But the APA establishes no formula for
the receipt of argument and evidence whose observance will (insofar as procedural
matters are concerned) automatically satisfy this test, and whose disregard will automatically fail it.

[169] See text *supra*, at note 81.

[170] Professor Davis's guess of 90 percent is as good as any. 1 DAVIS, note 74 *supra*, at 14.

[171] *Cf.* Goss v. Lopez, 419 U.S. 565 (1975). One could reasonably argue that—insofar
as hearing requirements are concerned—an interest which does not rise to the level of
entitlement to an "on-the-record" hearing does not rise to the level of any constitutional
protection under the Due Process Clause. But, as *Goss* indicates, such a "de minimis"
principle has no appeal to the present Court.

Circuit's *International Harvester* case:[172] denial of a manufacturer's application for a one-year suspension (as permitted by the statute) of the 1975 exhaust emission standards. This would appear to be informal adjudication. In the actual case, the statute itself had provided some requisite procedure—to wit, a "public hearing"—which the Court interpreted to require even "reasonable cross-examination" on remand. Suppose, however, that the statute had been completely silent as to procedures, so that such ready flight from the rigidities of the APA was not available. Is it conceivable that the only choices available to the Court would be: (1) to permit the Administrator to deny the application with no opportunity for any presentation of the applicant's case; or (2) to require that, in order to comply with constitutional due process, the entire matter must be made the subject of a full-dress adjudicatory proceeding? It is simply not likely that such a line can be held.

C. CONGRESSIONAL NONACQUIESCENCE

In addition to the drastic change in underlying law and the inherent inadequacy of the APA to begin with, there is yet a third reason why the Act cannot serve as the basic charter that the *Vermont Yankee* case envisions. The Congress has simply not accepted it as such in enacting the many substantive statutes to which the APA must apply.

The APA did not envision a rigid uniformity, but left it to each agency to adopt whatever procedures above the established minimum seemed desirable for its programs. Nonetheless the Act did assume and sought to codify a consensus as to what the legally enforceable minimum should be. Such a consensus could justify cases like *Allegheny-Ludlum*[173] and *Wong Yang Sung*,[174] which seek to squeeze not merely new statutes but even preexisting statutes and constitutional "due process" requirements into the APA mold. It is by now obvious, however, that the consensus either has evaporated or is too feeble to resist collateral, incidental attack in the course of congressional consideration of new substantive legislation. Either condition, it seems to me, eliminates the justification (not to mention the purpose) for imposing the APA's structure upon statutes, old or new, that seem ill designed and little intended to receive it; and for

---

[172] Note 30 *supra*.   [173] Note 77 *supra*.   [174] Note 81 *supra*.

restraining the courts from returning to their pre-APA ways of developing an administrative common law—a task they are at least as well equipped, and probably better motivated, to perform than are the substantive committees of Congress which consider procedural issues *en passant*.

The riotous growth of extra-APA procedural prescriptions in new legislation—particularly prescriptions relating to rulemaking—has been well documented elsewhere.[175] Suffice it to say here that they range from an imposed scheme of pre-rulemaking rulemaking[176] to an unfathomable prescription for "such cross-examination" as the agency determines to be (1) "appropriate" and (2) required for a "full and true disclosure" with respect to "disputed issues of material fact."[177] Professor Hamilton is quite correct when he concludes that "the procedural provisions of these statutes are almost unbelievably chaotic";[178] as is Judge Friendly when he observes that "one would almost think there had been a conscious effort never to use the same phraseology twice."[179] This statutory Babel displays, it should be added, not merely a devil-may-care attitude about departing from the APA, but—even worse—a profound ignorance concerning just what it is that is being departed from.[180]

There may be some debate concerning the virtue or vice of legislative activism in the area of administrative procedure—a subject to which I shall revert later on. What is unquestionable, however, is

---

[175] Hamilton, note 9 *supra*, at 1313–30; see also 1 DAVIS, note 74 *supra*, at 481–94.

[176] 15 U.S.C. § 2056 (consumer product safety standards under the Consumer Product Safety Act); see Scalia & Goodman, *Procedural Aspects of the Consumer Product Safety Act*, 20 U.C.L.A. L. REV. 899, 906–16 (1973).

[177] 15 U.S.C. § 57a(c)(1) (trade regulation rules under the FTC Improvement Act of 1975).

[178] Hamilton, note 9 *supra*, at 1315.

[179] Associated Industries v. United States Dept. of Labor, 487 F.2d 342, 345 n.2 (2d Cir. 1973).

[180] For one of many examples, see the National Traffic and Motor Vehicle Safety Act of 1966, now codified at 15 U.S.C. § 1391 *et seq.* This provides that "the Secretary shall establish by order appropriate Federal motor vehicle safety standards." 15 U.S.C. § 1392(a). Of course in APA terminology it does not mean "by order" but (quite the opposite) "by rule." The provision for judicial review of the "validity of any order" (*i.e.*, of the validity of any rule) requires the Secretary of Transportation to file in the court "the record of the proceedings on which [he] based his order." 15 U.S.C. § 1394 (a)(1). But, the proceeding below being informal rulemaking, there is no "record," either in the generally accepted legal sense, or in the sense in which the APA uses the term. See Hamilton, note 9 *supra*, at 1322–23. See also *Associated Industries*, 487 F.2d at 348–49.

that such activism cannot coexist with fundamental legislation of the sort the Court's opinion in *Vermont Yankee* pronounces the APA to be. Not only is legislative insouciance for the basic statute ultimately bound to infect the courts with its own spirit (as indeed it probably should), but the legislative prescription of particular variations from the procedural norm provides the pretext—and perhaps the necessity—for the addition of judge-made variations to the statutory scheme. Witness, for example, the D.C. Circuit's conclusions that legislative prescription (contrary to the APA) of a "substantial evidence" review test for rulemaking implicitly requires that the agency decision be made "on the record"[181] and that "some sort of adversary, adjudicative-type procedures" be used.[182] The former strikes me as reasonable enough, the latter not; but the point is that legislative variation from even a single APA provision has converted the statute into a proper subject for judicial law making. As the number of such statutes has multiplied, not only has the territory of APA sovereignty thereby been diminished, but the attitude of the courts toward the integrity of the APA, even in other areas, has been inevitably affected.

VII. The Effect of Vermont Yankee

On its face, *Vermont Yankee* seems to be a strong and categorical mandate for strict adherence to the original intent of the APA. The difficulty in assessing its real impact, however, is that the facts before the Court, to which the strong language was specifically addressed, presented, in several respects, the weakest possible case for nonadherence.

First of all, *Vermont Yankee* did not confront the Court with an instance of change in underlying law that would, unless the APA were modified to restore the balance, deprive parties of protections that were assumed in 1946. It is no doubt true that, thirty or even twenty years ago, a licensing proceeding would have been expected to include cross-examination on such issues as those involved in *Vermont Yankee*. But that would have been regarded as a protection for the benefit of the prospective licensee, rather than—as it was sought to be applied in *Vermont Yankee*—for the benefit of the

---

[181] *Public Service Comm'n for State of New York*, 487 F.2d at 1069.
[182] *Mobil Oil Corp.*, 483 F.2d at 1259.

public. That is to say, if the agency had, in those earlier days, decided that it would not cross-examine witnesses favoring the license application, though permitting cross-examination of opposing witness, there might have been criticism of the wisdom of the process, but hardly any claim that constitutionally or statutorily guaranteed rights had been violated.

Vermont Yankee would have been a better test, in other words, if the non-cross-examined testimony of the director of the Division of Waste Management and Transportation had been adverse, rather than favorable, to prospective licensees; and if it were they, rather than self-professed representatives of the public, who were seeking to overturn the Commission's reliance upon it. And it would have been a better test still if the matter at issue had not arisen under NEPA but under a hoary regulatory statute such as the Natural Gas Act, where it had originally been dealt with in adjudicatory proceedings but had only recently been slipped into rulemaking. The Supreme Court's opinion contains an explicit suggestion that this situation might be treated differently. After conceding that constitutional requirements of due process may sometimes require judicial supplementation of APA procedures, the Court floated this cryptic dictum: "It may also be true, although we do not think the issue is presented in this case and accordingly do not decide it, that a totally unjustified departure from well settled agency procedures of long standing might require judicial correction."[183] May this not be a suggestion that in some instances adherence to APA procedures in the application of those "more expeditious administrative methods" sanctioned (as described above) by post-APA case law will upset the original "settlement" to such a degree that it cannot be allowed?

In another respect, too, *Vermont Yankee* was the weakest possible case for nonadherence to the APA. One can establish an entire hierarchy of technical justifications for departure from the original text which might read (in ascending order of plausibility) as follows:

1. *Common-law power of the courts to supplement the APA.* This justification is rarely phrased so baldly by the courts, though it is by some commentators.[184] It underlies, presumably, expressions of judi-

---

[183] 435 U.S. at 542.

[184] *E.g.*, 1 Davis, note 74 *supra*, at 143–44: "Before the APA was adopted, courts were free to make common law requiring procedure of notice and written comment for issuing interpretative rules, and the courts still have that freedom after adoption of the APA."

cial reliance upon such concepts as "the interest of justice,"[185] "considerations of fairness,"[186] and "the very concept of fair hearing."[187] It also underlies (though less obtrusively) the imposition of extra-APA requirements by appeal to no more than the general judicial review provisions of the APA, *i.e.*, the finding that refusal to provide particular procedures in a particular case constitutes agency action which is "arbitrary, capricious [or] an abuse of discretion" and is therefore reversible by the courts under 5 U.S.C. § 706(2)(A).[188] Most subtle of all is the finding that final action (*e.g.*, an agency rule) whose validity has not been tested or established by certain procedures *ipso facto* lacks the necessary degree of credible factual support or rational justification and is therefore "arbitrary, capricious [or] an abuse of discretion."[189] All of these formulations are merely variants of the "common-law power" justification for supplementing the APA, because they all share (whether or not they express it) the assumption that the APA establishes only "minimum requirements," in the sense that it does not implicitly preclude the courts from imposing more.[190]

That assumption is definitively rejected by the Supreme Court's *Vermont Yankee* opinion, as is apparent throughout, but most clearly in the statement that § 553 "established the maximum procedural requirements which Congress was willing to have the courts impose upon agencies in conducting rulemaking procedures."[191] The opinion is also an explicit rejection of the most subtle variant of the common-law power justification,[192] since the D.C. Circuit had not only taken the direct route of finding the procedures themselves bad, but had also found the evidence inadequate to support the rule,

---

[185] *Kennecott Copper Corp.*, 462 F.2d at 850.

[186] O'Donnell v. Shaffer, 491 F.2d at 62.

[187] *American Airlines, Inc.*, 359 F.2d at 632.

[188] See, *e.g.*, *Kennecott Copper Corp.*, 462 F.2d at 850; *Nova Scotia Food Prods. Corp.*, 568 F.2d at 251; *Vermont Yankee*, 547 F.2d at 645–46, 655.

[189] See text *supra*, at notes 53–55.

[190] See *Kennecott Copper Corp.*, 462 F.2d at 850. Of course there is no question that the APA establishes only "minimum requirements" in the sense that the agencies themselves can impose still further (nonconstitutional) requirements in particular cases or classes of cases.

[191] 435 U.S. at 524; see also *id.* at 542–48.

[192] Text *supra*, at note 189.

partly (at least) because of the inadequacy of the procedures.[193] It
is clear from the Supreme Court's opinion that its remand in order
to permit the Court of Appeals to decide "whether the challenged
rule finds sufficient justification in the administrative proceedings"[194]
does not permit a finding of insufficient justification by reason of
procedures inadequate to test the evidence:[195]

> The Court below uncritically assumed that additional proce-
> dures will automatically result in a more adequate record. . . .
> But . . . the adequacy of the "record" in this type of proceed-
> ing is not correlated directly to the type of procedural devices
> employed, but rather turns on whether the agency has fol-
> lowed the statutory mandate of the Administrative Procedure
> Act or other relevant statutes.

Of course, it is not possible to maintain a complete dichotomy between the procedures used and the adequacy of evidentiary support.
Presumably the Court of Appeals is not being told unrealistically that
it cannot give greater weight to testimony which has firmly with-
stood the fire of cross-examination than to an internal agency memorandum. To this extent the Supreme Court is not putting the Court
of Appeals entirely out of the business of evaluating procedures. But
at least it is clear that particular procedures, or even (as in *Vermont
Yankee*) unspecified procedures "greater than X," can be prescribed
neither directly nor by reliance upon the necessity of weighing the
evidence.

Perhaps one limitation might be read into the Court's rejection of
the common-law power theory. *Vermont Yankee* involved only informal rulemaking. The quoted excerpts from the opinion demon-
strating rejection of the theory contain language limiting their application to that context. There is no conceivable justification for treating formal rulemaking and formal adjudication differently. But what
about informal adjudication—for which, as we have seen, the APA
did not establish any "maximum procedural requirements which
Congress was willing to have the courts impose upon agencies"?[196]
This gap can be taken as a congressional determination that the
courts will stay out of this area entirely. But it can also be taken as

---

[193] See note 54 *supra*.

[194] 435 U.S. at 549.

[195] *Id.* at 547.

[196] See note 191 *supra*.

a simple failure of the APA to address this field—perhaps because of its enormously diverse character—and thus as a preservation of the courts' common-law power in the area. As noted above,[197] it is unlikely that the courts will leave this broad area—which includes agency action of the sort involved in *Overton Park*[198] and in *International Harvester*[199]—to an all-or-nothing regime in which either the Constitution (cum *Wong Yang Sung*)[200] requires §§ 556–57 procedures or else the agency need provide no hearing at all.

As already suggested, one means of filling the vacuum would be the creation of constitutional "due process" requirements short of requirements for an "on-the-record" hearing.[201] A more flexible approach would be simply to restrict *Vermont Yankee*'s abnegation of common-law power to those areas of agency action for which the Congress has in fact prescribed procedures or (as with interpretative rulemaking[202] and the other specific exclusions of the APA)[203] for which it has apparently demonstrated an intent that no extraconstitutional procedures shall be imposed.

2. The second technical justification for departure from the original text of the APA, in ascending order of plausibility, is the *nature and general content (as opposed to specific provisions) of the substantive statute involved.* This is the justification used by the D.C. Circuit in *Mobil Oil*, for example, where it said that "a final determination of what procedures are appropriate here must turn upon an analysis of the regulatory scheme envisioned by Congress in passing the Natural Gas Act and a determination of what is necessary to effectuate the policies of this regulatory statute."[204] Obviously, the assertion that a court may consult the atmospherics of a substantive statute in order to divine what procedures the Congress would have thought best is barely distinguishable in its practical effect from the common-law power theory—since almost every federal agency ac-

---

[197] Text *supra*, at notes 168–72.

[198] *Citizens to Preserve Overton Park*, note 75 *supra*.

[199] *International Harvester Co.*, note 30 *supra*.

[200] *Wong Yang Sung*, note 81 *supra*.

[201] See text *supra*, at note 171.

[202] See text *supra*, at notes 165–67.

[203] *E.g.*, the exclusion of adjudications relating to federal employment or to military functions, § 554(a)(2), (4) (1976).

[204] *Mobil Oil Corp.*, 483 F.2d at 1254.

tion is taken pursuant to some statute, and since the courts have a
way of concluding that the Congress would have thought best what
the courts think best. In any case, what might be called the "statutory atmospherics" theory of judicial supplementation of the APA
was also attempted by the Court of Appeals in *Vermont Yankee*[205]
and was soundly rejected by the Supreme Court:[206] "[W]e search
in vain for something in NEPA which would mandate such a result.
. . . [I]t is clear NEPA cannot serve as the basis for a substantial revision of the carefully constructed procedural specifications of the
APA."

3. The third technical justification is a *specific overriding provision of the substantive statute*. I have put this in third place, though
in some cases it more properly belongs in fourth. Its plausibility obviously varies enormously according to the text of the provision in
question. It would appear very likely, for example, that a statutory
provision for "public hearing" mandates an oral hearing, but less
persuasive that it mandates cross-examination.[207] Similarly questionable is the mandate for "adversary, adjudicative-type procedures"
which the D.C. Circuit has extracted from a statutory provision for
"substantial evidence" review.[208] This type of justification for overriding the APA was not involved in *Vermont Yankee*. There is no
doubt that it must be accepted where the statutory intent is clear,
though the holding of *Florida East Coast*[209] and the strong, APA-

---

[205] The Court wrote: "A prominent feature of the statutory context created by NEPA
is the requirement that the agency acknowledge and consider 'responsible scientific
opinion concerning possible adverse environmental effects' which is contrary to the
official agency position. . . . NEPA requires that agencies see to it that 'the officials
making the ultimate decision [are] informed of the full range of responsible opinion on
the environmental effects in order to make an informed choice.' . . . At least in the NEPA
context, an agency has an affirmative obligation to explore the issues in depth, rather than
wait passively until an intervenor takes the initiative. . . . NEPA . . . mandates only a
'careful and informed decisionmaking process' to enlighten the decision maker and the
public. In the rulemaking context, that requires the Commission to identify and address
information contrary to its own position, to articulate its reasoning and to specify the
evidence on which it relies." 547 F.2d at 645, n.34, and 654. The quotations in these
excerpts are not from the statute, but from earlier D.C. Circuit opinions. There is no
language in NEPA that imposes upon the NRC any more of an "affirmative obligation to
explore the issues in depth, rather than wait passively" than does the NRC's substantive
statute—or almost any other agency's substantive statute, for that matter.

[206] 435 U.S. at 548.

[207] See *International Harvester Co.*, 478 F.2d at 630.

[208] See *Mobil Oil Corp.*, 483 F.2d at 1259.

[209] *Florida East Coast R. Co.*, note 79 *supra*.

supportive statements of *Vermont Yankee* suggest that only the plainest of language may satisfy the present Court.

4. The fourth technical justification is *an expansive interpretation of the language of the APA itself*. As noted above, the "notice and comment" provision of § 553 has been converted, contrary to its original intent, into a requirement that the agency disclose in advance the factual data to be relied upon in rulemaking;[210] and the "statement of basis and purpose" provision into a requirement that major arguments against a proposed rule be answered.[211] Not only does the Supreme Court's opinion in *Vermont Yankee* not expressly disapprove this technique, but its silence on the point seems to be an implicit approval. For although the Court chose to address only the Court of Appeals holding with respect to "the procedures afforded during the hearing," on the grounds that this was at least one of the bases of the decision, and probably "the principal" one,[212] the opinion below also contained several passages indicating that the statement of basis and purpose was inadequate because of its failure to address particular objections:[213]

> Since a reviewing court is incapable of making a penetrating analysis of highly scientific or technical subject matter on its own, it must depend on the agency's expertise, as reflected in the statement of basis and purpose, to organize the record, to distill the major issues which were ventilated and to articulate its reasoning with regard to each of them.
>
> [W]here apparently significant information has been brought to its attention, or substantial issues of policy or gaps in its reasoning raised, the statement of basis and purpose must indicate why the agency decided the criticisms were invalid. . . . [W]hat is required is a reasoned response, in which the agency points to particulars in the record which, when coupled with its reservoir of expertise, support its resolution of the controversy. An agency may abuse its discretion by proceeding to a decision which the record before it will not sustain, in the sense that it raises fundamental questions for which the agency had adduced no reasoned answers.
>
> The Commission disposed of these issues summarily in its statement of basis and purpose accompanying the promulgation of the rule without attempting to articulate responses to any of

---

[210] Text *supra*, at notes 151–53.

[211] Text *supra*, at notes 144–50.

[212] 435 U.S. at 542.

[213] 547 F.2d at 646, 652–53.

the points which had been raised regarding waste disposal. . . .
Thus, to the limited extent that any give-and-take was fostered
on the nuclear waste issues, the Commission, in its final decision, failed to address major contentions that were raised.

Not only were the generalities relied on in this case not subject
to rigorous probing—in any form—but when apparently substantial criticisms were brought to the Commission's attention,
it simply ignored them, or brushed them aside without answer.

Note that this asserted necessity of including within the statement
of basis and purpose a "reasoned response" to major objections is not
the same as the unquestioned necessity that the record contain material which could reasonably be considered to outweigh the objections. The Court of Appeals was asking the agency to identify those
elements which in its view did outweigh the objections, and to explain its rejection. As discussed above, there is simply no such requirement in the text of the APA, unless one stretches that text well
beyond its original meaning. Nonetheless, despite presentation of a
good occasion to squelch this heresy, the Supreme Court chose not
to do so—which makes one suspect that it is the new orthodoxy.

In sum, it would seem that *Vermont Yankee*'s demand for fealty
to the APA must be taken with a grain of salt. There is of course
room for any divergence that is specifically prescribed by the Congress (category 3 above)—and the degree of specificity that will be
required to deduce an intent to diverge remains to be seen, though
both *Florida East Coast* and *Vermont Yankee* suggest it is high.[214]
There is also room, apparently, for those more moderate distortions
of the APA that can be produced by a plausible reinterpretation of
its language (category 4 above)—at least where such distortions
seem necessary to make the APA work in its drastically new setting.[215] And finally, there may even be room for relatively brazen
distortions, such as the judicial importation of cross-examination requirements, where an ancient and well-established adjudicatory issue
has been kidnapped into rulemaking.[216] It would go too far, however, to suggest that *Vermont Yankee* is anything less than a major
watershed. It has put to rest the notion that the courts have a continuing "common-law" authority to impose procedures not required
by the Constitution in the areas covered by the APA. In that sense, at

---

[214] Text *supra*, at notes 207–09.
[215] Text *supra*, at notes 210–13.   [216] Text *supra*, at note 183.

least, "hybrid rulemaking" under the APA is dead. And, perhaps just as important, it has clearly established what is (for courts of appeals, at least) a new tone for the decision of administrative law cases—a tone of judicial restraint and of great deference to the text, if not entirely to the original meaning, of the APA.

It has accomplished all that, that is, if the D.C. Circuit deigns to follow it. Preliminary indications are that it will not, any more than it followed *Florida East Coast*. The undermining has already begun, with *United States Lines, Inc. v. FMC*[217] decided less than four months after *Vermont Yankee* was handed down. There is no space here for a thorough analysis of the case, but a few points must be made: As might have been expected, the D.C. Circuit took advantage of the most available justification for supplementing the APA which *Vermont Yankee* left open—a justification which can sometimes be the strongest but was in this case very weak, namely, congressional prescription. The Court found that a statutory requirement for a "hearing" implied: (1) a requirement to publish "for meaningful adversarial comment"[218] data upon which the agency relied;[219] and (2) a prohibition upon *ex parte* contacts.[220] In connection with the latter point, the Court of Appeals distinguished *Vermont Yankee* by observing that "the freedom of administrative agencies to fashion their procedures [which that case recognizes] does not encompass freedom to ignore statutory requirements."[221] The Court did not bother to distinguish *Florida East Coast*, which declined to give any extra-APA procedural effect to a similar statutory requirement for a "hearing," but treated the case (as it has in the past)[222] as though it concerned only the issue whether such a requirement triggers §§ 556–57 of the APA.[223]

Beyond using that loophole (which is fair enough—the Supreme Court will have to close it case by case), the Court resurrected several of its old theories which the Supreme Court had only just buried. As additional justification for both added procedural requirements, the Court employed the common-law power justification in various of its forms discussed above:[224]

---

[217] 584 F.2d 519 (D.C. Cir. 1978).

[218] *Id.* at 535.

[219] *Id.* at 536.

[220] *Id.* at 539–41.

[224] *Id.* at 534, 535, 541, 542, n.63.

[221] *Id.* at 542 n.63.

[222] See text *supra*, at notes 91–97.

[223] 584 F.2d at 536.

Our cases make clear the importance of [adversarial] comment in allowing a court to review the action taken by the agency.

[Data disclosure] requirements . . . provide a means by which a reviewing court, called upon to determine whether agency action is arbitrary and capricious, can secure needed guidance in the performance of this function from both the parties and the agency. . . .

[F]oreclosure of effective judicial review is itself sufficient reason for this court to require the FMC to disclose the information upon which it relies. . . .

Ex parte contacts . . . foreclose effective judicial review of the agency's final decision according to the arbitrary and capricious standard of the Administrative Procedure Act. . . .

[O]ur cases . . . make clear the critical role of adversarial comment in ensuring . . . effective judicial review.

Nor does *Vermont Yankee* provide a basis for agency procedures or practices which effectively foreclose judicial review where, as here, such review is provided for by statute. Nothing in that decision calls into question the well established principle, found in the Administrative Procedure Act and in the decisions of the Supreme Court that the court is required to conduct a "searching and careful" inquiry to determine whether agency action is arbitrary or capricious, or, in appropriate cases, supported by substantial evidence.

Compare all of this with the statement of the Supreme Court, quoted above:[225]

The Court below uncritically assumed that additional procedures will automatically result in a more adequate record. . . . But . . . the adequacy of the "record" in this type of proceeding is not correlated directly to the type of procedural devices employed, but rather turns on whether the agency has followed the statutory mandate of the Administrative Procedure Act or other relevant statutes.

Quite obviously, if the necessity of conducting judicial review under the "arbitrary or capricious" standard sufficed to support the imposition of extra-APA requirements in *United States Lines*, it could have sufficed (as it did not) in *Vermont Yankee* as well.

To appreciate fully the extent to which *United States Lines* flouts the Supreme Court's guidance in *Vermont Yankee*, one must

---

[225] 435 U.S. at 547.

read the whole opinion. It is full of the same exalted notion of the judicial role which *Vermont Yankee* criticizes. The text of the opinion cites repeatedly—it is a virtual rogue's gallery of—the swash-buckling D.C. Circuit opinions discussed at the outset of this article. Despite the fact that some of them have been cast in doubt by *Vermont Yankee*, they are alluded to (as is the D.C. Circuit's fashion) in a magisterial manner which is more customary for a court of last resort than for an intermediate court: "Our cases make clear";[226] "[W]e have required";[227] "[W]e have insisted";[228] "[We] have held before";[229] "Our cases . . . make clear."[230] The Supreme Court's *Overton Park* statement concerning "thorough, probing, in-depth review" also appears in text[231] (as in D.C. Circuit opinions it almost always does); and the *Overton Park* quote to the effect that the inquiry must be "searching and careful" is repeated no less than four times.[232] *Vermont Yankee*, on the other hand, unquestionably the most important precedent (on the assumption, of course, that the Supreme Court is a superior court), is cited only in two footnotes[233] and discussed only in the latter of them—almost as an afterthought, at the very end of the substantive discussion, appended to a section entitled "Summary."[234]

As was its custom before *Vermont Yankee*, so also after, the Court never does trouble to determine what the APA procedural requirements applicable to the action in question might be—for it never even considers whether the action is rulemaking or adjudication.[235] And of course the opinion also bears the hallmark of the

---

[226] 584 F.2d at 534.

[227] *Ibid.*

[228] *Ibid.*

[229] *Id.* at 536.

[230] *Id.* at 542.

[231] *Id.* at 526.

[232] *Id.* at 10, 25, 43, 44 n.63.

[233] *Id.* at 540 n.61, 542 n.63.

[234] It should not be thought that confining all mention and discussion of *Vermont Yankee* to footnote was an easy task. The aesthetic sacrifice alone was enormous: Foot-note 63 occupies about three-fifths of the last full page of the opinion and carries over to the portion of the next page that contains the headnotes for the following case. *Id.* at 542-43.

[235] This is not to suggest the court is not aware of the proper classification. To the contrary, its conspicuous failure to rely upon the APA's requirements for "an opportunity to participate" and a "statement . . . of basis and purpose," 5 U.S.C. § 553(c) (applicable only to rulemaking) abundantly displays its awareness that the action before it is adjudication. One might have thought that the court would have used this fact as the simplest way of distinguishing both *Florida East Coast* and *Vermont Yankee*. From the court's point of view, however, there would have been several problems with that: First, it was not particularly *interested* in distinguishing *Florida East Coast*, at least insofar as

D.C. Circuit's major opinions in this field: effective unappealability. Before even discussing the procedural issues, the Court determines that the case must be remanded to the agency for substantive reasons[236]—and for substantive reasons with which the Department of Justice agreed.[237] It was thus extremely unlikely, whatever absurdities the Court might pronounce with respect to the procedural issues, that the Solicitor General would support a petition for certiorari (if, perchance, the FMC might think it worth the trouble). Moreover, even within the certiorari-proof procedural portions of the opinion there is the usual protective duplication. All of the points relating to the necessity for publication of agency data are covered by a (much clearer) holding that the agency disregarded its own regulations.[238] And of course both procedural issues are decided on dual grounds: (1) statutory prescription and (2) common-law power (in the guise of enabling judicial review or applying the "arbitrary or capricious" standard).

The *United States Lines* case, and the whole trend of D.C. Circuit behavior of which it is merely the latest example, are cause for serious professional concern. If it was ever possible for the federal judicial system to function without courts of appeals that earnestly seek to apply the clear principles (and not merely the narrow holdings) enunciated by the Supreme Court, it certainly is not possible today. Mr. Justice White described the problem—with specific ref-

---

that case declines to permit the statutory requirement for a "hearing" to invoke §§ 556–57 procedures. See 548 F.2d at 536. (In fact, however, *Florida East Coast* went out of its way to point out that the effect of a statutory "hearing" requirement in triggering §§ 556–57 "undoubtedly will vary, depending on whether it is used in the context of a rulemaking-type proceeding or in the context of a proceeding devoted to the adjudication of particular disputed facts." 410 U.S. at 239.) More important, however, Judge Wright seemed hell-bent upon writing an opinion that would apply to rulemaking (whether or not that was involved) in order to rehabilitate, by sheer force of repetition, his opinion in *Home Box Office*, 567 F.2d 9, which Judge Tamm had demolished, by sheer force of logic, in *Action for Children's Television*, 564 F.2d at 468–78. The former case is cited and quoted to a degree that would be remarkable even if it were not in contradiction to another panel of the same court; the latter case, as noted earlier (note 128 *supra*), is consigned to an outer darkness even more profound than that reserved for *Vermont Yankee*: It does not even make the footnotes.

Unlike the ordinary rule-making case, *United States Lines* was in fact an appealing candidate for the imposition of some extra-APA procedural requirements—precisely because it involved (if the court's position as to the effect of the statutory "hearing" requirement upon §§ 556–57 applicability is accepted) informal adjudication, as to which the Congress has provided no structured procedural minimum. See text at notes 168–72 *supra*.

[236] 548 F.2d at 527–33.   [237] *Id*. at 527 n.23.   [238] *Id*. at 536.

erence to the area of law here under discussion—in a speech to the ABA Section on Administrative Law:[239]

> In the five-year period from 1956 through 1960, the Courts of Appeals averaged 386 administrative review decisions after argument or submission; an average of 80 petitions for certiorari were taken from these decisions each year; and the Supreme Court granted an average of 19 of these cases each year. In the five-year period from 1968 through 1972, as compared with the years 1956–60, the average number of decisions in the Courts of Appeals in administrative review situations was up from 386 to 650; the number of petitions for certiorari was up from 80 to 117; but the average number granted was 16 each year rather than 19.
>
> [A]s case loads in the District Courts and the Courts of Appeals continue to grow and our certiorari docket does likewise, a greater and greater proportion of administrative law decisions in the Courts of Appeals will receive no further review and the number of Supreme Court judgments in this area will decline relative to the total universe of reviewable judgments. The Court's overall participation in the development of administrative law will become increasingly spasmodic and episodic. The emerging question to which I do not know the answer is whether the appellate function contemplated for the Supreme Court is being or will be adequately performed. . . . That a constantly increasing proportion of the decisions of the Courts of Appeals on administrative law questions are, as a practical matter, beyond the reach of Supreme Court review is, at the very least, a matter of substantial legal significance.

The problem is even greater than Mr. Justice White describes, of course, if one assumes that the courts of appeals—and more specifically that court of appeals which handles the vast majority of significant administrative appeals—will not accept guidance even when it is given. A tongue-lashing having failed, it will be interesting to see what further steps the Supreme Court may take to bring the D.C. Circuit into line.

VIII. THE FUTURE OF ADMINISTRATIVE PROCEDURE: A LAMENT

I have discussed three major factors which have prevented the APA from fulfilling its intended role—and the role which the

---

[239] *Address of Justice Byron R. White*, 26 ADMIN. L. REV. 107, 108–09 (1974).

language of *Vermont Yankee* would reestablish—as the Magna Carta of administrative procedure. The first two of these can be eliminated or accommodated; the third gives every indication of being utterly intractable, permanently preventing not merely broad applicability of the APA, but any rationalization of the field. The first factor— drastic change in the underlying legal assumptions since 1946[240]— can be accommodated, as it has been, by judicial decisions reinterpreting the APA in a relatively permanent fashion. Both that and the second factor—the intrinsic inadequacy of the APA[241]—can be entirely eliminated by statutory amendment. Such legislative action is not beyond the pale of the possible. A major revision of the APA was pending before the Senate Judiciary Committee during the last session of Congress.[242] What is not in the stars, however, is any congressional willingness to stop tinkering with administrative procedures in every major regulatory statute that is passed.[243] Professor Davis sees this as a desirable practice:[244]

> What has happened during the 1970's is that the courts have been drawing good ideas from any and all sources, including statutes that do not apply to particular cases, for improving the legal requirements for rulemaking procedure. Indeed, in extraordinary fashion, the legal frontier has been pushed out by both judges and legislators, each stimulating the other with respect to the new ideas that may be needed. . . . [T]he degree of interaction between judicial thinking and legislative thinking is new. The partnership of legislators and judges in the grand enterprise of producing a better legal and governmental system may be superior to what either legislators or judges can produce without the partnership and the interaction.

I am willing to stipulate, for the sake of argument, that the Congress does a superb job of "producing a better legal and governmental system" when that is the subject before the house—as may be the case when it considers legislation designed to establish a procedural

---

[240] Text *supra*, at notes 130-58.

[241] Text *supra*, at notes 159-72.

[242] S. 2490, 95th Cong., 2d Sess. (1978), entitled "Regulatory Procedures Reform Act." See 124 Cong. Rec. S. 1196–1207 (February 6, 1978).

[243] Text *supra*, at notes 173-83.

[244] 1 Davis, note 74 *supra*, at 145.

framework, such as the APA. Such a bill would typically be considered at length by the Committees on the Judiciary and on Government Operations, predominantly (it is reasonable to believe) on the basis of those factors of fairness and efficiency which professors of administrative law think should govern the outcome. In fact, however, that is not the context in which the "legislative thinking" which has produced the continuing statutory erosion of the APA has occurred. The principal issue—the issue to which all the lobbying and horse trading which are an indispensable part of representative democracy were directed—was not, for example, "What are the most fair and efficient procedures for the Federal Trade Commission's adoption of trade practice rules?" but rather, "Should the Federal Trade Commission have rulemaking authority, and, if so, how actively do we want it exercised?" Not, for example, "What are the most fair and efficient procedures for Consumer Product Safety Commission rulemaking?"; but rather, "Should there be a Consumer Product Safety Commission and, if so, how intensively do we want it to regulate?" Such issues are thrashed out not before the Judiciary or Government Operations Committees, but before the Committees concerned with the substantive areas in question. Procedural efficiency and fairness are a side issue—and at least the first of them is inevitably regarded as negotiable in the interest of obtaining what are, in the context presented, more basic goals. An interest group which cannot achieve its goal of eliminating FTC rulemaking authority may, quite rationally, settle for imposition of cumbersome procedures that at least reduce the extent to which rulemaking can occur. It is not sheer accident that the most elaborate extra-APA procedural requirements have been attached to those agencies, or those new agency powers, whose existence aroused the most political opposition.[245] Nor is it coincidence that all of the congressional alterations of the APA go toward increasing its requirements (do fairness and efficiency never call for a reduction?).

I do not suggest that the legislative choice is in fact presented in such stark terms: "I propose that we give the FTC rulemaking au-

---

[245] See, *e.g.*, the Consumer Products Safety Act, establishing the Consumer Product Safety Commission, codified at 15 U.S.C. 2051–81 (1976): the Federal Trade Commission Improvement Act (Title II of the Magnuson-Moss Act), conferring upon the FTC statutory authority to adopt unfair trade practice rules, adding, *inter alia*, 15 U.S.C. §§ 52a, 57b.

thority, but make it tie one hand behind its back." One of the very reasons that procedural encumbrance is such a useful legislative bargaining chip is that its purpose and effect can be so well disguised— from the congressmen who deal in it and (just as important) from the public at large, which only knows whether a Brave New Agency has been created, not whether it has been endowed with a greater or lesser number of technical hobbles. Who is to demonstrate (if, remarkably, the inquiry ever captures the public attention and pierces the public understanding sufficiently to become of any political importance) that particular procedures are excessively burdensome and thus presumptively intended as procedural obstructionism? Such a demonstration, if ever possible, is doubly difficult now that the ad hoc statutory variations of the APA are so numerous that § 553 can no longer be pointed to as a generally accepted baseline of administrative due process. Indeed, is it even fair to characterize this phenomenon as procedural obstructionism? The lobbyist or congressman who does not believe, to begin with, that the matters in question should be handled by rulemaking rather than adjudication, or by an agency rather than the courts, is acting quite appropriately and in utter good faith when he insists that, if they are handled by agency rulemaking, it be with adjudicatory, courtlike procedures.

Moreover, legislators cannot be unaware that the prescription of procedure profoundly affects an agency's political capabilities, *i.e.*, its ability to reach decisions not solely on the basis of science and reason but also on the basis of what is acceptable to the most potent interest groups involved. Take, for example, the F.C.C.'s determination of the extent to which cable TV systems will be permitted to "siphon" feature films and sporting events away from over-the-air broadcasting. If such a determination must be made "on the record," with a prohibition against "ex parte" contacts, it becomes virtually impossible for the Commission to negotiate, among the principal contending interest groups (broadcasters, cable owners, film producers, and sports leagues), a political accommodation of the sort the Congress itself would produce if the issue were resolved there.[246] I would assert (though the issue may surely be debated) that the fashioning of such political accommodations—within the range of

---

[246] *Cf. Home Box Office, Inc.*, 567 F.2d 9.

what is consistent with the public interest—is one of the appropriate functions of administrative agencies, at least when they are operating under a legislative directive no more specific than to serve "the public interest, convenience and necessity."[247] Whether appropriate or not, however, it is assuredly something the agencies often do. And in the course of drafting new legislation a substantive committee of the Congress might reasonably engraft additional requirements upon informal rulemaking in order to reduce or eliminate such political decision making.

Five years ago, in the Foreword to the Annual Report of the Administrative Conference, I wrote the following:[248]

> The consultant's report pertaining to [Administrative Conference] Recommendation 72-5 . . . noted the recent tendency of the Congress to provide a variety of procedures in addition to or in variation of those set forth in the APA. That trend is still accelerating and extends well beyond merely the rulemaking field. It sometimes appears that Congress has lost confidence in the judgments it made in 1946, and feels obliged to reconsider the question of what constitutes fair and efficient procedure each time it writes new legislation. This is a major challenge facing the Conference in the years ahead: To prevent the balkanization of administrative law, by either re-establishing the validity of the general dispositions made in the Administrative Procedure Act or by achieving such fundamental changes in that Act as may be necessary to satisfy more recent standards of fairness and efficiency. Unless this is done, I fear that repeated Congressional attention to administrative procedure as a mere subsidiary issue in the context of more important substantive controversies will lead to an administrative process that is pointlessly diverse and frequently unsound.

I am today much less hopeful that the goal there expressed can ever be achieved, and somewhat doubtful whether—from the point of view of the society as a whole, rather than the small group of us who are intensely concerned with the integrity and rationality of the administrative process—it is worth achieving.

What this discussion of the legislative process was meant to emphasize is the fundamental point that one of the functions of proce-

---

[247] See Scalia, *Two Wrongs Make a Right*. REGULATION 38 (July–Aug. 1977).

[248] 1973–74 REPORT, ADMINISTRATIVE CONFERENCE OF THE UNITED STATES 2 (1974).

dure is to limit power—not just the power to be unfair, but the power to act in a political mode, or the power to act at all. Such limitation is sometimes an incidental result of pursuing other functions, such as efficiency and fairness; but it may be an end in itself. It is questionable, for example, whether the procedural requirement of a "case or controversy" for Supreme Court action,[249] which once served to sharpen the precise issues for decision and to assure vigorous, adversary presentation, has much continuing utility for those purposes in an age of enormously relaxed criteria for standing,[250] of publicly appointed counsel and public-interest law firms, and of opinions regularly drawn with legislative breadth.[251] It nonetheless continues to serve as a restriction upon the areas of law on which the Court may pronounce. Or if that particular procedural requirement seems too inherently jurisdictional to be an appropriate analogue, consider the basic requirement that courts proceed in an adjudicatory, adversary, on-the-record fashion, even with respect to resolution of those general issues of statutory interpretation that we permit the agencies to resolve through § 553 rulemaking. Why is a public notice-and-comment procedure fair and efficient in one case but not the other? Is not the procedural limitation principally a restriction upon the power of the courts, impairing (however crudely) their ability and thus their inclination to make social policy?

The procedural foundations of the judicial process were laid long ago, and the basic role of the courts seems firmly established by both tradition and constitutional prescription. There is little legislative inclination, therefore, to adjust upward and downward the power of the courts, and even less inclination to achieve this by fiddling with procedures. Not so with the agencies. Their powers are for the most part neither constitutionally prescribed nor well established, and their procedures are only recently formed. Thus, the tendency to alter procedures as a means of altering power is immeasurably stronger.

Of course, once it is accepted that procedures are to be used as a means of expanding or restricting the power to act, the idea of any genuinely stable APA based on fairness and efficiency alone be-

---

[249] See, *e.g*, Muskrat v. United States, 219 U.S. 346 (1911).

[250] *E.g.*, Flast v. Cohen, 392 U.S. 83 (1968); United States v. SCRAP, 412 U.S. 669 (1973).

[251] *E.g.*, Roe v. Wade, 410 U.S. 113 (1973).

comes visionary. It also becomes unrealistic to expect the framework of any such superstatute to contain only a few options of procedure among which later legislation must choose—such as the stark choice between formal and informal rulemaking offered under the current APA. Where fairness and efficiency are the values sought to be achieved, it is indeed possible to devise a few sets of procedures that can serve as the minimum (and the maximum, as far as judical imposition is concerned) for almost all agencies. Those values are relatively uniform in their application from one agency to the next. Not so with power. The degrees of activism and of political decision making which the Congress expects from (or, more precisely, which the legislative struggle finally induces its divergent factions to accord to) the FTC, the ICC, the INS, the FDA, and the CPSC may vary enormously—and so will the procedures which reflect those expectations.

One can argue that things should be otherwise. That the Congress should be induced to forswear the use of procedures as a means of restricting power, and to pursue that goal, when desired, by some more sensible means (such as cutting budgets) or by some other equally senseless means (such as blindfolding every third bureaucrat). If such congressional self-denial were achieved, one might think a truly stable framework of administrative procedure could be established. There are two problems, however: one practical, one theoretical. As a practical matter, both the Congress and the lobbyists who appear before it would be foolhardy from a selfish standpoint—and perhaps even from the standpoint of the public interest—to abandon a compromise device which is so well insulated from effective criticism. An incumbent can be excoriated by his opponent in the next election for permitting X million dollars to be slashed from the budget of the new and highly popular Federal Happiness Commission. The criticism has a good deal less bite when it degenerates into a debate over what procedures are appropriate. Thus, as a practical matter, as new agencies continue to be created and the activities of old agencies expanded into new areas of regulation, Congress is bound to fall back upon procedural elaboration as a means of adjusting power. While "hybrid rulemaking" may no longer be devised by the courts under the APA, it will continue to flourish in a multiplicity of special statutes that modify the APA's dispositions, at least so long as the APA itself provides so few variants (and those based on considerations of fairness and efficiency alone) from which to select.

And there is a theoretical reason why this ought to be so. Congress can, indeed, refrain from making use of the connection between procedure and power, but it cannot make that connection itself disappear. Thus, to the extent that the choice of procedures is left to the agencies themselves, to that same extent the agencies are left to determine a substantial aspect of their own power. It is cause for concern that much of the increased regulation which has appeared during the past two decades, and which is now the subject of national political attention, has occurred not by reason of new legislation, with the deliberate and visible political choice which that entails, but by reason of preexisting agencies' "contrivance of more expeditious administrative methods," that is, their massive new involvement in rulemaking. If the full political process had been consulted, perhaps expedition would not have been desired. In any case, it is in principle unsatisfactory to leave the actual scope of agencies' power largely indeterminate, which is the case when (as under the current APA) there is a vast divergence between the efficiency of formal adjudication and of informal rulemaking, and it is up to the agency to choose between the two for the resolution of most issues of policy.[252]

It seems to me, therefore, that if the continuing fragmentation of mandated administrative procedure is to be abated, what is called for is a more modest expectation of what the APA can and should

---

[252] Of course to some extent the indeterminateness of agency power may be attributable not to the divergence in efficiency between the two polar APA procedures (formal vs. informal), but to the divergence in scope and effect between the two basic modes of administrative action (adjudication vs. rulemaking), regardless of what procedures are applied to them. The choice between these modes is in large degree left to the agencies themselves. See SEC v. Chenery Corp., 332 U.S. 194 (1947); *American Airlines*, note 13 *supra*. It is difficult to analyze these two elements (procedure and mode of action) separately, since at present, by virtue of the APA, a change of procedure almost invariably accompanies a change in the mode of action for significant agency determinations. It would seem, however, that abstracting from the prodedures used, the differences between adjudication and rulemaking are not as great as commonly imagined. See Robinson, *The Making of Administrative Policy: Another Look at Rulemaking and Adjudication and Administrative Procedure Reform*, 118 U. PA. L. REV. 485 (1970); Shapiro, *The Choice of Rulemaking or Adjudication in the Development of Administrative Policy*, 78 HARV. L. REV. 921 (1965). But to the extent that those differences bear significantly upon agency power, leaving the choice between adjudication and rulemaking to the agencies raises the same issue of abdication of legislative responsibility discussed in the text.

achieve, and a design that will accord with the realities. The notion that the statute can somehow be prescriptive, establishing for Congressional selection in subsequent legislation only the number of procedural variables which the needs of fairness and efficiency can justify, must be abandoned. For better or for worse, Congress will often have other purposes in mind. I would settle for an APA that contains not merely three but ten or fifteen basic procedural formats—an inventory large enough to provide the basis for a whole spectrum of legislative compromises without the necessity for shopping elsewhere.[253] And to achieve that goal, of course, the formats would be based not merely upon lawyers' and scholars' notions of what is conducive to fairness and efficiency but also upon varying expectations of power. If there were added to this basic structure a requirement for the approval of the Judiciary Committees of both houses before a procedural format not inventoried in the APA is inserted in new legislation,[254] then there might be some chance of standardizing mandatory administrative procedures within a manageable number of well-known and well-litigated forms.[255] The alter-

---

[253] There are problems in implementing such an approach, the most substantial of which is the difficulty of determining which procedural variant will apply to preexisting statutes. Where the available selection of rulemaking procedure is limited to "formal" and "informal," it is simple enough (whether or not satisfactory) to make the determination turn upon an "on the record" requirement in the earlier statute. But how is the decision to be made if there are many available choices? There is no space to examine such difficulties here—except, perhaps, to note that even if the present "formal-informal" dichotomy were retained for pre-existing statutes the revised APA would at least regularize the procedural dispensations of future laws.

[254] Of course such a provision would amount to no more than an amendment of each House's rules of procedure, and could be disregarded by either House—as well as overridden by statutory provision. Nonetheless, established procedures usually are observed and would constitute a significant practical constraint against unthinking variation. A somewhat similar device—together with many other procedural restrictions—is contained in the legislative provisions for congressional approval of presidential reorganization plans. 5 U.S.C. §§ 908–912.

[255] That such a consummation is devoutly to be desired is exemplified—indeed, almost caricatured—by the recent case of Association of Nat'l Advertisers, Inc. v. FTC, Civil No. 78-1421, D.D.C. Nov. 3, 1978 (ATRR Nov. 9, 1978, p. F-1), involving a petition to disqualify the Chairman of the FTC for prejudice in a rulemaking proceeding conducted pursuant to the peculiar procedures of the FTC Improvement Act of 1975 (see note 107 supra). Chairman Pertschuk had forcefully expressed his firm views concerning the subject of the proceeding—FTC regulation of children's advertising. Such expression of prejudice would clearly have been disqualifying in formal adjudication and almost certainly in formal rulemaking. It has never been thought to be disqualifying in informal rulemaking, though it is admittedly difficult to recall so vigorous an expression of prejudgment in a pending proceeding. But the FTC Improvement Act had given what it called informal rulemaking so many of the characteristics of formal adjudication (or

natives, it seems me, are a continuation of ad hoc statutory variations and—whether or not the D.C. Circuit's judicial improvisation
can be controlled—an acceleration of our rush away from the kind
of fundamental statute *Vermont Yankee* seeks to preserve.

---

formal rulemaking) that it was difficult to decide which standard of conduct should
govern. As Judge Gesell noted, it was "in fact a hybrid proceeding, unique to the Federal
Trade Commission." The court's disqualification of Chairman Pertschuk was based on
constitutional grounds—to which the foregoing considerations should be irrelevant. I
think, however, that the issue should have turned upon statutory intent with respect to
a procedural area (expression of bias or prejudice) not specifically addressed by the APA.
On that point, the nature of the statutorily prescribed procedures would be crucial, and
infinite variation would make predictability most difficult.